The Three Regularities in Development

Moazam Mahmood

The Three Regularities in Development

Growth, Jobs and Macro Policy in Developing Countries

palgrave
macmillan

Moazam Mahmood
Lahore School of Economics
Lahore, Punjab, Pakistan

Capital University of Economics and Business
Beijing, China

ISBN 978-3-319-76958-5   ISBN 978-3-319-76959-2 (eBook)
https://doi.org/10.1007/978-3-319-76959-2

Library of Congress Control Number: 2018935242

© The Editor(s) (if applicable) and The Author(s) 2018
This work is subject to copyright. All rights are solely and exclusively licensed by the Publisher, whether the whole or part of the material is concerned, specifically the rights of translation, reprinting, reuse of illustrations, recitation, broadcasting, reproduction on microfilms or in any other physical way, and transmission or information storage and retrieval, electronic adaptation, computer software, or by similar or dissimilar methodology now known or hereafter developed.
The use of general descriptive names, registered names, trademarks, service marks, etc. in this publication does not imply, even in the absence of a specific statement, that such names are exempt from the relevant protective laws and regulations and therefore free for general use.
The publisher, the authors and the editors are safe to assume that the advice and information in this book are believed to be true and accurate at the date of publication. Neither the publisher nor the authors or the editors give a warranty, express or implied, with respect to the material contained herein or for any errors or omissions that may have been made. The publisher remains neutral with regard to jurisdictional claims in published maps and institutional affiliations.

Cover illustration: David Davis Photoproductions / Alamy Stock Photo

Printed on acid-free paper

This Palgrave Macmillan imprint is published by the registered company Springer International Publishing AG part of Springer Nature.
The registered company address is: Gewerbestrasse 11, 6330 Cham, Switzerland

This book is dedicated to Ghafooran, who brought me up on tales of her labour, share-picking cotton in Khanewal, Punjab, in the 1950s. And when the crop failed and pickings were scant, she would hold out her share to the landlord and say, 'Why don't you take it all?'
And to my mother, Suraiya, who taught me to work.

Foreword

This book by Moazam Mahmood is about poverty and economic development. In my own country, the United Kingdom, we are accustomed to think of poverty in relative terms, with household or individual poverty defined in relation to median income. In developing countries, a more relevant concept is absolute poverty. Globally, the total number of people living in extreme poverty (less than US$1.25 per day) has been gradually falling, but poverty of this variety is still extensive in the least developed countries where the 'bottom billion' live. These countries are mainly, but not exclusively, located in sub-Saharan Africa. This is of particular concern since these are also the countries with the highest fertility rates and population growth. Assuming a considerable decline in fertility, the UN projects that the population of today's least developed countries will rise from 1.0 billion at present to 4.0 billion by the end of the century. With an even larger decline in fertility, the projected population at the end of the period is 2.8 billion. It will be a major challenge to reduce poverty in the face of population growth on this scale.

As the author makes clear, economic growth is the key to any major improvement in living standards in the least developed countries. In countries higher up in the development ladder, productivity throughout the economy is typically higher than in the least developed countries, there are fewer people working in agriculture, and there are more people working in industry and services, where earnings are on average higher and more secure than in agriculture. However, one should not be too starry-eyed about the benefits of economic development. In 2013, some 65 percent of all employed persons in the least developed countries were classified as extremely poor or moderately poor (less than US$2 per day). In somewhat richer countries on the next rung of the development ladder, the figure was 48 percent. The really big change comes in the transition to emerging economy status where 'only' 10 percent of employed persons were extremely or moderately poor in 2013. This is a big improvement over the situation in the least developed countries, but it is still a long way behind the advanced economies.

Poverty can be alleviated through public transfer and expenditure programmes. These can take many forms, ranging from old-age pensions to subsidised or free food, health, and education. The generosity and form of such programmes depends, of course, on the wealth of the country concerned. Not surprisingly, they are more generous in richer countries, but they also exist to some extent in all countries. The authors estimate that, in 2012, US$72 billion would have been needed to eliminate extreme poverty in developing countries as a whole. This represents 0.16 percent of global income and 0.31 percent of developing country income. In the least developed countries the cost of eliminating extreme poverty would be 3.9 percent of their very small GDP.

The obstacles to rapid economic growth in the least developed countries are numerous, but the author singles out the following: a low share of manufacturing in national output and a low level of investment in physical and human capital. Moreover, much of the physical investment which does occur goes into resource extraction, which is of uncertain long-term benefit. Quite apart from their impact on economic growth, investment in human capital and an expansion of manufacturing have valuable spin-offs. The education of women, for example, is associated with lower fertility and smaller family size, and thereby a lower risk of poverty. Manufacturing jobs are relatively well-paid and secure, so an expansion of this sector helps to reduce poverty and insecurity.

An important, if unsurprising, finding in this book is the influence of demography (population) on the level and growth rate of employment in developing countries. With no alternative means of support, people must take whatever work that is available no matter how badly paid, and many of them end up working for a pittance in the unregulated informal sector which acts as a sponge to absorb excess labour. If the working-age population grows rapidly, employment will also grow rapidly, no matter how strong or weak the underlying demand for labour. If demand is weak, as is often the case in the least developed countries, the result will be an expansion in the number of working poor. Concern about the number of working poor is not confined to the least developed countries. It has been a common theme in recent years even in advanced economies, although the conventional poverty line in these economies is, of course, much higher than in many developing countries.

These are just some of the topics covered by Moazam Mahmood. In this absorbing book, he provides systematic and comprehensive evidence to support his numerous insights into economic conditions in developing countries. Before reading this book, I was familiar with the general theme, but was not really aware of the details or conversant with the evidence. Having read it, I now consider myself to be well informed.

King's College
Cambridge, UK
6 January 2017

Robert Rowthorn

Preface

This book makes one premise, and poses one question, which it then attempts to answer.

The Premise

The premise is that growth theory ought to apply to development economics. Its provenance is longer, making it richer, and more rigorous, to yield better analysis.

In academia, growth theory is taught and treated separately from development economics—as though models of economic growth are abstracted purely from the advanced economies (AEs), while models of economic development are abstracted purely from developing countries (DCs) seeking to catch up to the former. Both sets of models—growth and development—are agent-based. But the environments in which these agents operate are considered distinct, with AEs blessed with more complete markets for capital, labour, land, and outputs, and DCs with less complete markets in these. Hence, agent behaviour is said to vary between AEs and DCs to cope with the difference in completeness of markets.

This is the distinction largely used to justify the difference in models of growth between AEs and DCs, between growth theory and development economics.

But are there indeed special laws in economics, as in physics, that change with context, or are these laws general and universal? Precisely because the debate may be complex, I favour taking Occam's razor to it and working on the premise that the laws in economics are general and universal until there is serious empirical challenge. So, the book assumes that the same laws of economics govern DCs as AEs. And that, in the near future, these laws will be the same as in the near past. In the parlance of quantum physics, the laws in economics are not background-specific.

The Question and Entailed Methodology

Based on this premise of the universality of economic laws, across space and recent time, the book poses the question: what laws explain differences in per capita incomes among DCs and with AEs? Why do some countries move up the income ladder and others not? Is there a catch-up to AEs? And if so, why are some countries catching up better?

To answer this fundamental question, the book leads with empirics and a positivist methodology. An empirical answer is sought and then squared and supplemented with theory. And as warranted, the theory takes a modest step forward.

The resulting analysis and implied policy are heterodox. The book finds itself largely in the classical and Kaldorian tradition on growth, in a more development mode on informality-driven labour markets, riding classical and institutional public goods horses on accumulation, and supportive of enabling neoclassical macroprudential policies.

Specifically, the book examines over 140 DCs observed consistently over the past third of a century. In theory, this could yield over 140 distinctions between them. However, three categories of countries are observed to cluster, not just in the present but also in their change over the last 33 years. Least developed countries (LDCs), defined essentially as those below US$1000 per capita in 2012 US$, largely based on the UN definition, appear to be a distinct category of DCs over the past third of century, with more economic similarities than dissimilarities. Lower- and middle-income countries (LMICs), defined as falling between US$1000 and US$4000, based on the World Bank's definition, also prove to be a distinct and stable category of DCs over the past third of a century. Emerging economies (EEs), defined as falling between $4000 and US$12,000, again based on the World Bank's definition, are the third distinct and stable category of DCs over the past 33 years. AEs fall above US$12,000 per capita in 2012 US$, as a distinct and stable category of countries over the past 33 years.

To clarify, these three categories of DCs remain stable over the past third of a century: LDCs, LMICs, and EEs. This does not mean that each country remains trapped in the same category over time, for some countries do move up this income ladder. But it does mean that a distinct category of countries has remained trapped in this income band below US$1000 per capita over the past third of a century. Likewise, LMICs, EEs, and AEs are all stuck in their income bands. There has not been a bunching of these four categories over time, into three, two, or one.

Then the fundamental question of development can be reposed as: what laws explain why LDCs have remained trapped as LDCs over the past third of a century, and not become LMICs or EEs or AEs? Similarly, why have LMICs and EEs remain trapped in their income boundaries and not risen higher up the income ladder over such a long period?

The Answer in Three Regularities

The answer the book comes up with is: one law. It is not the quantum of growth that explains per capita incomes or their change over time. It is *en fait* the composition of this growth that explains per capita incomes and their change over time quite well.

This law is based on three regularities observed to hold for these 140-plus countries over the past third of a century.

One regularity holds in GDP growth. It is not the quantum of GDP growth that explains per capita incomes of a country. It is the composition of GDP growth that explains per capita incomes and their change over time. Specifically, it is the classical and Kaldorian emphasis on manufacturing which is vindicated through this large sample test. In a modest step forward in this tradition, the share of manufacturing is observed to explain per capita incomes, while growth in shares explains growth in GDP very well.

A second regularity holds in the labour market. It is not the quantum of job growth or unemployment that explains per capita incomes or their change over time. Quantum indicators are observed to be second-best indicators of weaknesses or strengths in the labour market in DCs, given the high levels of informality prevalent. Then, it is job quality that is seen to explain per capita incomes and change in them quite well. Further, job quality emerges not just as a residual spillover from GDP growth, but as a policy lever to leverage growth through higher-productivity forms of employment.

The third regularity holds in the macro drivers of growth and jobs. It is not just the quantum of accumulation that drives growth and jobs to determine the level of per capita incomes. It is the composition of the accumulation of capital which comes to explain per capita incomes across DCs. Specifically, accumulation in physical capital is observed to be as important as the accumulation in human capital, both coming to explain per capita incomes better than either one.

These three regularities are observed to hold over the past third of a century, despite a changing global and regional macro environment for DCs.

The macro environment in Latin America during the 1980s and the 1990s saw crises, with balance-of-payment concerns prompting depreciating exchange rates and falling employment and wage rates in turn. The macro environment in Africa was one of weak growth, pulled largely by commodity prices, but dampened by low investment, public and private, especially in infrastructure. The macro environment in Asia was better, with stronger growth, led especially by the East Asian tigers, China, Hong Kong (China), Indonesia, Malaysia, Singapore, South Korea, and Thailand.

The river of the global macroeconomy, into which the DCs stepped in the 1980s to the mid-1990s, was one of expanding aggregate demand and offshoring from AEs, leading to expanding demand for the products of the DCs, manufactures, and commodities.

But this river of the global macroeconomy changed course from the second half of the 1990s with the Asian crisis, prompted by weak macro fundamentals. Unsecured debt overhangs and unsustainable fixed exchange rates combined to reverse capital inflows into the East Asian tigers, minus China, depreciating exchange rates, depressing asset values, and deflating aggregate demand, exports, investment, employment, and wages. Multilateral policy advice to the beleaguered East Asian countries was largely, simply wrong. National policy responses were defensive and sensible, like capital controls in Malaysia, propping up minimum wages in Thailand and social floors in South Korea, but questioned under the neoclassical model of multilateral advice. China also saved the day by not devaluing its pegged exchange rate, which might have led to a beggar-thy-neighbour devaluation race to the bottom.

The Asian crisis tipped the global economy into a synchronised global recession at the start of the millennium, but it was short-lived and followed by a macro boom till 2007 and the onset of the global recession, led by macro headwinds in the AEs, which still lingers today.

The point is that the river of the global macroeconomy has varied, with booms and busts, global and regional. Global aggregate demand has often helped DCs, and then not. Multilateral advice, after a fashion, has helped, and then not, precipitating or supplementing, both booms and perversely busts.

This brings back the premise of the book. The DCs have, over the past third of a century, not always stepped into the same proverbial global macroeconomic river twice—but different rivers at different points in time—and yet the three regularities have held. Then, the laws of economics are not that background-dependent. If they held in the near past, with varying global macroeconomic contexts of booms and busts, then they should hold in the near future—until there is serious empirical challenge.

On this premise of the generalisation of economic laws, from the near past to the near future, the book uses each regularity to imply policy.

Policy

The first regularity on growth emphasises the composition of GDP growth over the quantum of GDP growth in determining the level of income of a country and catch-up—moving up the income ladder. This puts one policy caveat on growth—that it should be based on productive transformation, enhancing the share of manufacturing.

However, a policy prior on normative and welfare grounds is that growth should be poverty-reducing, providing a rising share of the caloric needs of the food-deficient. This makes for two policy caveats on growth—that growth should be more inclusive and based on productive transformation.

Hence, the policy chapter on growth first looks at the macro determinants of poverty reduction and the policy needs that stem from this. It then looks at the policy needs for productive transformation.

The second regularity on jobs prioritises job quality over job quantity in determining the level of income and movement up the income ladder. The limited size of the formal economy implies that more jobs are created in the informal economy, with a significant proportion among the working poor—workers whose incomes fail to meet even the caloric needs of their family. So, the quantum of jobs created matters less, with many of them being of very weak quality, with low productivity and incomes, and in onerous, often hazardous, working conditions.

With the informal, unregulated sector generating weak-quality jobs to absorb and match supply-side demographics, it is then the job quality rather than quantity which better reflects the state of the labour market and becomes a better predictor of country incomes—and a better policy lever to move countries up the income ladder.

A key element in improving job quality is the divide between the regulated formal economy and the unregulated informal economy. Policy to register and regulate the labour market is observed to improve forms of employment, with higher productivity, incomes, and access to national regulatory legislation, purview, and social floors.

The third regularity on the macro drivers of growth and jobs stresses the composition of accumulation as much as the quantum of accumulation in determining the level of income and movement up the income ladder. Investment in human capital is seen to be as important as investment in physical capital in explaining country income and change in it.

Policy incentives to increase the supply of physical capital are seen to turn crucially on lowering the cost of capital. Here, prudential macro policy plays as strong a role as regulatory policy on banking spreads. Policy incentives to increase the supply of human capital are seen to turn crucially on provisioning of public goods, especially primary and secondary education. Policy incentives to increase intangible capital are seen to depend on public provisioning of tertiary education.

Regularities Redux

In conclusion, the premise of the book seems warranted, with the regularities holding across the varying institutional space of over 140 DCs, and across time, a third of a century, with varying global macro contexts. The laws of economics are not that background-dependent. One such law appears to hold well for DCs and their comparator AEs—that to explain levels of per capita incomes across these countries, and changes in them over time, what matters less is the quantum of GDP growth, and more the composition of this growth. The law is based on the three regularities that appear to define recent development. The composition of growth matters, for it has to be poverty-reducing and transformative. Job quality matters, for it has to reduce vulnerability and increase productivity. And accumulation of capital has to be physical, human, and knowledge-based.

Lahore, Punjab, Pakistan Moazam Mahmood
Beijing, China

Acknowledgements

The work for this book was undertaken, and the book largely written, while I was at the International Labour Organization's (ILO) Research Department, latterly as director. I wish to thank a succession of research assistants for their hard work and support: Woori Lee, Mariano Mamertino, Jiaxian Zhang, Veronika Zhirnova, Marina Giovanzana, Veda Narasimhan, Zheng Wang, Maria Martha Sarabia, Nikita Grabher-Meyer, and Aimal Tanvir.

I must thank the ILO for giving me the opportunity and resources to undertake such a large project on development, especially the Director General, Guy Ryder, and then Deputy Director General, Sandra Polaski. The ILO Research Department has very kindly allowed me to publish this work independently.

The book has been authored by me except, very importantly, on Chap. 5 ('Putting Caveats on Growth: Policy for Inclusion and Productive Transformation'), where Florence Bonnet, senior economist at the ILO, has been a most valuable co-author.

I have tried out a number of arguments on my daughter Shanzeh baba and my wife Noreen, getting perhaps the severest responses.

Heartfelt thanks to Maheen Pracha, my editor at the Lahore School of Economics, and Rachel Sangster at Palgrave.

Many thanks to the Lahore School of Economics, where I currently have a chair in Economics, for their editorial support.

Contents

1 Introduction   1

Part I Three Empirical Regularities in Development: In
Growth, Jobs, and Macro Drivers   17

2 A Regularity in Growth Patterns in Developing Countries:
   The Quantum and Composition   19

3 A Regularity in Employment Patterns in Developing
   Countries: Jobs and Good Jobs   61

4 A Regularity in the Macro Drivers of Growth and Jobs:
   Accumulation of Physical Capital and Human Capital   107

Part II Three Policy Drivers of Development — 143

5 Putting Caveats on Growth: Policy for Inclusion and Productive Transformation — 147
Moazam Mahmood and Florence Bonnet

6 Policy for Jobs: Reducing Informality — 233

7 Macro Policy for Drivers of Growth and Jobs — 271

8 Regularities Redux: Success Stories and Traps—What Has Worked for Developing Countries? — 305

List of Figures

Fig. 2.1 GDP per capita ($ '000). (Note: *AE* advanced economy, *CAGR* compound annual growth rate, *DC* developing country, *EE* emerging economy, *GDP* gross domestic product, *LDC* least developed country, *LMIC* lower- or middle-income country. Source: Author's estimations at the ILO, based on data from ILO, *World of Work Report 2014: Developing with Jobs* (Geneva: ILO, 2014))   21

Fig. 2.2 GDP per capita (1980 = 100). (Note: *AE* advanced economy, *DC* developing country, *EE* emerging economy, *GDP* gross domestic product, *LDC* least developed country, *LMIC* lower- or middle-income country. Source: Author's estimations at the ILO, based on data from ILO, *World of Work Report 2014: Developing with Jobs* (Geneva: ILO, 2014))   22

Fig. 2.3 GDP per capita, average annual growth rate, 1980–2011. (Note: *EE* emerging economy, *GDP* gross domestic product, *LDC* least developed country, *LMIC* lower- or middle-income country. Source: Author's estimations at the ILO, based on data from ILO, *World of Work Report 2014: Developing with Jobs* (Geneva: ILO, 2014))   23

Fig. 2.4 Change in the share of manufacturing's contribution to GDP, 1980–2011 (percentage points). (Note: *EE* emerging economy, *GDP* gross domestic product, *LDC* least developed country, *LMIC* lower- or middle-income country. Source: Author's

Fig. 2.5   Effect of manufacturing and industry growth on GDP growth. (Note: *GDP* gross domestic product. The figures show the average annual percentage point change in GDP and GDP per capita with a 1 percentage point change in the average annual industrial and manufacturing sectors. All the estimated coefficients are statistically significant at the 1 percent confidence level. Econometric specifications available from the author. Source: Author's estimations at the ILO, based on data from the World Bank's World Development Indicators)   39

Fig. 2.6   Effect of sectoral shares on GDP per capita. (Note: *EE* emerging economy, *GDP* gross domestic product, *LDC* least developed country, *LMIC* lower- or middle-income country. Econometric specifications available from the author. Source: Author's estimations at the ILO, based on data from the World Bank's World Development Indicators)   40

Fig. 2.7   Effect of manufacturing (five-year average) growth on GDP growth. (Note: *EE* emerging economy, *GDP* gross domestic product, *LDC* least developed country, *LMIC* lower- or middle-income country. Econometric specifications available from the author. Source: Author's estimations at the ILO, based on data from the World Bank's World Development Indicators)   41

Fig. 3.1   Employment and working-age population growth rates. (Note: *p* projection; 2013 are preliminary estimates, *AE* advanced economy, *DC* developing country. Source: Author's estimations at the ILO, based on data from the ILO Trends Unit, Trends Econometric Models, October 2013)   67

Fig. 3.2   Employment and labour force growth rates, AEs and DCs. (Note: *p* projection; 2013 are preliminary estimates, *AE* advanced economy, *DC* developing country. Source: Author's estimations at the ILO, based on data from the ILO Trends Unit, Trends Econometric Models, October 2013)   68

Fig. 3.3   Employment and labour force growth rates, LDCs, LMICs, EEs. (Note: *p* projection; 2013 are preliminary estimates, *EE* emerging economy, *LDC* least developed country, *LMIC* lower- or middle-income country. Source: Author's estimations at the ILO, based on data from the ILO Trends Unit, Trends Econometric Models, October 2013)   69

(text above Fig. 2.5: estimations at the ILO, based on data from ILO, *World of Work Report 2014: Developing with Jobs* (Geneva: ILO, 2014))   24

Fig. 3.4	Share of employment, by status. (Note: *AE* advanced economy, *EE* emerging economy, *LDC* least developed country, *LMIC* lower- or middle-income country. Source: Author's estimations at the ILO, based on data from the ILO Trends Unit, Trends Econometric Models, October 2014)	77
Fig. 3.5	Change in the share of waged employment, 1991–2013. (Note: *EE* emerging economy, *LDC* least developed country, *LMIC* lower- or middle-income country. Source: Author's estimations at the ILO, based on data from the ILO Trends Unit, Trends Econometric Models, October 2013)	79
Fig. 3.6	Share of working poor (extreme poverty <$1.25/day), 1991 and 2013. (Note: *EE* emerging economy, *LDC* least developed country, *LMIC* lower- or middle-income country. Source: Author's estimations at the ILO, based on data from the ILO Trends Unit, Trends Econometric Models, October 2013)	82
Fig. 3.7	Share of working poor (moderate poverty <$2.00/day), 1991 and 2013. (Note: *EE* emerging economy, *LDC* least developed country, *LMIC* lower- or middle-income country. Source: Author's estimations at the ILO, based on data from the ILO Trends Unit, Trends Econometric Models, October 2013)	83
Fig. 3.8	Employment, by economic class. (Note: *DC* developing country, *EE* emerging economy, *LDC* least developed country, *LMIC* lower- or middle-income country. Source: Author's estimations at the ILO, based on October revisions to the model in Steven Kapsos and Evangelia Bourmpoula, 'Employment and Economic Class in the Developing World,' Research Paper 6 (Geneva: ILO, 2013); and data from the ILO Trends Unit, Trends Econometric Models, October 2013)	85
Fig. 3.9	Labour productivity. (Note: *p* projection; 2013 are preliminary estimates, *AE* advanced economy, *DC* developing country, *EE* emerging economy, *LDC* least developed country, *LMIC* lower- or middle-income country. Source: Author's estimations at the ILO, based on data from the ILO Trends Unit, Trends Econometric Models, October 2013; and the World Bank's World Development Indicators, 2013)	88

Fig. 3.10	Productivity growth rate, 1991–2013. (Note: *EE* emerging economy, *LDC* least developed country, *LMIC* lower- or middle-income country. Source: Author's estimations at the ILO, based on data from the ILO Trends Unit, Trends Econometric Models, October 2013; and the World Bank's World Development Indicators, 2013)	89
Fig. 3.11	Effect of log GDP per capita on sectoral shares of employment: fixed-effects (within) estimator. (Note: *GDP* gross domestic product, *L* labour. All coefficients are significant at the 0.01 level. Econometric specifications available from the author. Source: Author's estimations at the ILO, based on data from the ILO Trends Unit, Trends Econometric Models, October 2013)	92
Fig. 3.12	Effect of sectoral shares of labour on vulnerable employment and shares of waged and salaried workers: fixed-effects (within) estimator. (Note: *GDP* gross domestic product, *L* labour. All coefficients are significant at the 0.05 level. Econometric specifications available from the author. Source: Author's estimations at the ILO, based on data from the ILO Trends Unit, Trends Econometric Models, October 2013)	93
Fig. 3.13	Effect of sectoral shares of labour and log GDP per capita on log productivity: fixed-effects (within) estimator. (Note: *GDP* gross domestic product, *L* labour. *** significant at the 0.01 level. Econometric specifications available from the author. Source: Author's estimations at the ILO, based on data from the ILO Trends Unit, Trends Econometric Models, October 2013)	97
Fig. 3.14	Employment in manufacturing and extractives, 2000–12. (Note: *EE* emerging economy, *LDC* least developed country, *LMIC* lower- or middle-income country. Source: Author's estimations at the ILO, based on data from the ILO's Key Indicators of the Labour Market)	99
Fig. 3.15	Growth decomposition. (Note: *EE* emerging economy, *LDC* least developed country, *LMIC* lower- or middle-income country. Source: Author's estimations at the ILO, based on data from the ILO Trends Unit, Trends Econometric Models, October 2013; the World Bank's World Development Indicators; and UN, *World Population Prospects: The 2012 Revision* (New York: UN, 2013))	100

Fig. 3.16	Productivity decomposition. (Note: *EE* emerging economy, *LDC* least developed country, *LMIC* lower- or middle-income country. Growth decomposition is based on data for 66 countries (13 LDCs, 26, LMICs, 27 EEs) and follows the methodology described in ILO, *Global Employment Trends 2013* (Geneva: International Labour Office, 2013, chap. 4). Source: Author's estimations at the ILO, based on data from the ILO Trends Unit, Trends Econometric Models, October 2013; the World Bank's World Development Indicators; and UN, *World Population Prospects: The 2012 Revision* (New York: UN, 2013))	101
Fig. 3.17	Share of waged and salaried workers, and productivity. (Source: Author's estimations at the ILO, based on data from the ILO Trends Unit, Trends Econometric Models, October 2013)	103
Fig. 4.1	Drivers of growth, contribution to average annual GDP growth, 1980–2010. (Note: *EE* emerging economy, *GDP* gross domestic product, *LDC* least developed country, *LMIC* lower- or middle-income country. Source: Author's estimations at the ILO, based on data from IMF, *World Economic Outlook, April 2013, Hopes, Realities, Risks* (Washington, DC: IMF, 2013); and the World Bank's World Development Indicators, 2013)	114
Fig. 4.2	Gross fixed capital formation as a percentage of GDP, 1980 and 2007. (Note: *EE* emerging economy, *GDP* gross domestic product, *GCF* gross capital formation, *LDC* least developed country, *LMIC* lower- or middle-income country. Source: Author's estimations at the ILO, based on data from IMF, *World Economic Outlook, April 2013, Hopes, Realities, Risks* (Washington, DC: IMF, 2013); and the World Bank's World Development Indicators, 2013)	115
Fig. 4.3	Savings as a percentage of GDP, 1980 and 2007. (Note: *EE* emerging economy, *GDP* gross domestic product, *LDC* least developed country, *LMIC* lower- or middle-income country. Source: Author's estimations at the ILO, based on data from IMF, *World Economic Outlook, April 2013, Hopes, Realities, Risks* (Washington, DC: IMF, 2013); and the World Bank's World Development Indicators, 2013)	118

Fig. 4.4	Direction of the Granger causality relationship found for gross capital formation and GDP per capita. (Note: *EE* emerging economy, *GDP* gross domestic product, *K* gross capital formation, *LDC* least developed country, *LMIC* lower- or middle-income country. Source: Author's estimations at the ILO, based on data from the World Bank's World Development Indicators, 2013)	121
Fig. 4.5	Direction of the Granger causality relationship found for savings and GDP per capita. (Note: *EE* emerging economy, *GDP* gross domestic product, *LDC* least developed country, *LMIC* lower- or middle-income country, *SAV* savings. Source: Author's estimations at the ILO, based on data from the World Bank's World Development Indicators, 2013)	122
Fig. 4.6	Effect of gross capital formation, tertiary gross enrolment ratio, and average years of schooling on GDP per capita: fixed-effects (within) estimator. (Note: *AYS* average years of schooling, *GCF* gross capital formation, *GDP* gross domestic product, *TGER* tertiary gross enrolment ratio. The figure displays the coefficient estimates from a regression of GDP per capita on gross capital formation, tertiary gross enrolment, and average years of schooling. All coefficients are significant at the level of 0.01. Econometric specifications are available from the author. Source: Author's estimations at the ILO, based on data from the World Bank's World Development Indicators, 2013)	123
Fig. 4.7	Direction of the Granger causality relationship found for primary enrolment and GDP per capita and for tertiary enrolment and GDP per capita. (Note: *EE* emerging economy, *GDP* gross domestic product, *LDC* least developed country, *LMIC* lower- or middle-income country. Source: Author's estimations at the ILO, based on data from the World Bank's World Development Indicators, 2013)	124
Fig. 4.8	Decomposition of GDP growth into physical capital, human capital, employment, and TFP components, 1991–2011. (Note: *AE* advanced economy, *DC* developing country, *EE* emerging economy, *GDP* gross domestic product, *LDC* least developed country, *LMIC* lower- or middle-income country, *TFP* total factor productivity. Growth decompositions are based on data for 55 DCs (12 LDCs, 16 LMICs, 27 EEs)	

	and 37 AEs. Source: Author's estimations at the ILO, based on data from Christian Viegelahn, 'Decomposition of GDP Growth', unpublished manuscript (ILO, Geneva, forthcoming); IMF, *World Economic Outlook, October 2013, Transitions and Tensions* (Washington, DC: IMF, 2013); ILO Trends Unit, Trends Econometric Models, October 2013; and Groningen Growth and Development Centre, Penn World Tables Version 8.0)	125
Fig. 4.9	Average number of years of schooling for adults over 25 years of age, 1980–2007. (Note: *EE* emerging economy, *LDC* least developed country, *LMIC* lower- or middle-income country. Source: Author's estimations at the ILO, based on data from the World Bank's World Development Indicators, 2013)	127
Fig. 4.10	Exports as a percentage of GDP, 1980 and 2007. (Note: *EE* emerging economy, *GDP* gross domestic product, *LDC* least developed country, *LMIC* lower- or middle-income country. Source: Author's estimations at the ILO, based on data from the World Bank's World Development Indicators, 2013)	131
Fig. 4.11	Ratio of consumption over exports, as a percentage of GDP, 1980 and 2007. (Note: *EE* emerging economy, *GDP* gross domestic product, *LDC* least developed country, *LMIC* lower- or middle-income country. Source: Author's estimations at the ILO, based on data from the World Bank's World Development Indicators, 2013)	132
Fig. 4.12	Direction of the Granger causality relationship found for exports (EXP) and GDP per capita. (Note: *EE* emerging economy, *GDP* gross domestic product, *LDC* least developed country, *LMIC* lower- or middle-income country. Source: Author's estimations at the ILO, based on data from the World Bank's World Development Indicators, 2013)	133
Fig. 4.13	Effect of manufacturing, industry, and services on exports: fixed-effects (within) estimator. (Note: *GDP* gross domestic product. Standard errors in parentheses. *** $p < 0.01$, ** $p < 0.05$, * $p < 0.1$. Source: Author's estimations at the ILO, based on data from the World Bank's World Development Indicators)	133
Fig. 5.1	Relationship between GDP growth and poverty rate. (Note: *GDP* gross domestic product. Source: Authors' estimations at the ILO, based on data from the World Bank, PovcalNet, April 2016 (available at http://iresearch.worldbank.org/PovcalNet/))	160

Fig. 5.2	Effect on poverty rate of 1 percentage point increase in share of GDP components, by poverty measure, 1991–2014 (percentage). (Note: *GDP* gross domestic product. Source: Authors' estimations at the ILO, based on data from the World Bank's World Development Indicators)	161
Fig. 5.3	Distribution of total GDP and extreme income gap in DC categories. (Note: *DC* developing country, *EE* emerging economy, *GDP* gross domestic product, *LDC* least developed country, *LMIC* lower- or middle-income country, *PPP* purchasing power parity. Global and regional estimates based on 65 DCs (20 LDCs, 23 LMICs, and 24 EEs). See Table 5.12 in the Appendix for detailed data sources. Extreme poverty and extreme associated income gap are defined as the share of those with per capita income or consumption below US$1.90 PPP per day. Source: Authors' estimations at the ILO, based on national household survey data)	163
Fig. 5.4	Total income gap and expenditure on public social protection as a percentage of GDP, 2012. (Note: *EE* emerging economy, *GDP* gross domestic product, *LDC* least developed country, *LMIC* lower- or middle-income country, *PPP* purchasing power parity. In panel A, in countries on the right side of the red line, the estimated income gap to eliminate extreme poverty in LDCs is superior to the actual total public investment in social protection. In countries on the right side of the blue line, the estimated income gap accounts for more than half of actual public social protection expenditure, which is still above the proportion of social protection that reaches the poor in many countries (see Sect. 5.2). Country names associated with ISO3 codes and detailed data sources are presented in Table 5.12 in the Appendix. Source: Authors' estimations at the ILO, based on national household survey data for the income gap; and on data from ILO, Social Security Inquiry, April 2016 (available at http://www.ilo.org/dyn/ilossi/ssimain.home); OECD, Social Expenditure Database, April 2016 (available at http://www.oecd.org/social/expenditure.htm); ADB, Social Protection Index, April 2016 (available at http://spi.adb.org/spidmz/index.jsp); and European System of Integrated Social Protection Statistics, February 2016 (available at http://ec.europa.eu/eurostat/web/social-protection/overview) for social protection expenditure data)	167

Fig. 5.5	Composition of the total income gap, 2012. (Note: *EE* emerging economy, *LDC* least developed country, *LMIC* lower- or middle-income country, *PPP* purchasing power parity. Global estimates based on 103 countries representing close to 85 percent of the world population. Source: Authors' estimations at the ILO, based on national household survey data)	168
Fig. 5.6	Short working hours and poverty in DCs (hours per week), latest year available. (Note: *DC* developing country, *EE* emerging economy, *LDC* least developed country, *LMIC* lower- or middle-income country, *PPP* purchasing power parity. Global weighted estimates based on 65 DCs, representing 74 percent of total employment. Hours of work refer to usual hours of work from all jobs when available, otherwise from main and second jobs. Panels A and B: common poverty line of US$3.10 PPP per day and per capita. The population of reference covers people in employment aged 15–64. Data is for the latest year available, which ranges between 2005 and 2013. One-fourth of the country data refers to 2005–09 and nearly 60 percent is for 2012 or 2013. Source: Authors' estimations at the ILO, based on national household survey data)	173
Fig. 5.7	Excessive hours of work and poverty in DCs (hours per week), latest year available. (Note: *DC* developing country, *EE* emerging economy, *LDC* least developed country, *LMIC* lower- or middle-income country, *PPP* purchasing power parity. Global weighted estimates based on 47 DCs representing more than 74 percent of total employment. The population of reference covers people in employment aged 15–64. Data is for the latest year available, which ranges between 2005 and 2013. One-fourth of the country data refers to 2005–09 and nearly 60 percent is for 2012 or 2013. Source: Authors' estimations at the ILO, based on national household survey data)	175
Fig. 5.8	Permanent contracts among wage and salaried workers: comparison between poor and non-poor (percentage), latest year available. (Note: *EE* emerging economy, *LDC* least developed country, *LMIC* lower- or middle-income country, *PPP* purchasing power parity. This figure covers wage and salaried workers aged 15–64. The dark grey dots are for LDCs, the	

black dots for LMICs, and the light grey dots for EEs. All of them refer to the extreme and moderate poverty line of US$3.10 PPP per capita per day. Any dot above the diagonal means that the proportion of the non-poor in wage and salaried employment with a permanent contract is higher than the corresponding proportion among the poor. Country names associated with ISO3 codes and detailed data sources are presented in Table 5.12 in the Appendix. Data is for the latest year available, which ranges between 2005 and 2013. One-fourth of the country data refers to 2005–09 and nearly 60 percent is for 2012 or 2013. Source: Authors' estimations at the ILO, based on national household survey data) 176

Fig. 5.9 Affiliation to contributory social protection (pension mainly), poor and non-poor workers (percentage of total employment), latest year available. (Note: *DC* developing country, *EE* emerging economy, *LDC* least developed country, *LMIC* lower- or middle-income country, *PPP* purchasing power parity. Contribution to social protection (at least for pensions). All dots refer to the extreme and moderate poverty line of US$3.10 PPP per capita per day. Any dot above the diagonal means that the proportion of the non-poor contributing to social protection (at least for pensions) is higher than the proportion among the poor. Country names associated with ISO3 codes and detailed data sources are presented in Table 5.12 in the Appendix. Panel B: Global estimates based on 34 DCs representing 75 percent of total employment. The population of reference covers people in employment aged 15–64. Data are for the latest year available, which ranges from 2007 to 2013. Source: Authors' estimations at the ILO, based on national household survey data) 177

Fig. 5.10 Percentage of the poor and non-poor receiving benefits and proportion of social protection benefits expenditure going to the poor, latest year available. (Note: *EE* emerging economy, *LDC* least developed country, *LMIC* lower- or middle-income country, *PPP* purchasing power parity. The analysis of the shares of public expenditure on social protection benefits going to the poor versus the non-poor should take into consideration that many people are above the poverty threshold because they receive social protection benefits. Panel A compares the proportions of the poor (horizontal axis) and non-poor (vertical axis) receiving social protection benefits (any type). Any dots below the diagonal highlight a situation where the percentage of the poor receiving benefits (independently of the level of benefit received) exceeds the proportion of the non-poor. Panel B considers the incidence of poverty (or the proportion of the poor in total population, horizontal axis) compared to the share of the total value of social protection benefits going to the poor (vertical axis). Any dot below the diagonal means that the cumulative value of benefits from social protection received by the poor is lower than their representation in the total population and that the level of benefit per beneficiary is lower for the poor than for the non-poor. Country names associated with ISO3 codes and detailed data sources are presented in Table 5.12 in the Appendix. Source: Authors' estimations at the ILO, based on national household survey data) 179

Fig. 5.11 Public social protection expenditure (percentage of GDP) and impact of social transfers (percentage points), latest year available. (Note: *DC* developing country, *EE* emerging economy, *GDP* gross domestic product, *LDC* least developed country, *LMIC* lower- or middle-income country, *PPP* purchasing power parity. The impact of social protection transfers is measured as the difference between poverty rates before and after social protection transfers. Only the direct reduction of income poverty through the transfer of purchasing power to the beneficiaries is considered here. Calculations based on a common poverty line of US$3.10 PPP per capita per day. In panel A, the figures relate total public social protection expenditure as a percentage of GDP to the impact for individuals of social protection transfers on poverty reduction (differences in poverty rates before and after social transfers in percentage points). In panel B, the horizontal axis presents public social protection benefits for older persons (either in cash or in kind) as a percentage of GDP and the vertical axis the differences (in percentage points) in poverty rates resulting from the income received from social protection (all types of benefits) for people aged 65 and over. In the latter case, all social protection transfers are taken into account and not only old-age or survivors' pensions or benefits in kind directed specifically to the elderly. Country names associated with ISO3 codes and detailed data sources are presented in Table 5.12 in the Appendix. DCs include 32 countries. Source: Authors' estimations at the ILO, based on national household survey data) 180

Fig. 5.12 Impact of social protection on poverty reduction and prevention by age group and economic status, country data (latest year available). (Note: *DC* developing country, *EE* emerging economy, *LDC* least developed country, *LMIC* lower- or middle-income country, *PPP* purchasing power parity. Common poverty line of US$3.10 PPP per capita per day all DCs. Impact on poverty reduction and prevention calculated on a per capita basis, to be consistent with other results presented in this report. This methodological choice explains some of the differences between these and other results published in Eurostat or OECD using the same original data. 'Inactive unable to work' are people with disability not in the labour force and not looking for work, being unable to work because of their disability (identified in household surveys). Source: Authors' estimations at the ILO, based on national household survey data) 181

Fig. 5.13 Impact of social protection investment on poverty reduction and prevention (percentage), latest year available. (Note: *DC* developing country. The impact of social protection benefits on poverty reduction and prevention in the various subgroups of the population results not only from specific benefits targeting those groups but from all social protection benefits received by household members and equally shared between them. Public social protection expenditure covers all measures that provide benefits, whether in cash or in kind, to secure protection from a lack of work-related income (or insufficient income) caused by sickness, disability, maternity, employment injury, unemployment, old age, or death of a family member; lack of (affordable) access to healthcare; insufficient family support, in particular for children and adult dependants; general poverty; and social exclusion (ILO 2014b). Data is for the latest year available, which ranges from 2007 to 2013. Nearly 70 percent of the country data is for 2012 or 2013. The 32 DCs represent 72 percent of the

	total population of DCs. Source: Authors' estimations at the ILO, based on national household survey data)	183
Fig. 5.14	Simplified cases and most appropriate policy responses. (Source: Authors' illustration)	185
Fig. 5.15	Proportions of the gap, respectively, filled by social protection transfers and increases in labour earnings, 2012. (Note: *DC* developing country, *EE* emerging economy, *LDC* least developed country, *LMIC* lower- or middle-income country, *PPP* purchasing power parity. Calculation for US$3.10 PPP. 103 countries covered, representing 85 percent of the global population. The proportion of the income gap calling for social protection transfers is determined for each household and applied to its household members. The share to be covered by an increase in labour income is the complement to 100 percent. Econometric specifications available from the authors. Source: Authors' estimations at the ILO, based on national household survey data)	189
Fig. 5.16	Size of government expenditure and public social protection expenditure (percentage of GDP) and GDP per capita, latest available year. (Note: *EE* emerging economy, *GDP* gross domestic product, *LDC* least developed country, *LMIC* lower- or middle-income country, *PPP* purchasing power parity. For a given level of GDP per capita, the figure displays both the size of government expenditure (circles) and, as part of it, public social protection expenditure (triangles), the two indicators expressed as a percentage of GDP. Taking the examples of Brazil and Mexico, their GDP per capita are comparable (around US$16,000 PPP per capita per year) but both total government expenditure and public social protection spending are significantly lower in Mexico than in Brazil. The total size of government expenditure as a percentage of GDP amounts to 39 percent in Brazil compared to 28 percent in Mexico. While public social protection expenditure in Brazil constitutes more than half of the amount of government expenditure (55 percent), in Mexico, this ratio is lower by half (28 percent). Country names associated with ISO3 codes are presented in Table 5.12 in the Appendix. Source: Authors' estimations at the ILO, based on data from the IMF's World Economic Outlook Database, January 2016)	191

Fig. 5.17	Out-of-school children (percentage), by country income group. (Source: Authors' estimations at the ILO, based on data from UNICEF (available at https://data.unicef.org/))	196
Fig. 5.18	Out-of-school children (percentage), by regional group. (Source: Authors' estimations at the ILO, based on data from UNICEF (available at https://data.unicef.org/))	197
Fig. 5.19	Correlation between government expenditure on education and school attendance. (Note: *GDP* gross domestic product. Source: Authors' estimations at the ILO, based on data from UNICEF (available at https://data.unicef.org/))	198
Fig. 5.20	Correlation between pupil-teacher ratio in primary school and school attendance. (Source: Authors' estimations at the ILO, based on data from UNICEF (available at https://data.unicef.org/))	200
Fig. 5.21	Assistance during delivery (any skilled personnel) (percentage of births). (Source: Authors' estimations at the ILO, based on data from the World Bank, ASPIRE: The Atlas of Social Protection Indicators of Resilience and Equity, April 2016 (available at http://datatopics.worldbank.org/aspire/))	201
Fig. 5.22	Under-five mortality rate (per 1000 live births). (Source: Authors' estimations at the ILO, based on data from the World Bank, ASPIRE: The Atlas of Social Protection Indicators of Resilience and Equity, April 2016 (available at http://datatopics.worldbank.org/aspire/))	202
Fig. 5.23	Correlation between government expenditure on health (percentage) and under-five child mortality. (Source: Authors' estimations at the ILO, based on data from the World Bank, ASPIRE: The Atlas of Social Protection Indicators of Resilience and Equity, April 2016 (available at http://datatopics.worldbank.org/aspire/))	203
Fig. 5.24	Correlation between out-of-pocket health expenditure (percentage of total health expenditure) and under-five child mortality. (Source: Authors' estimations at the ILO, based on data from the World Bank, ASPIRE: The Atlas of Social Protection Indicators of Resilience and Equity, April 2016 (available at http://datatopics.worldbank.org/aspire/))	205
Fig. 5.25	Correlation between medical staff density and under-five child mortality. (Source: Authors' estimations at the ILO, based on data from the World Bank, ASPIRE: The Atlas of	

	Social Protection Indicators of Resilience and Equity, April 2016 (available at http://datatopics.worldbank.org/aspire/))	206
Fig. 5.26	Change in GDP sector share. (Note: *GDP* gross domestic product. Source: Authors' estimations at the ILO, based on data from the World Bank's World Development Indicators and PovcalNet (available at http://iresearch.worldbank.org/PovcalNet/))	211
Fig. 6.1	Poverty rates among workers in informal and formal employment. (Note: *PPP* purchasing power parity. Extreme and moderate poverty = <$3.10 PPP per capita per day. Source: Calculations by Florence Bonnet at the ILO, based on national household survey data)	251
Fig. 6.2	Old-age pension and survivors' legal coverage, 1990–2013. (Note: Global estimates based on 178 countries in 2013, 173 countries in 1990 and 2000, weighted by the working-age population. Source: Calculations by Florence Bonnet at the ILO, based on data from ILO, *World Employment and Social Outlook 2015: The Changing Nature of Jobs* (Geneva: International Labour Office, 2015); data on legal and social protection coverage from the ILO Research Department, International Social Security Association, European Commission, United Nations, ILO Trends Unit (Trends Econometric Models), and national legislation and statistical offices)	260
Fig. 7.1	Official policy rates. (Source: Author's calculations at the ILO, based on data from the central banks' websites; and Charles Bean, Christian Broda, Takatoshi Ito, and Randall Kroszner, 'Low for Long? Causes and Consequences of Persistently Low Interest Rates', Geneva Reports on the World Economy 17 (ICMB, Geneva; CEPR, London, 2015))	277
Fig. 7.2	Balance between the determinants of growth. (Source: Author's illustration)	297

List of Tables

Table 1.1	Country classifications	13
Table 2.1	Annual real GDP growth rate, period average	27
Table 2.2	Annual real GDP growth rates	28
Table 2.3	Annual value-added growth rates, by sector, period average	32
Table 2.4	Annual growth rates, by sector, period average	34
Table 2.5	Value added, by sector, as a percentage of GDP (nominal values at constant 2005 US$)	36
Table 2.6	Share of manufacturing as a percentage of GDP	45
Table 3.1	Employment growth rate, by sex and age group	65
Table 3.2	Unemployment rate, by sex and age group	71
Table 3.3	Youth-to-adult ratio of unemployment rate	72
Table 3.4	Labour force participation rates	74
Table 3.5	Working poverty	80
Table 3.6	Percentage share of total employment, by economic class	84
Table 3.7	Labour productivity growth rates	86
Table 3.8	Share of employment, by sector	91
Table 3.9	Labour productivity, by sector	95
Table 3.10	Labour productivity growth rate, by sector	96
Table 4.1	Aggregate demand components as percentages of GDP	111
Table 4.2	Aggregate demand components as percentages of GDP, 2000–10	112
Table 4.3	Drivers of growth, contribution to average annual GDP growth, 1980–2010	113

Table 4.4	Savings and capital inflows as percentages of GDP		116
Table 4.5	Savings and capital inflows as percentages of GDP		117
Table 4.6	Resource-based economies, aggregate demand components as a percentage of GDP		134
Table 5.1	Poverty rates (percent)		151
Table 5.2	Population in DCs, by poverty and employment status, 2012		152
Table 5.3	Percentage of the poor/non-poor living in rural/urban areas		155
Table 5.4	Decomposition of the poor and non-poor in DCs, by broad employment sector, 2012		157
Table 5.5	Decomposition of the poor and non-poor in DCs, by specific employment sector, 2012		159
Table 5.6	Global income gap, by region and poverty line, 2012		163
Table 5.7	Size of household and percentage of household members in paid employment, latest year available		169
Table 5.8	Additional investment in social protection to close the income gap, 2012		190
Table 5.9	Government expenditure on food subsidies as a percentage of GDP		207
Table 5.10	Impact of food subsidies on poverty		208
Table 5.11	Characteristics of different country groups		215
Table 5.12	List of household surveys consulted		218
Table 6.1	Average share of informal employment in total non-agricultural employment		238
Table 6.2	Informal employment as a percentage share of total non-agricultural employment, by country (ILO estimates)		239
Table 6.3	Informal employment as a percentage share of total non-agricultural employment, by country (ILO and OECD estimates)		241
Table 6.4	Productivity ratios		246
Table 6.5	Correlations with informality		250
Table 7.1	Total investment as a percentage of GDP		273
Table 7.2	Real interest rates		274
Table 7.3	Lending interest rates		274
Table 7.4	Gross domestic savings as a percentage of GDP		275
Table 7.5	Percentage change in inflation, average consumer prices		282
Table 7.6	Government budget balance as a percentage of GDP		282
Table 7.7	Current account balance as a percentage of GDP		283

Table 7.8	General government gross debt as a percentage of GDP	283
Table 7.9	FDI net inflows as a percentage of GDP	285
Table 7.10	Gross enrolment ratios	289
Table 7.11	Public expenditure on education as a percentage of GDP	290
Table 7.12	Survival rate to the last grade of primary school	291
Table 7.13	Out-of-school rate (percent) for children of lower secondary school age	291
Table 7.14	Average years of total schooling, children aged 15 or above	292
Table 7.15	Patent applications by non-residents and residents	295
Table 7.16	R&D expenditure as a percentage of GDP	296
Table 8.1	Average change in value-added share as a percentage of GDP	311
Table 8.2	Average change in employment shares	312
Table 8.3	Average change in selected labour market variables	313
Table 8.4	Average change in aggregate demand components as a percentage of GDP	314
Table 8.5	Average change in selected human capital variables	314
Table 8.6	Average growth in public social protection expenditure per capita	316

1

Introduction

The crisis persisting in the advanced economies (AEs) and its spillovers into developing countries (DCs) has put the longer-term agenda of development—the development of countries and people—somewhat on the analytic and policy backburner. Day-to-day management of macro fundamentals in the global economy and the labour market have consumed decision makers and analysts with faltering gross domestic product (GDP) growth, elevated unemployment, and a continuing threat of deflation. The aim of this book is to bring back some balance through focus on the bigger and more intractable problem of development facing some 145 countries. Indeed, the vulnerability of these DCs to the crisis and their recovery, which is their cyclical problems, are bound to their longer-run, more structural challenges of development.

1.1 The Immense Contextual Literature on Development

Development theory and its empirical moorings are myriad. Two distinctions in this iconography stand out. There are explanations of the quantum of growth, which is the central concern of both neoclassical and accumulation arguments, the exemplars par excellence being the Harrod–Domar growth model (see Harrod 1948) and Solow (1956)[1] on the one hand, and Mill (1848), Say (1821), and Marshall (1920) on the other, which are indeed important to consider. And then there are explanations of the content of this growth, which is the more prolific literature emphasising a variety of structural constraints. These go from sectors, with progenitors like Verdoorn (2002), Lewis (1954), and Kaldor (1966) among the classics, to the emphasis on tradeables versus primary production like Singer (1950) and Prebisch (1962); to the latter-day structural transformationists like Chang (2002, 2005), Lin (2011), Lin and Chang (2009), Hausmann et al. (2005), and Hausmann et al. (2008); to the institutionalists like North (2008) and Acemoglu et al. (2000). And then there are the crossovers, where the quantum of growth depends on both the quantum of investment and the content of investment, which is an endogenous growth theory emphasising human capital (see Lucas 1988; Mankiw et al. 1992; Easterly and Levine 2001), the inability to capture human capital in embodied investment emphasised by Robinson (1953, 1962), and some innovations suggested by intangible knowledge-based capital for example by Dutz et al. (2012).

The labour market appears on the surface to be orthogonal to this macro literature on growth for development.[2] But it comes in very strongly in the content of growth literature, through the examination of output per person—labour productivity—and the returns to work, the wage, especially emphasised by the classics, Verdoorn (2002), Lewis (1954), and Kaldor (1966). The labour market and work also comes in through the determination of labour productivity through the sectoral transformation literature and the human capital literature.

Which gives a very rich literature to guide this book.

1.2 This Book's Take on Development

The message of this book is that development can be well defined in terms of empirically observed regularities in three principal areas: growth, jobs, and the macro drivers of growth and jobs. And these regularities show that development can be about the quantum of change, but is much more about the composition of this change.

The yardstick of development in the areas of growth, jobs, and their macro drivers arguably returns to the individual. Increasing the returns to the individual is good and desirable, which implies increasing individuals' productivity. Hence per capita incomes and their increase over time becomes a good benchmark of development in both growth and jobs. It makes sense then to categorise DCs in terms of their per capita incomes, to observe what separates higher- from lower-income countries, and to explain the differences in their behaviour. It is these differences that allow them to move up the per capita income ladder.

1.3 The Methodology of the Book

This book then examines growth and employment in 145 countries defined as DCs, over the long run of the past third of a century—from 1980 to 2013. DCs are defined, after the World Bank's criteria, as those with per capita incomes falling below US$12,000. To facilitate analysis of such a large number of countries, there had to be some aggregation of these 145 DCs. But to also acknowledge their immense diversity, they have for a start been divided into three income categories.[3] Least developed countries (LDCs) are defined by the United Nations' criteria, which are those that fall below US$1000 per capita, but additionally a few whose structural characteristics bring them into this group. Lower- and middle-income countries (LMICs) lie between US$1000 and US$4000 per capita. Emerging economies (EEs) lie between US$4000 and US$12,000 per capita. AEs then fall above US$12,000 per capita.

The book examines differences in growth and employment patterns between these income categories of DCs, and their policy drivers.

The typology of country categories is widened in the search for explanations of distinguishing between better and worse outcomes amongst the 145 DCs and the policy explanations sought for them. One such categorisation is the degree of reliance on extractives. Another categorisation is country reliance on macro drivers of growth, such as being investment-led or investment-shy, export-led, and being both export-led and consumption-led.

1.4 The Structure of the Book

Three Regularities Shaping Development

The book argues that development can be well defined in terms of empirically observed regularities in three principal areas: growth, jobs, and macro drivers of growth and jobs. And these regularities show that development can be about the quantum of change, but is much more about the composition of this change. Each of these empirical regularities, derived in the first part of the book, implies a specific set of policies in the second part.

Part 1. Three Empirical Regularities in Development: In Growth, Jobs, and Macro Drivers

Chapter 2. A Regularity in Growth Patterns in DCs: The Quantum and Composition

The quantum of growth does not explain the wide variety in different levels of income per capita amongst DCs. The composition of growth, in terms of productive transformation and structural change, explains this wide heterogeneity better.

GDP growth rates for the three income categories, LDCs, LMICs, and EEs, have converged over time. Hence GDP growth rates per se do not distinguish well between these income categories. So, the quantum of change does not explain well why LDCs do not become LMICs, LMICs do not become EEs, or EEs do not become AEs. What consistently discriminate between LDCs, LMICs, and EEs, over the past third of a century, is the development of manufacturing. The range in manufacturing shares over the past 33 years moves in lockstep up the income ladder. LDCs have remained trapped below a 10 percent share in GDP for manufacturing over this period, LMICs in the teens and EEs in the twenties.

Hence the composition of change appears to explain how countries move up the income ladder. This striking empirical regularity in productive transformation may not imply specific industrial policy for each DC, but it is broadly indicative of what has worked in the past, and can be a major policy for the future.

Chapter 3. A Regularity in Employment Patterns in DCs: Jobs and Good Jobs

Employment growth is demographically led in DCs. Hence job quality, that is, composition of employment, is a better indicator of labour market success or distress in DCs.

This chapter sets out to examine the patterns of employment across DCs, in terms of distinguishing between the characteristics of LDCs, LMICs, and EEs. It does not find the quantum of employment growth to be the best estimator of improvement or distress in the labour markets of DCs. The reason is that in DCs, lack of social protection compels the poor and low-income part of the labour force to work, which causes employment growth to be largely determined by labour force growth. Employment growth is then determined more by demographic supply-side factors, than by economic demand-side factors. This makes job quality a better estimator of labour market improvement or distress. Job quality is demonstrated to be correlated to employment in the informal economy, where workers are not registered. These unregistered workers are employed in both unregistered enterprises and registered ones. Using these statistical definitional building blocks, estimates are derived for informality for a large number of DCs. Such a large-scale empirical estimate is rare. Further, this estimate of informality is decomposed to indicate vulnerability, and correlated to other indicators of job quality, like the working poor.

A question of causality arises, as to whether job quality is merely a trickle-down effect of higher incomes, or whether job quality can leverage countries up the income ladder. Some evidence is provided showing the circularity and cumulativeness of the development process, with job quality and productivity and hence incomes all moving together up the income ladder. That is, job quality need not lag behind growth.

Chapter 4. A Regularity in the Macro Drivers of Growth and Jobs: Accumulation of Physical Capital and Human Capital

Quantitative change in macro aggregates driving growth, like investments and savings, matter. However, the composition of the drivers of growth between investment in physical capital, human capital, and intangibles matters even more.

The third empirical regularity emerges in the macro drivers of GDP growth and jobs. The conventional macro drivers of GDP growth and jobs are borne out in the form of investment and savings, climbing in lockstep up the income ladder. LDCs are particularly seen to be trapped at low levels of savings and investment. Interestingly, exports do not provide such a consistent explanation of moving up the income ladder, nor do other macro drivers like consumption and government expenditure. However, a more comprehensive explanation of moving up the income ladder is provided by examining the composition of capital accumulation. While physical capital is observed to be important, investment in human capital is seen to discriminate very well between DCs as a whole and AEs. The explanation improves further in considering different forms of human capital, going from investment in primary education to investment in higher-skilled intangibles.

Part 2. Three Policy Drivers of Development

Chapter 5. Putting Caveats on Growth: Policy for Inclusion and Productive Transformation

This first policy chapter on growth harks back to the first empirical chapter's finding on growth—that the quantum of growth does not explain DCs moving up the per capita income ladder as well as the composition of this growth explains it. So, growth, to explain catch-up in country incomes, needs a caveat on it, which is that the composition of this growth must exhibit structural change. But arguably, and with a large literature to support it, growth should in the first instance be poverty reducing. If we are to prioritise the needs of the population, then the first priority should be, meeting the caloric needs of the population falling below the required dietary allowance. This puts two policy caveats on growth. That it should be poverty-reducing. And that it should be based on productive transformation of the structure of the economy. The chapter examines the policy conditions required to meet these two caveats on growth.

This policy chapter on inclusive growth is structured into four parts. Section 5.1 looks at some key determinants of poverty based on an empirical analysis of some 75 DCs. Section 5.2 looks at the policy needs to fill the income gap of the poor, through transfers and enhanced labour incomes. Section 5.3 looks at the non-income needs of the poor, and the role of public goods in meeting those needs. Strategic policy to fill the income and non-income gaps is discussed. Section 5.4 looks at the policy needs for productive transformation.

In Sect. 5.1, the empirical analysis of poverty in DCs is based on identifying who the poor are. It shows the largest quantitative determinants to be a demographic drag, comprising the children and the elderly, and vulnerable workers. Both pull these populations below the poverty line.

In Sect. 5.2, the identification of the poor then allows an estimation of the income gap, and what kinds of income would be needed to fill this gap. The young and the elderly, not being of working age, would require more transfer incomes, to fill their gaps. Vulnerable workers would require enhanced labour incomes, through higher productivity, wages, and employment levels. Policy on transfers and enhancing labour incomes is examined in the light of the literature and country experiences.

Non-income gaps to reduce poverty (Sect. 5.3) are identified in three key areas, health, education, and subsidies on consumption. The role of public goods in these areas is seen as being indispensable in filling in the gaps for the poor in health, education, and nutrition.

Turning to the second caveat on growth, in Sect. 5.4, policy on productive transformation is examined. A strategic area focussed on is country experiences in industrial catch-up, with educational attainments and capabilities playing key roles.

Chapter 6. Policy for Jobs: Reducing Informality

The second policy chapter, on jobs, harks back to the findings of the empirical second chapter on jobs, that the quantum of employment growth does not explain per capita incomes, while job quality does. This policy chapter argues that a major determinant of job quality is arguably informality, with wide-ranging weaknesses in informal jobs. Hence policy to reduce informality is seen as a strategic policy lever to improve job quality. Employment policies should then focus on enforcing registration of both workers and enterprises to reduce informality and improve job quality. They should also be complemented by social provision policies which have an impact on workers' vulnerability and on productivity and internal demand.

Given the empirical regularity found between per capita income levels and job quality, the notion of informality suggests itself as a policy lever. The chapter provides the first estimates of informality, based on a more comprehensive definition of informality, for a large sample of DCs. The new estimates lead to two important policy implications.

One, they allow a comparison of job quality between the formal and informal economies. The demonstration of weaker job quality in informality gives a broad policy handle with which to improve jobs. Two, the new estimates allow a better decomposition of informality, showing the significance of not just informal employment in unregistered firms, but also the considerable share of informal employment in formally registered firms. Policy on informality hence needs to be derived through an instrument to register not just enterprises but also workers.

Contractual provisioning is seen to climb up the income ladder across DCs, implying the need to enhance both the number of provisions and their coverage. Enhanced security in employment, and therefore enhanced duration of employment, increases capabilities through learning by doing effects, and therefore productivity. Registration of workers is also seen as a policy instrument enabling them to potentially access social protection, earn minimum wages, and benefit from national legislation on a raft of improved conditions and rights. Social health provisioning becomes a key area of policy intervention as it provides a micro floor for the individual and their family, and hence a macro floor for consumption and aggregate demand for the economy.

Chapter 7. Macro Policy for Drivers of Growth and Jobs

The third policy chapter, on macro drivers (in symmetry with the policy chapters on growth and jobs), also bases itself on the findings of the empirical chapter on macro drivers. That accumulation of physical capital explains per capita incomes as much as human capital. This policy chapter then examines macro policy which enables increases in both types of investment, in gross fixed capital formation and in human capital through education and training.

The third empirical regularity, that the quantum of accumulation is as important as the composition of accumulation—that is, investment in both physical and human capital explains per capita incomes—leads to a broad policy implication for both physical capital and human capital.

Country policy on investment in physical and human capital is examined not through de jure proclamations, but de facto policy as revealed by national income accounts, budgets, and effective resource allocation towards these expenditure heads. Domestic resource mobilisation is seen to be more important for such investment, rather than inflows.

On investment in physical capital, the chapter finds that looser monetary policy and interest rate structures climb up the per capita income ladder. Hence the lower cost of borrowing is seen to enable higher levels of investment. However, this lower cost of borrowing is seen to be enabled in turn by more stringent macroprudential regimes, tightening fiscal policy, and controlling inflation, which in turn allow lower interest rate structures. Therefore, good governance of macro fundamentals through both fiscal and monetary policy is seen to enable higher levels of investment. Further, sequencing is seen to be at the heart of this policy, in that reversing the sequence, to loosen monetary policy, prior to lowering inflation, would simply raise the nominal interest rates and therefore not be sustainable.

On investment in human capital, the key enabling policy variable is seen to be government expenditure on both basic and tertiary education.

But the chapter ends on a note of caution. While stressing that investment in both physical and human capital has been observed to work, to explain higher per capita incomes, there is a broader policy argument to be made for more balanced growth. Balance in the reliance between the drivers of investment, exports and consumption, leads to a better balance between incentives to raise productivity and incomes, and incentives to raise aggregate demand.

Chapter 8. Regularities Redux: Success Stories and Traps—What Has Worked for DCs?

The concluding chapter starts by taking a quick stock of the theoretical and empirical contributions of the volume. It highlights the analytical framework chosen, the empirical findings, and the policy derivations. It goes back to the central argument of the volume, picking up the key determinants of per capita incomes as they emerged in each chapter, the regularities in growth, jobs, and macro drivers, to empirically demonstrate that they can also be observed to have worked over time.

The logic of the central argument of the book is to determine what works—what has been empirically demonstrated to explain income differences between LDCs, LMICs, and EEs. This gives the three empirical regularities and in turn allows policies to leverage what works. A more stringent test of what works would be to regroup the DCs, not by income, but by growth of income, in terms of those that doubled their incomes, those that raised them by only half, and those that stagnated. So, this is a final test to see if the regularities observed to explain levels of income also explain change in these incomes over time.

This more stringent test largely confirms the explanatory and policy variables, especially linking productive transformation and productive jobs.

1.5 The Current Global Context for DCs: The Crisis Has Affected the Economy and Labour Markets of Both AEs and DCs

Day-to-day management of macro fundamentals in the global economy and the labour market have consumed decision makers and concerned organisations, with still low GDP growth, elevated unemployment, and an abiding threat of price and wage deflation, at the time of writing. Global GDP after the initial recovery from the onslaught of the crisis has declined on trend, falling from 4.2 percent in 2011 to 3.4 percent in 2012, to 3.3 percent in 2013, 3.4 percent in 2014, and 3.1 percent for both 2015 and 2016, far from the pre-crisis growth of 5.3 percent seen in 2007 (IMF 2016). October-based estimation for 2017 has come in at 3.6 percent, and projections for 2018 stood at 3.7 percent (IMF 2017).

Global unemployment rose from its pre-crisis 2007 level of 5.5 percent to peak at 6.2 percent in 2009, was still stuck at 5.7 percent by 2016, and is in fact estimated to have risen marginally to 5.8 percent for 2017 and 2018.[4] Men's unemployment may have crept down from its peak of 5.9 percent in 2009, to flatline at about 5.5 percent for the past two years. But women's unemployment has persistently increased on trend since the start of the crisis level of 5.8 percent in 2007 to about 6.2 percent for the past two years. Similarly, youth unemployment has seen no recovery whatsoever, increasing on trend from 11.5 percent in 2007 to 13.1 percent for 2017.

The number of the unemployed has steadily plodded up, from 170 million in 2007 to 198 million in 2016, and 202 million for 2017—the crisis adding this 32 million, with 3 million being added in 2016 and another 4 million in 2017. If the discouraged worker effect on the falling labour force participation rate is taken into account, the jobs gap due to the crisis mounts to 62 million. Nor is the crisis in labour markets restricted to the AEs, with about one-third of the jobs lost there, but the other two-thirds lost in the DCs, prominently, 35 million in South Asia, 4 million in sub-Saharan Africa, almost 2 million in the Middle East, and 6 million in Latin America and the Caribbean.[5]

The macro explanation for the faltering global economy appears to be the huge macro headwinds blowing largely from the AEs, leading to a deficit in aggregate demand. Households and firms have continued deleveraging, and not consuming and investing enough. Banks have continued to labour under infected portfolios, reluctant to lend, especially to small and medium enterprises. Corporate debt has translated through much needed financial support for it, into government debt. The need to restore fiscal balances has led to reductions in public expenditures and in significant part through reductions in public wage bills. Weak domestic consumption has led to the need to restore export competitiveness through internal devaluations, again through cuts in the wage bill. These negative private and public feedback loops have all contributed to the weakness in aggregate demand. The problem of the persistence of high unemployment into the longer term has raised structural supply-side issues of deskilling, and scarring for youth, further weighing down on global employment growth rates which continue at 1.4 percent to be a half of global GDP growth rates.

A consequence of the cyclical slowdown in growth in the AEs, both cyclical and structural slowdown in the EEs, especially China, has beckoned the end of the commodities supercycle that began in 2003–04. Commodity prices have been increasing on trend since then, to falter with the initial onslaught of the crisis in 2009, to recover and peak in 2011/12. But by 2016, the cycle had ended, with oil having lost virtually any gains since the start of the cycle, and metals 50 percent above that. This huge fall in commodity prices has affected the earnings, growth, and budgets of the primary commodity producers significantly.

A moot point is whether this depressed state of the global economy and labour market represents a new normal, from which DCs will have to rebound harder in their quest for moving up the income ladder and catch up to the AEs.

Management of a crisis of such proportions in the short run has also detracted from the longer-run issue of development—of growth and jobs in DCs, of the crisis before the crisis—to which we now turn.

Introduction 13

Appendix

Table 1.1 Country classifications

LDCs 49 countries	Afghanistan, Angola, Bangladesh, Benin, Bhutan, Burkina Faso, Burundi, Cambodia, Central African Rep., Chad, Comoros, Dem. Rep. Congo, Djibouti, Equatorial Guinea, Eritrea, Ethiopia, Guinea, Guinea-Bissau, Haiti, Kiribati, Lao PDR, Lesotho, Liberia, Madagascar, Malawi, Mali, Mauritania, Mozambique, Myanmar, Nepal, Niger, Rwanda, Samoa, São Tomé and Príncipe, Senegal, Sierra Leone, Solomon Islands, Somalia, South Sudan, Sudan, Tanzania, The Gambia, Timor-Leste, Togo, Tuvalu, Uganda, Vanuatu, Yemen, Zambia The United Nations defines LDCs according to income criterion (GNI per capita <$992 for inclusion, >$1190 for graduation), human assets index, and economic vulnerability index
LMICs 44 countries	Albania, Armenia, Belize, Bolivia, Cameroon, Cape Verde, Rep. Congo, Côte d'Ivoire, Egypt Arab Rep., El Salvador, Fiji, Georgia, Ghana, Guatemala, Guyana, Honduras, India, Indonesia, Iraq, Kenya, Dem. Rep. Korea, Kosovo, Kyrgyz Republic, Marshall Islands, Micronesia Fed. Sts., Moldova, Mongolia, Morocco, Nicaragua, Nigeria, Pakistan, Papua New Guinea, Paraguay, Philippines, Sri Lanka, Swaziland, Syrian Arab Republic, Tajikistan, Tonga, Ukraine, Uzbekistan, Vietnam, West Bank and Gaza, Zimbabwe World Bank income category: lower-middle income (GNI per capita US$1026–4035) + low-income (GNI per capita <$1025) countries that are not classified as LDCs
EEs 52 countries	Algeria, American Samoa, Antigua and Barbuda, Argentina, Azerbaijan, Belarus, Bosnia and Herzegovina, Botswana, Brazil, Bulgaria, Chile, China, Colombia, Costa Rica, Cuba, Dominica, Dominican Republic, Ecuador, Gabon, Grenada, Iran, Jamaica, Jordan, Kazakhstan, Latvia, Lebanon, Libya, Lithuania, Macedonia FYR, Malaysia, Maldives, Mauritius, Mexico, Montenegro, Namibia, Palau, Panama, Peru, Romania, Russian Federation, Serbia, Seychelles, South Africa, St Lucia, St Vincent and the Grenadines, Suriname, Thailand, Tunisia, Turkey, Turkmenistan, Uruguay, Venezuela RB World Bank income category: upper-middle income (GNI per capita US$4036–12,475) less Angola and Tuvalu (LDCs)

Note: *EE* emerging economy, *GNI* gross national income, *LDC* least developed country, *LMIC* lower- or middle-income country

Notes

1. With Solow going from investment to endogenous growth theory.
2. Which is to purposively ignore for the moment a prolific micro literature on development and labour markets.
3. Largely following the World Bank's categorisation.
4. Data from the ILO Trends Unit, Trends Econometric Models, November 2016 and November 2017.
5. Data from the ILO Trends Unit, Trends Econometric Models, November 2016 and November 2017.

References

Acemoglu, Daron, Simon Johnson, and James A. Robinson. 2000. The Colonial Origins of Comparative Development: An Empirical Investigation. Working Paper 7771, National Bureau of Economic Research, Cambridge, MA.

Chang, Ha-Joon. 2002. *Kicking Away the Ladder: Development Strategy in Historical Perspective*. London: Anthem Press.

———. 2005. *Why Developing Countries Need Tariffs: How WTO NAMA Negotiations Could Deny Developing Countries' Right to a Future*. Geneva: South Centre.

Dutz, Mark A., Sérgio Kannebley Jr., Maira Scarpelli, and Siddharth Sharma. 2012. Measuring Intangible Assets in an Emerging Market Economy: An Application to Brazil. Policy Research Working Paper 6142, World Bank, Washington, DC.

Easterly, William, and Ross Levine. 2001. It's Not Factor Accumulation: Stylized Facts and Growth Models. *World Bank Economic Review* 15 (2): 177–220.

Harrod, Roy. 1948. *Towards a Dynamic Economics: Some Recent Developments of Economic Theory and Their Application to Policy*. London: Macmillan.

Hausmann, Ricardo, Lant Pritchett, and Dani Rodrik. 2005. Growth Accelerations. *Journal of Economic Growth* 10 (4): 303–329.

Hausmann, Ricardo, Dani Rodrik, and Andrés Velasco. 2008. Growth Diagnostics. In *The Washington Consensus Reconsidered: Towards a New Global Governance*, ed. Narcís Serra and Joseph E. Stiglitz, 324–355. New York: Oxford University Press.

IMF (International Monetary Fund). 2016. *World Economic Outlook October 2016: Subdued Demand; Symptoms and Remedies*. Washington, DC: IMF.

———. 2017. *World Economic Outlook October 2017: Seeking Sustainable Growth: Short-Term Recovery, Long-Term Challenges*. Washington, DC: IMF.

Kaldor, Nicholas. 1966. *Causes of the Slow Rate of Economic Growth of the United Kingdom: An Inaugural Lecture*. Cambridge: Cambridge University Press.

Lewis, W. Arthur. 1954. Economic Development with Unlimited Supplies of Labour. *The Manchester School* 22 (2): 139–191.

Lin, Justin Yifu. 2011. New Structural Economics: A Framework for Rethinking Development. *World Bank Research Observer* 26 (2): 193–221.

Lin, Justin, and Ha-Joon Chang. 2009. Should Industrial Policy in Developing Countries Conform to Comparative Advantage or Defy it? A Debate Between Justin Lin and Ha-Joon Chang. *Development Policy Review* 27 (5): 483–502.

Lucas, Robert E., Jr. 1988. On the Mechanics of Economic Development. *Journal of Monetary Economics* 22 (1): 3–42.

Mankiw, N. Gregory, David Romer, and David N. Weil. 1992. A Contribution to the Empirics of Economic Growth. *Quarterly Journal of Economics* 107 (2): 407–437.

Marshall, Alfred. 1920. *Principles of Economics*. 8th ed. London: Macmillan.

Mill, John Stuart. 1848. *Principles of Political Economy, with Some of Their Applications to Social Philosophy*. 2 vols. London: John W. Parker.

North, Douglass C. 2008. Institutions and the Performance of Economies Over Time. In *Handbook of New Institutional Economics*, ed. Claude Ménard and Mary M. Shirley, 21–30. Berlin: Springer.

Prebisch, Raúl. 1962. The Economic Development of Latin America and its Principal Problems. *Economic Bulletin for Latin America* 7 (1): 1–22. Originally published as *The Economic Development of Latin America and its Principal Problems* (New York: United Nations, Department of Economic Affairs, 1950).

Robinson, Joan. 1953. The Production Function and the Theory of Capital. *Review of Economic Studies* 21 (2): 81–106.

———. 1962. *Essays in the Theory of Economic Growth*. London: Palgrave Macmillan.

Say, Jean-Baptiste. 1821. *A Treatise on Political Economy; or, The Production, Distribution, and Consumption of Wealth*. Translated from the fourth edition of the French, by C. R. Prinsep. London: Longman, Hurst, Rees, Orme and Brown.

Singer, Hans W. 1950. The Distribution of Gains Between Investing and Borrowing Countries. *American Economic Review* 40 (2): 473–485.

Solow, Robert M. 1956. A Contribution to the Theory of Economic Growth. *Quarterly Journal of Economics* 70 (1): 65–94.

Verdoorn, P.J. 2002. Factors That Determine the Growth of Labour Productivity. Translated by A. P. Thirlwall. In *Productivity Growth and Economic Performance: Essays on Verdoorn's Law*, edited by John McCombie, Maurizio Pugno, and Bruno Soro, 28–36. London: Palgrave Macmillan. Originally published as 'Fattori the regolano lo sviluppo della produttività del lavoro,' *L'Industria* 1 (1949): 3–10.

Part I

Three Empirical Regularities in Development: In Growth, Jobs, and Macro Drivers

2

A Regularity in Growth Patterns in Developing Countries: The Quantum and Composition

This chapter sets out to examine the pattern of gross domestic product (GDP) growth across developing countries (DCs), to discern distinguishing characteristics between different income levels for least developed countries (LDCs), lower- and middle-income countries (LMICs) and emerging economies (EEs). It does not find that the quantum of GDP growth distinguishes consistently well between these income groups. However, what it does find is that the composition of GDP growth over the past third of a century does set them consistently and distinctly apart. The share of manufacturing moves in lockstep up the income ladder in this long run. This striking empirical regularity about productive transformation may not imply specific industrial policy for each DC, but it is broadly indicative of what has worked in the past, and can be a major policy driver for the future.

2.1 Three Fundamental Questions About Growth

To capture the immense economic and social diversity amongst the 145 DCs, they initially have been classified after the World Bank into per capita income categories of LDCs below US$1000, in 2012 US$, LMICs between US$1000 and US$4000, and EEs between US$4,000 and US$12,000. With advanced economies (AEs) lying above US$12,000. This categorisation allows the posing of three fundamental questions about growth in DCs.

(a) Are DCs converging with AEs—that is, are DCs catching up to AEs in terms of per capita incomes?
(b) If convergence and comparison between DCs and AEs is a far shot, then what distinguishes DCs amongst themselves? What distinguishes LDCs from LMICs and EEs? That is, why are LDCs trapped in lower per capita incomes compared to LMICs, and both in turn compared to EEs? Is it the quantum of their long-run GDP growth?
(c) Or, does the composition of GDP growth also fundamentally distinguish and trap LDCs from LMICs and from EEs?

This logic also establishes the broad methodology of the book. The first part of the book asks the main question—what growth, employment, and macro patterns distinguish and characterise LDCs from LMICs and from EEs? The second part of the book then focuses on the policy drivers for these distinguishing characteristics between LDCs, LMICs, and EEs.

There are of course multiple other cross-cutting categories besides per capita income, by which DCs could be classified. This book goes on to consider a few typologies, such as extractives, and macro drivers of growth, such as investment, export, and consumption-led countries. The World Bank's (2012) *Jobs* report uses to good effect a typology of major characteristics of societies, such as agrarian, conflict-affected, urbanising, resource-based, island, high youth unemployment, formalising, and ageing. The development literature is replete with such rich typologies, with good arguments for their use (see, for instance, Boserup 1981). The choice of typology used, however, should depend on the objective of the enquiry. The objective of this book is to examine development in the areas of growth and jobs using the yardstick of returns to the individual and their productivity. Per capita incomes, and their distribution, then come to a close approximation as the basis for categorising DCs, given this perspective of examining and benchmarking development. Other forms of categorisation, like extractives, or macro drivers of growth like accumulation, exports, and consumption, can then serve to explain what distinguishes growth and employment outcomes between LDCs, LMICs, and EEs. They add to the causal explanation of what distinguishes and traps LDCs from LMICs and from EEs.

2.2   Is There Convergence Between DCs and AEs?

The economist's two-handed answer is, in principle, yes, but effectively no.

Look at Figs. 2.1 and 2.2, which track GDP per capita for 145 DCs and the AEs, in constant US$ over the last third of a century, from 1980 to 2012. There are two critical variables to track here. One is the relative GDP growth rates for DCs and their composite LDCs, LMICs, and EEs,

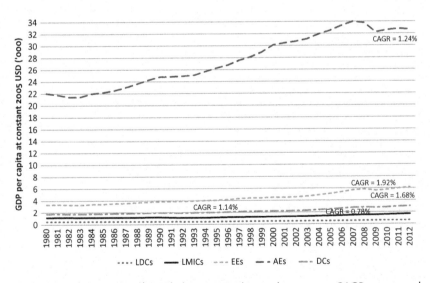

Fig. 2.1 GDP per capita ($ '000). (Note: *AE* advanced economy, *CAGR* compound annual growth rate, *DC* developing country, *EE* emerging economy, *GDP* gross domestic product, *LDC* least developed country, *LMIC* lower- or middle-income country. Source: Author's estimations at the ILO, based on data from ILO, *World of Work Report 2014: Developing with Jobs* (Geneva: ILO, 2014))

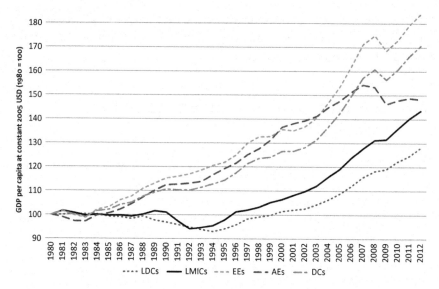

Fig. 2.2 GDP per capita (1980 = 100). (Note: *AE* advanced economy, *DC* developing country, *EE* emerging economy, *GDP* gross domestic product, *LDC* least developed country, *LMIC* lower- or middle-income country. Source: Author's estimations at the ILO, based on data from ILO, *World of Work Report 2014: Developing with Jobs* (Geneva: ILO, 2014))

on the one hand, and for AEs on the other. Figures 2.1 and 2.2 are in constant 2005 US$.

Further, Figs. 2.3 and 2.4 separate out a terms-of-trade effect which is estimated to be very small for DCs, −0.1 percent of GDP per capita growth between 1980 and 2011, comprising +0.2 percent for LDCs and −0.1 percent each for LMICs and EEs.

Between 1980 and 2012, AEs have had a long-run growth rate of GDP per capita of 1.2 percent per annum. Compared to this, DCs have had a long-run growth rate over this period of 1.7 percent per annum, higher than AEs by 0.5 percent per annum. So, in theory, there has been convergence in terms of GDP per capita over the past 32 years. Further, from amongst DCs, EEs have had a higher growth rate for GDP per capita, of 1.9 percent per annum over this period, beckoning an earlier crossover with AEs compared to the average DC. But LMICs have had a slightly lower growth rate for GDP per capita over this period, of 1.1 percent

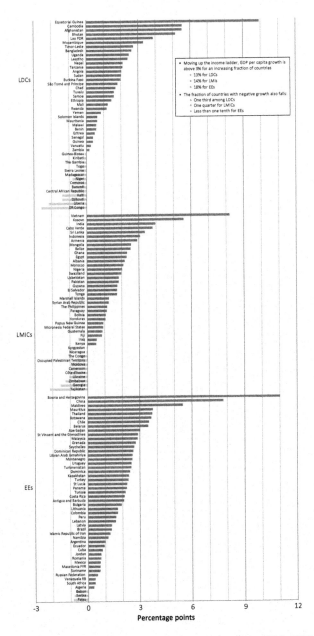

Fig. 2.3 GDP per capita, average annual growth rate, 1980–2011. (Note: *EE* emerging economy, *GDP* gross domestic product, *LDC* least developed country, *LMIC* lower- or middle-income country. Source: Author's estimations at the ILO, based on data from ILO, *World of Work Report 2014: Developing with Jobs* (Geneva: ILO, 2014))

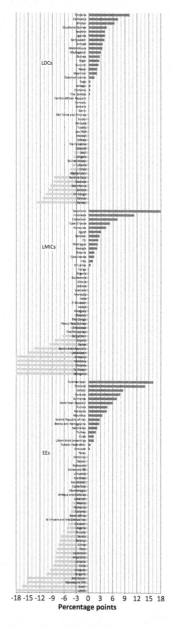

Fig. 2.4 Change in the share of manufacturing's contribution to GDP, 1980–2011 (percentage points). (Note: *EE* emerging economy, *GDP* gross domestic product, *LDC* least developed country, *LMIC* lower- or middle-income country. Source: Author's estimations at the ILO, based on data from ILO, *World of Work Report 2014: Developing with Jobs* (Geneva: ILO, 2014))

per annum, and compared to AEs, beckoning that an eventual crossover with AEs is farther. And LDCs have had an even lower growth rate of GDP per capita over this period, of 0.8 percent per annum, compared to AEs' higher growth rate of 1.2 percent per annum, indicating no convergence over the past 32 years.

Figure 2.2 illustrates this convergence, by pretending as if there were no gap between AEs and DCs in 1980. Starting from this common point, EEs would cross AEs' GDP per capita in about 20 years, EEs would take 30 years, and LMICs a lot longer than the scale of the projections made.

So, there has been convergence in GDP per capita, between AEs, EEs, and LMICs over the past 32 years. However, returning to Fig. 2.1, it shows the immense per capita gap between AEs and DCs. The gap implies that the convergence is at a very low rate, and therefore so far off to be effectively negligible.

In 1980, AEs had an average GDP per capita of US$22,000 (in 2005 US$). Compared to this, DCs had an average GDP per capita of just US$2000. Giving a gap between them of US$20,000. By 2012, the gap between them had widened to about US$30,000. Which illustrates the simple arithmetic of convergence, that the larger the gap in per capita incomes to be overcome, the higher the growth rates of per capita incomes of DCs need to be compared to AEs. That is, the higher the income per capita gap, the higher the growth rate of income needs to overcome the income gap.

So, even the GDP per capita gap for EEs widens from about US$18,000 in 1980 to about US$26,000 by 2012, despite their higher growth rate of 0.7 percent per annum compared to AEs. The GDP per capita gap for LMICs widens from US$21,000 in 1980 to US$31,000 by 2012, given almost equal growth rates with AEs of about 1.2 percent per annum. And the GDP per capita gap for LDCs widens the most, from about US$21,000 in 1980 to US$32,000 in 2012, given their lower growth rates by 0.4 percent compared to AEs.

An important caveat to this convergence exercise has to be noted. Just because the average DC is a far cry from converging with the average AE does not mean that some DCs, especially some EEs, will not converge earlier. Indeed, as seen ahead, there have been a number of graduations from EEs to AEs, and even a few from LMICs to AEs, over the last third of a century examined here. However, the point of this analysis and indeed the whole project of examining a group of countries categorised as DCs is that despite the graduations, a large number of countries characterised as DCs remains very far away from convergence and graduation. Hence it becomes important to examine the immense variety of DCs by themselves, to establish what growth and employment characteristics distinguish between them, and trap them into LDCs, LMICs, and EEs.

2.3 Does the Quantum of Growth Differentiate DCs into LDCs, LMICs, and EEs?

Since convergence between DCs and AEs is a long shot yet, the fundamental question to be asked is, amongst the wide variety of DCs with per capita incomes ranging from LDCs under US$1000 to EEs with up to US$12,000, what growth, employment, and macroeconomic characteristics distinguish and trap them into these per capita incomes. The development policy challenge is then to change these binding growth, employment, and macroeconomic characteristics, to move them up the income ladder.

A prior to these fundamental questions is: does the quantum of GDP growth distinguish LDCs, LMICs, and EEs? And the answer is not lately.

True, Figs. 2.1 and 2.2 showed that long-term growth over the past third of a century, between 1980 and 2012, did give LDCs, LMICs, and EEs significantly different growth rates. LDCs were trapped into growth of GDP per capita of 0.8 percent per annum over this period. LMICs had higher growth of 1.1 percent per annum over this period. And EEs had the highest growth rates of 1.9 percent per annum over this period—higher than AEs by 0.7 percent per annum. Table 2.1 splits this long period into three decades: 1980s, 1990s, and 2000s. It shows that DC growth rates of GDP have picked up from near 4 percent per annum in the 1980s to 5 percent per annum in the 1990s, to 6.5 percent per annum in the 2000s. This applies to each of the three income categories, LDCs, LMICs, and EEs, each climbing up in their GDP growth rates by the decade. In the 2000s, LDCs had GDP growth rates of 6.5 percent

Table 2.1 Annual real GDP growth rate, period average

Classification	1980–89	1990–99	2000–11
DCs	3.81	5.01	6.53
LDCs	2.64	4.03	6.29
LMICs	4.67	4.63	6.33
EEs	3.53	5.20	6.62
Non-extractives			
LDCs	2.82	3.91	5.58
LMICs	4.66	4.88	6.53
EEs	4.12	5.47	7.02
Extractives			
LDCs	1.94	1.06	6.16
LMICs	4.67	4.03	5.86
EEs	1.33	3.97	4.56

Note: *DC* developed country, *EE* emerging economy, *GDP* gross domestic product, *LDC* least developed country, *LMIC* lower- or middle-income country
Source: Author's estimations at the ILO, based on data from IMF, *World Economic Outlook, April 2013, Hopes, Realities, Risks* (Washington, DC: IMF, 2013)

per annum, LMICs 6.3 percent per annum, and EEs 6.6 percent per annum. So LDCs, LMICs, and EEs have been doing equally well in GDP growth in the past 12 years, in the band range of 6.3–6.6 percent. LDCs began the 1980s with much lower GDP growth rates of 2.6 percent per annum, which were 1.5–2.0 percent lower than for the EEs and LMICs. But this early difference in GDP growth rates was largely ironed out by the 2000s.

Table 2.1 also shows that natural resources helped the lower-income categories more in the last decade, giving LDCs and LMICs higher GDP growth rates compared to EEs amongst the DCs more reliant on extractives.[1] Amongst the less extractive-reliant DCs, EEs had the highest GDP growth rates in the last decade of 7 percent per annum, LMICs next at 6.5 percent per annum, and LDCs lowest at 5.6 percent per annum.

Table 2.2 shows that LDC growth was also hardest hit by the end of the decade crisis. The crisis lowered pre-crisis DC growth of 6.7 percent per annum over 2000–07, to 5.9 percent per annum over 2008–13, by about 0.8 percent per annum. LDCs had their GDP growth lowered by 1.9 percent per annum by the crisis, compared to a drop of 0.5 percent per annum for LMICs, and 0.8 percent per annum for EEs.

Table 2.2 Annual real GDP growth rates

	2000	2001	2002	2003	2004	2005	2006	2007	2008	2009	2010	2011	2012	2013	2000–07	2008–13
DCs	5.6	3.6	4.9	6.1	7.5	7.5	8.4	9.1	6.2	3.9	8.2	6.6	5.3	5.7	6.7	5.9
LDCs	5.8	6.0	5.5	6.1	7.4	7.0	7.6	8.3	6.9	4.3	5.3	4.7	5.1	5.6	6.9	5.0
LMICs	4.9	3.8	4.9	5.9	6.7	7.3	7.6	8.2	5.8	4.4	8.6	6.5	4.5	5.5	6.4	5.9
EEs	5.9	3.4	4.9	6.1	7.9	7.7	8.7	9.4	6.3	3.7	8.2	6.7	5.7	5.8	6.8	6.0

Note: *DC* developed country, *EE* emerging economy, *GDP* gross domestic product, *LDC* least developed country, *LMIC* lower- or middle-income country

Source: Author's estimations at the ILO, based on data from IMF, *World Economic Outlook, April 2013, Hopes, Realities, Risks* (Washington, DC: IMF, 2013)

So, in the long run of the past 33 years, the quantum of GDP growth per capita does serve to distinguish between LDCs, LMICs, and EEs, but in the past decade GDP growth rates for all three income categories have picked up and converged in the range of 6.3–6.6 percent. This leads to the next fundamental question, that if the quantum of GDP growth does not consistently distinguish over time between these income categories of LDCs, LMICs, and EEs, does the composition of GDP growth afford more time-consistent distinguishing characteristics?

Some Growth Theory to Contextualise These Findings

Growth theory for development is myriad and arcane. For the purpose of this enquiry, to differentiate between income groups in terms of growth and employment outcomes, and their policy drivers, growth literature is divided into two broad sets. One set explains economic change in terms of the quantum of growth. Another set seeks to explain this change in terms of the composition of growth. And then there is a crossover literature which explains the quantum of growth through its composition.

Essentially, the quantum literature, with its genesis in Mill (1848), Marshall (1920), and Say (1821), has explained macroeconomic change in countries through growth rates determined by the accumulation of physical capital. Their neoclassical successors Solow (1956, 1994) and Harrod (1948) pondered challenges to long-run steady-state growth, stemming from exogenous factors like the rate of population growth having to equal the rate of investment growth (divided by the capital-output ratio). The logical implication of these models seeking to explain economic change in terms of simply the quantum of growth was that there would be eventual convergence across countries from different income groups. The Swan–Solow model in fact predicts just that (see Solow 1994; Thirlwall 1983, 2002). The empirical literature has not borne this out. And the findings above also show convergence to be effectively negligible—a long shot for the group of EEs and LMICs, leave alone LDCs. Which implies the need to rely more (although not solely as seen ahead) on the second literature set emphasising the explanatory power of the composition of growth.

The sea change in growth literature came with the realisation that the economic change could not be explained well by the quantum of growth alone. The components of this growth mattered very much. Without a strict chronology, the progenitors in this realisation stem from Lewis (1954), Verdoorn (2002), Kaldor (1966, 1967, 1975), and the structural transformationists like Chang and Lin (Lin and Chang 2009; Lin 2011) and Hausmann et al. (2008). Lewis comes first because his is the broadest model of macroeconomic change being determined not just by the quantum of growth, but by sectoral change from a subsistence to a capitalist sector. Verdoorn focused on industry, Kaldor on the role of manufacturing, with the transformationists following in that tradition with their own nuances.

The crossover literature seeks to explain the quantum of growth through the composition of growth, principally manufacturing, à la the structural transformationists. But it also seeks to differentiate capital into physical and human capital, à la Arrow (1962), Becker (1962), Lucas (1988), and Mankiw et al. (1992). A more latter-day interpretation by Dutz et al. (2012) seeks to use intangible knowledge-based capital.

2.4 Does the Composition of Growth Differentiate and Lock in DCs into LDCs, LMICs, and EEs?

So, the empirical finding is that the quantum of GDP growth does not offer a time-consistent explanation of the vast income difference within DCs, between LDCs, LMICs, and EEs. Nor does the literature support an explanation of economic change purely in terms of the quantum of GDP growth. This implies that an explanation must be sought for what distinguishes between LDCs, LMICs, and EEs being locked into their separate trajectories, in terms of the composition of their growth.

And the first clear explanation emerges, that a long-run time-consistent difference between LDCs, LMICs, and EEs is due to their differences in the development of manufacturing. Manufacturing shares appear to strongly differentiate and lock in DCs into LDCs, LMICs, and EEs in the long run.

Sectoral Growth

The importance of manufacturing in explaining the long-run differences in income between LDCs, LMICs, and EEs is implied by sectoral growth rates, but only comes out stridently through sectoral shares—the structure of the economy.

Sectoral growth in Table 2.3 follows a Lewisian pattern, in being led by non-agriculture. Lewis (1954) argued that a movement of surplus labour from a low-productivity subsistence sector, say agriculture, to a higher-productivity capitalist sector, say industry, would raise the economy's GDP and growth. A lower increase in the wage compared to the productivity increase provided a surplus to the capitalist to increase investment in this budding sector.

Table 2.3 shows that the earlier observed pick up in DC growth from 3.8 percent in the 1980s to 5 percent in the 1990s, to 6.5 percent in the 2000s, was not led by agriculture, and marginally by manufacturing. Agriculture growth over this period trends at about 3.5 percent per annum. Manufacturing growth over this period picks up from 4.7 percent per annum to 7.2 percent per annum. Industrial growth follows, with a pickup over this period from 3.5 percent per annum to 6.8 percent per annum. Services growth also follows, with a pickup over this period from 3.7 percent per annum to 6.4 percent per annum.

It is important to distinguish between industry and manufacturing. The two main components of industry are manufacturing and extractives. Hence the implication of Table 2.3 is that DC growth over the past third of a century has been led a bit more by manufacturing, a bit less by extractives and services. And this is where the first pattern emerges in sectoral differences between the three income groups, LDCs, LMICs, and EEs.

The three income categories of DCs, LDCs, LMICs, and EEs, all followed the broad Lewisian pattern over the 1980s to the 2000s, of growth being led by non-agriculture. However, Table 2.3 shows that growth for the higher-income groups, EEs and LMICs, was consistently slightly higher for manufacturing over this period than for industry. Conversely, LDCs' growth over this period was more consistently led by industry than manufacturing.

Table 2.3 Annual value-added growth rates, by sector, period average

	Agriculture			Industry			Manufacturing			Services		
	1980–89	1990–99	2000–11	1980–89	1990–99	2000–11	1980–89	1990–99	2000–11	1980–89	1990–99	2000–11
DCs	3.6	2.8	3.5	3.5	5.8	6.8	4.7	7.0	7.2	3.7	4.9	6.4
LDCs	2.7	3.2	4.3	4.1	4.0	7.5	3.8	5.6	5.8	2.8	2.2	6.7
LMICs	3.1	2.8	3.2	4.9	4.9	5.8	5.9	5.3	5.9	5.3	5.3	7.3
EEs	3.9	2.8	3.5	3.2	6.0	7.0	4.4	7.5	7.4	3.4	4.9	6.1

Note: *DC* developed country, *EE* emerging economy, *LDC* least developed country, *LMIC* lower- or middle-income country
Source: Author's estimations at the ILO, based on data from IMF, *World Economic Outlook, April 2013, Hopes, Realities, Risks* (Washington, DC: IMF, 2013); and the World Bank's World Development Indicators, July 2013

Hence the higher-income groups amongst DCs, EEs and LMICs, tend to have relied more on manufacturing growth to lead their GDP growth over the past third of a century. Compared to lower-income DCs like LDCs which have more consistently relied on extractive growth to lead their GDP growth. Services growth pretty much consistently comes third in leading GDP growth for all three DCs' income categories.

The relatively greater reliance of LDCs' growth on extractives also made them more vulnerable to the global crisis. Table 2.4 shows that for DCs' pre-crisis GDP growth over 2000–07 of 6.7 percent per annum, dropped by a half percent per annum with the crisis over 2008–11. From amongst the DCs, the largest drop in GDP growth over this period was for the LDCs of over 2 percentage points per annum, followed by EEs with a drop in GDP growth of 0.6 percentage points per annum. The table shows that the large drop in LDC growth over the crisis is largely accounted for by a more than halving of their industrial growth rates, while their manufacturing growth rates remained constant over this period. The table further shows that industrial growth rates plunged for the more extractive-reliant of LDCs, and indeed the more extractive-reliant of EEs as well.

A general tension also emerges between growth of manufacturing and growth of extractives. A recap of Table 2.4 shows that a high reliance on natural resource rent appears to inhibit manufacturing growth. The table separates the more extractive-reliant DCs from the less extractive-reliant. And it shows that manufacturing growth rates over the 1980s to the 2000s have been largely consistently higher for the less extractive-reliant LDCs, LMICs, and EEs.

Sectoral Shares

So, higher-income DCs, EEs and LMICs, appear to have relied more on manufacturing growth to lead their GDP growth, while lower-income DCs like LDCs appear to have relied more on extractive growth to lead their GDP growth over the past third of a century. This implies that EEs and LMICs will have built up higher shares in manufacturing compared to LDCs.

Table 2.4 Annual growth rates, by sector, period average

	GDP		Agriculture		Industry		Manufacturing		Services	
	2000–07	2008–11	2000–07	2008–11	2000–07	2008–11	2000–07	2008–11	2000–07	2008–11
DCs	6.7	6.2	3.4	3.5	7.1	6.7	7.9	5.8	6.7	6.0
LDCs	6.9	4.8	3.7	4.8	9.4	3.9	6.5	6.5	7.0	5.8
LMICs	6.4	6.5	3.3	3.7	6.1	5.6	6.3	5.6	7.2	7.5
EEs	6.8	6.2	3.4	3.3	7.2	7.0	8.3	5.6	6.5	5.5
Non-extractives										
LDCs	5.5	5.5	3.6	3.9	7.0	7.0	6.3	6.2	5.9	5.7
LMICs	6.5	6.8	3.2	3.8	6.9	6.1	6.7	6.2	7.4	7.9
EEs	7.2	6.7	3.4	3.4	7.7	7.6	8.6	5.9	6.6	5.7
Extractives										
LDCs	7.4	2.8	3.9	6.7	11.5	1.3	7.2	7.4	9.2	6.1
LMICs	5.9	5.6	3.5	3.3	4.7	4.8	5.5	4.4	6.4	6.3
EEs	5.1	3.6	4.2	2.7	3.6	0.8	4.5	0.8	6.3	3.8

Note: *DC* developed country, *EE* emerging economy, *GDP* gross domestic product, *LDC* least developed country, *LMIC* lower- or middle-income country

Source: Author's estimations at the ILO, based on data from IMF, *World Economic Outlook, April 2013, Hopes, Realities, Risks* (Washington, DC: IMF, 2013); and the World Bank's World Development Indicators, July 2013

Indeed, neither shares of extractives in GDP, nor services show any consistent pattern moving up the income ladder in DCs between 1980 and 2010. Shares in manufacturing, however, move in serial lockstep moving up the income ladder, from LDCs to LMICs to EEs.

Table 2.5 shows that the share of agriculture in DCs goes down in expected Lewis fashion, from 15 percent of GDP in 1980 to about 10 percent in 2010, which is by a third. Also in keeping with Lewis, the shares in agriculture over the past three decades have been the lowest for EEs, followed by LMICs and followed by LDCs.

Table 2.5 separates manufacturing from industry, so there are value-added shares in GDP for agriculture, extractives cum construction and utilities, manufacturing, and services. For DCs as a whole, the share of extractives drops marginally between 1980 and 2010 from about 17 percent of GDP to about 16 percent. There is some pattern to the drop in extractive shares. Moving up the income ladder, the share in extractives drops more. So LDCs actually increased their share of extractives in GDP over these last three decades by 7 percent. LMICs reduced their share of extractives in GDP marginally by about 1 percent, while EEs reduced also their share in extractives by less than 1 percent.

The share of services does not show any consistent pattern moving up the income ladder. The share of services in DCs as a whole has remained virtually constant at about 50 percent of GDP for these last three decades. It dropped marginally for LDCs, rose for LMICs, and dropped again for EEs. It is vaguely symptomatic of a backward bending curve moving up the income ladder, but not consistently so either.

Then it is only manufacturing shares which move consistently up the income ladder in DCs, between 1980 and 2010. The manufacturing share in DCs as a whole increased from about 18 percent of GDP to about 24 percent, over the last three decades. LDCs have remained locked in to a very low band in manufacturing shares, ranging between 9 percent in 1980 and 10 percent in 2010. Moving up the income ladder, LMICs have had a significantly higher band in manufacturing, ranging from 16 percent in 1980 to near 19 percent in 2010, while EEs have had the highest band range in manufacturing, ranging from near 19 percent in 1980 to 26 percent in 2010.

Table 2.5 Value added, by sector, as a percentage of GDP (nominal values at constant 2005 US$)

	Agriculture				Industry (excl. manufacturing)				Manufacturing				Services			
	1980	1990	2000	2010	1980	1990	2000	2010	1980	1990	2000	2010	1980	1990	2000	2010
DCs	15.0	15.0	12.2	9.5	16.8	16.0	16.0	16.4	17.6	18.9	22.2	23.8	49.9	50.2	50.6	51.5
LDCs	29.7	29.4	29.4	23.3	14.3	15.0	16.8	21.4	9.0	9.1	10.4	10.2	47.4	47.0	43.9	45.7
LMICs	27.5	23.7	19.6	14.8	14.3	13.8	13.8	13.3	16.0	17.8	18.8	18.6	41.7	44.5	47.5	53.1
EEs	11.2	11.9	9.6	7.5	17.7	16.8	16.6	17.1	18.5	19.7	23.6	25.9	52.1	52.0	51.7	51.3
EEs, excl. China	7.8	7.8	6.8	6.2	19.2	19.2	18.4	17.2	17.4	18.0	19.0	18.4	55.0	55.6	57.5	59.8

Note: *DC* developed country, *EE* emerging economy, *GDP* gross domestic product, *LDC* least developed country, *LMIC* lower- or middle-income country

Source: Author's estimations at the ILO, based on data from IMF, *World Economic Outlook, April 2013, Hopes, Realities, Risks* (Washington, DC: IMF, 2013); and the World Bank's World Development Indicators, July 2013

Hence long-run manufacturing shares in GDP appear to explain per capita *incomes very well for DCs and consistently over the past three decades. It is not the quantum of growth—GDP growth rates having converged across* per capita *incomes in the last decade—that explains the large variation in* per capita *incomes. It is the nature of growth that explains this variation in country incomes. It is the long-run manufacturing share in GDP that appears to distinguish countries in different* per capita *income groups.*

That said, manufacturing has had a very rough ride in an increasingly competitive market. So this result could be based on the manufacturing gains of few large countries, at the expense of a number of small ones whose manufacturing sectors have shrunk over time. The first test for this is the removal of one such manufacturing giant from amongst the EEs, China. That still leaves EEs in the same band as LMICs, with a manufacturing share in GDP ranging between 17 percent in 1980 and 18 percent in 2010. The manufacturing share still separates LDCs, from LMICs and EEs quite consistently over the last three decades.

The second test is to examine in how many countries manufacturing dropped its share significantly in the last three decades. Figure 2.4 shows that only 13 out of 49 LDCs saw a reduction in their manufacturing shares of greater than 3 percent, over the last three decades. Sixteen out of 44 LMICs saw such significant drops over this period. And 24 out of 52 EEs saw such significant drops over this period. So, while there has been much churning in the manufacturing sector shares in these 145 DCs, stability and even rise in manufacturing shares has been a majority phenomenon, and not restricted to a minority of winners. Figure 2.4 shows the substantial variation between the countries within each of these country groups.

Some Econometric Support for Three Key Propositions

So, there are two key propositions made about long-run growth in DCs stretching back to the past third of a century. These have been made through tabular findings, and could use econometric support.

Proposition 1: GDP growth is more consistently led by manufacturing growth than by growth in other sectors.

Proposition 2: The share of manufacturing moves up the per capita *GDP ladder, hence explaining the long-run persistence of different income levels of LDCs, LMICs, and EEs.*

Which implies Proposition 3: If GDP growth is led by manufacturing growth, and manufacturing shares move up the per capita *income ladder, then manufacturing growth will help GDP growth more moving up the* per capita *income ladder. That is higher* per capita *income countries with higher manufacturing shares will have higher GDP growth.*

Hence manufacturing growth becomes a key determinant of moving up the per capita income ladder for DCs.

Figure 2.5 lends more econometric robustness to the tabular results in Tables 2.3 and 2.5 driving these two propositions. First in support of Proposition 1, manufacturing is strongly, significantly, and positively correlated to GDP growth and GDP per capita growth, supporting the tabular result in Fig. 2.5 showing that manufacturing growth may have more consistently led GDP growth in the past three decades. A coefficient of 0.42 shows that a 1 percentage point increase in manufacturing growth rate is associated with a 0.4 percentage point increase in GDP growth rates. A coefficient of 0.4 shows that a 1 percentage point increase in manufacturing growth rates is associated with a 0.4 percentage point increase in GDP per capita. The R-squared shows that about 44 percent of the variation in GDP growth is explained by manufacturing growth.

Figure 2.5 further shows that in running both manufacturing and the rest of industry—largely extractives—manufacturing has a coefficient of 0.34, twice the coefficient for the rest of industry with 0.17. So, a 1 percentage point increase in manufacturing growth leads to a 0.34 percentage point increase in GDP growth. Compared to this, a 1 percentage point increase in the rest of industry's growth rate, leads to a much smaller 0.17 percentage point increase in GDP growth. The R-squared shows that about 60 percent of the variation in GDP growth is explained by both manufacturing and extractives.

Second, in support of Proposition 2, Fig. 2.6 shows that the share of manufacturing in GDP is also positively and significantly correlated to

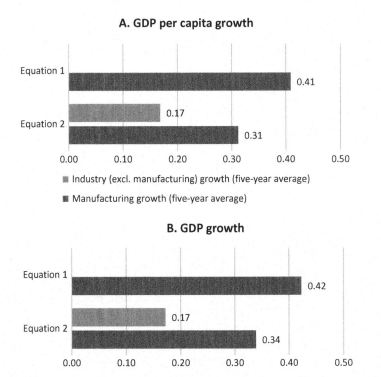

Fig. 2.5 Effect of manufacturing and industry growth on GDP growth. (Note: *GDP* gross domestic product. The figures show the average annual percentage point change in GDP and GDP per capita with a 1 percentage point change in the average annual industrial and manufacturing sectors. All the estimated coefficients are statistically significant at the 1 percent confidence level. Econometric specifications available from the author. Source: Author's estimations at the ILO, based on data from the World Bank's World Development Indicators)

GDP per capita. As is the rest of industry. Both more so than services. The coefficients for both manufacturing and the rest of industry are low at 0.03, because of the huge variation in per capita incomes to be explained. But sectoral variation in shares explains about two-thirds of the variation in GDP per capita. Further, Fig. 2.6 also shows that the

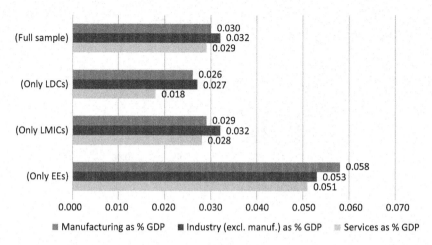

Fig. 2.6 Effect of sectoral shares on GDP per capita. (Note: *EE* emerging economy, *GDP* gross domestic product, *LDC* least developed country, *LMIC* lower- or middle-income country. Econometric specifications available from the author. Source: Author's estimations at the ILO, based on data from the World Bank's World Development Indicators)

coefficients increase moving up the income ladder. The manufacturing coefficient goes up from 0.026 for LDCs to 0.029 for LMICs, to 0.058 for EEs.

Third, Fig. 2.7 gives support for Proposition 3, that manufacturing growth will contribute more to GDP growth in going up the income ladder. The figure shows that the coefficient for manufacturing growth contributing to per capita GDP growth goes up from 0.235 for LDCs, to 0.506 for LMICs, to 0.516 for EEs. The R-squared explains about 40 percent of the variation in GDP per capita growth.

Support for Classical Growth Theory

Proposition 1, that manufacturing growth is the more important determinant of GDP growth, harks back to classical growth theory whose progenitors were Kaldor and Verdoorn. Proposition 2, that manufacturing shares explain

A Regularity in Growth Patterns in Developing Countries... 41

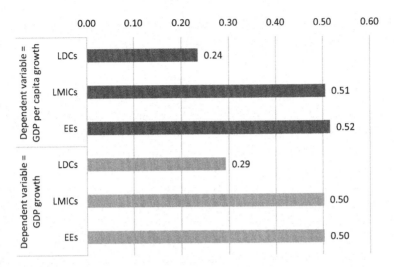

Fig. 2.7 Effect of manufacturing (five-year average) growth on GDP growth. (Note: *EE* emerging economy, *GDP* gross domestic product, *LDC* least developed country, *LMIC* lower- or middle-income country. Econometric specifications available from the author. Source: Author's estimations at the ILO, based on data from the World Bank's World Development Indicators)

per capita *incomes of countries, and hence their movement up the* per capita *income ladder, is a modest advance in that tradition. Proposition 3, ergo that manufacturing growth will contribute more to GDP growth for higher* per capita *income countries, is again a modest advance in the Kaldorian tradition.*

Lewis (1954) implied that GDP growth would be led by (a) the increasing share and (b) the higher productivity of the capitalist modern sector, as a result of workers moving to it from the lower-productivity subsistence sector. Kaldor (1966, 1967, 1975) identified that GDP growth would be led by manufacturing (see also Thirlwall 1983). Kaldor was seeking to explain why growth rates for Great Britain had lagged behind those of the other industrialised economies like the US, France, and Germany. His hypothesis was that the decline in manufacturing in the UK was responsible for the relatively low GDP growth rate experienced. Manufacturing was the driving force for growth and development.

Kaldor's first law sets out this hypothesis clearly: higher growth of manufacturing causes higher growth of aggregate output.[2] Since manufacturing is also a part of aggregate output, part of the law could be true by definition. But Kaldor's argument was that output growth in manufacturing contributed to output growth in non-manufacturing because it provided capital goods to the other sectors. Four other key rationales have been added along the way (see Andreoni and Gregory 2013). First, there are more opportunities for capital accumulation and intensification in manufacturing, given greater economies of scale allowing for technological indivisibilities. Second, there is a higher income elasticity of demand for manufactured goods, so as incomes rise, higher manufactures constitute a higher proportion of consumption. Third, manufactures help ease balance-of-payments problems because of their exportability. And fourth, the possibility of higher technical change in manufacturing permits greater learning opportunities enhancing supply-side capabilities.

What can work against Kaldor's first law is that since his first arguments were made, freer movement of capital and technology could have vitiated the preferential role of manufacturing in leading technological change and growth. However, two factors also work to support the law. One, increasing global competition within manufacturing has served to keep its growth and shares in country's GDP in check. Two, increasing competition in manufacturing has also driven up technical change within it. A large debate on the complementary role of services and outsourcing some manufacturing processes to services is addressed in the following chapter five on productive transformation. Hence the persistence in the literature with a preferential role for manufacturing in both DCs and AEs.

Empirical results testing Kaldor's first law have been good. Kaldor himself used data from 12 technically advanced economies over 1953–1963, regressing GDP growth on manufacturing growth. He found a significant coefficient of 0.64 with an R-squared value of 0.959. The result for 145 DCs given above is a bit weaker, with a lower coefficient of 0.4 and a lower R-squared of 0.44, but very much supportive of

Kaldor's first law applied to DCs. A number of other empirical results have been supportive of Kaldor, including Thirlwall's (1983) rerun, McCombie and de Ridder (1984) for states in the US, Hansen and Zhang (1996) for provinces in China, Bernat (1996) for the US, Bairam (1991) for Turkey, Drakopoulos and Theodossiou (1991) for Greece, and Atesoglu (1993) for the US.

There are a number of theoretical problems with Kaldor's first law, but they are not overriding. The source of demand has to be assumed to be exogenous. Manufacturing does not produce just capital goods but also consumption goods. The empirical results are based on the mechanism of increasing returns to scale in manufacturing, and transfer of labour from less productive sectors to manufacturing.

Hence a host of current literature takes manufacturing as the engine of growth and development, for instance, Cohen and Zysman (1988) and Toner (1999) and the structural transformationists par excellence being Lin and Chang (2009), Lin (2011), and McMillan and Rodrik (2011). McMillan and Rodrik have a more nuanced position amongst the structural transformationists in first using country data for 39 DCs, including China, Turkey, and countries from Latin America and Africa, for the period 1990–2005. They specify that labour flows have to be from low- to higher-productivity sectors for structural transformation to have a positive impact on growth.

In essence, the results obtained here for 145 DCs observed over the past three decades support Kaldor's first law. Proposition 1, that manufacturing growth is the more important determinant of GDP growth, follows and supports Kaldor's first law. Proposition 2, that manufacturing shares move up the income ladder, explaining the variation in GDP per capita between LDCs, LMICs, and EEs, is a modest step forward in the Kaldorian tradition. Proposition 3, which is implied from the first two propositions, that manufacturing growth will contribute more towards GDP growth going up the income ladder from LDCs to LMICs to EEs, is also a modest step forward in this tradition.

2.5 Conclusions

This chapter sets out to examine the pattern of GDP growth across DCs, to see what distinguishes LDCs from LMICs and from EEs. It does not find that the quantum of growth does this well and consistently over time, because of a convergence in GDP growth rates in the last decade plus. What it does find is that the composition of growth distinguishes between LDCs, LMICs, and EEs consistently and well—in the form of the development of the manufacturing sector. This empirical regularity does not of itself a development strategy make—based on industrial policy to develop manufacturing. There must be important caveats to this. Principally, the analysis of DCs' manufacturing shares over the past third of a century do show a reduction in a minority of the countries. Competition within global manufacturing being intense would account for the falls in these countries' shares. There may also be limits on the size of the sector imposed by non-price factors as seen ahead in the policy chapter five also focussing on productive transformation. And in some cases, factor endowments could be not just non-conducive and therefore amenable to aggressive industrial policy, but could down right militate against manufacturing.

All said, however, this chapter does find a striking empirical regularity in manufacturing differentiating between LDCs, LMICs, and EEs. As such it does provide a broad indicator for development policy, of what has worked in the past, and indicative of future policy drivers.

Appendix

Table 2.6 Share of manufacturing as a percentage of GDP

	1980	1981	1982	1983	1984	1985	1986	1987	1988	1989	1990	1991	1992	1993	1994	1995
Afghanistan																
Angola	13.83	13.73	13.71	14.70	14.27		10.92	7.31	8.24	6.14	5.00	6.24	4.96	5.65	4.94	4.01
Bangladesh	7.97	6.64	9.10	8.67	7.93	14.16	13.96	13.25	13.18	12.78	13.10	13.41	13.91	14.91	15.29	15.33
Benin	2.89	5.71	5.62	6.43	6.47	7.89	7.18	7.17	8.13	7.84	7.38	7.16	7.94	7.43	8.05	8.08
Bhutan						5.95	5.16	5.81	5.42	7.57	7.91	8.76	9.02	9.09	9.49	10.70
Burkina Faso	15.24	14.87	14.87	16.36	15.44	13.83	14.39	15.56	15.80	15.16	15.38	14.02	15.16	14.76	14.50	15.23
Burundi	7.44	7.71	8.91	8.94	8.62	8.06	8.77	11.54	11.01	13.31	12.94	14.20	9.59	9.40	10.74	9.46
Cambodia														8.85	9.27	9.51
Central African Republic	7.19	7.43	7.72	8.68	8.35	9.83	8.23	8.85	9.91	9.95	11.26	11.90	11.05	11.05	10.00	10.16
Chad				11.11	13.29	10.43	11.90	11.41	10.71	13.38	14.41	10.61	10.58	11.15	9.22	11.23
Comoros	3.91	3.85	3.67	3.57	0.36	3.67	3.66	3.74	3.84	4.00	4.21	4.18	4.45	4.50	5.97	4.16
Congo, Dem. Rep.	15.18	15.64	14.99	14.16	10.47	10.49	10.65	9.62	11.33	10.34	11.30	7.40	4.96	6.89		
Djibouti																
Equatorial Guinea										5.49	3.65	3.64	3.39	3.35	2.81	2.80
Eritrea												1.72	1.68	1.60		
Ethiopia		4.91	4.63	4.44	5.39	4.34	4.63	5.51	5.13	5.15	4.79	3.03	8.25	9.03	7.74	9.04
Gambia, The	4.88	5.67	4.65	6.65	8.68	6.67	6.26	5.99	4.80	4.93	5.53	9.21	2.81	3.93	4.45	4.80
Guinea									4.52	4.54	4.56	4.04	8.90	8.70	8.02	8.15
Guinea-Bissau							14.42	8.50	6.46	7.61	8.40	3.81	4.64	4.76	4.67	3.98
Haiti													2.50	3.54	7.23	7.89
Kiribati	2.11	2.11	1.95	2.05	0.45	0.69	0.60	0.33	0.67	0.63	1.23	7.04	6.17	6.36	6.01	6.19
Lao PDR										9.27	9.96	12.49	13.41	13.08	12.91	14.27
Lesotho	8.42	9.12	11.53	12.66	13.93	13.21	14.07	16.30	15.48	15.77	14.50	14.64	16.16	15.98	16.80	16.31

(continued)

Table 2.6 (continued)

	1980	1981	1982	1983	1984	1985	1986	1987	1988	1989	1990	1991	1992	1993	1994	1995
Liberia	7.69	5.70	5.30	5.14	5.15	4.91	4.76									2.74
Madagascar					11.18	11.26	10.64	11.43	10.74	12.86	11.15	11.01	10.42	9.86	8.02	7.94
Malawi	13.66	14.04	13.56	14.33	13.80	14.46	14.76	16.80	15.80	18.48	19.47	17.97	21.17	15.66	17.39	15.82
Mali	6.54	6.93	6.42	6.52	6.79	7.33	7.24	8.67	8.89	8.55	8.55	8.52	7.50	7.55	7.72	7.98
Mauritania																
Mozambique						12.88	13.09	12.08	13.15	11.58	10.28	7.59	8.49	9.79	8.66	8.30
Myanmar	9.54	9.35	9.29	9.58	9.85	9.93	9.23	7.77	7.51	8.61	10.17	10.97	11.36	8.46	8.95	7.61
Nepal	4.28	4.12	4.28	4.61	4.91	5.70	6.17	6.19	6.39	5.75	7.78	6.99	6.93	6.83	6.24	6.88
Niger	3.74	3.93	3.86	6.24	7.02	7.14	7.75	6.17	5.90	6.27	6.09	6.73	8.83	8.81	9.55	9.54
Rwanda	15.26	15.74	13.48	15.35	13.96	13.72	15.93	10.76	10.35	10.44	6.59	6.21	6.47	6.52	6.31	6.40
Samoa											18.30	16.14	12.11	11.48	17.25	10.22
São Tomé and Príncipe														19.61		19.32
Senegal	13.50	13.10	14.14	14.34	14.42	13.79	13.70	13.71	14.61	14.35	15.26	15.43	16.38	15.73	16.03	16.59
Sierra Leone	5.29	6.56	6.93	6.76	5.73			4.00	3.00	6.00	4.61	5.32	7.21	10.14	9.90	9.27
Solomon Islands											2.35	9.86	8.81	8.04	8.96	7.15
Somalia	4.74	4.60	5.26	4.90	4.69	4.98	5.50	5.22	5.29	4.55	4.62					
South Sudan																
Sudan	7.46	7.41	7.13	7.60	8.32	8.62	8.63	8.78	8.71	8.70	8.67	6.49	5.96	5.50	5.36	4.80
Tanzania											9.27	8.97	8.20	7.49	7.41	7.17
Timor-Leste																
Togo	7.83	7.07	7.37	6.75	6.37	6.74	7.27	8.28	7.67	8.94	9.93	11.12	11.59	9.10	9.12	9.89
Tuvalu											3.08	3.21	3.39	2.59	2.42	3.88
Uganda	4.28	1.87	6.68	5.73	6.74	5.81	6.45	5.88	5.78	5.94	5.67	5.82	6.17	5.98	6.52	6.79
Vanuatu	4.22	4.23	4.50	3.39	3.47	4.20	4.24	5.09	5.33	5.40	5.19	5.06	4.64	4.37	4.65	4.63
Yemen, Rep.											19.04	17.98	16.80	16.25	15.15	12.34
Zambia	18.26	19.77	20.57	23.38	23.05	25.46	25.24	28.48	32.72	34.37	36.06	36.75	37.16	27.94	11.24	11.22
Albania																

(continued)

Table 2.6 (continued)

	1980	1981	1982	1983	1984	1985	1986	1987	1988	1989	1990	1991	1992	1993	1994	1995
Armenia											32.79	37.33	33.13	22.86	30.08	25.20
Belize	23.91	20.34	16.50	18.27	19.65	16.72	15.58	18.55	18.50	16.43	13.09	12.01	11.77	11.14	11.29	11.23
Bolivia	14.45	16.42	8.22	12.75	11.97	17.34	20.42	18.69	19.45	18.55	18.50	19.50	19.07	18.81	18.70	19.01
Cameroon	9.60	10.46	12.07	11.65	12.14	11.53	12.39	13.20	13.57	14.38	14.52	14.48	14.29	21.45	22.30	21.66
Cape Verde							7.38	8.44	7.28	8.70	9.02	10.58	10.87	7.13	9.57	10.10
Congo, Rep.	7.49	6.33	4.77	5.52	4.85	5.62	9.64	8.65	8.64	6.86	8.35	8.94	7.90	7.99	7.76	8.13
Côte d'Ivoire	12.81	11.78	14.22	14.45	14.01	14.59	17.63	18.78	19.53	19.11	20.90	19.43	19.07	15.43	14.74	15.05
Egypt, Arab Rep.	12.25	12.95	13.29	13.20	13.23	13.51	13.26	16.49	17.74	18.10	17.76	16.57	16.58	16.71	17.20	17.45
El Salvador											22.12	22.61	24.40	23.98	23.48	23.10
Fiji	11.94	10.50	10.67	9.15	10.14	9.45	10.30	11.84	9.57	12.72	13.55	13.94	13.39	14.62	14.89	13.93
Georgia																
Ghana	8.10	6.22	3.73		6.74	12.44	11.21	9.90	9.58	10.10	9.81	9.28	9.37	10.51	10.12	10.27
Guatemala																
Guyana	12.13	14.89	14.32	13.17	13.03	13.88	14.75	13.92	12.78	13.35	10.31	12.91	14.28	11.62	11.60	11.40
Honduras	14.96	14.42	14.68	15.06	15.41	14.52	14.28	14.54	15.14	15.01	16.34	16.94	17.82	17.73	17.26	17.83
India	16.18	16.25	15.88	16.10	16.11	15.98	15.84	15.87	15.68	16.41	16.16	15.21	15.36	15.32	16.20	17.30
Indonesia	12.99	12.10	11.94	12.75	14.59	15.98	16.74	16.95	19.70	19.74	20.66	21.35	21.96	22.30	23.35	24.13
Iraq																
Kenya	12.84	12.34	12.21	11.75	11.89	11.72	11.89	11.55	11.89	11.67	11.72	12.05	10.79	10.01	10.69	9.88
Korea, Dem. Rep.																
Kosovo																
Kyrgyz Republic											27.11	28.82	33.68	26.33	21.83	9.25
Marshall Islands																
Micronesia, Fed. Sts.			0.40													

(continued)

Table 2.6 (continued)

	1980	1981	1982	1983	1984	1985	1986	1987	1988	1989	1990	1991	1992	1993	1994	1995
Moldova														35.99	30.90	25.71
Mongolia			17.46	18.53	18.41	18.39	17.36	18.72	18.04	32.70	20.99	18.82	19.78	17.64	17.88	18.25
Morocco	16.87	18.09	17.46	18.53	18.41	18.39	17.36	18.72	18.04	18.35	18.99	17.75	18.98	18.85	17.55	18.95
Nicaragua															15.19	15.14
Nigeria																
Pakistan	15.93	15.11	15.13	15.29	16.13	15.90	16.28	16.65	16.79	16.61	17.41	17.13	16.86	16.67	16.78	16.31
Papua New Guinea	10.16	10.63	10.19	10.92	11.92	11.84	10.94	10.38	10.19	11.85	9.55	10.14	9.69	8.80	8.01	8.41
Paraguay												14.97	14.90	14.88	15.31	15.86
Philippines	25.70	25.51	25.10	24.24	24.63	25.15	24.63	24.84	25.62	24.87	24.83	25.32	24.18	23.71	23.26	22.99
Sri Lanka	17.75	16.24	14.37	14.01	14.92	14.73	15.19	16.02	15.38	15.32	14.84	14.76	15.33	15.20	15.38	15.73
Swaziland	20.94	20.94	21.40	17.90	18.59	16.17	21.66	29.21	34.26	35.84	36.82	36.72	35.02	36.14	36.05	39.06
Syrian Arab Republic											21.48	19.12	14.86	15.35	15.19	15.46
Tajikistan						31.30	27.62	29.95	26.65	22.98	24.85	24.38	34.07	32.37	27.70	28.11
Tonga	7.01	4.82	4.68	4.60	5.97	5.67	5.20	4.86	5.37	6.06	6.10	5.35	5.13	5.44	9.64	9.19
Ukraine										39.26				29.88	39.03	34.62
Uzbekistan								27.98	25.11	22.10			43.54		14.19	11.86
Vietnam					20.51		22.37	22.37	18.05	15.15	12.26	13.10	15.39	15.17	14.91	14.99
West Bank and Gaza																
Zimbabwe	21.58	21.77	20.88	23.01	22.65	19.85	21.45	22.69	21.51	25.60	22.76	27.16	29.54	23.01	21.17	21.80
Algeria	10.55	10.59	11.15	11.81	13.83	13.70	15.71	14.88	14.89	12.32	11.38	11.45	12.31	13.13	12.36	11.50
American Samoa																
Antigua and Barbuda	5.33	5.05	5.30	4.94	4.78	4.32	3.89	3.56	3.14	3.13	3.38	3.03	2.76	2.44	2.27	2.31
Argentina	29.48	28.77	31.36	30.67	29.71	29.64	27.42	27.50	28.00	30.95	26.79	24.39	21.86	19.50	19.07	18.36
Azerbaijan											19.30	17.66	23.93	18.81	12.92	12.50

(continued)

	1980	1981	1982	1983	1984	1985	1986	1987	1988	1989	1990	1991	1992	1993	1994	1995
Belarus											39.17	42.17	40.54	30.00	29.82	30.98
Bosnia and Herzegovina															11.51	11.44
Botswana	5.09	6.99	7.71	6.70	5.60	5.44	5.97	5.88	5.41	5.24	5.12	5.31	5.48	4.77	4.87	5.47
Brazil	33.49	32.92	34.56	33.19	33.87	33.75	32.97	31.96	30.95	29.53		25.34	24.66	24.95	23.66	18.62
Bulgaria																
Chile	21.52	22.27	18.49	21.18	24.23	16.20	18.69	18.37	18.89	18.87	19.57	20.46	20.49	18.55	18.36	18.09
China	40.23	38.32	37.13	36.37	35.29	34.73	34.98	34.45	34.60	34.30	32.66	32.49	32.74	33.97	33.63	33.65
Colombia	23.93	21.93	21.83	21.50	22.61	21.97	23.19	21.05	21.95	21.62	20.58	20.90	19.77	20.49	16.13	15.92
Costa Rica				24.76	25.86	25.12	24.42	24.03	24.48	23.96	22.62	22.84	23.34	22.24	21.74	21.84
Cuba	8.68	8.69	8.61	8.57	8.48	9.05	8.74	8.23	8.39	8.02	7.66	8.15	9.43	9.60	13.02	14.58
Dominica	4.80	6.67	8.19	7.82	6.12	6.45	6.67	6.45	6.58	7.27	7.15	7.54	8.16	8.22	7.14	7.42
Dominican Republic	15.31	15.59	18.27	17.71	16.53	12.26	12.68	12.79	12.11	17.67	17.96	28.36	27.43	26.65	26.52	25.56
Ecuador	17.52	16.57	17.30	18.21	21.41	20.58	20.22	20.74	21.65	21.03	21.73	23.10	24.27	20.95	20.81	20.32
Gabon	4.56	4.03	4.29	4.48	5.37	7.25	9.32	8.48	7.60	6.40	5.58	6.17	6.19	6.29	4.73	4.52
Grenada	3.76	3.50	5.48	4.66	5.45	6.07	5.60	5.92	6.38	6.26	6.55	6.45	7.00	6.06	6.33	6.58
Iran, Islamic Rep.	7.77	8.19	7.89	7.33	7.68	7.17	7.37	8.18	9.04	8.73	11.78	13.08	13.22	10.61	12.14	11.88
Jamaica														17.22	17.01	16.04
Jordan	12.68	14.50	13.91	12.70	14.00	11.52	10.65	11.37	10.12	12.07	14.85	13.72	14.21	13.29	15.88	15.10
Kazakhstan																15.27
Latvia	45.97	45.15	42.17	37.32	35.18	37.07	38.90	40.09	36.88	37.00	34.47	35.70	28.21	23.06	19.94	20.68
Lebanon															13.98	13.98
Libya																
Lithuania											20.88	45.28	34.42	31.70	25.05	19.13
Macedonia, FYR											35.67	29.23	32.89	28.11	23.71	23.24
Malaysia	21.55	20.92	19.06	19.31	19.31	19.32	19.33	19.80	21.82	23.80	24.22	25.55	25.82	25.93	26.64	26.38

(continued)

Table 2.6 (continued)

	1980	1981	1982	1983	1984	1985	1986	1987	1988	1989	1990	1991	1992	1993	1994	1995
Maldives																7.88
Mauritius	15.77	16.25	16.10	16.35	18.73	21.34	24.08	25.30	25.13	24.48	24.37	23.94	23.83	23.31	22.63	22.95
Mexico	22.26	21.95	21.72	21.26	22.66	23.97	24.78	26.38	23.86	21.90	20.80	20.59	20.25	19.04	18.71	20.81
Montenegro																
Namibia	9.15	11.27	11.77	12.17	11.95	11.08	11.45	12.53	11.79	11.97	13.78	12.95	13.74	14.14	13.17	12.99
Palau													0.72	0.74	0.86	0.91
Panama	10.97	9.77	9.31													
Peru				10.21	10.64	12.33	11.31	10.79	9.46	9.33	9.75	9.88	9.64	9.20	8.95	9.13
Romania																
							23.69	28.82	28.82	25.27	17.83	17.52	17.74	17.80	17.70	16.76
Russian Federation												33.84	30.61	28.73	31.09	28.66
Serbia																
Seychelles	7.38	8.53	8.52	9.63	9.39	9.66	9.27	9.79	10.50	9.43	10.10	10.82	11.90	10.67	11.42	12.66
South Africa	21.63	24.00	23.72	23.48	23.01	21.80	21.93	22.39	22.93	23.50	23.64	22.87	21.86	21.14	20.92	21.22
St. Lucia	10.45	9.27	9.09	9.52	8.90	8.50	8.20	8.48	8.41	8.26	8.12	7.94	7.52	7.48	6.21	6.87
St. Vincent and the Grenadines	10.46	10.82	10.93	10.25	12.56	11.60	10.26	10.26	10.45	10.76	8.50	8.94	9.54	9.30	9.21	8.37
Suriname	18.56	17.98	14.24	12.68	13.04	13.21	13.70	11.46	12.84	12.90	10.29	8.22	7.76	8.17	9.95	13.66
Thailand	21.51	22.64	21.32	22.13	22.91	21.92	23.88	24.25	25.84	26.75	27.20	28.24	27.52	29.65	29.55	29.90
Tunisia	13.62	13.57	12.64	16.60	17.02	17.29	18.08	17.23	19.27	19.11	19.05	19.37	19.08	19.84	21.25	21.75
Turkey	17.32	19.72	20.30	19.51	18.47	18.78	22.87	22.64	23.74	23.84	22.73	22.98	22.47	21.70	22.87	23.42
Turkmenistan														5.52	28.64	40.45
Uruguay				25.36	27.28	29.40	29.72	28.95	27.26	26.83	27.97	28.31	24.78	21.10	18.88	19.69
Venezuela, RB	16.02	14.90	15.90	16.33	18.21	18.94	19.76	18.95	18.06	16.69	14.94	15.52	14.95	14.71	14.63	15.11

(continued)

Table 2.6 (continued)

	1996	1997	1998	1999	2000	2001	2002	2003	2004	2005	2006	2007	2008	2009	2010	2011
Afghanistan	3.45	4.38	6.32	3.22	2.89	3.87	18.75	17.08	17.88	16.94	16.74	18.05	18.20	13.56	12.94	14.09
Angola	15.43	15.61	16.24	15.47	15.23	15.61	3.66	3.88	4.00	4.07	4.85	5.20	4.80	6.07	6.12	5.97
Bangladesh	8.28	8.47	7.99	8.14	8.20	8.52	15.86	15.80	16.13	16.53	17.21	17.77	17.83	17.92	17.89	17.63
Benin	11.60	10.23	9.55	8.94	8.38	8.55	8.49	8.28	7.83	7.84	7.54	7.52	7.17	7.46	7.71	
Bhutan	14.48	15.65	14.93	16.85	16.33	13.13	7.66	7.43	7.50	7.39	7.88	8.40	8.65	8.43	9.09	9.31
Burkina Faso	6.72	7.64	7.89	8.20	14.88	14.67	11.11	14.26	14.41	11.69	11.34	11.06	8.32	8.84	7.80	6.73
Burundi	10.58	12.13	13.19	13.98	16.87	17.67	14.35	14.02	13.52	12.95	12.69	12.44	11.45	11.60	10.52	9.85
Cambodia	9.82	9.58	9.37	9.00	7.34	7.12	18.59	19.13	19.91	18.79	19.55	18.61	16.33	15.35	15.62	16.11
Central African Republic							7.37	7.31								
Chad	10.52	12.03	11.28	10.21	8.93	9.56	9.43	7.98	5.15	5.34	5.61	6.18	6.56			
Comoros	4.16	4.16	4.16	4.16	4.53	4.57	4.36	4.36	4.42	4.35	4.19	4.20	4.25	4.29		
Congo, Dem. Rep.	8.92	6.33	6.07	5.05	4.82	4.86	5.42	5.42	5.39	5.40	5.24	5.12	4.96	4.97	4.68	4.55
Djibouti	2.89	2.89	2.70	2.58	2.61	2.61	2.64	2.67	2.66	2.59	2.52	2.45				
Equatorial Guinea					1.44	6.18	6.43	6.73	5.73	6.15						
Eritrea	9.56	10.70	9.38	10.04	9.93	9.57	10.09	9.90	9.33	7.31	6.35	5.71	6.76	5.65		
Ethiopia	5.13	5.04	4.94	5.48	5.52	5.72	5.68	5.67	5.32	4.78	4.54	5.02	4.76	3.99	3.90	3.56
Gambia, The	7.57	8.02	7.54	7.15	6.77	6.63	7.02	5.92	5.60	6.64	6.85	6.68	5.79	4.98	4.73	5.16
Guinea	3.82	3.62	3.83	4.02	4.03	4.03	4.10	6.37	6.09	6.60	6.16	7.02	6.83	7.38	7.25	7.24
Guinea-Bissau	7.41	11.20	9.29	10.73	10.50	10.16	10.60									
Haiti																
Kiribati	5.61	5.50	5.01	5.19	4.99	4.88	4.45	4.52	4.97	5.49	5.48	6.23	5.83	5.53	5.55	
Lao PDR	15.92	15.89	17.02	17.01	6.31	6.24	8.96	8.66	8.91	9.94	8.39	8.63	8.88	8.55	7.47	7.56
Lesotho	17.63	18.62	18.32	17.85	13.55	18.87	22.54	21.21	21.95	19.38	21.00	18.98	18.95	15.94	13.48	12.41
Liberia		5.51	4.81	4.84	4.05	4.18	3.24	4.13	7.73	7.23	7.58	7.34	6.01	4.30	4.03	3.53
Madagascar	9.66	11.29	11.61	11.73	12.24	12.43	12.50	13.71	14.19	13.99	14.34	14.47	14.34	14.14		

(continued)

Table 2.6 (continued)

	1996	1997	1998	1999	2000	2001	2002	2003	2004	2005	2006	2007	2008	2009	2010	2011
Malawi	14.30	13.55	13.61	13.38	12.88	11.53	10.59	11.86	10.00	9.18	10.71	11.39	12.67	12.31	12.04	11.94
Mali	7.64	4.15	4.33	4.06	3.81	3.09	3.17	2.83	3.37	3.19	3.08	3.11				
Mauritania	8.52	9.13	14.62	15.21	13.20	13.64	13.75	11.87	11.63	10.01	7.51	6.10	3.80	4.24	3.63	3.40
Mozambique	8.84	9.78	11.13	11.77	12.24	13.89	13.89	16.58	17.20	15.13	15.57	14.99	14.89	13.98	13.67	13.52
Myanmar	7.15	7.06	7.01	6.54	7.16	7.83	9.18	9.80	11.57							
Nepal	9.62	9.45	9.57	9.46	9.44	9.29	8.77	8.43	8.32	8.18	7.83	7.72	7.57	7.20	6.55	6.38
Niger	6.47	6.59	6.19	6.49	6.79	6.56	6.59	6.35								
Rwanda	11.54	12.04	11.23	7.54	6.97	6.91	7.49	6.79	6.94	7.03	6.80	6.10	6.16	6.38	6.64	6.61
Samoa	18.52	16.61	13.89	14.67	14.77	16.00	16.68	18.21	16.14	15.72	13.26	13.67	11.40	8.62	9.99	8.26
São Tomé and Príncipe						5.70	5.78	5.98	6.83	6.37	5.20					
Senegal	16.98	16.46	16.00	15.89	14.65	16.90	17.24	16.32	16.32	15.16	14.19	14.31	12.95	12.99	13.31	13.91
Sierra Leone	8.49	4.89	3.98	3.07	3.55	3.83	3.46	2.95	2.78	2.64	2.76	2.59	2.56	2.24	2.31	2.35
Solomon Islands	7.24	7.58	8.19	8.69	8.00	7.93	7.63	6.41	6.42	5.68	4.85	3.92	3.86	3.76		
Somalia																
South Sudan																
Sudan	9.15	8.78	8.88	8.72	8.61	7.99	8.18	7.48	7.41	6.91	6.07	6.17	5.66	6.03	6.03	6.86
Tanzania	7.37	6.90	10.55	9.68	9.39	8.98	8.89	8.89	8.71	8.69	8.57	8.56	8.62	9.54	9.90	10.22
Timor-Leste				2.78	2.76											
Togo	9.23	8.42	6.94	6.41	8.58	8.85	9.08	9.09	8.20	8.54	9.26	9.18	8.49	7.91	7.81	8.24
Tuvalu	3.35	4.09	4.21	4.85	0.76	0.76	0.88	1.23	0.94	0.83	0.89	0.77	1.06	1.05	1.33	1.52
Uganda	7.86	8.58	9.11	9.83	7.58	7.53	7.82	7.53	6.73	7.46	7.55	7.56	7.77	8.03	8.31	8.23
Vanuatu	4.70	4.34	4.41	4.47	4.51	4.50	4.20	4.10	4.03	3.80	3.61	3.05	2.49	2.86	4.77	4.24
Yemen, Rep.	8.82	7.67	8.36	6.26	5.73	6.05	6.39	6.47	7.37	7.13	7.76	8.57	7.07	7.76	6.06	
Zambia	13.37	13.20	12.97	12.08	11.34	11.02	11.53	12.02	11.89	11.65	11.14	10.20	9.96	9.66	8.85	8.39
Albania	14.42	13.26	11.07	10.90	11.44	10.35	9.89	12.34			0.00	18.80	18.71	18.23	16.06	15.82
Armenia	24.79	24.41	21.92	23.12	18.53	17.36	16.74	16.84	14.81	14.82	11.85	10.41	9.98	9.72	10.66	10.56
Belize	11.62	11.16	11.00	10.35	10.87	10.31	9.67	9.06	9.07	9.05	11.94	13.14	14.29			

(continued)

Table 2.6 (continued)

	1996	1997	1998	1999	2000	2001	2002	2003	2004	2005	2006	2007	2008	2009	2010	2011
Bolivia	18.96	16.78	16.26	15.49	15.33	15.32	14.99	14.68	14.43	14.18	14.38	14.68	14.41	14.41	13.94	13.26
Cameroon	20.06	19.52	20.72	21.00	20.83	20.94	20.64	20.25	19.29	17.71	16.79	16.72				
Cape Verde	10.06	9.73	9.20	8.76												
Congo, Rep.	6.70	5.46	6.96	5.46	3.48	4.51	5.32	6.02	4.98	4.00	3.57	4.03	3.46	4.47	3.78	3.63
Côte d'Ivoire	18.21	21.38	19.55	20.49	21.68	21.03	19.50	17.85	18.61	19.29	17.84	17.53	18.02			
Egypt, Arab Rep.	17.71	17.56	18.29	19.54	19.39	19.09	19.15	17.83	17.57	16.95	16.55	15.69	15.73	15.98	15.80	15.21
El Salvador	22.72	22.51	22.91	24.16	24.70	24.82	24.82	24.32	23.82	23.09	22.22	21.86	21.54	20.50	20.40	20.30
Fiji	13.28	14.77	15.06	13.42	13.97	15.63	14.90	13.83	15.01	14.23	14.95	14.17	13.74	13.61	14.57	14.31
Georgia	11.13	10.66	8.93	8.76	9.10	8.26	8.98	13.88	13.36	13.67	12.73	12.73	12.06	11.47	12.17	13.24
Ghana	9.73	10.13	10.04	10.07	10.08	10.05	10.07	9.88	9.57	9.46	10.24	9.15	7.94	6.95	6.75	6.95
Guatemala						21.28	20.14	20.05	20.50	20.20	20.26	19.82	19.82	19.88	19.87	20.19
Guyana	10.32	11.44	9.40	10.06	8.15	8.25	8.84	9.24	9.64	3.68	4.50	4.50	4.33	4.30	4.05	3.76
Honduras	18.11	17.95	18.62	19.60	22.69	21.76	21.96	21.72	21.03	20.89		19.60	19.21	18.20	18.42	19.23
India	16.94	15.85	15.00	14.68	15.38	14.69	14.91	14.92	15.25	15.39	16.06	15.99	15.43	15.10	14.87	14.39
Indonesia	25.62	26.79	25.00	25.99	27.75	29.05	28.72	28.25	28.07	27.41	27.54	27.05	27.81	26.36	24.75	24.30
Iraq		0.65	0.86	0.58	0.91	1.57	1.51	1.71								
Kenya	13.26	12.91	12.30	11.43	11.62	11.00	11.07	10.92	11.25	11.82	11.55	11.79	12.29	11.28	11.29	10.98
Korea, Dem. Rep.																
Kosovo											19.27	17.61	17.09	17.13	16.76	15.76
Kyrgyz Republic	8.49	14.81	15.50	14.01	19.46	19.02	14.29	14.63	17.05	14.41	12.56	11.47	15.22	15.99	18.89	20.62
Marshall Islands																
Micronesia, Fed. Sts.																
Moldova	24.01	21.33	17.24	14.67	16.26	18.12	17.03	18.26	16.90	15.88	15.00	14.19	13.70	12.58	12.72	13.46
Mongolia	8.18	9.11	7.66	7.71	7.55	9.46	7.27	7.48	6.24	6.42	6.04	6.93	7.31	7.08	7.28	7.06

(continued)

Table 2.6 (continued)

	1996	1997	1998	1999	2000	2001	2002	2003	2004	2005	2006	2007	2008	2009	2010	2011
Morocco	17.33	18.07	17.29	17.93	17.46	16.30	16.42	17.20	17.31	16.28	15.68	15.04	14.04	15.92	15.30	15.50
Nicaragua	14.78	14.92	14.02	13.12	13.67	14.82	16.14	15.26	15.36	14.92	15.21	15.91	15.91	16.50	17.04	17.41
Nigeria							3.43	3.39	3.06	2.83	2.58					
Pakistan	16.05	15.88	15.85	15.48	14.68	15.50	15.50	16.00	17.19	18.56	19.15	19.03	19.66	17.09	17.71	18.62
Papua New Guinea	9.40	9.70	9.75	8.70	7.55	7.41	6.58	6.82	7.05	6.48	6.07	6.06	5.59	5.94	5.90	5.92
Paraguay	15.59	14.89	14.88	15.26	14.68	14.38	13.52	13.58	13.34	12.86	12.91	12.39	12.52	12.72	12.36	11.68
Philippines	22.81	22.26	23.46	23.47	24.47	24.67	24.69	24.64	23.95	24.05	23.62	22.74	22.81	21.26	21.44	21.03
Sri Lanka	16.20	16.41	16.54	16.40	16.83	15.95	18.48	18.59	18.72	19.51	19.23	18.50	17.95	18.11	18.00	18.21
Swaziland	37.83	39.46	39.34	38.73	38.67	39.68	39.19	39.88	39.56	38.93	41.35	41.72	42.23	42.27		43.83
Syrian Arab Republic	23.31				6.55	8.48	7.99									
Tajikistan	20.38	22.31	20.91	21.13	33.66	34.12	34.24	31.32	24.29	23.72	22.21	18.85	14.42	12.53	9.48	8.35
Tonga	8.99	9.43	8.76	9.43	10.46	9.76	9.33	9.40	8.95	8.56	8.21	8.45	8.11	7.49	6.91	6.65
Ukraine	31.05	28.37	29.79	32.75	19.23	19.72	20.07	20.69	22.84	19.61	23.08	23.07	19.99	17.81	17.51	16.41
Uzbekistan	13.13	12.11	10.49	9.99	9.44	9.46	9.18	9.23	10.20	9.10	10.76	12.57	12.08	13.04	12.90	12.80
Vietnam	15.18	16.48	17.15	17.69	18.56	19.78	20.59	20.45	20.34	20.63	21.25	21.38	20.35	20.09	19.68	19.27
West Bank and Gaza																
Zimbabwe	18.78	18.01	16.63	16.35	15.61	14.56	13.25	13.65	15.12	16.38	16.89	16.40	16.66	17.75	17.92	17.09
Algeria	9.04	8.72	9.91	9.17	7.46	7.90	7.82	7.10	6.49	5.94	5.54	5.28	4.63	5.62		
American Samoa																
Antigua and Barbuda	2.20	2.22	2.24	2.26	1.93	2.02	2.06	2.14	2.09	2.01	2.01	1.85	1.73	2.26	2.16	1.80
Argentina	18.74	19.55	19.08	18.02	17.52	16.96	21.30	23.92	24.08	23.15	22.27	21.28	21.24	21.20	20.53	20.62
Azerbaijan	11.59	9.06	8.68	6.29	5.64	6.72	8.08	9.36	8.93	7.02	6.11	4.09	5.04	6.00	5.84	
Belarus	33.33	34.84	33.90	32.51	31.64	30.52	30.19	31.49	33.32	33.08	32.51	32.23	33.40	30.34	30.38	36.56

(continued)

	1996	1997	1998	1999	2000	2001	2002	2003	2004	2005	2006	2007	2008	2009	2010	2011
Bosnia and Herzegovina	13.93	13.67	14.70	13.03	10.10	10.37	10.25	10.61	11.37	11.26	11.89	14.22	14.06	13.00	13.69	12.51
Botswana	5.42	5.39	5.27	4.59	4.54	4.10	3.79	4.11	3.88	3.65						
Brazil	16.80	16.67	15.72	16.12	17.22	17.13	16.85	18.02	19.22	18.09	17.37	17.03	16.63	16.65	16.23	14.60
Bulgaria	25.61	18.98	18.97	16.66	17.57	17.32	16.34	16.96	16.84	16.27	15.96	15.25	14.36	15.40	16.22	16.56
Chile	19.36	19.21	18.93	19.17	16.89	17.58	17.57	16.14	15.61	14.67	13.22	12.85	12.23	12.22	11.70	11.91
China	33.51	33.18	31.84	31.59	32.12	31.64	31.42	32.85	32.37	32.51	32.92	32.91	32.65	32.30	29.62	
Colombia	15.49	14.92	15.07	14.78	15.01	15.25	15.17	15.45	15.70	15.45	15.65	15.90	15.20	14.26	13.93	13.56
Costa Rica	22.11	22.39	23.03	29.01	25.33	21.87	21.52	21.16	21.74	21.70	21.68	21.38	20.31	17.83	17.43	17.51
Cuba	13.85	14.02	14.65	15.56	17.74	16.39	14.88	12.23	10.87	9.48	9.36	10.06	10.92	10.69	10.56	
Dominica	7.34	7.62	8.68	8.09	8.07	8.34	10.13	6.15	5.50	4.85	5.15	4.41	3.88	2.73	2.80	2.51
Dominican Republic	26.93	26.59	26.74	26.72	26.13	24.94	25.39	25.45	24.95	22.87	22.08	21.20	23.16	24.47	24.07	24.60
Ecuador	20.18	18.72	18.20	19.19	19.42	17.44	15.92	14.40	13.51	13.10	12.91	12.53	12.51	13.05	12.99	12.77
Gabon	4.06	4.40	5.61	4.73	3.72	4.56	4.84	4.72	4.55	4.12	4.10	4.06				
Grenada	6.75	6.93	7.02	7.22	5.26	5.18	5.02	4.51	3.88	3.36	3.94	4.18	3.82	3.79	4.52	4.61
Iran, Islamic Rep.	13.23	13.97	13.28	13.03	13.16	13.36	11.39	11.25	11.27	10.74	10.87	10.55				
Jamaica	15.48	14.86	11.70	11.30	10.60	10.19	9.50	9.45	9.40	8.83	8.73	8.84	9.23	9.36	9.03	9.15
Jordan	13.76	13.97	15.72	15.64	15.66	15.74	16.89	17.18	18.26	18.20	19.38	21.24	20.99	20.12	19.16	19.38
Kazakhstan	13.94	13.98	12.78	14.93	17.66	17.64	15.59	15.25	14.17	12.83	12.44	12.38	12.66	11.40	13.11	13.51
Latvia	19.03	20.21	16.36	14.03	13.73	13.87	13.70	13.29	13.15	12.58	11.79	11.39	10.76	9.94	12.18	
Lebanon	13.98	13.98	14.11	13.71	13.01	12.91	12.75	12.87	12.87	12.69	11.40	10.39	9.30	9.20	8.42	8.22
Libya							3.14	6.28	5.09	4.71	4.51	4.51	4.49			
Lithuania	18.16	18.54	18.31	17.83	19.34	19.91	18.75	19.28	20.89	20.83	20.08	18.60	18.09	16.37		
Macedonia, FYR	23.01	21.96	20.92	20.50	20.74	20.28	19.10	17.55	16.54	17.35	17.96	20.44	19.76	16.17	14.37	13.85
Malaysia	27.84	28.38	28.78	30.94	30.86	29.34	29.25	29.93	30.38	27.55	27.57	26.12	24.56	23.80	24.56	24.36
Maldives	7.19	7.56	7.71	7.98	7.96	6.15	5.83	5.90	6.09	6.54	5.71	5.47	5.97	4.68	4.34	5.73

(continued)

Table 2.6 (continued)

	1996	1997	1998	1999	2000	2001	2002	2003	2004	2005	2006	2007	2008	2009	2010	2011
Mauritius	23.38	23.58	23.96	23.88	23.48	23.33	22.44	21.68	20.96	19.85	19.97	19.22	19.39	18.81	17.04	16.91
Mexico	21.49	21.38	21.29	20.99	20.31	19.56	18.62	18.78	18.69	18.40	18.68	18.41	17.80	17.81	18.11	18.19
Montenegro					10.23	12.78	11.61	10.25	10.25	9.78	9.40	6.80	6.72	5.90	5.59	6.01
Namibia	9.97	11.07	12.18	11.38	12.83	12.61	13.05	14.80	13.63	13.56	15.62	17.02	14.02	14.74	13.90	12.86
Palau	0.93	1.26	1.48	1.45	1.59	1.79	2.07	0.75	0.75	0.84	0.80	0.78	1.00	0.94	0.89	0.94
Panama	12.73	11.42	11.12	10.92	10.05	9.29	8.47	8.08	8.32	7.44	7.07	6.64	6.61	6.31	5.91	4.81
Peru	16.47	16.40	15.73	15.35	15.81	16.00	16.09	15.69	16.33	16.40	16.01	15.97	15.94	14.03	14.45	14.00
Romania	30.83	27.97	25.70	16.49	14.54	16.90		30.55	29.92							
Russian Federation							17.08	16.33	17.44	18.30	17.91	17.64	17.52	14.79	14.99	15.99
Serbia					23.77	22.12	19.05	16.96	17.49	17.44	17.38	17.00	16.76	16.32	15.63	15.62
Seychelles	13.02	14.38	15.06	15.12	19.21	18.08	18.25	16.41	7.66	8.74	8.96	9.57	9.29	7.82	8.01	7.16
South Africa	20.18	19.87	19.40	18.55	18.98	19.06	19.16	19.38	19.20	18.49	17.46	16.99	16.80	15.23	14.20	12.81
St. Lucia	6.75	6.10	5.56	5.44	4.37	4.41	4.44	4.55	4.90	5.50	5.29	5.17	4.52	4.05	3.76	3.81
St. Vincent and the Grenadines	8.30	7.87	6.83	6.22	5.80	6.42	5.43	5.54	5.86	5.91	5.03	5.54	4.88	5.43	5.64	5.75
Suriname	10.75	10.43	9.14	9.04	9.00	6.75	14.65	14.11	16.62	18.39	25.12	25.54	27.17	22.07	22.61	23.30
Thailand	29.72	30.17	30.87	32.65	33.59	33.43	33.69	34.84	34.45	34.70	35.04	35.63	34.84	34.15	35.62	
Tunisia	20.97	18.77	18.80	18.64	18.47	18.76	18.60	17.97	17.54	17.29	17.67	18.34	19.51	18.38	18.38	18.07
Turkey	21.82	22.32	26.04	24.06	22.50	21.47	20.25	20.35	20.02	19.93	19.82	19.13	18.31	17.20	17.91	18.59
Turkmenistan	25.54	24.76	18.03	18.08	10.64	14.65	15.25	18.55	21.67							
Uruguay	19.26	16.86	16.04	15.08	14.05	14.30	14.69	16.90	17.16	17.13	16.97	15.97	17.18	15.88	14.24	13.26
Venezuela, RB	13.65	23.17	20.83	19.22	19.83	18.24	17.53	18.08	17.87	16.42	15.13	14.43	14.93	15.42	13.92	

Note: *EE* emerging economy, *GDP* gross domestic product, *LDC* least developed country, *LMIC* lower- or middle-income country

Notes

1. Extractive-reliant countries being classified as those with extractive revenues above 40 percent of GDP.
2. Kaldor's second and third laws relate to productivity and are examined ahead in that context.

References

Andreoni, Antonio, and Mike Gregory. 2013. Why and How Does Manufacturing Still Matter: Old Rationales, New Realities. *Revue d'économie industrielle* 144 (4): 21–57.
Arrow, Kenneth J. 1962. The Economic Implications of Learning by Doing. *Review of Economic Studies* 29 (3): 155–173.
Atesoglu, H. Sonmez. 1993. Manufacturing and Economic Growth in the United States. *Applied Economics* 25 (1): 67–69.
Bairam, Erkin. 1991. Economic Growth and Kaldor's Law: The Case of Turkey, 1925–78. *Applied Economics* 23 (8): 1277–1280.
Becker, Gary S. 1962. Investment in Human Capital: A Theoretical Analysis. *Journal of Political Economy* 70 (5): 9–49.
Bernat, G. Andrew, Jr. 1996. Does Manufacturing Matter? A Spatial Econometric View of Kaldor's Laws. *Journal of Regional Science* 36 (3): 463–477.
Boserup, Ester. 1981. *Population and Technological Change: A Study of Long-Term Trends*. Chicago: University of Chicago Press.
Cohen, Stephan S., and John Zysman. 1988. *Manufacturing Matters: The Myth of the Post-industrial Economy*. New York: Basic Books.
Drakopoulos, S.A., and I. Theodossiou. 1991. Kaldorian Approach to Greek Economic Growth. *Applied Economics* 23 (10): 1683–1689.
Dutz, Mark A., Sérgio Kannebley Jr., Maira Scarpelli, and Siddharth Sharma. 2012. Measuring Intangible Assets in an Emerging Market Economy: An Application to Brazil. Policy Research Working Paper 6142, World Bank, Washington, DC.
Hansen, Jorgen Drud, and Jie Zhang. 1996. A Kaldorian Approach to Regional Economic Growth in China. *Applied Economics* 28 (6): 679–685.
Harrod, Roy. 1948. *Towards a Dynamic Economics: Some Recent Developments of Economic Theory and Their Application to Policy*. London: Macmillan.

Hausmann, Ricardo, Dani Rodrik, and Andrés Velasco. 2008. Growth Diagnostics. In *The Washington Consensus Reconsidered: Towards a New Global Governance*, ed. Narcís Serra and Joseph E. Stiglitz, 324–355. New York: Oxford University Press.

Kaldor, Nicholas. 1966. *Causes of the Slow Rate of Economic Growth of the United Kingdom: An Inaugural Lecture*. Cambridge: Cambridge University Press.

———. 1967. *Strategic Factors in Economic Development*. Ithaca: Cornell University Press.

———. 1975. What is Wrong with Economic Theory. *Quarterly Journal of Economics* 89 (3): 347–357.

Lewis, W. Arthur. 1954. Economic Development with Unlimited Supplies of Labour. *The Manchester School* 22 (2): 139–191.

Lin, Justin Yifu. 2011. New Structural Economics: A Framework for Rethinking Development. *World Bank Research Observer* 26 (2): 193–221.

Lin, Justin, and Ha-Joon Chang. 2009. Should Industrial Policy in Developing Countries Conform to Comparative Advantage or Defy it? A Debate Between Justin Lin and Ha-Joon Chang. *Development Policy Review* 27 (5): 483–502.

Lucas, Robert E., Jr. 1988. On the Mechanics of Economic Development. *Journal of Monetary Economics* 22 (1): 3–42.

Mankiw, N. Gregory, David Romer, and David N. Weil. 1992. A Contribution to the Empirics of Economic Growth. *Quarterly Journal of Economics* 107 (2): 407–437.

Marshall, Alfred. 1920. *Principles of Economics*. 8th ed. London: Macmillan.

McCombie, J.S.L., and J.R. de Ridder. 1984. The Verdoorn Law Controversy: Some New Empirical Evidence Using US State Data. *Oxford Economic Papers* 36 (2): 268–284.

McMillan, Margaret S., and Dani Rodrik. 2011. Globalization, Structural Change and Productivity Growth. Working Paper 17143, National Bureau of Economic Research, Cambridge, MA.

Mill, John Stuart. 1848. *Principles of Political Economy, With Some of Their Applications to Social Philosophy*. Vol. 2 vols. London: John W. Parker.

Say, Jean-Baptiste. 1821. *A Treatise on Political Economy; Or, The Production, Distribution, and Consumption of Wealth*. Translated from the fourth edition of the French, by C. R. Prinsep. London: Longman, Hurst, Rees, Orme and Brown.

Solow, Robert M. 1956. A Contribution to the Theory of Economic Growth. *Quarterly Journal of Economics* 70 (1): 65–94.

———. 1994. Perspectives on Growth Theory. *Journal of Economic Perspectives* 8 (1): 45–54.
Thirlwall, A.P. 1983. A Plain Man's Guide to Kaldor's Growth Laws. *Journal of Post Keynesian Economics* 5 (3): 345–358.
———. 2002. *The Nature of Economic Growth: An Alternative Framework for Understanding the Performance of Nations.* Cheltenham: Edward Elgar.
Toner, Philip. 1999. *Main Currents in Cumulative Causation: The Dynamics of Growth and Development.* London: Macmillan.
Verdoorn, P.J. 2002. Factors That Determine the Growth of Labour Productivity. Translated by A. P. Thirlwall. In *Productivity Growth and Economic Performance: Essays on Verdoorn's Law*, edited by John McCombie, Maurizio Pugno, and Bruno Soro, 28–36. London: Palgrave Macmillan. Originally published as 'Fattori the regolano lo sviluppo della produttività del lavoro,' *L'Industria* 1 (1949): 3–10.
World Bank. 2012. *World Development Report 2013: Jobs.* Washington, DC: World Bank.

3

A Regularity in Employment Patterns in Developing Countries: Jobs and Good Jobs

This chapter sets out to examine the patterns of employment across DCs, in terms of distinguishing between the characteristics of least developed countries (LDCs), lower- and middle-income countries (LMICs), and emerging economies (EEs). It does not find the quantum of employment growth to be the best estimator of either improvement or distress in the labour markets of DCs. The reason is that in DCs, lack of social protection compels the poor and low-income part of the labour force to work, which causes employment growth to be largely determined by labour force growth. Employment growth is then determined more by demographic supply-side factors, than by economic demand-side factors. This makes job quality a better estimator of labour market improvement or distress.

Job quality, measured in terms of three key indicators, the working poor, vulnerability, and labour productivity, are all observed to consistently climb up the per capita *income ladder across DCs. This empirical regularity of a strong correlation between job quality and* per capita *incomes must however be viewed as a two-way relationship. Climbing up the* per capita *income ladder may well allow improvements in job quality. However, equally, improvements in job quality can also lead to climbing up the income ladder—to development. In this chapter, rates of reduction in vulnerability are seen to explain increases in labour productivity well. In the following chapter four on*

© The Author(s) 2018
M. Mahmood, *The Three Regularities in Development*,
https://doi.org/10.1007/978-3-319-76959-2_3

drivers of jobs and growth, this causality is established further. Human capital is seen to climb the per capita *income ladder. This empirical regularity of human capital clearly works to improve job quality—through productivity, allowing DCs to climb up the income ladder.*

3.1 Introduction

Chapter 2 posed and set out to answer three fundamental questions about DCs. One was about catch-up with advanced economies (AEs) in terms of incomes per capita, and was seen to be far distant. The second was about what distinguished DCs amongst themselves—what factors characterised LDCs, LMICs, and EEs, almost trapping them into their growth and income trajectories. And the answer was that, while long-term gross domestic product (GDP) growth had varied and moved up the income ladder in the past decade or so, GDP growth rates had converged across LDCs, LMICs, and EEs. The third question was that if the quantum of growth did not consistently differentiate between income groups, then the content of growth could. And this was indeed seen to be so, with manufacturing affecting GDP growth the most, and the share of manufacturing climbing in lockstep up the income ladder, from LDCs to LMICs to EEs. Hence the impact of manufacturing on GDP growth also climbed up the income ladder. This was not to discount the role and importance of the other sectors in growth, but merely to emphasise the well-observed lead taken by manufacturing.

The fundamental questions posed for GDP growth outcomes in DCs can be reposed for labour market outcomes in DCs, albeit with an important nuance. The quantum of employment growth is an important indicator of labour market outcomes in DCs, but less so than in AEs, for several reasons to do with essential differences in the nature of labour markets between DCs and AEs. A key stylised characteristic of labour markets in DCs, as observed below, is the relative lack of significant social protection, compared to AEs. Which vitiates the indicators of employment and unemployment as measures of labour market outcomes in DCs. The fairly robust logic is that the majority of the low-income population in DCs cannot afford not to work, given the lack of social protection or the adequacy of any other forms of transfers. Hence the lack of formal waged employment simply impels the need to accept employment with weaker remuneration and more onerous working conditions, often in self-employment, all too often outside the working age. Hence employment growth has been observed to track labour force growth, become supply-led by demographics rather than demand-led by economics (ILO 2011). Resultantly unemployment in DCs becomes minimised, and a weaker indicator of labour market outcomes.

With this relative de-emphasis on the quantum of employment as an indicator of labour market outcomes in DCs comes the greater importance of the quality and nature of jobs. There have been in fact three key indicators for the first Millennium Development Goal (MDG) on halving global poverty, which have also succeeded to the Sustainable Development Goal (SDG) 8 on full and productive employment and decent work for all. These three key indicators of the nature of jobs include the incidence of the working poor falling below agreed norms, the incidence of vulnerable workers, and productivity per worker.

Hence four key questions arise for labour market development in DCs:

One, what has quantitative job growth been like in DCs in the long run?
Two, has there been catch-up with AEs in terms of the quality and nature of jobs in the long run?
Three, what differentiates between—and so, characterises—LDCs from LMICs, from EEs, in terms of the quality and nature of jobs generated in the long run? Further, if higher manufacturing shares give better growth outcomes as observed in Chap. 2, do they also provide more and better jobs?
Four, if job quality moves up the income ladder, then is this a two-way relationship, with higher incomes affording better jobs, but also better jobs enabling higher incomes? Does job quality also drive growth?

3.2 Quantum Indicators of Job Growth for DCs

Quantum indicators of job growth for DCs are less revealing than for AEs, particularly so for employment and unemployment.

Employment and Unemployment Are More Labour Supply-Driven

Beginning with job growth. Job growth lags behind GDP growth axiomatically, if there is to be productivity growth. This is so simply because job growth and productivity growth must sum up to GDP growth.[1] Hence GDP growth over 1991–2013 of 2.1 percent per annum for AEs exceeds employment growth over this period seen in Table 3.1 of 0.8 percent, giving a gap of about 1.3 percent per annum. For DCs over this period, GDP growth of 6.5 percent per annum exceeded employment growth of 1.7 percent per annum, which is near 5 percent per annum. Leaving aside the gap representing some form of productivity for later, the point to be made here is that on the face of it, employment growth in DCs was more than double that in AEs, not just over the last decade, but in the long run for which there is consistent employment data presented in Table 3.1, from 1990 onwards. However, the difference narrows for women's employment growth, while youth employment growth was negligible for DCs and negative for AEs over this period.

While the near-double employment growth rate for DCs compared to AEs shows twice the absorption of labour in the DCs, it need not reflect twice the demand for labour. Figure 3.1 shows employment growth and the growth of the working-age population over the last two decades. And the growth of the working-age population in DCs over this period has been double that of AEs. Hence the first point to note is that the demographically given supply of the working-age population in DCs approximates their long-run trend in employment growth.

The second point to note is that in Fig. 3.2, employment growth hugs labour force growth quite closely for DCs, over the last two decades. Much more so than for AEs. Hence for DCs, employment growth seems more driven by supply-side demographics, than by demand-side economics. Which implies that within DCs, employment growth has been driven much more so by demographic growth for the lowest income group (LDCs, as Fig. 3.3 shows), a little less so for LMICs, and even less so for EEs. As labour force growth goes down, moving up the income ladder, from LDCs to LMICs, to EEs, the demographic supply-side pressure for labour absorption weakens, and demand-side economics begins

Table 3.1 Employment growth rate, by sex and age group

Region	2000	2001	2002	2003	2004	2005	2006	2007	2008	2009	2010	2011	2012	2013p	1991–2000	2000–2013	1991–2013
															Average annual growth rates (%)		
Total employment, annual growth rates (%)																	
AEs	1.4	0.6	0.2	0.8	1.2	1.5	1.9	1.7	0.9	−1.7	0.2	0.8	0.7	0.6	0.9	0.7	0.8
DCs	1.6	1.9	1.8	1.9	2.1	2.0	1.5	1.6	1.1	0.9	1.4	1.6	1.5	1.5	1.8	1.6	1.7
LDCs	2.5	2.9	3.1	2.7	3.0	2.9	2.6	2.8	2.6	2.6	2.9	2.7	2.8	2.8	2.8	2.8	2.8
LMICs	1.5	2.4	2.0	2.4	2.5	2.3	1.4	1.6	1.1	1.1	1.5	1.5	1.4	1.9	2.1	1.8	1.9
EEs	1.4	1.3	1.3	1.3	1.6	1.5	1.3	1.3	0.6	0.2	1.0	1.3	1.2	0.9	1.4	1.1	1.2
Male employment, annual growth rates (%)																	
AEs	1.3	0.3	−0.0	0.4	1.2	1.4	1.7	1.7	0.6	−2.4	0.1	1.1	0.8	0.7	0.6	0.6	0.6
DCs	1.5	1.8	1.6	1.8	2.0	1.9	1.7	1.7	1.3	1.0	1.7	1.6	1.5	1.5	1.8	1.6	1.7
LDCs	2.4	2.7	2.9	2.6	2.8	2.9	2.3	2.6	2.4	2.4	2.6	2.7	2.7	2.8	2.9	2.6	2.7
LMICs	1.5	2.4	1.7	2.1	2.2	2.2	1.8	1.8	1.6	1.6	2.1	1.7	1.6	1.8	2.1	1.9	2.0
EEs	1.3	1.2	1.3	1.4	1.6	1.5	1.4	1.4	0.7	0.2	1.1	1.3	1.1	0.9	1.3	1.2	1.2
Female employment, annual growth rates (%)																	
AEs	1.7	1.1	0.5	1.2	1.2	1.7	2.0	1.8	1.2	−0.9	0.2	0.3	0.6	0.5	1.2	0.9	1.0
DCs	1.7	1.9	2.1	1.9	2.2	2.0	1.2	1.5	0.7	0.6	0.9	1.5	1.4	1.5	1.9	1.5	1.7
LDCs	2.7	3.2	3.3	2.9	3.1	3.0	2.9	3.2	2.8	2.8	3.1	2.8	2.9	2.8	2.8	3.0	2.9
LMICs	1.5	2.4	2.7	2.9	3.1	2.7	0.5	1.0	0.2	0.1	−0.0	1.0	1.1	2.0	2.3	1.5	1.8
EEs	1.6	1.4	1.5	1.1	1.5	1.4	1.2	1.3	0.5	0.2	0.8	1.4	1.2	0.8	1.5	1.1	1.3
Youth employment, annual growth rates (%)																	
AEs	1.5	−1.8	−2.2	−1.7	0.6	0.9	1.7	0.2	−1.5	−6.9	−3.4	−0.6	−0.9	−0.6	−1.0	−1.3	−1.2
DCs	−0.4	1.1	1.0	1.4	1.8	1.1	0.0	0.3	−0.9	−1.6	−1.3	−0.4	−1.2	−0.9	−0.4	0.0	−0.1
LDCs	2.5	2.9	3.1	2.7	3.0	2.9	2.6	2.8	2.6	2.6	2.9	2.7	2.8	2.8	2.5	2.2	2.3
LMICs	1.5	2.4	2.0	2.4	2.5	2.3	1.4	1.6	1.1	1.1	1.5	1.5	1.4	1.9	1.2	0.0	0.5
EEs	1.4	1.3	1.3	1.3	1.6	1.5	1.3	1.3	0.6	0.2	1.0	1.3	1.2	0.9	−2.3	−0.9	−1.5

(continued)

Table 3.1 (continued)

Region	2000	2001	2002	2003	2004	2005	2006	2007	2008	2009	2010	2011	2012	2013p	1991–2000	2000–2013	1991–2013
Adult employment, annual growth rates (%)															Average annual growth rates (%)		
AEs	1.4	1.0	0.6	1.1	1.3	1.6	1.9	1.9	1.2	−1.1	0.6	0.9	0.9	0.7	1.2	1.0	1.1
DCs	2.1	2.1	2.0	2.0	2.1	2.2	1.9	1.9	1.5	1.4	2.0	2.0	2.1	2.0	2.5	1.9	2.2
LDCs	2.8	2.9	3.1	2.6	3.1	3.3	3.1	3.1	3.0	3.0	3.0	3.0	3.0	3.0	2.9	3.0	3.0
LMICs	2.0	2.5	2.4	2.5	2.7	2.7	2.0	2.1	1.8	1.7	2.3	1.9	1.9	2.2	2.4	2.2	2.3
EEs	2.1	1.6	1.6	1.5	1.5	1.5	1.5	1.6	1.0	0.9	1.6	1.9	1.9	1.7	2.4	1.5	1.9

Note: *p* projection; 2013 are preliminary estimates, *AE* advanced economy, *DC* developing country, *EE* emerging economy, *LDC* least developed country, *LMIC* lower- or middle-income country

Source: Author's estimations at the ILO, based on data from the ILO Trends Unit, Trends Econometric Models, October 2013

A Regularity in Employment Patterns in Developing Countries...

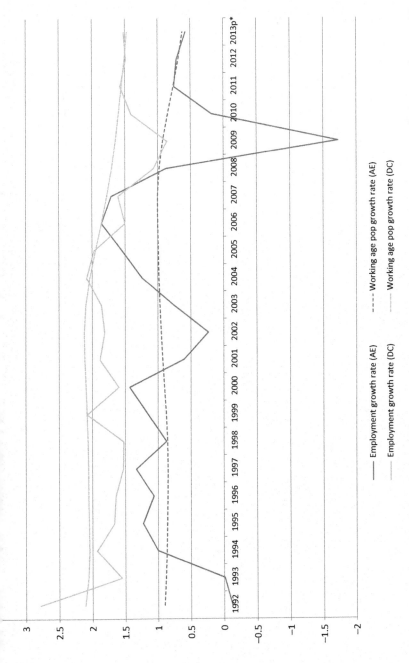

Fig. 3.1 Employment and working-age population growth rates. (Note: *p* projection; 2013 are preliminary estimates, *AE* advanced economy, *DC* developing country. Source: Author's estimations at the ILO, based on data from the ILO Trends Unit, Trends Econometric Models, October 2013)

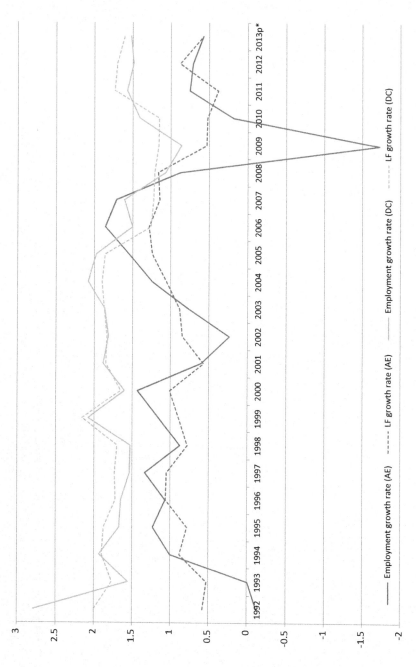

Fig. 3.2 Employment and labour force growth rates, AEs and DCs. (Note: *p* projection; 2013 are preliminary estimates, *AE* advanced economy, *DC* developing country. Source: Author's estimations at the ILO, based on data from the ILO Trends Unit Trends Econometric Models, October 2013)

A Regularity in Employment Patterns in Developing Countries...

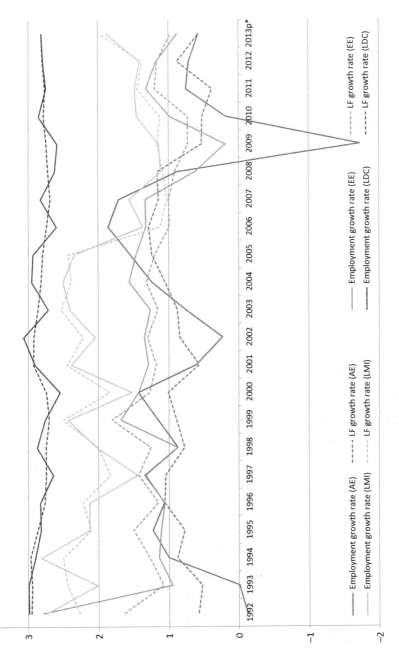

Fig. 3.3 Employment and labour force growth rates, LDCs, LMICs, EEs. (Note: *p* projection; 2013 are preliminary estimates, *EE* emerging economy, *LDC* least developed country, *LMIC* lower- or middle-income country. Source: Author's estimations at the ILO, based on data from the ILO Trends Unit, Trends Econometric Models, October 2013)

to play a greater role in determining employment growth. Observe that the global crisis hit employment growth in AEs and EEs starkly, but not apparently LMICs and LDCs.

If employment has been more demographically driven amongst DCs, then the level of unemployment becomes minimised, and therefore not the best indicator of labour market distress. Table 3.2 shows that the impact of the crisis had raised unemployment in AEs from under 6 percent pre-crisis, to 8 percent in 2009. For DCs as a whole, unemployment only rose over this period from 5.4 to 5.8 percent. LDCs saw a rise of only 0.2 percent over this period, LMICs no rise, while EEs saw a rise of 0.8 percent.

But the crisis did hit youth unemployment in DCs more visibly in Table 3.2, with DCs seeing a rise of 0.8 percent between 2007 and 2009, 0.6 percent for LDCs, 0.7 percent for LMICs, and 1.5 percent for EEs. And again, while long-run unemployment rates over the past two decades remain within a pretty constant band range of 5.5 percent to 6 percent for DCs, the ratio of youth unemployment to adult unemployment does show a gradual increase over this period. This is more pronounced for LMICs in Table 3.3, rising from a ratio of 3.5 in 1991 to 3.8 by 2013, and for EEs rising from 2.5 to 2.8 over this period. It also appears to be more pronounced for women in EEs.

Joining the Labour Force Is More Compulsive and Complex in DCs

The factors that vitiate quantum indicators of job growth, like employment and unemployment into second-best measures of labour market success or distress in DCs, work through the labour force. But a number of behavioural factors can further complicate this indicator of labour market outcomes. Making labour force participation difficult to read as an unambiguous good or bad labour market outcome in DCs.

Absence of significant social protection or transfers, low incomes, and high demographic growth of the working-age population in DCs, make joining the labour force more compulsive going down the income ladder. This can be labelled an income effect, and implies a linear increase in the

Table 3.2 Unemployment rate, by sex and age group

Region	1991	1992	1993	1994	1995	1996	1997	1998	1999	2000	2001	2002	2003	2004	2005	2006	2007	2008	2009	2010	2011	2012	2013p
Total unemployment rate (%)																							
AEs	6.9	7.5	8.0	7.9	7.5	7.5	7.2	7.1	6.9	6.5	6.5	7.0	7.1	7.0	6.7	6.1	5.6	5.9	8.0	8.3	8.0	8.1	8.1
DCs	6.1	5.4	5.6	5.6	5.8	5.8	6.0	6.2	6.3	6.3	6.3	6.3	6.3	6.1	6.0	5.8	5.4	5.6	5.8	5.6	5.5	5.5	5.6
LDCs	5.8	5.8	5.8	5.8	5.9	5.8	5.9	5.8	5.7	5.9	5.9	5.8	5.9	5.8	5.7	5.8	5.7	5.8	5.9	5.9	5.9	5.9	5.9
LMICs	5.5	5.1	5.5	5.2	5.2	5.3	5.6	5.6	5.7	5.9	6.0	6.2	6.3	6.2	6.2	6.0	5.5	5.5	5.5	5.2	5.2	5.1	5.2
EEs	6.6	5.6	5.7	5.8	6.2	6.3	6.3	6.7	6.8	6.6	6.5	6.5	6.4	6.2	5.9	5.6	5.3	5.6	6.1	5.9	5.7	5.7	5.8
Male unemployment rate (%)																							
AEs	6.4	7.1	7.6	7.4	7.0	7.0	6.7	6.6	6.4	6.0	6.1	6.7	6.9	6.6	6.3	5.8	5.3	5.7	8.2	8.4	7.9	8.0	8.0
DCs	6.0	5.3	5.5	5.5	5.6	5.7	5.8	5.9	6.0	6.2	6.0	6.1	6.1	5.9	5.7	5.5	5.2	5.4	5.7	5.3	5.2	5.3	5.3
LDCs	5.2	5.1	5.1	5.2	5.1	5.1	5.1	5.0	5.0	5.1	5.2	5.1	5.3	5.1	4.9	5.1	5.0	5.1	5.2	5.2	5.2	5.2	5.2
LMICs	5.1	4.7	5.1	4.8	4.8	4.9	5.3	5.1	5.3	5.7	5.5	5.7	5.8	5.7	5.6	5.5	5.1	5.1	5.1	4.6	4.6	4.6	4.7
EEs	6.8	5.8	5.9	6.1	6.4	6.4	6.5	6.8	6.9	6.8	6.7	6.7	6.5	6.3	6.0	5.7	5.4	5.7	6.2	5.9	5.8	5.8	6.0
Female unemployment rate (%)																							
AEs	7.6	8.1	8.6	8.5	8.2	8.2	7.9	7.8	7.5	7.1	6.9	7.4	7.4	7.4	7.1	6.6	6.0	6.1	7.7	8.1	8.1	8.3	8.3
DCs	6.4	5.6	5.8	5.8	6.0	6.1	6.3	6.6	6.6	6.5	6.6	6.6	6.7	6.5	6.5	6.2	5.8	5.9	6.1	6.1	6.0	6.0	6.0
LDCs	6.7	6.7	6.6	6.7	6.8	6.7	6.9	6.8	6.7	6.9	6.9	6.8	6.8	6.7	6.7	6.7	6.5	6.6	6.8	6.7	6.7	6.7	6.7
LMICs	6.4	5.8	6.3	6.1	5.9	6.0	6.3	6.5	6.4	6.5	7.1	7.1	7.2	7.2	7.4	7.1	6.3	6.2	6.3	6.4	6.4	6.2	6.3
EEs	6.4	5.2	5.4	5.5	5.9	6.0	6.2	6.5	6.7	6.5	6.3	6.3	6.3	6.1	5.9	5.6	5.2	5.5	5.9	5.7	5.6	5.6	5.6
Youth unemployment rate (%)																							
AEs	14.0	14.8	15.9	15.7	15.2	15.2	14.8	14.4	14.1	13.3	13.4	14.3	14.7	14.4	14.2	13.3	12.5	13.3	17.1	17.6	17.1	17.6	17.9
DCs	11.6	10.5	11.0	10.9	11.3	11.5	12.0	12.5	12.4	12.8	12.7	13.0	12.9	12.7	12.7	12.3	11.5	11.8	12.3	12.2	12.1	12.3	12.5
LDCs	10.2	10.4	10.3	10.3	10.4	10.1	10.4	10.1	10.3	10.7	10.6	10.2	9.7	9.5	9.7	10.1	9.8	10.0	10.4	10.1	10.2	10.3	10.4
LMICs	11.7	10.6	11.6	11.2	11.1	11.4	12.2	12.8	12.2	13.0	13.0	13.7	13.8	13.6	14.0	13.6	12.5	12.5	12.6	13.0	12.9	13.0	13.2
EEs	11.8	10.4	10.7	10.9	11.7	12.0	12.3	13.1	13.3	13.3	13.2	13.4	13.4	13.0	12.6	12.0	11.4	11.9	12.9	12.5	12.4	12.6	12.9
Adult unemployment rate (%)																							
AEs	5.4	6.1	6.5	6.5	6.1	6.1	5.9	5.9	5.7	5.4	5.3	5.9	6.0	5.8	5.5	5.1	4.6	4.8	6.8	7.1	6.8	6.9	6.9
DCs	4.2	3.6	3.8	3.8	4.0	4.1	4.2	4.3	4.5	4.5	4.5	4.4	4.5	4.3	4.2	4.0	3.8	4.0	4.2	4.0	4.0	4.0	4.1
LDCs	4.0	3.8	3.9	3.9	4.0	4.0	4.0	4.0	3.8	3.9	4.0	4.0	4.4	4.3	4.1	4.1	4.1	4.1	4.2	4.3	4.3	4.2	4.2
LMICs	3.4	3.2	3.5	3.3	3.3	3.3	3.5	3.4	3.6	3.8	3.9	3.9	4.0	3.9	4.0	3.9	3.6	3.6	3.7	3.2	3.3	3.3	3.4
EEs	4.7	3.9	4.0	4.2	4.5	4.6	4.7	5.0	5.2	5.0	4.9	4.9	4.8	4.6	4.4	4.2	3.9	4.2	4.6	4.5	4.4	4.4	4.6

Note: *p* projection; 2013 are preliminary estimates, *AE* advanced economy, *DC* developing country, *EE* emerging economy, *LDC* least developed country, *LMIC* lower- or middle-income country

Source: Author's estimations at the ILO, based on data from the ILO Trends Unit, Trends Econometric Models, October 2013

Table 3.3 Youth-to-adult ratio of unemployment rate

Region	1991	1992	1993	1994	1995	1996	1997	1998	1999	2000	2001	2002	2003	2004	2005	2006	2007	2008	2009	2010	2011	2012	2013p
Youth-to-adult ratio of unemployment rate																							
LDCs	2.6	2.7	2.7	2.6	2.6	2.5	2.6	2.5	2.7	2.7	2.6	2.6	2.2	2.2	2.4	2.5	2.4	2.4	2.5	2.4	2.4	2.4	2.5
LMICs	3.4	3.3	3.4	3.4	3.4	3.4	3.4	3.8	3.4	3.5	3.4	3.5	3.4	3.5	3.6	3.5	3.5	3.5	3.4	4.0	3.9	4.0	3.9
EEs	2.5	2.7	2.7	2.6	2.6	2.6	2.6	2.6	2.6	2.7	2.7	2.7	2.8	2.8	2.9	2.9	2.9	2.9	2.8	2.8	2.8	2.8	2.8
Male youth-to-adult ratio of unemployment rate																							
LDCs	2.8	3.0	2.9	2.9	2.9	2.8	2.9	2.8	2.9	3.0	2.9	2.8	2.4	2.4	2.5	2.7	2.6	2.6	2.7	2.5	2.6	2.6	2.7
LMICs	3.5	3.4	3.4	3.5	3.5	3.5	3.5	3.9	3.4	3.5	3.5	3.7	3.6	3.6	3.7	3.7	3.5	3.5	3.4	4.3	4.2	4.3	4.1
EEs	2.6	2.8	2.8	2.7	2.7	2.7	2.7	2.7	2.7	2.7	2.7	2.8	2.8	2.9	2.9	2.9	2.9	2.9	2.8	2.8	2.8	2.8	2.8
Female youth-to-adult ratio of unemployment rate																							
LDCs	2.4	2.5	2.4	2.4	2.3	2.2	2.3	2.2	2.4	2.4	2.4	2.3	2.0	2.0	2.2	2.3	2.2	2.2	2.3	2.2	2.2	2.2	2.3
LMICs	3.3	3.1	3.3	3.2	3.3	3.3	3.4	3.5	3.3	3.4	3.2	3.3	3.3	3.3	3.4	3.3	3.3	3.4	3.4	3.6	3.5	3.6	3.5
EEs	2.4	2.6	2.6	2.5	2.5	2.5	2.5	2.5	2.5	2.6	2.6	2.7	2.8	2.8	2.8	2.9	2.8	2.8	2.8	2.8	2.8	2.8	2.9

Note: *p* projection; 2013 are preliminary estimates, *EE* emerging economy, *LDC* least developed country, *LMIC* lower- or middle-income country
Source: Author's estimations at the ILO, based on data from the ILO Trends Unit, Trends Econometric Models, October 2013

labour force participation rate going down the income ladder. Hence an increase in or high labour force participation need not be a good outcome, if based on lowered or low incomes. Both over time and across income groups—LDCs, LMICs, and EEs.

Another effect, labelled a behavioural factor, of sending more young people to school or college, is the obverse of the income effect. So, this education effect implies that the ability to educate reduces going down the income ladder. Which implies a linear increase in the labour force participation rate going down the income ladder. However, over time, all income groups—LDCs, LMICs, and EEs—should be sending more of their kids to school, so lowering their labour force participation rates.

A second behavioural factor, sending more women to work could have a nonlinear effect across income groups, even a U-shape. Low incomes could push more women into the labour force for LDCs. Higher incomes could enable them to leave the labour force for LMICs (ILO 2012). While the highest incomes amongst DCs, for EEs, could again push up their labour force participation reflecting global mores and practices of more women in work.

This complex set of factors, demographic, income, and behavioural, makes labour force participation as an outcome indicator difficult to read.

Table 3.4 illustrates all three kinds of effects working on the labour force participation rate. The income effect is visible in Table 3.4, panel (a), with the labour force participation rate for DCs higher at 65 percent in 2013 compared to AEs at 60 percent. Positive income and education effects, a good outcome, are also evident over time, with the labour force participation rate for DCs falling from 68 percent in 1990 to 65 percent by 2013. A negative income effect, the income compulsion to work, a bad, kept the labour force participation rate high and constant for LDCs at 74 percent over this long run. But positive income and education effects, a good, lowered labour force participation rates for LMICs and EEs over this long run.

Corroboration for the education effect comes from Table 3.4, panels (d) and (e). DCs lowered their labour force participation rates for youth from 60 percent in 1990 to 48 percent by 2013. And the drops were bigger going up the income ladder—affording more education—from LDCs

Table 3.4 Labour force participation rates

Region	1990	1991	1992	1993	1994	1995	1996	1997	1998	1999	2000	2001	2002	2003	2004	2005	2006	2007	2008	2009	2010	2011	2012	2013p
(a) Total labour force participation rate (%)																								
AEs	60.5	60.7	60.5	60.3	60.3	60.3	60.4	60.5	60.5	60.5	60.5	60.3	60.3	60.2	60.3	60.4	60.6	60.6	60.8	60.5	60.3	60.1	60.2	60.2
DCs	68.0	67.9	67.8	67.6	67.5	67.4	67.2	67.0	66.7	66.8	66.5	66.3	66.1	66.0	65.9	65.8	65.4	65.1	64.8	64.4	64.2	64.3	64.4	64.5
LDCs	74.6	74.5	74.4	74.2	74.0	73.9	73.7	73.6	73.5	73.5	73.4	73.5	73.6	73.7	73.7	73.8	73.8	73.9	73.9	74.0	74.0	74.1	74.1	74.1
LMICs	61.6	61.5	61.4	61.4	61.5	61.3	61.2	60.9	60.6	60.7	60.4	60.6	60.6	60.8	61.0	61.2	60.6	60.0	59.5	59.0	58.6	58.3	58.0	58.1
EEs	71.5	71.5	71.4	71.1	70.9	70.8	70.5	70.4	70.1	70.2	69.8	69.3	68.9	68.4	68.1	67.8	67.4	67.2	67.0	66.7	66.5	66.6	66.8	66.9
(b) Male labour force participation rate (%)																								
AEs	72.8	72.7	72.3	71.9	71.6	71.4	71.3	71.2	71.0	70.8	70.7	70.3	70.0	69.7	69.6	69.6	69.7	69.7	69.6	69.1	68.7	68.5	68.5	68.5
DCs	82.6	82.5	82.3	82.1	81.9	81.8	81.6	81.3	81.0	81.0	80.6	80.3	80.0	79.8	79.6	79.4	79.1	78.9	78.7	78.5	78.3	78.4	78.5	78.6
LDCs	84.2	84.1	83.9	83.7	83.6	83.5	83.4	83.2	83.2	83.0	82.9	82.9	82.9	82.9	82.9	82.8	82.8	82.7	82.7	82.7	82.6	82.6	82.6	82.6
LMICs	82.5	82.3	82.1	81.9	81.8	81.7	81.6	81.2	80.8	81.0	80.7	80.7	80.6	80.6	80.6	80.7	80.3	79.9	79.6	79.4	79.1	79.0	78.8	78.8
EEs	82.4	82.3	82.2	82.0	81.7	81.5	81.2	80.9	80.6	80.5	80.0	79.4	78.9	78.3	78.0	77.6	77.3	77.1	76.9	76.6	76.4	76.6	76.8	77.0
(c) Female labour force participation rate (%)																								
AEs	49.0	49.5	49.4	49.4	49.7	49.8	50.1	50.4	50.5	50.7	50.9	50.9	51.0	51.2	51.3	51.6	51.9	52.0	52.2	52.3	52.2	52.0	52.2	52.2
DCs	53.1	53.1	53.1	52.9	52.9	52.8	52.6	52.5	52.3	52.5	52.2	52.2	52.1	52.1	52.1	52.1	51.6	51.2	50.8	50.4	50.0	50.1	50.2	50.3
LDCs	65.1	65.2	65.0	64.8	64.6	64.4	64.2	64.1	64.0	64.0	64.1	64.3	64.5	64.6	64.7	64.9	65.1	65.2	65.4	65.5	65.7	65.7	65.7	65.8
LMICs	40.1	40.1	40.1	40.4	40.6	40.4	40.3	40.0	40.0	39.9	39.7	40.0	40.1	40.5	40.9	41.3	40.5	39.7	39.0	38.3	37.6	37.3	36.9	37.0
EEs	60.5	60.5	60.5	60.1	60.0	60.1	59.8	59.8	59.6	59.9	59.6	59.3	59.0	58.6	58.2	58.0	57.6	57.3	57.0	56.8	56.5	56.6	56.8	56.9
(d) Youth labour force participation rate (%)																								
AEs	54.7	53.9	52.9	52.1	51.9	51.5	51.2	50.9	50.9	50.7	51.0	50.1	49.3	48.5	48.5	48.7	48.9	48.4	48.1	46.9	45.8	45.4	45.5	45.7
DCs	60.4	59.9	59.4	58.6	58.0	57.3	56.5	55.7	54.7	54.5	53.6	53.1	52.6	52.2	51.9	51.6	50.8	50.0	49.4	48.7	48.0	48.2	48.2	48.2
LDCs	63.9	63.7	63.4	63.1	62.8	62.5	62.3	62.0	61.8	61.6	61.4	61.3	61.3	61.2	61.2	61.0	60.8	60.5	60.3	60.2	60.1	60.0	59.9	59.9
LMICs	50.2	49.8	49.5	48.9	48.5	48.3	48.1	47.7	46.8	47.4	46.9	46.9	46.9	47.0	47.1	47.1	45.9	44.6	43.5	42.6	41.7	41.1	40.6	40.5
EEs	67.9	67.5	67.0	66.0	65.2	64.4	63.0	61.7	60.4	59.4	58.1	56.8	55.7	54.4	53.7	53.1	52.3	51.9	51.6	51.0	50.3	50.6	50.7	50.7
(e) Adult labour force participation rate (%)																								
AEs	61.9	62.3	62.3	62.2	62.2	62.2	62.4	62.5	62.4	62.5	62.5	62.4	62.4	62.5	62.5	62.7	62.8	63.0	63.1	63.0	63.0	62.7	62.8	62.7
DCs	71.3	71.3	71.4	71.3	71.4	71.4	71.4	71.3	71.3	71.4	71.4	71.3	71.2	71.2	71.2	71.2	70.9	70.7	70.4	70.1	69.8	69.8	69.8	69.8
LDCs	80.4	80.4	80.3	80.1	80.0	79.9	79.9	79.8	79.8	79.8	79.9	80.1	80.2	80.3	80.4	80.5	80.7	80.8	81.0	81.1	81.1	81.1	81.2	81.2
LMICs	66.8	66.8	66.7	67.0	67.2	67.1	67.0	66.7	66.7	66.5	66.4	66.5	66.5	66.7	66.8	67.1	66.7	66.3	65.9	65.5	65.2	64.9	64.6	64.6
EEs	73.0	73.0	73.1	72.9	72.9	73.1	73.0	73.2	73.2	73.5	73.4	73.2	73.1	72.9	72.7	72.5	72.2	71.9	71.7	71.4	71.1	71.1	71.0	71.0

Note: p projection; 2013 are preliminary estimates, *AE* advanced economy, *DC* developing country, *EE* emerging economy, *LDC* least developed country, *LMIC* lower- or middle-income country

Source: Author's estimations at the ILO, based on data from the ILO Trends Unit, Trends Econometric Models, October 2013

with 4 percent, to LMICs with 10 percent, to EEs with 17 percent. In contrast, the negative income effect—a bad—kept drops in the adult labour force participation rate low over this period, for DCs at 1.5 percent over this long run, raised them for LDCs by about 1 percent, while lowering them for LMICs and EEs by 2 percent.

The gender effect is complicated over time, and going across income groups, in Table 3.4, panels (b) and (c). The income effects are visible for men across income groups, a bad, with their labour force participation rates highest for LDCs at 83 percent, lower for LMICs at 79 percent, and lowest for EEs at 77 percent. And the income and education effects are also visible for men over time—a good—with their labour force participation rates falling over time for all income groups, LDCs 2 percent and LMICs and EEs 3 percent each.

But for women, the gender effect as expected is a nonlinear U-shape across income groups. Women's labour force participation rate in 2013 was the highest for LDCs at 66 percent, lower at 37 percent for LMICs, and higher again for EEs at 57 percent. This nonlinear U-shape for women's participation in the labour force across income groups gives the same nonlinear U-shape for the aggregate labour for participation rate across income groups, with LDCs at 74 percent, LMICs at 58 percent, and EEs at 67 percent.

Note that the income compulsion on women's participation over time, a bad, can be seen clearly in Table 3.4, panel (c). Women's labour force participation went up for LDCs between 1990 and 2013, by near 1 percent, while falling for LMICs and EEs by 3 percent each.

In summary, over the long run, income compulsions have kept labour force participation rates up for LDCs, particularly for women. But at the same time, increasing incomes and education have lowered labour force participation rates for LMICs and EEs, for youth, and for men.

3.3 Catch-Up in Job Quality Across the DCs: Indicators of Job Quality and Informality

With quantum indicators of labour market development like employment, unemployment, and labour force participation strongly demographically supply-led, rather than being led by economic demand, they become second best. To observe the economic impact and the role of the labour market in growth and development in DCs, the first best indicators of labour market outcomes must be job quality.

There are three key indicators of job quality. These are the working poor, the vulnerable, and labour productivity. The working poor gives a headcount of the proportion of workers living below the poverty line. The vulnerable gives a headcount of the population judged to be more at risk of weak incomes and variation in it. Two categories of employment fall into the vulnerable definition currently, contributing family workers and the self-employed. Labour productivity indicates at the micro level potential income for the workers. At the macro level it indicates output capacity, technological change, and competitiveness.

All three of these indicators are tied into the key DC labour market concept of informality. Informality is essentially defined as unregistered work.[2] Chapter 6 estimates informality across DCs. Here its consonance with vulnerability and weaker job quality is simply noted.

What makes formality preferable to informality is: (a) greater stability in the duration of work and in income; (b) more rights at work; (c) the possibility of some modicum of social protection both in work and out of it. The indicator of vulnerability captures some of these characteristics of informality in DC labour markets. The two categories of employment falling into the vulnerable, contributing family workers, and the self-employed, are judged to be more at risk of: (a) instability of work, instability of wage rates and prices of their products, and therefore instability of their incomes; (b) rights at work would be non-existent for family work and for the unregistered self-employed; (c) institutionalised social protection for family workers and the unregistered self-employed would again be virtually non-existent.

The indicator of the working poor captures the combined effects on income, of informality characteristics (a) to (c). The capture lies in the indicator of the working poor being largely a subset of informality.[3] The indicator of labour productivity has great potential in capturing the low-income potential in informality, but there are data limitations in estimating it for the unregistered self-employed.

Catch-Up in Vulnerability

Waged work has long been the norm in AEs, with its reciprocal vulnerability, comprising self-employment and contributing family work, being quite low. DCs have seen catch-up with AEs in the long run, and increasing going up the income ladder.

Figure 3.4 shows that AEs already had a high waged share in employment of 81 percent in 1991, which increased by 5 percentage points to 86 percent by 2013. Conversely, their share in vulnerable employment dropped down from 13 to 9 percent over this period. Self-employment had a near stable 9 percent share over the last decade at least. Contributing family work had been driven down to just 1 percent by 2013.

In DCs, waged work was just a third of total employment in 1991, and this increased by 10 percentage points to 43 percent by 2013. This 10 percentage point increase in waged work led to a 10 percentage point reduction in vulnerability from two-thirds of employment to 55 percent over this period. The interesting point to note is that DCs' self-employment share actually increased by 5 percentage points over this

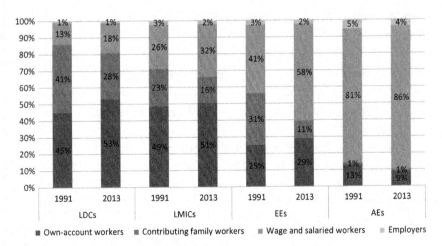

Fig. 3.4 Share of employment, by status. (Note: *AE* advanced economy, *EE* emerging economy, *LDC* least developed country, *LMIC* lower- or middle-income country. Source: Author's estimations at the ILO, based on data from the ILO Trends Unit, Trends Econometric Models, October 2014)

period, to 40 percent. So, the gross reduction in vulnerability came from a halving in the share of contributing family labour over this period, coming down to 15 percent by 2013.

The increase in the waged share in DCs over time, and converse drop in vulnerability over time, climbs up the income ladder. LDCs saw a 5 percentage point increase in their waged share between 1991 and 2013, with a 5 percentage point decrease in their vulnerability down to 81 percent by 2013 (Fig. 3.5). LMICs also saw a 6 percentage point increase in their wage share over this period, with a 6 percentage point drop in their vulnerability down to two-thirds of total employment by 2013. EEs saw a much higher increase in their waged share by 17 percentage points over this period, with their vulnerability dropping down to 40 percent.

Vulnerability in DCs has continued to be highly feminised, albeit dropping at the same rate as for men between 1991 and 2013, but coming down to 58 percent for women's employment in 2013, and 54 percent for men's employment. This gender gap in vulnerable employment does reduce going up the income ladder. In 2013, it was 12 percent for LDCs, 6 percent for LMICs, and 7 percent for EEs.

The Working Poor and the Distribution of Income in DCs

DCs have made a substantive reduction in their working poor in the long run. Again, the drop in the working poor goes up the income ladder. A developing middle class expanded its share in employment, again more so going up the income ladder.

The poverty line used to measure the headcount, those falling under it, has changed between finalisation of the MDGs, targeted for 2015, and the framing of the SDGs, spanning the next 15 years to 2030. The older poverty line of US$1.25 should be used to judge the old goal of the MDGs, which is done here. A more forward-looking exercise of eliminating poverty over the course of the SDGs uses the newer poverty line of US$1.90, in Chap. 5.

Table 3.5 shows that DCs had a US$1.25 working-poor share in total employment of 45 percent in 1991, which dropped near 30 percentage points by 2013, coming down to 14 percent of employment. This still

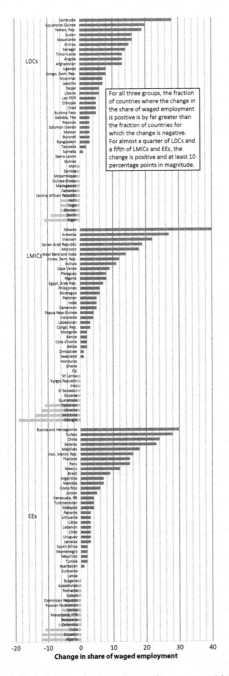

Fig. 3.5 Change in the share of waged employment, 1991–2013. (Note: *EE* emerging economy, *LDC* least developed country, *LMIC* lower- or middle-income country. Source: Author's estimations at the ILO, based on data from the ILO Trends Unit, Trends Econometric Models, October 2013)

Table 3.5 Working poverty

Region	1991	1992	1993	1994	1995	1996	1997	1998	1999	2000	2001	2002	2003	2004	2005	2006	2007	2008	2009	2010	2011	2012p	2013p
Total US$1.25 (PPP) working poor (millions)																							
DCs	811	800	817	765	713	699	676	688	710	693	675	661	625	579	537	519	491	483	464	436	406	385	375
LDCs	133	138	142	144	145	147	150	154	156	156	156	157	157	154	150	148	146	144	145	144	143	140	138
LMICs	293	296	296	293	291	288	286	293	295	292	288	286	280	271	263	260	245	241	231	218	202	194	190
EEs	384	366	379	327	277	263	240	241	259	245	231	217	189	155	124	111	100	98	88	74	62	51	47
Share of working poor in total employment, US$1.25 (PPP) (%)																							
DCs	45.1	43.3	43.5	39.9	36.6	35.3	33.6	33.7	34.1	32.7	31.3	30.1	27.9	25.3	23.0	21.9	20.4	19.9	18.9	17.5	16.1	15.0	14.4
LDCs	65.8	66.4	66.3	65.7	64.2	63.4	62.7	62.6	61.7	60.4	58.6	57.3	55.6	52.9	50.3	48.2	46.2	44.6	43.6	42.2	40.7	38.9	37.4
LMICs	45.7	44.9	43.9	42.3	41.2	39.9	39.1	39.2	38.5	37.5	36.2	35.3	33.7	31.8	30.1	29.4	27.3	26.5	25.1	23.4	21.4	20.2	19.4
EEs	40.3	37.3	38.3	32.6	27.4	25.7	23.1	23.1	24.4	22.6	21.1	19.6	16.8	13.5	10.7	9.5	8.4	8.1	7.4	6.1	5.0	4.1	3.7
Total US$2 (PPP) working poor (millions)																							
DCs	1234	1238	1254	1228	1184	1193	1182	1195	1211	1198	1188	1174	1142	1096	1049	1027	989	977	954	912	878	850	839
LDCs	176	182	189	193	196	202	206	211	216	219	222	227	230	231	231	231	232	233	236	237	239	240	242
LMICs	475	486	492	499	504	507	509	520	528	530	533	536	535	530	524	528	514	511	505	490	479	472	471
EEs	583	569	573	536	484	485	468	463	467	450	432	411	377	336	293	268	243	233	213	184	159	138	126
Share of working poor in total employment, US$2 (PPP) (%)																							
DCs	68.6	66.9	66.8	64.2	60.9	60.3	58.9	58.6	58.1	56.6	55.1	53.4	51.0	48.0	45.0	43.4	41.1	40.2	38.9	36.7	34.7	33.2	32.2
LDCs	87.1	87.9	88.3	88.0	86.8	86.6	86.2	86.1	85.5	84.6	83.5	82.7	81.5	79.6	77.4	75.5	73.6	72.1	71.0	69.6	68.2	66.6	65.2
LMICs	74.0	73.6	73.1	72.2	71.3	70.2	69.5	69.7	69.0	68.2	67.1	66.1	64.3	62.2	60.1	59.7	57.3	56.4	55.0	52.7	50.7	49.3	48.2
EEs	61.1	58.0	57.8	53.4	47.8	47.3	45.1	44.2	43.8	41.6	39.4	37.0	33.5	29.4	25.3	22.8	20.4	19.4	17.7	15.2	13.0	11.1	10.0

Note: *p* projection; 2013 are preliminary estimates, *DC* developing country, *EE* emerging economy, *LDC* least developed country, *LMIC* lower- or middle-income country

Source: Author's estimations at the ILO, based on data from the ILO Trends Unit, Trends Econometric Models, October 2013

left 375 million working poor in 2013. LDCs and LMICs reduced their share of the working poor in employment over this period in the band range of 26–28 percentage points. EEs reduced their share of the working poor over this period by 36 percent. This left LDCs with still over a third of their employment in the working poor, LMICs with 20 percent, and EEs with just 4 percent.

In terms of timing, the larger reductions in the working poor seem to have come not in the 1990s, but in the 2000s, especially for LDCs and LMICs, more evenly for EEs (see Figs. 3.6 and 3.7). If the MDG 1 aim of halving poverty by 2015 is extended to the working poor, then DCs as whole had already met this goal well before, LDCs were scheduled to meet it by 2015, while LMICs and EEs had already met it before.

Table 3.6 and Fig. 3.8 give the total distribution of income for DCs. There are five income classes, the extremely poor being the working poor under US$1.25, the moderately poor between US$1.25 and US$2, the near poor between US$2 and US$4, the developing middle class between US$4 and US$13, and the developed middle class above US$13. The table shows that the bottom two classes have shrunk over time, from over two-thirds of total employment in 1991 to just under a third by 2013. Unfortunately, the near poor, bunched just above US$2, have increased their share to a quarter of employment. However, the developing middle class has more than doubled its share of employment in this period, to just under a third. This developing middle class just doubled for LDCs between 1991 and 2013, to 7 percent of employment, more than doubled for LMICs to 17 percent of employment, and tripled to a half of employment for EEs.

Catch-Up in Labour Productivity

Labour productivity growth for DCs was higher than for AEs. Again, it goes up the income ladder for DCs. However, catch-up in the level of productivity, with the huge gap to AEs, seems very far away.

Table 3.7 shows that between 1991 and 2013, AEs had a labour productivity growth rate of 1.4 percent per annum. Compared to this, DCs as a whole had a labour productivity growth rate of more than double that of AEs, of 3.2 percent per annum. The labour productivity growth

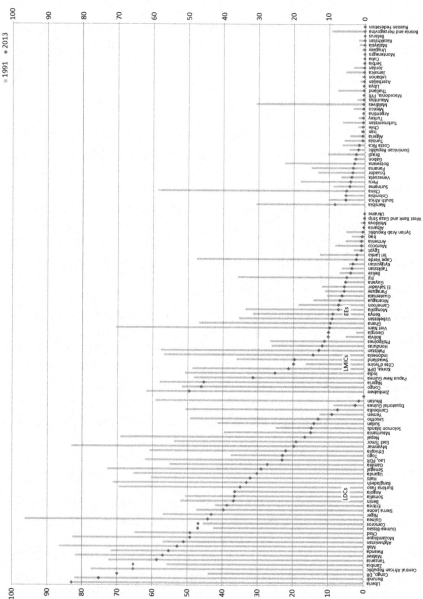

Fig. 3.6 Share of working poor (extreme poverty <$1.25/day), 1991 and 2013. (Note: *EE* emerging economy, *LDC* least developed country, *LMIC* lower- or middle-income country. Source: Author's estimations at the ILO, based on data from the

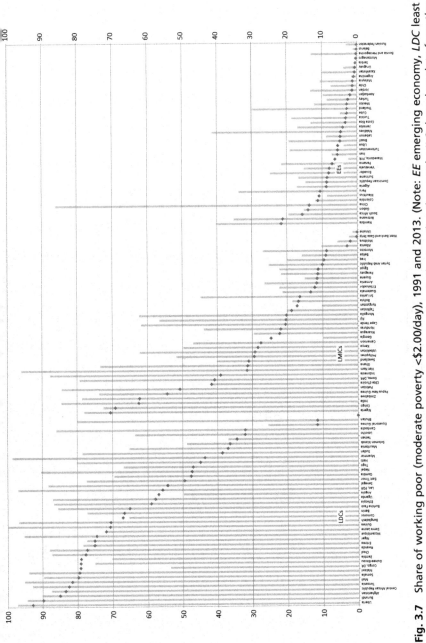

Fig. 3.7 Share of working poor (moderate poverty <$2.00/day), 1991 and 2013. (Note: *EE* emerging economy, *LDC* least developed country, *LMIC* lower- or middle-income country. Source: Author's estimations at the ILO, based on data from the ILO Trends Unit, Trends Econometric Models, October 2013)

Table 3.6 Percentage share of total employment, by economic class

Economic class	1991	1992	1993	1994	1995	1996	1997	1998	1999	2000	2001	2002	2003	2004	2005	2006	2007	2008	2009	2010	2011	2012p	2013p
DCs																							
Extremely poor	45.1	43.3	43.5	39.9	36.6	35.3	33.6	33.7	34.1	32.7	31.3	30.1	27.9	25.3	23.0	21.9	20.4	19.9	18.9	17.5	16.1	15.0	14.4
Moderately poor	23.5	23.7	23.3	24.2	24.2	25.0	25.2	24.8	24.1	23.9	23.8	23.4	23.1	22.6	21.9	21.5	20.7	20.4	20.0	19.1	18.7	18.2	17.8
Near poor	14.9	16.5	17.5	19.5	21.3	22.0	22.9	23.0	22.7	23.2	23.9	24.3	25.2	26.0	26.7	26.6	26.6	26.4	26.3	26.4	26.4	26.2	26.3
Developing middle class	12.0	12.3	11.6	12.5	14.0	13.8	14.5	14.8	15.5	16.3	17.3	18.4	19.7	21.3	23.0	24.0	25.5	26.1	27.2	28.6	29.7	30.6	31.3
Developed middle class and above	4.6	4.2	4.0	3.9	3.9	3.9	3.8	3.6	3.7	3.8	3.8	3.8	4.1	4.7	5.3	6.0	6.7	7.3	7.6	8.3	9.1	9.9	10.2
LDCs																							
Extremely poor	65.8	66.4	66.3	65.7	64.2	63.4	62.7	62.6	61.7	60.4	58.6	57.3	55.6	52.9	50.3	48.2	46.2	44.6	43.6	42.2	40.7	38.9	37.4
Moderately poor	21.2	21.5	22.0	22.3	22.7	23.3	23.5	23.4	23.8	24.2	24.9	25.4	25.9	26.6	27.2	27.3	27.4	27.5	27.4	27.3	27.5	27.7	27.8
Near poor	8.5	8.3	8.3	8.7	9.6	10.2	10.7	10.9	11.4	12.2	13.1	13.8	14.8	16.4	17.9	19.3	20.6	21.6	22.2	22.8	23.8	24.8	25.7
Developing middle class	3.7	3.2	2.8	2.8	3.0	2.6	2.5	2.5	2.6	2.6	2.8	2.9	3.1	3.5	3.9	4.4	4.9	5.3	5.7	6.3	6.7	7.2	7.7
Developed middle class and above	0.7	0.6	0.6	0.5	0.6	0.5	0.6	0.6	0.6	0.5	0.5	0.5	0.6	0.6	0.8	0.9	1.0	1.0	1.1	1.2	1.3	1.4	1.4
LMICs																							
Extremely poor	45.7	44.9	43.9	42.3	41.2	39.9	39.1	39.2	38.5	37.5	36.2	35.3	33.7	31.8	30.1	29.4	27.3	26.5	25.1	23.4	21.4	20.2	19.4
Moderately poor	28.3	28.7	29.2	29.8	30.1	30.3	30.4	30.5	30.5	30.7	30.9	30.8	30.7	30.4	30.0	30.3	30.0	29.8	29.9	29.2	29.3	29.1	28.8
Near poor	16.3	17.0	17.7	18.9	19.6	20.4	20.7	20.7	21.3	21.9	22.7	23.4	24.4	25.5	29.1	26.7	28.0	28.6	29.5	30.4	31.3	31.7	32.2
Developing middle class	6.9	6.8	6.9	7.0	7.3	7.6	8.0	8.0	8.1	8.4	8.8	9.1	9.8	10.8	11.7	11.8	12.6	12.9	13.4	14.6	15.5	16.3	16.8
Developed middle class and above	2.8	2.5	2.3	1.9	1.8	1.7	1.8	1.7	1.6	1.5	1.5	1.5	1.5	1.5	1.7	1.8	2.1	2.2	2.1	2.3	2.5	2.7	2.8
EEs																							
Extremely poor	40.3	37.3	38.3	32.6	27.4	25.7	23.1	23.1	24.4	22.6	21.1	19.6	16.8	13.5	10.7	9.5	8.4	8.1	7.4	6.1	5.0	4.1	3.7
Moderately poor	20.8	20.7	19.6	20.8	20.4	21.6	21.9	21.2	19.5	19.0	18.4	17.5	16.7	15.8	14.5	13.3	12.0	11.3	10.4	9.0	7.9	7.0	6.3
Near poor	15.3	17.9	19.4	22.3	25.0	25.8	27.2	27.4	26.4	26.8	27.3	27.5	28.3	28.8	29.1	28.4	27.2	26.1	25.1	24.3	23.4	22.4	21.8
Developing middle class	17.1	17.9	16.8	18.4	21.2	20.8	21.8	22.6	23.9	25.3	26.9	29.1	31.2	33.7	36.4	38.3	40.6	41.6	43.6	45.6	47.2	48.5	49.6
Developed middle class and above	6.5	6.2	6.0	5.9	6.0	6.1	6.0	5.8	5.9	6.2	6.3	6.4	7.0	8.2	9.2	10.5	11.8	12.9	13.6	15.0	16.5	18.0	18.5

Note: p projection, DC developing country, EE emerging economy, LDC least developed country, LMIC lower- or middle-income country. Extremely poor (less than US$1.25, PPP); moderately poor (between US$1.25 and US$2, PPP); near poor (between US$2 and US$4, PPP); developing middle class (between US$4 and US$13, PPP); developed middle class and above (US$13, PPP).

Source: Author's estimations at the ILO, based on October revisions to the model in Steven Kapsos and Evangelia Bourmpoula, 'Employment and Economic Class in the Developing World,' Research Paper 6 (Geneva: ILO, 2013); and data from the ILO Trends Unit, Trends Econometric Models, October 2013

A Regularity in Employment Patterns in Developing Countries...

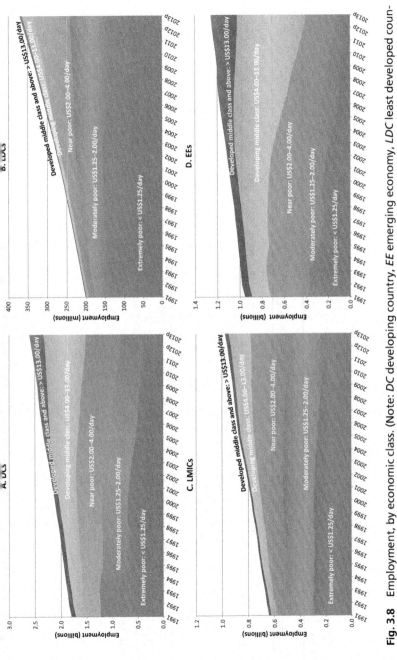

Fig. 3.8 Employment, by economic class. (Note: *DC* developing country, *EE* emerging economy, *LDC* least developed country, *LMIC* lower- or middle-income country. Source: Author's estimations at the ILO, based on October revisions to the model in Steven Kapsos and Evangelia Bourmpoula, 'Employment and Economic Class in the Developing World,' Research Paper 6 (Geneva: ILO, 2013); and data from the ILO Trends Unit, Trends Econometric Models, October 2013)

Table 3.7 Labour productivity growth rates

Output per worker (constant 2005 international $), annual growth rates (%)

Region	2000	2001	2002	2003	2004	2005	2006	2007	2008	2009	2010	2011	2012	2013p	Average annual growth rates (%)	
															1991–2000	2000–2013	1991–2013p
AEs	2.6	0.9	1.4	1.4	2.0	1.1	1.3	1.1	−0.5	−1.6	2.7	1.1	0.6	0.6	2.0	0.9	1.4
DCs	3.9	1.7	2.5	3.9	5.4	5.3	6.6	7.1	4.6	2.0	6.1	4.3	3.4	3.0	1.6	4.3	3.2
LDCs	2.4	2.8	2.0	2.7	4.3	4.9	4.9	5.8	3.9	2.1	2.7	1.4	2.2	2.6	1.0	3.3	2.3
LMICs	2.2	1.3	1.2	2.9	4.9	4.5	6.0	6.2	3.3	3.9	6.4	4.2	2.6	2.3	1.5	3.8	2.9
EEs	4.8	2.2	3.3	4.7	6.0	5.9	7.1	7.8	5.5	1.7	6.6	4.8	4.0	3.8	1.9	4.9	3.7

Note: *p* projection; 2013 are preliminary estimates, *AE* advanced economy, *DC* developing country, *EE* emerging economy, *LDC* least developed country, *LMIC* lower- or middle-income country

Source: Author's estimations at the ILO, based on data from the ILO Trends Unit, Trends Econometric Models, October 2013; and the World Bank's World Development Indicators, 2013

rates climbed up the income ladder across DCs, going from 2.3 percent per annum for LDCs, to 2.9 percent per annum for LMICs, to 3.7 percent for EEs.

Convergence in the level of productivity between DCs and AEs, however, seems far away in Fig. 3.9. The figure shows that AEs increased their labour productivity from US$55,000 in 1992 by near US$20,000 to US$74,000 by 2013. The gap in labour productivity between AEs and DCs increased over this period from US$50,000 to US$60,000. DCs almost doubled their labour productivity from near US$7,000 to near US$14,000. This left LDCs with a labour productivity of near US$4000 in 2013, LMICs with US$9000, and EEs with near US$20,000. Figure 3.10 again confirms labour productivity climbing up the income ladder, with fewer countries with negative growth rates.

In summary, quantitative indicators of labour market outcomes become moot and second best, because they are observed to be driven more by supply-side demographics, rather than demand-side economic factors. Which places the onus of indicating labour market outcomes—success or distress—on job quality. Then, GDP growth in DCs has been seen to be coupled with significant improvement in job quality. There have been notable reductions in the working poor, meeting an extended definition of MDG 1. The developing middle class has expanded its share in employment significantly. Waged employment too has gone up, bringing down vulnerable employment. Labour productivity growth in DCs has been double that in AEs, even if convergence seems far away.

The point however is to determine causality—to determine which factors have led to better labour market outcomes in job quality. One factor has been seen clearly to be income. There have been distinctly more improvements in job quality going up the income ladder. So LDCs, LMICs, and EEs are seen to be locked into different employment trajectories. Much as Chap. 2 showed that LDCs, LMICs, and EEs were locked into different growth trajectories. A major factor in differentiating growth outcomes between LDCs, LMICs, and EEs was seen to be the sectoral composition of growth, specifically the development of manufacturing. It now needs to be determined whether the sectoral composition of employment and growth, particularly manufacturing, has produced better jobs.

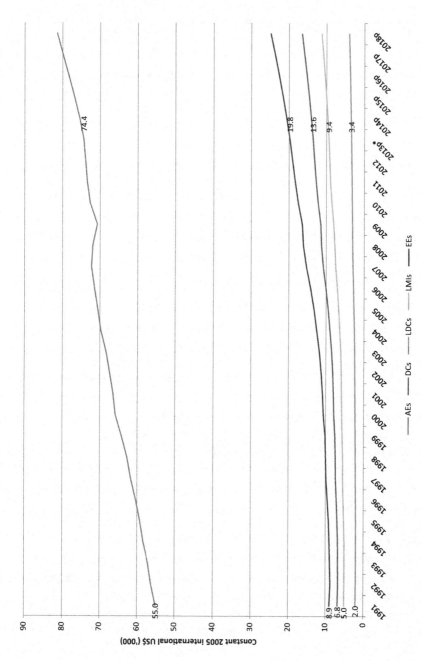

Fig. 3.9 Labour productivity. (Note: *p* projection; 2013 are preliminary estimates, *AE* advanced economy, *DC* developing country, *EE* emerging economy, *LDC* least developed country, *LMIC* lower- or middle-income country. Source: Author's estimations at the ILO, based on data from the ILO Trends Unit, Trends Econometric Models, October 2013; and the World Bank's World Development Indicators, 2013)

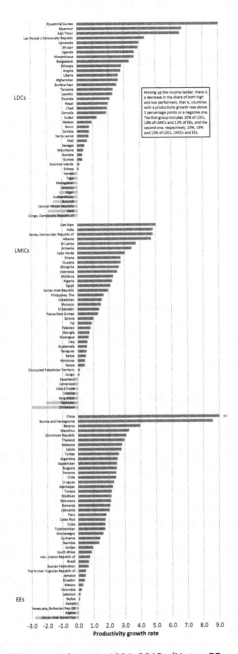

Fig. 3.10 Productivity growth rate, 1991–2013. (Note: *EE* emerging economy, *LDC* least developed country, *LMIC* lower- or middle-income country. Source: Author's estimations at the ILO, based on data from the ILO Trends Unit, Trends Econometric Models, October 2013; and the World Bank's World Development Indicators, 2013)

3.4 Sectoral Employment, Sectoral Growth, and Job Quality

Sectoral employment in DCs follows the Lewisian model, but with a spin. The services sector has continued to be the largest sector, rather than manufacturing for the last two decades. However, the industrial sector has led more consistently in terms of improvement in job quality. Separating out manufacturing employment from the rest of the industry reduces the number of countries that can be examined, but where possible, it shows that manufacturing provides the bulk of jobs in industry as opposed to extractives.

Sectoral Employment

DCs have followed the Lewisian model over the last two decades, in reducing the share of their employment in agriculture. Table 3.8 shows that DCs had 54 percent of their employment in agriculture in 1991, and reduced it to 38 percent by 2013. AEs in contrast halved their agricultural employment shares from 6 to 3 percent over this period. For DCs, this still left LDCs' agricultural shares just under two-thirds of total employment, LMICs with 42 percent, and EEs with just over a quarter, over this period.

The spinoff from Lewis (1954) is that for DCs industrial employment only went up by 4.5 percentage points between 1991 and 2013, from 19 percent of total employment to 23 percent. There is an interesting coincidence with AEs, whose industrial employment shares went down over this period, from 30 percent of total employment to 23 percent.

Within DCs, another important long-run characteristic emerges, differentiating LDCs from LMICs and from EEs. Between 1991 and 2013, LDCs' industrial employment share barely inched up, from 8.1 percent of total employment to 9.5 percent. For LMICs, their industrial employment share went up from 17 percent of total employment to 22 percent over this period. For EEs, their industrial employment share also went up from 23 percent of total employment to 28 percent. *So, industrial employment shares in total employment have moved in lockstep up the income ladder over the past two decades.*

Table 3.8 Share of employment, by sector

Region	1991	1992	1993	1994	1995	1996	1997	1998	1999	2000	2001	2002	2003	2004	2005	2006	2007	2008	2009	2010	2011	2012	2013p
Employment in agriculture, total (%)																							
AEs	6.6	6.4	6.0	5.9	5.6	5.4	5.2	5.1	4.8	4.7	4.5	4.4	4.1	3.9	3.8	3.6	3.5	3.3	3.3	3.3	3.2	3.2	3.2
DCs	53.7	53.3	52.3	51.3	50.2	49.3	48.7	48.7	48.7	48.5	47.9	47.4	46.8	45.6	44.5	43.2	42.1	41.4	40.7	40.0	38.9	37.8	37.6
LDCs	73.7	73.7	73.7	73.4	72.7	72.0	71.7	71.4	71.1	70.9	69.8	68.6	67.4	67.1	66.4	65.9	65.5	65.3	65.1	65.0	64.9	64.5	64.9
LMICs	55.9	56.1	55.3	54.6	53.8	53.3	52.3	52.6	52.3	52.4	51.7	51.0	50.6	49.7	49.1	48.0	47.3	46.5	45.8	45.0	43.8	42.5	41.8
EEs	48.1	47.2	45.7	44.4	42.8	41.4	40.9	40.6	40.9	40.4	39.9	39.7	38.9	37.1	35.5	33.8	32.2	31.2	30.2	29.2	27.9	26.6	26.4
Employment in industry, total (%)																							
AEs	30.9	30.4	29.6	29.1	28.9	28.5	28.3	27.9	27.4	27.1	26.7	26.1	25.5	25.2	24.9	24.9	24.7	24.2	22.4	21.9	22.5	22.9	23.2
DCs	19.4	19.3	19.4	19.4	19.4	19.5	19.6	19.3	19.1	19.0	19.1	19.0	19.2	19.7	20.3	20.9	21.6	21.8	22.0	22.3	22.6	23.0	23.0
LDCs	8.1	7.8	7.5	7.3	7.3	7.2	7.4	7.4	7.6	7.7	8.0	8.4	8.8	8.7	8.9	9.1	9.2	9.2	9.3	9.3	9.4	9.5	9.5
LMICs	17.1	16.9	17.0	17.3	17.4	17.4	17.6	17.1	17.2	17.2	17.7	18.1	18.4	18.7	19.2	19.6	20.0	20.2	20.5	20.8	21.3	21.8	22.1
EEs	23.2	23.2	23.5	23.5	23.5	23.8	23.8	23.6	23.1	22.9	22.8	22.3	22.4	23.1	24.0	25.0	26.0	26.3	26.5	26.9	27.3	27.7	27.5
Employment in services, total (%)																							
AEs	62.5	63.2	64.4	65.0	65.5	66.1	66.5	67.0	67.8	68.2	68.8	69.5	70.4	70.9	71.3	71.5	71.8	72.4	74.3	74.8	74.3	73.9	73.7
DCs	26.9	27.4	28.3	29.2	30.4	31.2	31.7	32.0	32.2	32.5	33.0	33.6	34.0	34.8	35.2	35.9	36.3	36.8	37.3	37.8	38.5	39.2	39.4
LDCs	18.1	18.6	18.8	19.3	20.0	20.8	20.9	21.1	21.3	21.5	22.2	23.0	23.8	24.2	24.7	25.1	25.3	25.5	25.6	25.7	25.7	26.0	25.6
LMICs	26.9	27.0	27.6	28.1	28.9	29.3	30.1	30.3	30.5	30.4	30.6	30.9	31.1	31.6	31.7	32.4	32.8	33.2	33.7	34.2	34.9	35.7	36.1
EEs	28.7	29.6	30.7	32.2	33.8	34.8	35.3	35.8	36.0	36.7	37.3	38.0	38.6	39.8	40.5	41.2	41.7	42.5	43.3	43.9	44.7	45.7	46.0

Note: *p* projection, *AE* advanced economy, *DC* developing country, *EE* emerging economy, *LDC* least developed country, *LMIC* lower- or middle-income country
Source: Author's estimations at the ILO, based on data from the ILO Trends Unit, Trends Econometric Models, October 2013

The spinoff from Lewis (1954) continues in the growing predominance of services in total employment. Table 3.8 shows that DCs' share of services rose from 27 percent of total employment in 1991 to near 40 percent by 2013. AEs' share in services by 2013 neared three quarters of total employment. Within DCs, LDCs' share in services rose from 18 percent of total employment to a quarter, over this period. LMICs' share in services rose from 27 percent of total employment to 36 percent over this period. And EEs' share in services rose from 29 percent of total employment to 46 percent over this period.

The econometric results in Fig. 3.11 support the tabular results, showing the falling share of agricultural employment, and the rising shares of industry and manufacturing, going up the GDP per capita ladder.

While the services sector does emerge as the predominant employer in DCs, the quantum of job growth has been observed above to be a second-best indicator of labour market outcomes, being more demographically led by labour force growth, rather than economic demand. Hence job quality had been adjudged to be a complementary if not better indicator

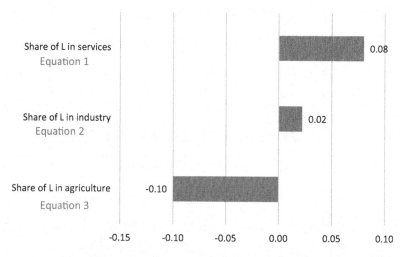

Fig. 3.11 Effect of log GDP per capita on sectoral shares of employment: fixed-effects (within) estimator. (Note: GDP gross domestic product, L labour. All coefficients are significant at the 0.01 level. Econometric specifications available from the author. Source: Author's estimations at the ILO, based on data from the ILO Trends Unit, Trends Econometric Models, October 2013)

of labour market outcomes in DCs. Two key indicators of job quality, vulnerability, and labour productivity show industrial employment to be better than employment in services.

Vulnerability Across Sectors

If the Lewis model is interpreted in terms of improvement in job quality, in going from agriculture to a modern sector, then industry trumps services consistently.

Figure 3.12 shows that in DCs, as a whole, the share of vulnerable employment is reduced by the share of labour in industry by a significantly negative coefficient of −0.27. In the same equation, the share of vulnerable employment is reduced by services by a significant but much smaller coefficient of −0.087. The R-squared term shows that 72 percent of the variation in vulnerability shares is explained by these two sectors (econometric specifications available from the author).

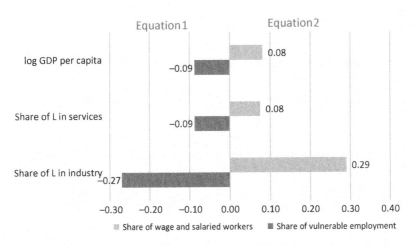

Fig. 3.12 Effect of sectoral shares of labour on vulnerable employment and shares of waged and salaried workers: fixed-effects (within) estimator. (Note: *GDP* gross domestic product, *L* labour. All coefficients are significant at the 0.05 level. Econometric specifications available from the author. Source: Author's estimations at the ILO, based on data from the ILO Trends Unit, Trends Econometric Models, October 2013)

The reciprocal of vulnerability, waged employment shares, are also improved more by industrial shares in employment than by the share of services in employment. The second equation in Fig. 3.12 shows that for DCs as a whole, the share of the waged in total employment is increased by a significantly positive coefficient of 0.29. In the same equation, the share of waged employment is increased by a significantly positive but much smaller coefficient of 0.08. The R-squared term shows that 72 percent of the variation in waged employment shares is explained by these two sectors (econometric specifications available from the author).

Hence from the point of view of vulnerability, there does seem to be some evidence that some part of the services sector in DCs may simply be a refuge sector led by demographic labour supply. Hence its predominance in employment in DCs may not necessarily be a good and desirable labour market outcome in terms of job quality. Another indicator of job quality, labour productivity, also supports industry over services.

Labour Productivity Across Sectors

For DCs as a whole, sectoral labour productivity levels and their growth over the long run have been higher in industry than in services. Further, aggregate labour productivity increases with industrial employment shares in total employment, and decreases with services employment shares.

Table 3.9 shows that from 1994 onwards, industrial labour productivity levels have been the highest amongst DCs as a whole at US$5000, followed by services just below this level, and agriculture below US$700. By 2011, industry's labour productivity was about US$8700, services labour productivity was US$7200, while agriculture was near US$1200. Hence Table 3.10 shows that over the entire period of 1991–2011, industry had higher growth rates for labour productivity, which at 2.7 percent per annum were almost double those for services at 1.5 percent per annum. True, agriculture had an even higher growth rate of labour productivity, of 3 percent per annum over this period, but from the extremely low base seen.

The more worrying labour market outcome is for LDCs' services which had a long-run growth rate of labour productivity of zero, over this

Table 3.9 Labour productivity, by sector

Region	1991	1992	1993	1994	1995	1996	1997	1998	1999	2000	2001	2002	2003	2004	2005	2006	2007	2008	2009	2010	2011
Output per worker in agriculture (constant 2005 USD)																					
AEs	14,003	15,232	15,619	15,906	16,260	17,316	18,238	18,871	20,293	21,334	21,396	22,062	24,050	26,483	26,544	26,884	27,575	30,392	31,754	31,206	30,775
DCs	654	654	670	683	700	740	744	749	756	766	789	794	822	860	900	955	996	1046	1080	1126	1191
LDCs	282	266	267	259	269	280	281	276	283	281	289	290	299	306	316	325	334	346	355	363	367
LMICs	597	594	603	621	614	656	651	659	664	662	686	667	698	707	727	768	798	820	843	891	936
EEs	786	795	827	848	892	946	961	972	979	1009	1038	1065	1103	1192	1276	1381	1464	1579	1658	1740	1884
Output per worker in industry (constant 2005 USD)																					
AEs	51,418	52,391	53,763	56,099	57,569	58,849	60,275	61,320	63,483	65,667	65,545	67,250	69,409	72,429	73,425	74,632	75,917	75,264	75,275	81,786	80,777
DCs	5099	4950	4952	5010	5184	5365	5569	5672	5840	6156	6182	6405	6661	6943	7097	7353	7633	7898	7961	8453	8730
LDCs	2185	2263	2231	2380	2532	2740	2814	2903	2957	2987	2898	2857	2721	2909	3131	3315	3579	3744	3758	3768	3791
LMICs	3342	3350	3228	3174	3318	3453	3497	3474	3498	3619	3532	3547	3574	3652	3707	3863	4006	4062	4131	4293	4299
EEs	6052	5799	5853	5987	6185	6383	6687	6846	7133	7583	7750	8206	8680	9091	9292	9583	9895	10,305	10,397	11,130	11,610
Output per worker in services (constant 2005 USD)																					
AEs	62,540	63,312	63,332	63,751	64,290	65,072	66,144	67,208	67,835	69,010	69,771	70,233	70,088	70,500	71,138	71,807	72,194	71,451	69,290	69,935	71,109
DCs	5366	5217	5037	4949	4836	4839	4930	4924	4969	5137	5179	5265	5388	5524	5749	6031	6435	6696	6830	7020	7207
LDCs	2109	1985	1807	1706	1657	1621	1650	1664	1672	1702	1653	1618	1583	1598	1608	1699	1798	1905	1964	2037	2127
LMICs	2773	2780	2771	2702	2724	2749	2790	2766	2828	2943	3010	3077	3195	3296	3480	3649	3884	4104	4266	4482	4620
EEs	7261	6961	6670	6553	6338	6336	6479	6488	6542	6719	6768	6896	7056	7227	7501	7873	8416	8716	8849	9049	9273

Note: *AE* advanced economy, *DC* developing country, *EE* emerging economy, *LDC* least developed country, *LMIC* lower- or middle-income country

Source: Author's estimations at the ILO, based on data from the ILO Trends Unit, Trends Econometric Models, October 2013; the World Bank's World Development Indicators, 2013; and the UN Statistics Division

Table 3.10 Labour productivity growth rate, by sector

Region	2000	2001	2002	2003	2004	2005	2006	2007	2008	2009	2010	2011	1991–2000	2000–2011	1991–2011
													Average annual growth rate (%)		
Output per worker in agriculture (constant 2005 USD), annual growth rates (%)															
AEs	5.1	0.3	3.1	9.0	10.1	0.2	1.3	2.6	10.2	4.5	−1.7	−1.4	4.8	3.4	4.0
DCs	1.4	3.0	0.6	3.6	4.6	4.6	6.2	4.2	5.1	3.2	4.2	5.8	1.8	4.1	3.0
LDCs	−0.8	2.9	0.4	2.8	2.4	3.3	3.0	2.8	3.5	2.6	2.2	1.2	−0.0	2.5	1.3
LMICs	−0.4	3.6	−2.7	4.6	1.4	2.8	5.5	3.9	2.8	2.8	5.7	5.1	1.2	3.2	2.3
EEs	3.0	2.9	2.6	3.5	8.1	7.1	8.2	6.1	7.8	5.0	5.0	8.2	2.8	5.8	4.5
Output per worker in industry (constant 2005 USD), annual growth rates (%)															
AEs	3.4	−0.2	2.6	3.2	4.4	1.4	1.6	1.7	−0.9	0.0	8.6	−1.2	2.8	1.9	2.3
DCs	5.4	0.4	3.6	4.0	4.2	2.2	3.6	3.8	3.5	0.8	6.2	3.3	2.1	3.2	2.7
LDCs	1.0	−3.0	−1.4	−4.8	6.9	7.7	5.9	8.0	4.6	0.3	0.3	0.6	3.5	2.2	2.8
LMICs	3.4	−2.4	0.4	0.8	2.2	1.5	4.2	3.7	1.4	1.7	3.9	0.1	0.9	1.6	1.3
EEs	6.3	2.2	5.9	5.8	4.7	2.2	3.1	3.3	4.1	0.9	7.0	4.3	2.5	3.9	3.3
Output per worker in services (constant 2005 USD), annual growth rates (%)															
AEs	1.7	1.1	0.7	−0.2	0.6	0.9	0.9	0.5	−1.0	−3.0	0.9	1.7	1.1	0.3	0.6
DCs	3.4	0.8	1.7	2.3	2.5	4.1	4.9	6.7	4.1	2.0	2.8	2.7	−0.5	3.1	1.5
LDCs	1.8	−2.9	−2.1	−2.1	1.0	0.6	5.7	5.8	5.9	3.1	3.7	4.4	−2.4	2.0	0.0
LMICs	4.0	2.3	2.2	3.8	3.1	5.6	4.9	6.4	5.7	3.9	5.1	3.1	0.7	4.2	2.6
EEs	2.7	0.7	1.9	2.3	2.4	3.8	5.0	6.9	3.6	1.5	2.3	2.5	−0.9	3.0	1.2

Note: *AE* advanced economy, *DC* developing country, *EE* emerging economy, *LDC* least developed country, *LMIC* lower- or middle-income country

Source: Author's estimations at the ILO, based on data from the ILO Trends Unit, Trends Econometric Models, October 2013; the World Bank's World Development Indicators, 2013; and the UN Statistics Division

A Regularity in Employment Patterns in Developing Countries...

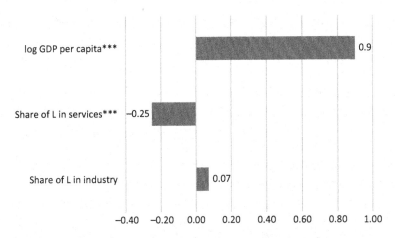

Fig. 3.13 Effect of sectoral shares of labour and log GDP per capita on log productivity: fixed-effects (within) estimator. (Note: *GDP* gross domestic product, *L* labour. *** significant at the 0.01 level. Econometric specifications available from the author. Source: Author's estimations at the ILO, based on data from the ILO Trends Unit, Trends Econometric Models, October 2013)

period. Compared to this, LDCs' industrial labour productivity grew at 2.8 percent over 1991–2011. So, at the bottom of the income ladder, services were entirely a refuge sector for labour.

The econometric results in Fig. 3.13 confirm these tabular results. Aggregate labour productivity in DCs is seen to be determined by the industrial employment share with a positively significant coefficient of 0.07. In the same equation, aggregate labour productivity is negatively determined by the services employment share with a significantly negative coefficient of −0.25. The R-squared term shows that 89 percent of the variation in aggregate labour productivity in the DCs is explained by the variation in these two sectoral shares (econometric specifications available from the author).

Manufacturing and Job Quality

Then in DCs, while the industrial sector may have a smaller employment share than services, but it has better job quality in terms of vulnerability and labour productivity compared to the service sector. In fact, the service sector was seen at the lower end of the income ladder, for LDCs, to have stagnant long-run productivity. Implying it to be entirely a refuge sector driven by supply-side labour force growth rather than expansion to meet economic demand.

Chapter 2 had implied that DCs were locked into separate growth trajectories between LDCs, LMICs, and EEs by their manufacturing shares moving up the income ladder in virtual lockstep. Which implies that if labour market outcomes move in symmetry with growth outcomes, that manufacturing should produce better jobs. Industry has just been observed to produce better jobs than services. So, manufacturing employment has to be separated out from industrial employment.

Figure 3.14 separates industrial employment into its two major components, manufacturing and extractives.[4] It shows that, for countries for which data was available, employment in manufacturing predominated over extractives on average over the period 2000–12. The only exceptions were Sierra Leone, Samoa, and Ukraine amongst the LDCs, Mongolia and Morocco amongst the LMICs, and Suriname amongst the EEs. Ipso facto, manufacturing employment predominating over extractive employment within industrial employment, and industrial employment producing better jobs in DCs, manufacturing has actually created the better jobs.[5]

Further corroborative evidence is provided by Fig. 3.15, which decomposes total GDP growth into productivity growth and employment growth. Employment growth is further decomposed into an economic employment effect, a behavioural labour force participation effect, and a demographic working-age population effect. The figures confirm that total employment growth is driven almost entirely by working-age demographics. But in addition, they show the relative roles of productivity and employment (for which, read demographics). The share of productivity goes up the income ladder, from LDCs to LMICs to EEs. The share also goes up for more non-extractive-based countries amongst the DCs. Hence also supporting the role of manufacturing as opposed to extractives in generating productivity—and by extension, more productive jobs.

Figure 3.16 further decomposes productivity growth into two sources. One source of productivity growth is through structural change, with labour moving from lower-productivity sectors to higher-productivity sectors. A second source of productivity growth is through within-sector

A Regularity in Employment Patterns in Developing Countries...

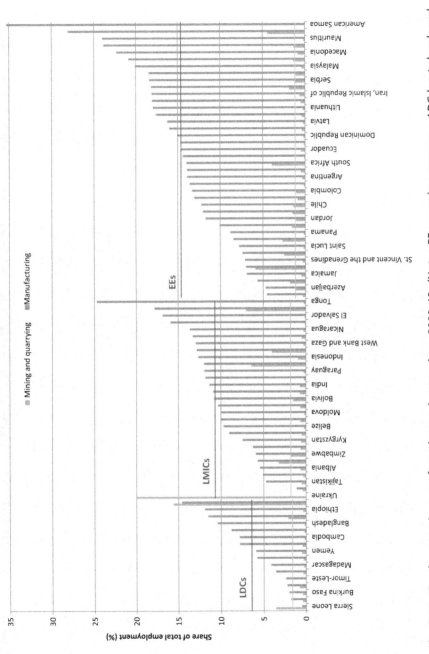

Fig. 3.14 Employment in manufacturing and extractives, 2000–12. (Note: *EE* emerging economy, *LDC* least developed country, *LMIC* lower- or middle-income country. Source: Author's estimations at the ILO, based on data from the ILO's Key Indicators of the Labour Market)

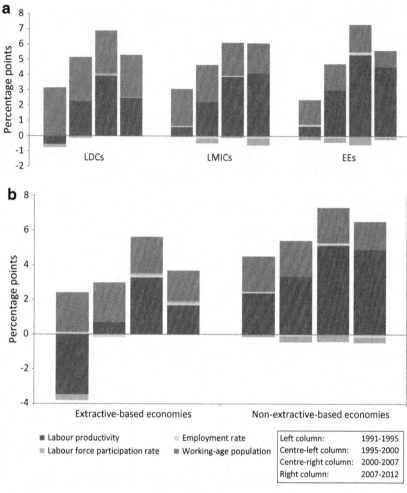

Fig. 3.15 Growth decomposition. (Note: *EE* emerging economy, *LDC* least developed country, *LMIC* lower- or middle-income country. Source: Author's estimations at the ILO, based on data from the ILO Trends Unit, Trends Econometric Models, October 2013; the World Bank's World Development Indicators; and UN, *World Population Prospects: The 2012 Revision* (New York: UN, 2013))

technical change. Structural change seems more consistently higher moving up the income ladder. It is higher more often for EEs and LMICs than for LDCs. And it accounts for about a quarter of productivity growth from 1995 onwards. Within-sector technical change accounts for the other three quarters of productivity growth in this last decade.

A Regularity in Employment Patterns in Developing Countries... 101

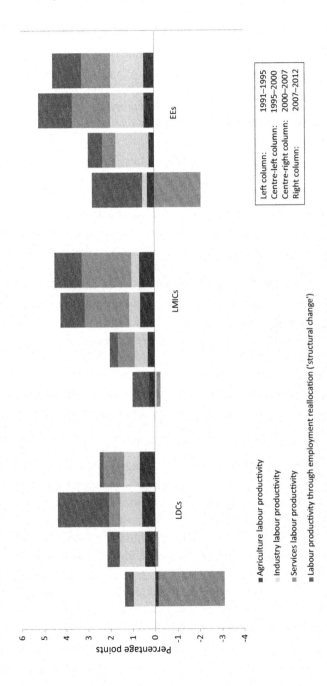

Fig. 3.16 Productivity decomposition. (Note: *EE* emerging economy, *LDC* least developed country, *LMIC* lower- or middle-income country. Growth decomposition is based on data for 66 countries (13 LDCs, 26 LMICs, 27 EEs) and follows the methodology described in ILO, *Global Employment Trends 2013* (Geneva: International Labour Office, 2013, chap. 4). Source: Author's estimations at the ILO, based on data from the ILO Trends Unit, Trends Econometric Models, October 2013; the World Bank's World Development Indicators; and UN, *World Population Prospects: The 2012 Revision* (New York: UN, 2013))

3.5 Job Quality and Climbing Up the Income Ladder

Across DCs then, job quality climbs consistently up the income ladder, from LDCs to LMICs to EEs. All three indicators of job quality, the working poor, vulnerability, and labour productivity, improve going up the income ladder, from LDCs to LMICs to EEs.

This correlation can cut both ways, with higher per capita incomes affording better job quality. And improving job quality could lead to higher incomes. This can be tested using productivity as a proxy variable for growth, and waged employment as an indicator of job quality.

GDP growth is accounted for in larger part by productivity growth as Fig. 3.15 shows. Hence it becomes a good proxy variable for GDP growth. Waged employment is the reciprocal of vulnerability. As the share of vulnerable employment goes down, the share of waged employment goes up. The waged share in employment also goes up with structural change, given the observed prevalence of the Lewis (1954) model. Since self-employment and vulnerability have been amassed in agriculture, as agricultural employment goes down, the waged share in employment tends to go up.

Figure 3.17 shows the scatter of the two variables, the share of wage earners in employment, and the level of productivity. There is a clear positive correlation, with a third of the variation in productivity explained by variation in the share of wage earners. Again, the correlation could go both ways, with higher productivity enabling waged employment, or waged employment enabling higher productivity. But causality is aided by the observation about structural change. Structural change implies a simultaneous increase in waged employment and an increase in labour productivity. Within sector, increases in labour productivity need not necessarily be associated with a simultaneous increase in the waged employment in that sector.

Hence job quality becomes not only a good indicator of labour market success or distress, but in its climbing up the income ladder, it becomes an important determinant of higher per capita *incomes.*

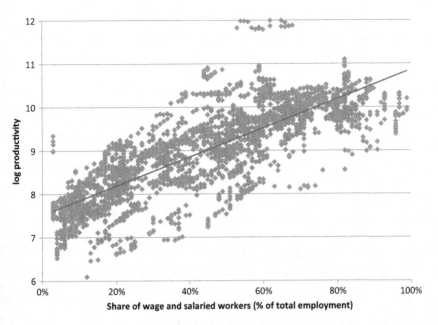

Fig. 3.17 Share of waged and salaried workers, and productivity. (Source: Author's estimations at the ILO, based on data from the ILO Trends Unit, Trends Econometric Models, October 2013)

3.6 Conclusions About the Pattern of Development in Growth and Jobs

The pattern of development in growth and labour markets for DCs gives support to some main conclusions:

- Within DCs, LDCs, LMICs, and EEs appear to be locked into different growth trajectories, primarily by their development of manufacturing, whose share in GDP moves up the income ladder.
- Confirmation of Kaldor's first law, that manufacturing growth has driven GDP growth more, for these 145 DCs over the last three decades.
- Implying, and observed, that GDP per capita growth will also move in lockstep up the income ladder, again differentiating LDCs from LMICs and from EEs.
- But manufacturing shares have declined significantly in about a third of DCs, reflecting not just intense competition, but also factor endow-

ments that may militate against the development of manufacturing. Hence manufacturing may be one well-observed path in climbing up the income ladder for DCs, but certainly not the only one.
- The quantum of job growth accompanying GDP growth is much more supply-led by demographics rather than being led by economic demand, and ambiguous to interpret in terms of desirability. Hence a complementary if not better indicator of labour market outcomes is job quality.
- Improvements in job quality, in terms of vulnerability in employment, the working poor, and labour productivity, all move up the income ladder, again differentiating between LDCs, LMICs, and EEs.
- Service shares predominate in total employment in DCs.
- But industrial employment improves job quality more, specifically vulnerability and labour productivity.
- Industrial employment shares in total employment move in lockstep up the income ladder in the long run, hence again differentiating between LDCs, LMICs, and EEs.
- Within industry, manufacturing employment predominates over employment in extractives. Hence manufacturing employment leads to better jobs.
- At the lower end of the income ladder, LDCs saw no productivity growth in their services sector, defining it pretty much as a refuge sector led more by supply-side labour force growth than by economic demand.
- Again, employment in manufacturing may be preferable in terms of job quality and moving up the income ladder, but may have reached its limits in terms of further absorption of surplus labour from agriculture. Hence the flooding into services.
- But job quality climbing up the income ladder gives an important determinant of attaining higher incomes for DCs. The correlation can of course run both ways, with higher incomes affording better job quality, and better job quality enabling higher incomes. A good correlation between waged employment and labour productivity, and another correlation between structural transformation and labour productivity help establish some causality here. Structural transformation, from agriculture to other sectors, makes it more probable that the

increase in waged employment accompanies increases in labour productivity. Within sector, increases in labour productivity may have a lower probability of being accompanied by increases in waged employment.

The next chapter on drivers of jobs and growth helps establish this causality between jobs and growth more comprehensively, through human capital and knowledge-based capital.

Notes

1. The mathematical expression is more complex because it is not additive but multiplicative.
2. Informality is strictly defined according to the International Conference of Labour Statisticians as employment without legal protection, or social protection, and comprising employment both in the informal sector and the formal sector.
3. But allowing for the possibility of formality also contributing to the working poor—albeit a smaller part compared to informality.
4. Strictly, industry comprises manufacturing plus extractives, plus construction, plus utilities, but the latter two sectors are very small.
5. It must be noted that between 1990 and 2012, manufacturing employment went down by more than 1 percentage point of the labour force in a quarter of LDCs and in half of LMICs and EEs for which data was available (ILO database).

References

ILO (International Labour Organization). 2011. *Growth, Productive Employment and Decent Work in the Least Developed Countries*. Geneva: ILO.
———. 2012. *Global Employment Trends for Women*. Geneva: ILO.
Lewis, W. Arthur. 1954. Economic Development with Unlimited Supplies of Labour. *The Manchester School* 22 (2): 139–191.

4

A Regularity in the Macro Drivers of Growth and Jobs: Accumulation of Physical Capital and Human Capital

4.1 Introduction

Chapters 2 and 3 have shown evidence of growth and employment outcomes improving going up the per capita income ladder. Long-run gross domestic product (GDP) per capita, that is, income growth over the past third of a century has been the highest for emerging economies (EEs), followed by lower- and middle-income countries (LMICs) and then least developed countries (LDCs). The quantum of employment growth accompanying this GDP growth, however, was not judged to be the best indicator of labour market outcomes in developing countries (DCs), being driven more by supply-side demographics, than by demand-side economics. The quality of employment was seen to be a complementary if not a better indicator of labour market outcomes. And internationally agreed upon indicators of job quality, which are vulnerability, the working poor, and labour productivity, again were observed to improve, in their growth over the past two decades for which this data was available, and in their levels, in moving up the income ladder.

However, if income per capita is such a strong determinant of long-run growth and employment, then there is a conundrum of a vicious circle for policy. If LDCs, LMICs, and EEs are locked into separate per capita income trajectories, giving distinct growth and employment trajectories, how can they break out of their predetermining income trajectories? The answer to this conundrum is to explain what determines income levels. And the first part of this book showed some evidence that per capita incomes depended on the sectoral composition of growth, in the manufacturing sector. There was also some evidence adduced, that manufacturing shares improved both GDP growth and job quality more than other sectors. Hence manufacturing allows a way out of the policy impasse. If manufacturing climbs up the per capita income ladder for DCs, then development of manufacturing would allow countries to climb up the income ladder, and hence also the GDP growth and job quality ladder.

But manufacturing is one determinant of income and growth à la Kaldor. Growth and development theory offer a number of other tested determinants of growth and incomes. The key determinants of long-run growth and incomes in the literature begin with the macro determinants. These are pre-eminently capital investment, from the classical tradition begun by Mill (1848), Marshall (1920), and Say (1821). There are the balanced versions of growth from Rosenstein-Rodan (1943), and the unbalanced version of growth from Hirschman (1958). Then there is the neoclassical tradition of growth models led by Harrod and Domar (see Harrod 1948) and Solow (1956, 1994). Endogenous growth theory makes a powerful distinction between physical capital and human capital, with its progenitors in Frankel (1962), Solow (1956), and Romer (1986). More sophisticated endogenous growth models like Grossman and Helpman (1991) have knowledge spillovers, of learning by doing, and increasing allocation of resources to these sectors increases the sustainability of growth. Kaldor (1966, 1967, 1975) and Joan Robinson (1953, 1962) posed a conceptual problem in separating physical from human capital when so much of both was embodied in technology. This conceptual knot is perhaps best untangled by the current literature on the contribution of intangibles to growth as in Dutz et al. (2012).

If accumulation of some sort is taken in the literature as a key determinant of growth, then a second body of literature focuses on the sources of demand, a major strand arguing for the primacy of exports, running from Ricardo (1821: chap. 7) and Mill (1844) to Heckscher (1991) and Ohlin (1935). A counter-strand to this ubiquitous theory of comparative advantage comes from Myrdal (1957) arguing that DCs are pressured by advanced economies (AEs) into primary commodity production. Singer (1950) and Prebisch (1962) show the declining terms of trade for such primary commodity producers compared to manufacturing. And Corden and Neary (1982: 829–31) demonstrate the prevalence of the Dutch Disease of exporting extractives appreciating the exchange rates and so driving down the competitiveness of manufacturing. Lin gives a more current version of comparative advantage, while Chang argues against it, to develop manufacturing to move up the income ladder. Hausmann et al. (2007) move the argument further into the content of exports, showing that complexity and sophistication in the goods exported explain growth better. Palley (2011) and UNCTAD (2013) echo Joan Robinson's concerns about exports beggaring thy neighbour. The ILO has concerns about the unbalanced reliance of demand based on exports, leading to wage competition and the risk of a race to the bottom (Mahmood 2007; Mahmood and Charpe 2013).

This literature basically points to growth policy being based on three major drivers of growth. One is accumulation of capital, which is investment and savings. Another is exports. And a third, in juxtaposition to exports, is relatively greater balance in demand, between exports and consumption. Keynesian pump priming to raise aggregate demand also raises the possibility of government expenditures boosting growth.

This chapter finds that investment and savings shares explain per capita *income consistently and well, in moving up the income ladder virtually in lockstep from LDCs to LMICs and to EEs. Export shares do not explain* per capita *incomes so consistently in moving up the income ladder. But most importantly, human capital and knowledge-based capital explain* per capita *incomes and their growth, in complement with physical capital, very well. This is a major macro argument demonstrating the impact of productive employment on growth itself. It is complemented in the next chapter by examining at the sectoral level, the impact of capabilities on enabling productive transformation.*

4.2 Accumulation of Capital and Growth

All DCs have chosen to increase their accumulation of capital over time, observed from 1980 to 2010. They have done so in two ways, by increasing their share of investment in GDP, and by increasing their share of domestic savings in GDP. The shares of investment and savings climb up the income ladder, virtually in lockstep, from LDCs to LMICs and to EEs. It has also been possible to observe the separation of investment into physical capital and human capital. And the further separation of human capital into basic education, and more intangible knowledge-based capital. Such a complex growth equation does explain per capita *incomes across DCs with a good level of significance.*

Investment

Table 4.1 disaggregates GDP into its macro drivers of growth, consumption, investment, exports, and government expenditure. Consumption is axiomatically the largest driver of growth. And being a negative function of income, its share goes down from LDCs in the long-run band range of 70–80 percent of GDP, to LMICs with band range of 60–70 percent of GDP, and EEs with a band range of 45–60 percent of GDP.

Apart from consumption, the driver of growth that consistently separates LDCs from LMICs, from EEs, is investment. For LDCs, investment was in the long-run band range of 15–24 percent of GDP between 1980 and 2010. For LMICs, investment over this period picks up in lockstep to a band range of 22–32 percent of GDP. And for EEs, investment picks up further over this period to a band range of 27–36 percent of GDP.

Exports do not distinguish between LDCs, LMICs, and EEs, anywhere near as consistently as investment. In 1980, exports for LDCs were 16 percent of GDP, for LMICs 18 percent, and for EEs 17 percent. By 2010, exports for LDCs were 27 percent of GDP, for LMICs 24 percent, and for EEs 31 percent.

Table 4.2 shows that the global crisis hit exports over 2008–10, the most for EEs by 5 percent of GDP, and LMICs and LDCs by 2 percent of GDP each. The crisis does not appear to have affected investment in

Table 4.1 Aggregate demand components as percentages of GDP

	1980	1990	2000	2010
LDCs				
Household consumption expenditure	79.53	75.66	73.72	71.82
Government consumption expenditure	13.41	12.32	11.35	10.66
Gross capital formation	15.35	14.66	19.98	23.83
Exports	16.65	16.35	23.58	27.07
Imports	25.03	21.11	28.65	33.23
LMICs				
Household consumption expenditure	69.44	66.22	66.76	61.53
Government consumption expenditure	11.55	11.93	11.17	10.99
Gross capital formation	21.96	24.81	22.29	31.26
Exports	18.26	16.34	22.79	23.83
Imports	21.21	19.29	23.02	27.61
EEs				
Household consumption expenditure	61.90	59.16	56.56	46.54
Government consumption expenditure	12.40	13.55	14.80	14.22
Gross capital formation	27.17	26.61	26.77	36.35
Exports	16.63	19.73	27.42	30.60
Imports	18.11	19.05	25.55	27.71

Note: *EE* emerging economy, *GDP* gross domestic product, *LDC* least developed country, *LMIC* lower- or middle-income country. Shares are weighted by PPP country share of world GDP total

Source: Author's estimations at the ILO, based on data from IMF, *World Economic Outlook, April 2013, Hopes, Realities, Risks* (Washington, DC: IMF, 2013); and the World Bank's World Development Indicators, 2013

DCs in the same way. Which shows a logical decoupling between DCs and AEs in their domestic policy decisions, but an expected continued coupling in their trade links.

It is important to distinguish between shares in GDP, as given in Tables 4.1 and 4.2, and contribution to GDP growth as given in Table 4.3 and Fig. 4.1. In the 1980s, exports for LDCs and LMICs were weak, with investment contributing to growth more. In the 1990s, export growth picked up across all DCs, contributing to growth more. In the 1990s, both investment and exports have contributed almost equally to growth.

Observed at a country level, gross fixed capital formation is again seen to climb the income ladder. Figure 4.2 shows that, for countries with gross fixed capital formation below 20 percent of GDP, this share was highest for LDCs, falling for LMICs and lowest for EEs by 2007, just on the eve of the crisis before investment levels became volatile.

Table 4.2 Aggregate demand components as percentages of GDP, 2000–10

	2000	2001	2002	2003	2004	2005	2006	2007	2008	2009	2010
LDCs											
Household consumption expenditure	73.7	76.8	76.1	75.3	73.3	73.3	70.5	70.9	73.1	75.5	71.8
Government consumption expenditure	11.4	10.9	11.1	11.2	11.3	11.0	11.1	10.9	11.0	11.1	10.7
Gross capital formation	20.0	20.5	21.3	21.8	21.9	22.2	22.8	22.9	22.2	23.3	23.8
Exports	23.6	22.3	22.0	22.1	24.6	27.1	28.3	29.6	30.3	24.8	27.1
Imports	28.7	30.7	30.5	30.3	31.2	33.6	32.8	34.4	36.6	34.7	33.2
LMICs											
Household consumption expenditure	66.8	66.3	67.0	65.5	63.6	63.4	62.5	61.9	63.7	62.4	61.5
Government consumption expenditure	11.2	11.1	11.1	11.1	12.0	10.7	10.6	10.4	10.9	11.4	11.0
Gross capital formation	22.3	23.2	22.7	23.9	26.9	28.4	29.4	31.1	30.5	30.6	31.3
Exports	22.7	22.1	22.2	22.3	24.7	25.8	26.1	25.2	26.6	22.4	23.8
Imports	22.9	22.8	23.0	22.7	26.0	28.3	28.5	28.5	31.7	26.9	27.5
EEs											
Household consumption expenditure	56.6	56.5	54.9	53.6	52.1	50.7	48.5	48.4	47.4	46.9	46.5
Government consumption expenditure	14.8	15.2	15.2	14.6	14.0	14.2	14.2	13.8	13.8	14.4	14.2
Gross capital formation	26.8	26.8	27.6	29.4	31.2	30.9	32.1	32.3	34.3	35.4	36.4
Exports	27.4	26.7	28.2	30.1	33.0	34.8	36.1	35.5	34.1	28.0	30.6
Imports	25.5	25.2	25.9	27.7	30.3	30.6	30.9	30.0	29.6	24.7	27.7

Note: *EE* emerging economy, *GDP* gross domestic product, *LDC* least developed country, *LMIC* lower- or middle-income country. Shares are weighted by PPP country share of world GDP total

Source: Author's estimations at the ILO, based on data from IMF, *World Economic Outlook, April 2013, Hopes, Realities, Risks* (Washington, DC: IMF, 2013); and the World Bank's World Development Indicators, 2013

Table 4.3 Drivers of growth, contribution to average annual GDP growth, 1980–2010

	GDP (%)	Household consumption (%)	Government consumption (%)	Gross capital formation (%)	Exports (%)	Imports (%)
LDCs						
1980–1990	2.5	79.8	0.0	20.1	−0.5	0.6
1990–2000	4.0	63.8	5.7	32.6	34.4	−36.5
2000–2010	6.3	67.9	10.3	32.2	31.8	−42.2
LMICs						
1980–1990	4.2	57.2	12.8	28.0	12.7	−10.7
1990–2000	3.2	78.7	12.2	3.5	30.6	−25.0
2000–2010	6.4	56.9	10.1	40.5	33.1	−40.5
EEs						
1980–1990	3.2	49.0	19.2	15.2	23.5	−6.8
1990–2000	3.1	64.3	13.4	8.1	47.2	−32.9
2000–2010	6.0	41.6	12.7	43.2	45.7	−43.2

Note: *EE* emerging economy, *GDP* gross domestic product, *LDC* least developed country, *LMIC* lower- or middle-income country
Source: Author's estimations at the ILO, based on data from IMF, *World Economic Outlook, April 2013, Hopes, Realities, Risks* (Washington, DC: IMF, 2013); and the World Bank's World Development Indicators, 2013

Savings and Inflows

Savings as a share of GDP also moves up the per capita *income ladder for DCs over the long run of 1980–2010.*

Table 4.4 shows that savings have increased over time, for LDCs, LMICs, and EEs, from 1980 to 2010. Further, savings climb up the income ladder. For LDCs, the saving share in GDP was in a band range of 7 percent of GDP in 1980 and 18 percent in 2010. For LMICs, savings were in a band range of 19–28 percent of GDP over this period. And for EEs, savings were in the band range of 26–39 percent of GDP over this period.

The table also shows inflows between 1980 and 2010. Foreign direct investment (FDI) goes from under 1 percent of GDP for each of the income groups, LDCs, LMICs, and EEs, in 1980, to 3 percent of GDP for LDCs and EEs each, and near 2 percent of GDP for LMICs.

Official development assistance (ODA) and remittances have been more important for LDCs. ODA for LDCs has fluctuated between 1980

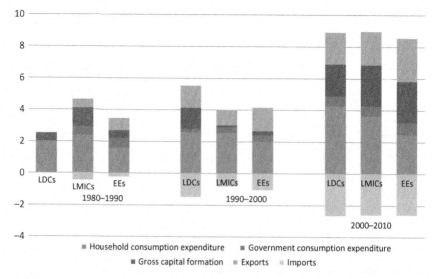

Fig. 4.1 Drivers of growth, contribution to average annual GDP growth, 1980–2010. (Note: *EE* emerging economy, *GDP* gross domestic product, *LDC* least developed country, *LMIC* lower- or middle-income country. Source: Author's estimations at the ILO, based on data from IMF, *World Economic Outlook, April 2013, Hopes, Realities, Risks* (Washington, DC: IMF, 2013); and the World Bank's World Development Indicators, 2013)

and 2010, but trends at just under 7 percent of their GDP. Remittances have increased over this period for LDCs, from 2 percent of GDP to over 6 percent. For LMICs, ODA has tapered off over this period, from under 3 percent of their GDP to 0.6 percent. For EEs, ODA has been negligible over this period. Remittances in LMICs have picked up over this period, from 2.5 percent of their GDP, to 4 percent. Remittances for EEs have remained under 1 percent of their GDP over this whole period.

Table 4.5 shows that the global crisis hit FDI by about half a percent for both LDCs, and EEs, and by about 1.5 percent for LMICs. ODA tapered off with the crisis by almost 1 percent for LDCs, negligibly for LMICs.

Observed at a country level, again, savings as a share of GDP climb up the income ladder. A higher incidence of countries has a higher share of savings in GDP, going from LDCs to LMICs to EEs (Fig. 4.3).

A Regularity in the Macro Drivers of Growth and Jobs...

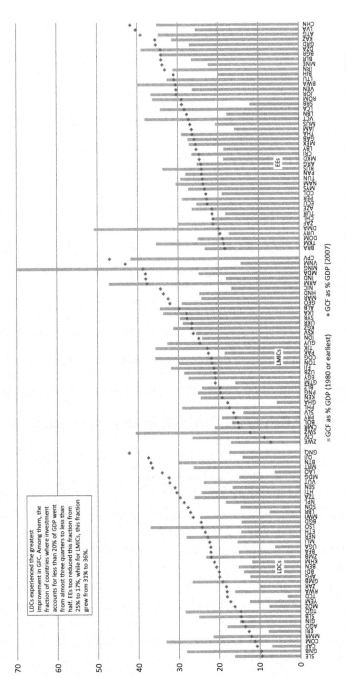

Fig. 4.2 Gross fixed capital formation as a percentage of GDP, 1980 and 2007. (Note: *EE* emerging economy, *GDP* gross domestic product, *GCF* gross capital formation, *LDC* least developed country, *LMIC* lower- or middle-income country. Source: Author's estimations at the ILO, based on data from IMF, *World Economic Outlook, April 2013, Hopes, Realities, Risks* (Washington, DC: IMF, 2013); and the World Bank's World Development Indicators, 2013)

Table 4.4 Savings and capital inflows as percentages of GDP

	1980	1990	2000	2010
LDCs				
Gross fixed capital formation	14.7	14.7	19.1	22.6
Gross domestic savings	7.0	9.4	14.9	17.5
Foreign direct investment	0.8	0.2	2.4	3.5
Official development assistance	6.6	10.7	7.2	6.6
Personal remittances received	2.2	2.6	3.7	6.2
LMICs				
Gross fixed capital formation	20.8	23.5	21.2	28.0
Gross domestic savings	19.0	21.9	22.1	27.5
Foreign direct investment	0.4	0.6	0.5	1.8
Official development assistance	2.7	3.4	1.1	0.6
Personal remittances received	2.5	2.1	2.8	4.0
EEs				
Gross fixed capital formation	24.6	22.5	25.1	34.1
Gross domestic savings	25.7	27.3	28.6	39.2
Foreign direct investment	0.7	0.8	3.0	3.2
Official development assistance	0.4	0.5	0.2	0.1
Personal remittances received	0.6	0.6	0.8	0.7

Note: *EE* emerging economy, *GDP* gross domestic product, *LDC* least developed country, *LMIC* lower- or middle-income country. Shares are weighted by PPP country share of world GDP total

Source: Author's estimations at the ILO, based on data from IMF, *World Economic Outlook, April 2013, Hopes, Realities, Risks* (Washington, DC: IMF, 2013); and the World Bank's World Development Indicators, 2013

Estimation of Drivers of Growth in the Literature: Accumulation

So, a long classical tradition in growth theory and development theory stretching from Mill (1848), Marshall (1920) and Say (1821) to Kaldor (1966) and Kuznets (1973) has considered the accumulation of physical capital as the major determinant of growth. This relationship between GDP growth and investment growth is on the whole largely well supported by the empirical literature. Kuznets (1973) finds that East Asian growth of over 8 percent per annum over a long period was well explained by investment levels in excess of 30 percent of GDP. Blomstrom et al. (1993, 1996), for 100 country data from 1965 to 1985, find that growth Granger-causes investment, but not vice versa, that investment Granger-causes growth.[1] Young (1994) again finds growth in the Asian newly industrialised countries

A Regularity in the Macro Drivers of Growth and Jobs... 117

Table 4.5 Savings and capital inflows as percentages of GDP

	2000	2001	2002	2003	2004	2005	2006	2007	2008	2009	2010
LDCs											
Gross fixed capital formation	19.1	19.7	20.8	20.8	21.1	21.1	21.9	22.1	22.3	22.3	22.6
Gross domestic savings	14.9	12.3	12.8	13.5	15.4	15.6	18.4	18.2	15.9	13.4	17.5
Foreign direct investment	2.4	4.2	4.0	5.2	3.2	2.3	2.8	3.3	4.0	3.7	3.5
Official development assistance	7.2	7.7	9.0	11.1	10.2	8.7	8.3	7.5	7.1	7.3	6.6
LMICs											
Gross fixed capital formation	21.2	22.2	21.3	21.7	24.4	25.8	26.7	28.1	28.3	27.8	28.0
Gross domestic savings	22.1	22.5	21.8	23.4	25.6	25.9	26.9	27.7	25.4	26.1	27.5
Foreign direct investment	0.5	0.6	1.1	0.7	1.0	1.8	2.7	2.8	3.3	2.4	1.8
Official development assistance	1.1	1.3	1.2	1.0	1.0	1.0	0.8	0.7	0.6	0.7	0.6
EEs											
Gross fixed capital formation	25.1	25.3	26.1	27.4	28.6	28.9	29.8	29.8	31.2	33.9	34.1
Gross domestic savings	28.6	28.3	29.8	31.8	33.9	35.0	37.3	37.8	38.8	38.7	39.2
Foreign direct investment	3.0	3.4	3.0	2.5	2.8	3.6	3.5	3.8	3.4	2.3	3.2
Official development assistance	0.2	0.1	0.1	0.1	0.1	0.1	0.1	0.1	0.1	0.1	0.1

Note: *EE* emerging economy, *GDP* gross domestic product, *LDC* least developed country, *LMIC* lower- or middle-income country. Shares are weighted by PPP country share of world GDP total

Source: Author's estimations at the ILO, based on data from IMF, *World Economic Outlook, April 2013, Hopes, Realities, Risks* (Washington, DC: IMF, 2013); and the World Bank's World Development Indicators, 2013

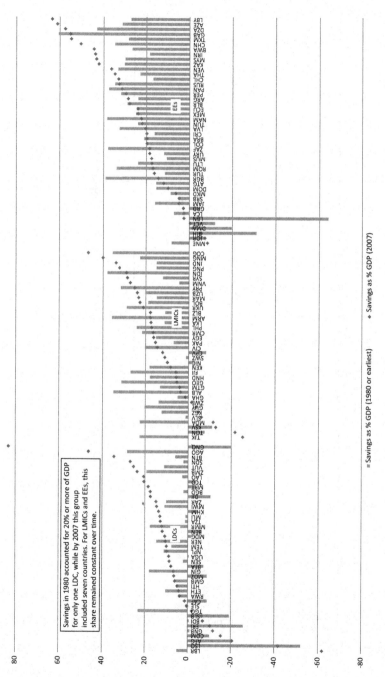

Fig. 4.3 Savings as a percentage of GDP, 1980 and 2007. (Note: *EE* emerging economy, *GDP* gross domestic product, *LDC* least developed country, *LMIC* lower- or middle-income country. Source: Author's estimations at the ILO, based on data from IMF, *World Economic Outlook, April 2013, Hopes, Realities, Risks* (Washington, DC: IMF, 2013); and the World Bank's World Development Indicators, 2013)

correlated to capital accumulation. De Long and Summers (1991, 1993) find good correlations between investment shares and GDP for two samples of countries, and stronger for developing economies. Easterly and Rebelo (1993) also find this correlation for a cross section of 100 countries for 1970–1988. A dissenting note is struck by Auerbach et al. (1993).

Accumulation of capital comprises both investment and savings. The role of savings highlights the two-way causality possible with GDP growth. In the short run, savings could be a function of income à la Friedman's (1957) permanent income hypothesis. But in the long run, growth becomes a function of savings. Hence this emphasis on savings from the Marshall–Mill tradition, to Rosenstein-Rodan (1943), to Lewis (1954), and the two-gap models of Chenery and Bruno (1962) with savings as one major gap.

The relationship between savings and GDP growth is largely well reported in the literature even if some ambiguity remains on the direction of causation. So, Carroll and Weil (1994) show a significant positive correlation between GDP growth and savings rates for a cross section of 64 countries. They also find that GDP growth Granger-causes savings, but not that savings Granger-cause GDP growth. Agrawal (2001), for seven Asian countries, and Anoruo and Ahmad (2001), for seven African countries, find two-way feedbacks between savings and GDP growth. Tang and Ch'ng (2012), for five ASEAN countries for 1970–2010, find that savings Granger-cause GDP growth.

But this rich strand of literature on physical capital accumulation makes a demarche from the neoclassical tradition of Harrod–Domar and Solow's exogenously given growth, to differentiating between physical and human capital, never to return. Harrod and Domar (see Harrod 1948) take GDP growth to be determined by investment divided by the capital-output ratio. This ratio runs into a knife-edge problem of maintaining a steady state, because it has to equal the growth of the labour force and change in labour productivity. This is the first formal introduction of technical change. Solow (1956), to solve the Harrod–Domar knife-edge problem, allows the capital-output ratio to adjust over time, by making technical change exogenous. Kaldor (1957) and Joan Robinson (1967) acknowledged the role of technical change, but found it difficult to account for it, given that technical change was embodied in capital equipment.

While the role of technical change was accepted, Solow's exogenous determination of it drew criticism from Schultz (1963), Arrow (1962), and Becker (1962), who argued for endogeneity of technical change through learning by doing. Endogenous growth theory takes off with Frankel's (1962) model of a composite capital good which lumps physical capital with a technology level. Romer (1986) moves away from this notion of mongrel capital combining physical capital and human knowledge, by basing his empirical estimates of human capital on years of schooling and years of job training. This sparked off new growth theory, epitomised by Mankiw et al. (1992), with GDP growth established as a function of physical capital and human capital.

Human capital itself has come to be further differentiated, between lower-level skills associated with basic education, and the use of higher-skilled IT services associated with higher-level skills. Such intangible, knowledge-based capital is seen to account in early studies of the US for 10–20 percent of firm's investment (Corrado et al. 2009; Dutz et al. 2012; Hulten and Hao 2012). One indicator of such intangible capital would be research and development (R&D) expenditure. However, Fennel (2014) notes a downward bias with low R&D estimates for low-income countries. For a better proxy available for LDCs, LMICs, and EEs, tertiary education is seen to be related to R&D expenditure, and much needed for higher-skill formation.

Econometric Estimation of Accumulation for 145 DCs

The tabular results for 145 DCs given above are not only well in keeping with the growth and development literature, but go a bit further. They show that physical investment and savings climb up the per capita income ladder, from LDCs to LMICs to EEs, explaining the separate trajectories of these income groups quite consistently. Exports too, climb up the income ladder, but not so consistently. This implies that DCs have used investment and savings as policy tools to climb up the per capita income ladder. It also implies that DCs can rely on this policy tool to further climb up the income ladder. Some econometric results add to this explanation of the use and impact of drivers of growth.

Figure 4.4 tests for Granger causality in examining these correlations. It shows that two-thirds of the DCs for which this data was available for the period 1980–2010 showed a significant positive correlation between investment and GDP per capita. In a quarter of the DCs, investment Granger-caused GDP. In 18 percent of the countries, GDP Granger-caused investment. While in another 21 percent of the DCs, there was two-way feedback. This is a more robust support for the general policy result that investment has been used to leverage DCs up the per capita income ladder and a viable policy tool for the future.

Figure 4.4 also shows that 61 percent of the DCs tested showed a significant positive correlation between investment and growth of GDP per capita. In 30 percent of the DCs, investment Granger-caused growth of GDP per capita. In 11 percent of the countries, growth of GDP per capita Granger-caused investment. In another 20 percent of the DCs, there was two-way feedback.

Hence there is a two-step argument here:

(a) *Physical investment Granger-caused GDP* per capita *in 25 percent of DCs tested over 1980–2010*

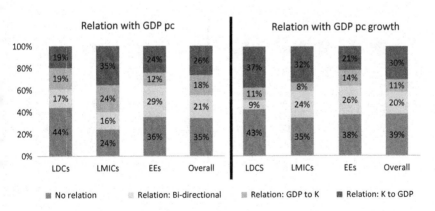

Fig. 4.4 Direction of the Granger causality relationship found for gross capital formation and GDP per capita. (Note: *EE* emerging economy, *GDP* gross domestic product, *K* gross capital formation, *LDC* least developed country, *LMIC* lower- or middle-income country. Source: Author's estimations at the ILO, based on data from the World Bank's World Development Indicators, 2013)

(b) *Physical investment Granger-caused growth in GDP* per capita *in 30 percent of the DCs tested over 1980–2010*

Which implies that physical investment can be used by DCs to leverage both their incomes and its growth over time.

Figure 4.5 gives symmetric results for savings. In 57 percent of the DCs that could be tested for data between 1980 and 2010, savings were significantly positively correlated to GDP per capita. In 21 percent of the DCs, savings Granger-caused GDP per capita. In 18 percent of the DCs, GDP per capita Granger-caused savings. While in another 18 percent of the DCs, there was two-way feedback.

Further, analogous to the investment result, in 52 percent of the DCs tested, savings were positively and significantly correlated to growth of GDP per capita. In 21 percent of the DCs, savings Granger-caused growth of GDP per capita. In 18 percent of the DCs, growth of GDP per capita Granger-caused savings. While in 13 percent of the DCs there was two-way feedback.

Which implies that savings can also be used by DCs to leverage their incomes and its growth over time.

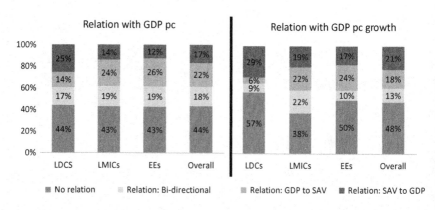

Fig. 4.5 Direction of the Granger causality relationship found for savings and GDP per capita. (Note: *EE* emerging economy, *GDP* gross domestic product, *LDC* least developed country, *LMIC* lower- or middle-income country, *SAV* savings. Source: Author's estimations at the ILO, based on data from the World Bank's World Development Indicators, 2013)

4.3 Investment in Human Capital

Beyond investment in physical capital, it is important to examine the pattern of investment in human capital: that is, the contribution that education and training of the labour force make to growth. While the quantum of physical capital does play a role in explaining differences in GDP per capita, the relative investment in human capital adds more explanatory power, not least because physical and human capital may be complements. More broadly, human capital is a key factor in enhancing labour productivity and job quality, and hence GDP.

Moving from physical capital to human capital and intangibles. Figure 4.6 uses an OLS regression with fixed country effects to determine the impact of physical capital investment, human capital, and intangible knowledge-based capital on GDP per capita, for the DCs for which data

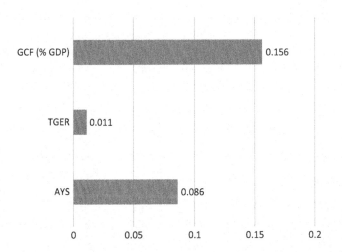

Fig. 4.6 Effect of gross capital formation, tertiary gross enrolment ratio, and average years of schooling on GDP per capita: fixed-effects (within) estimator. (Note: *AYS* average years of schooling, *GCF* gross capital formation, *GDP* gross domestic product, *TGER* tertiary gross enrolment ratio. The figure displays the coefficient estimates from a regression of GDP per capita on gross capital formation, tertiary gross enrolment, and average years of schooling. All coefficients are significant at the level of 0.01. Econometric specifications are available from the author. Source: Author's estimations at the ILO, based on data from the World Bank's World Development Indicators, 2013)

was available from 1980 to 2012. The proxy variable used for human capital was average years of schooling, as the literature advocates. The proxy variable used for intangible knowledge-based capital was gross tertiary enrolment, again as the literature prompts.

The equation shows a positive and significant correlation for all three variables. Physical capital has a coefficient of 0.16, showing that a 1 percent increase in physical capital investment leads to a 0.16 percent increase in GDP per capita. Average years of schooling has a coefficient of 0.09, which implies that a one-year increase in average years of schooling raise GDP per capita by 0.09 percent. Finally, gross tertiary enrolment has a coefficient of 0.01, which means that a 1 percent increase in tertiary enrolment increases GDP per capita by 0.01 percent.

So, in addition to accumulation of physical capital, DCs can also use human capital and intangible knowledge-based capital to leverage their income levels over time.

Further evidence is provided on causality by Fig. 4.7, which shows that in 56 percent of the DCs for which data was available, there was a positive correlation between primary enrolment as a proxy for human capital and GDP. In 16 percent of the DCs, enrolment Granger-caused GDP, while in

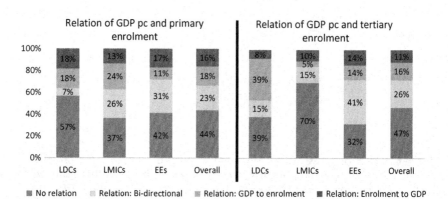

Fig. 4.7 Direction of the Granger causality relationship found for primary enrolment and GDP per capita and for tertiary enrolment and GDP per capita. (Note: *EE* emerging economy, *GDP* gross domestic product, *LDC* least developed country, *LMIC* lower- or middle-income country. Source: Author's estimations at the ILO, based on data from the World Bank's World Development Indicators, 2013)

18 percent of the DCs, GDP Granger-caused enrolment. In 23 percent of the DCs, there was two-way feedback between GDP and enrolment.

The result for tertiary enrolment, as a proxy for intangibles and GDP is broadly similar. But there is a key difference in the variation across LDCs, LMICs, and EEs. Primary enrolment and human capital have the largest impact on GDP in LDCs. Tertiary enrolment and intangibles have the largest impact on GDP in EEs.

Figure 4.8 provides further detail of the channel through which human capital affects GDP growth, by decomposing this growth between 1991 and 2011 into physical capital, labour, human capital, and a residual taken to be total factor productivity (TFP) (see Inklaar and Timmer

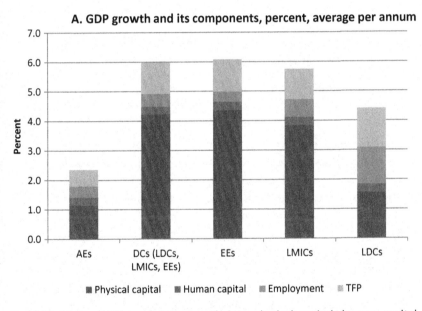

Fig. 4.8 Decomposition of GDP growth into physical capital, human capital, employment, and TFP components, 1991–2011. (Note: *AE* advanced economy, *DC* developing country, *EE* emerging economy, *GDP* gross domestic product, *LDC* least developed country, *LMIC* lower- or middle-income country, *TFP* total factor productivity. Growth decompositions are based on data for 55 DCs (12 LDCs, 16 LMICs, 27 EEs) and 37 AEs. Source: Author's estimations at the ILO, based on data from Christian Viegelahn, 'Decomposition of GDP Growth', unpublished manuscript (ILO, Geneva, forthcoming); IMF, *World Economic Outlook, October 2013, Transitions and Tensions* (Washington, DC: IMF, 2013); ILO Trends Unit, Trends Econometric Models, October 2013; and Groningen Growth and Development Centre, Penn World Tables Version 8.0)

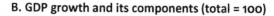
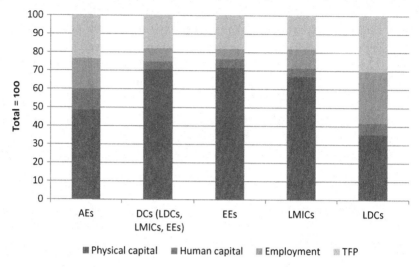

Fig. 4.8 (continued)

2013). The traditional decomposition of GDP growth over time is usually in terms of just three elements: capital, labour, and TFP. However, the Penn World Tables and their methodology permit labour to be differentiated by educational levels. These educational levels allow labour to be weighted by primary-, middle-, and higher-level educational attainment. In effect this allows GDP growth to be decomposed into a fourth element, human capital.

In comparing AEs with DCs as a group, physical capital does not appear to be a constraint for DCs (Fig. 4.8, panel A). However, physical capital does appear to be constrained for LDCs as it accounts for only 35 percent of GDP growth between 1991 and 2011. For LMICs, physical capital accounts for about 66 percent of GDP growth over this period, while for EEs it accounts for about 72 percent of GDP growth. But the more critical finding (Fig. 4.8, panel B) is in the role of human capital in AEs compared with DCs. Human capital accounted for about 11 percent of GDP growth between 1991 and 2011 for AEs. This was more than double the share of human capital in GDP for DCs. It is this difference

A Regularity in the Macro Drivers of Growth and Jobs... 127

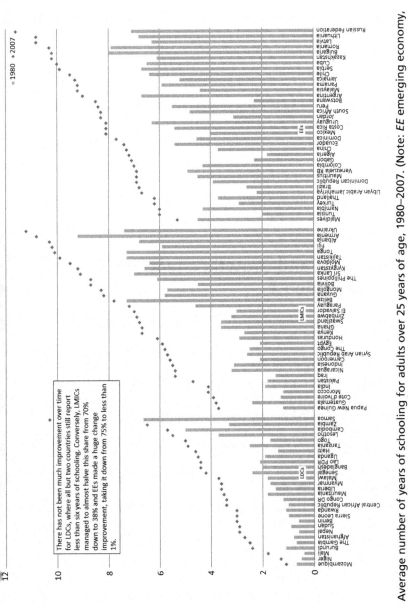

Fig. 4.9 Average number of years of schooling for adults over 25 years of age, 1980–2007. (Note: *EE* emerging economy, *LDC* least developed country, *LMIC* lower- or middle-income country. Source: Author's estimations at the ILO, based on data from the World Bank's World Development Indicators, 2013)

in human capital that is likely to explain the much higher relative contribution of TFP for AEs, of almost one-quarter of total GDP growth compared with 18 percent of GDP growth for DCs.

All DCs improved their educational outcomes between 1980 and 2007 (Fig. 4.9). In terms of attainment of an arbitrary threshold, say six years of schooling, the LDCs' much lower base meant they have struggled to catch up with LMICs and EEs. Despite big improvements by LDCs, only two had average years of schooling above six years in 2007, compared with only one in 1980. The number of LMICs with above six years of schooling more than doubled, from 30 percent in 1980 to 62 percent in 2007. EEs made a huge improvement, from 25 percent above six years of schooling in 1980 to all but one country in 2007.

4.4 Exports and Growth: Literature and Evidence

The Literature

Trade theory has myriad strands to it, but focussing here on empirical evidence of its impact on growth. Ricardian specialisation on comparative lower cost advantage is meant to increase output in a two-country case, and by extension in a multi-country case (Ricardo 1821: chap. 7). Mill's (1844) formalisation of Ricardo allows for the possibility of net loss for one country and gain for the second, if the exchange rate favours the cost ratio of the second country. Neoclassical comparative advantage in Heckscher–Ohlin also argues for country specialisation using its more abundant and hence cheaper factor. Trade is meant to result in equalisation of goods prices, factor prices, and wages (Heckscher 1991, Ohlin 1935). Hence the upward impact on DCs' incomes. Evidence however is against factor price equalisation in Tovias (1982) and Bernard et al. (2002).

Myrdal (1957) observed trade specialisation of DCs in primary commodities, driven more by AE demand rather than the neoclassical notion of comparative advantage. Which would strengthen the backwash effects and maintain primary commodity sectors in DCs, rather than developing new ones. Prebisch (1962) and Singer (1950) observed declining terms of trade for primary commodities produced largely by DCs, from

1870 to the Second World War, giving rise to balance-of-payments problems, low-income growth, and increasing aid dependency. Much of the evidence from Singer and Gray (1988), Linnemann et al. (1987), and Kindleberger (1960: 367–68) concurs with declining terms of trade for primary commodities. Corden and Neary (1982: 829–31) observe that a Dutch disease of exporting extractive could appreciate the exchange rate and so lower the competitiveness of manufacturing and its development. Considerable evidence, for instance from Sachs and Warner (1995, 1999), Ismail (2010), and Cavalcanti et al. (2011), largely supports the Dutch disease argument.

Lin observes that industry plays a major role in economic growth, but that industrial strategy should not defy comparative advantage (Lin and Chang 2009; Lin 2011). Stiglitz (2011) disagrees with such a static notion of comparative advantage since it does not incorporate learning by doing to increase productivity. Chang elaborates that comparative advantage will not allow accumulation of human capital, because there will be no significant manufacturing sector to demand that human capital (Lin and Chang 2009). Chang cites Japan and South Korea as evidence of comparative advantage-defying strategies which moved into industries and adopted technologies that high-income countries had not done at similar stages of their development. McMillan and Rodrik (2011) specify that, to increase growth, such structural change must always ensure the movement of workers from less productive sectors to more productive ones. Hausmann et al. (2007) further show for 80 countries for 1994–2003 that exports matter, with the sophistication of the export basket increasing growth.

Further reservations on export-led growth come from Palley (2011) who recalls Joan Robinson's beggar-thy-neighbour argument about one DC increasing its export competitiveness at the expense of others, especially given constant demand for exports. UNCTAD (2013) again cites reduced demand from AEs, and competition amongst DCs to provide bases for multinational corporations. The ILO has had a longstanding concern about wage competition and a race to the bottom in DCs' attempts to increase their competitiveness (Mahmood and Charpe 2013). Favouring instead more balance in demand between exports and domestic consumption (Mahmood 2007).

Econometric Evidence on Exports and Growth for 145 DCs

The tabular evidence on exports seen above showed that the export share in GDP moved up the income ladder, but not as consistently as investment and savings. Figure 4.10 shows the considerable jump up in the share of exports in GDP, for most DCs across LDCs, LMICs, and EEs. Figure 4.11 shows its inverse, the ratio of consumption to export shares in GDP, to have fallen over time between 1980 and 2007, and to be the lowest for EEs, higher for LMICs and highest for LDCs.

Figure 4.12 concurs by showing that while exports were significantly positively correlated to GDP per capita for 59 percent of the DCs tested, only in 17 percent of the DCs did exports Granger-cause GDP per capita. In 16 percent of the DCs, GDP per capita Granger-caused exports. While in 25 percent of the DCs, there was two-way feedback.

However, the figure also shows that in a third of the DCs, exports Granger-caused growth in GDP per capita. In 8 percent of the DCs, GDP per capita growth Granger-caused exports. While in 18 percent of the DCs there was two-way feedback. Hence a somewhat nuanced finding on exports as a driver of growth. Exports are not observed to help all DCs consistently in moving up the per capita ladder. However, they do Granger-cause growth.

Which recalls from the literature, that what you export matters. Figure 4.13 runs an OLS regression with fixed country effects for DCs that could be tested. It shows that the export share in GDP was significantly positively correlated to manufacturing, which had a coefficient of 0.71, and to industry with a higher coefficient of 1.0. Services had a much smaller coefficient, 0.19. The difference between industry and manufacturing is extractives. Hence while manufacturing did lead to increasing export shares, extractives increased export shares by more. The R-squared was low at just 0.2 (econometric specifications available from the author). Table 4.6 in the Appendix splits LDCs, LMICs, and EEs into more extractive-based countries and less extractive-based ones. It shows that for each of LDCs, LMICs, and EEs, non-extractive countries had a much lower share of exports compared to extractive-based countries.

A Regularity in the Macro Drivers of Growth and Jobs... 131

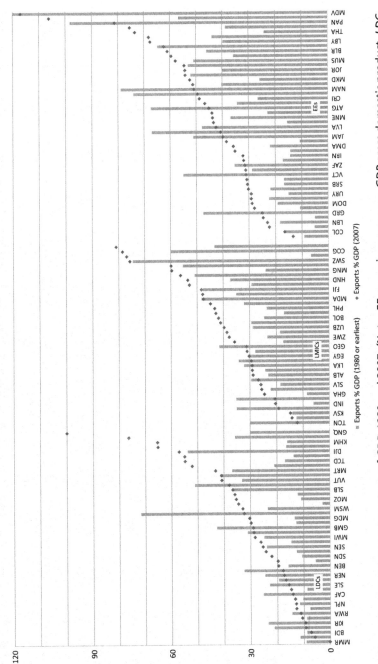

Fig. 4.10 Exports as a percentage of GDP, 1980 and 2007. (Note: *EE* emerging economy, *GDP* gross domestic product, *LDC* least developed country, *LMIC* lower- or middle-income country. Source: Author's estimations at the ILO, based on data from the World Bank's World Development Indicators, 2013)

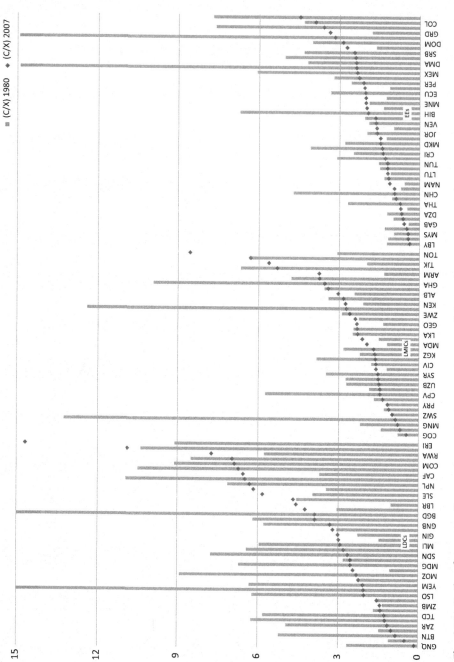

Fig. 4.11 Ratio of consumption over exports, as a percentage of GDP, 1980 and 2007. (Note: *EE* emerging economy, *GDP*

A Regularity in the Macro Drivers of Growth and Jobs...

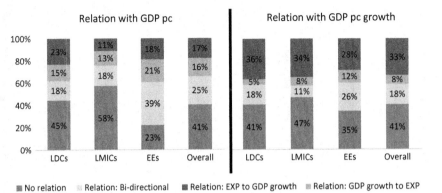

Fig. 4.12 Direction of the Granger causality relationship found for exports (EXP) and GDP per capita. (Note: *EE* emerging economy, *GDP* gross domestic product, *LDC* least developed country, *LMIC* lower- or middle-income country. Source: Author's estimations at the ILO, based on data from the World Bank's World Development Indicators, 2013)

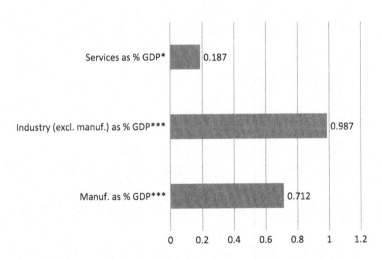

Fig. 4.13 Effect of manufacturing, industry, and services on exports: fixed-effects (within) estimator. (Note: *GDP* gross domestic product. Standard errors in parentheses. *** $p < 0.01$, ** $p < 0.05$, * $p < 0.1$. Source: Author's estimations at the ILO, based on data from the World Bank's World Development Indicators)

Appendix

Table 4.6 Resource-based economies, aggregate demand components as a percentage of GDP

	Resources rent as % GDP	Household consumption expenditure				Government consumption expenditure				Gross capital formation				Exports				Imports			
		1980	1990	2000	2010	1980	1990	2000	2010	1980	1990	2000	2010	1980	1990	2000	2010	1980	1990	2000	2010
LDCs																						
Extractives																						
Equatorial Guinea	75.8	...	80.3	9.8	11.7	...	39.7	4.6	4.4	...	17.4	72.3	64.0	30.1	32.2	99.5	82.7	39.6	69.6	86.1	62.8
Angola	65.9	39.3	35.8	30.0	50.3	32.4	34.5	30.4	17.6	18.0	11.7	12.8	12.7	35.7	38.9	89.6	62.4	25.3	20.9	62.8	42.9
Chad	62.2	98.3	97.6	86.8	40.6	5.5	10.0	7.7	13.2	3.2	6.8	23.3	32.7	16.9	13.5	16.9	41.4	28.9	27.9	34.7	28.0
Yemen, Rep.	39.7	...	77.0	60.1	80.6	...	15.5	13.6	11.8	...	12.4	18.9	11.7	...	12.2	41.4	30.5	...	17.2	34.0	34.6
Mauritania	24.8	58.2	69.2	74.5	69.8	45.3	25.9	20.2	16.3	26.3	20.0	20.6	26.9	36.8	45.6	30.0	56.3	66.7	60.7	45.3	69.3
Congo, Dem. Rep.	22.4	81.5	79.1	87.4	76.2	8.4	11.5	7.5	9.8	10.0	9.1	3.4	23.6	16.5	29.5	22.4	68.3	16.4	29.2	20.7	77.9
Sudan	20.1	81.9	86.1	63.5	63.5	16.0	5.8	9.1	10.8	14.7	11.2	24.9	23.2	10.6	4.0	16.0	20.0	23.1	7.1	13.4	17.5
Guinea	16.3	...	66.9	76.9	82.6	...	11.0	7.1	15.0	...	24.5	20.5	10.6	...	31.1	24.5	28.4	...	33.4	29.0	36.5
Solomon Islands	15.4	...	...	84.3	81.9	21.3	...	...	39.2	25.1	20.3	6.6	14.6	...	30.1	24.1	31.1	79.3	64.7	38.6	61.5
Liberia	15.1	73.7	83.2	85.7	122.4	21.3	...	7.5	14.2	...	...	7.5	26.4	36.9	55.2	26.1	19.1	71.8	43.9	26.9	82.1
Zambia	13.3	55.2	64.4	87.0	49.2	25.5	19.0	9.5	16.4	23.3	17.3	17.4	22.6	71.8	35.9	26.5	46.8	45.4	36.6	40.4	34.9
Burundi	11.6	91.4	94.5	88.2	78.7	9.2	10.8	14.9	31.6	13.9	14.5	2.8	20.0	41.4	7.9	6.3	8.9	23.3	27.8	16.2	39.2
Mozambique	11.5	96.7	92.3	80.6	83.3	12.2	13.5	9.0	13.4	7.6	22.1	31.0	21.8	8.8	8.2	16.5	26.1	27.4	36.1	37.0	44.7
LDCs		86.2	83.0	78.6	78.0	10.3	9.6	9.8	8.9	15.7	16.4	20.6	25.8	12.6	11.5	17.4	19.2	24.9	20.4	26.5	31.7
Non-extractives																						

(continued)

Table 4.6 (continued)

	Resources rent as % GDP	Household consumption expenditure				Government consumption expenditure				Gross capital formation				Exports				Imports			
		1980	1990	2000	2010	1980	1990	2000	2010	1980	1990	2000	2010	1980	1990	2000	2010	1980	1990	2000	2010
LMICs Extractives																						
Iraq	107.4	...	...	...	...	...	...	...	...	...	...	...	...	...	...	...	...	...	...	...	...
Uzbekistan	105.9	...	61.4	55.4	48.4	...	25.4	18.7	23.5	...	32.2	22.9	24.9	...	28.8	24.6	31.9	...	47.8	21.5	28.8
Congo, Rep.	74.7	46.8	31.8	29.1	38.6	17.6	19.6	11.6	10.4	35.8	15.9	22.6	20.5	60.0	51.8	80.3	85.1	60.1	19.0	43.6	54.7
Papua New Guinea	44.8	60.9	59.0	44.6	70.0	24.1	24.8	16.6	9.5	25.2	24.4	21.9	17.8	43.2	40.6	66.2	55.9	53.3	48.9	49.2	53.1
Nigeria	43.4	...	...	...	...	...	...	...	...	...	...	...	...	29.4	43.4	54.0	35.2	19.2	28.8	32.0	29.9
Bolivia	38.9	67.3	76.9	76.4	62.3	13.8	11.8	14.5	13.8	16.6	12.5	18.1	17.0	24.5	22.8	18.3	41.2	22.3	23.9	27.3	34.3
Syrian Arab Republic	29.7	64.8	68.7	63.5	71.5	23.2	14.3	12.4	10.1	29.6	16.5	17.3	18.8	18.6	28.3	35.4	35.3	36.1	28.0	28.6	35.8
Egypt, Arab Rep.	24.3	69.2	72.6	75.9	74.7	15.7	11.3	11.2	11.2	27.5	28.8	19.6	18.9	30.5	20.0	16.2	21.3	42.9	32.7	22.8	26.1
Mongolia	21.3	52.3	68.7	69.6	53.1	24.9	24.4	15.3	13.7	70.0	29.1	29.0	40.8	23.9	18.3	54.0	54.7	71.0	40.3	67.9	62.4
Vietnam	18.6	...	84.3	66.4	64.9	...	12.3	6.4	6.5	...	12.6	29.6	38.9	...	36.0	55.0	77.5	...	45.3	57.5	87.8
Indonesia	16.1	51.4	58.9	60.7	56.8	10.5	8.8	6.5	9.0	24.1	30.7	22.2	32.5	34.2	25.3	41.0	24.6	20.2	23.7	30.5	22.9
Cameroon	11.0	68.6	66.6	68.5	73.1	9.7	12.8	10.1	14.2	21.0	17.8	17.0	16.1	27.9	20.2	29.2	25.5	27.1	17.3	24.8	28.9
LMICs		73.8	67.2	67.3	61.0	10.8	12.5	12.1	11.3	20.6	23.5	22.8	32.7	12.8	13.1	18.8	23.2	18.0	16.3	21.0	28.2
Non-extractives																						

(continued)

Table 4.6 (continued)

	Resources rent as % GDP	Household consumption expenditure				Government consumption expenditure				Gross capital formation				Exports				Imports			
		1980	1990	2000	2010	1980	1990	2000	2010	1980	1990	2000	2010	1980	1990	2000	2010	1980	1990	2000	2010
EEs Extractives																						
Libya	70.5	...	48.4	45.7	22.9	...	24.4	20.8	9.3	...	18.6	13.4	27.9	...	39.7	35.6	67.4	...	31.1	15.5	27.5
Azerbaijan	65.0	...	51.2	69.2	38.1	...	17.6	9.5	11.1	...	26.5	20.7	16.8	...	43.9	39.0	54.0	...	39.2	38.4	19.9
Gabon	57.9	26.1	49.7	32.2	35.9	13.2	13.4	9.6	8.9	27.5	21.7	21.9	25.9	64.7	46.0	69.0	62.2	31.6	30.9	32.7	32.9
Kazakhstan	52.2	...	51.6	62.3	49.1	...	18.2	12.1	10.8	...	31.5	18.1	25.4	...	74.0	56.6	44.0	...	75.3	49.1	29.2
Iran, Islamic Rep.	51.6	59.0	59.3	47.9	45.0	22.5	12.1	13.9	11.2	31.1	37.2	33.0	33.2	14.4	14.5	22.7	32.2	27.1	23.1	17.4	21.5
Venezuela RB	47.9	54.9	62.1	51.7	55.9	11.8	8.4	12.4	11.2	26.4	10.2	24.2	22.0	28.8	39.5	29.7	28.5	21.8	20.2	18.1	17.6
Algeria	42.9	41.7	56.8	41.6	34.7	15.2	16.1	13.6	14.2	39.1	28.6	25.0	41.5	34.3	23.4	41.2	30.9	30.3	24.9	21.4	21.5
Russian Federation	38.4	...	48.9	46.2	51.5	...	20.8	15.1	18.2	...	30.1	18.7	22.2	...	18.2	44.1	29.2	...	17.9	24.0	21.1
Ecuador	26.0	57.1	62.7	64.6	63.9	18.3	12.3	9.4	13.1	25.4	24.1	21.3	27.0	17.1	22.8	32.1	28.7	17.9	21.8	27.3	32.7
Malaysia	19.4	54.2	51.7	43.8	47.5	16.0	13.8	10.2	12.2	27.4	32.4	26.9	23.1	56.7	74.5	119.8	93.7	54.3	72.4	100.6	76.6
Chile	13.9	70.7	61.4	65.0	58.5	12.5	10.0	11.6	11.9	21.0	25.2	22.7	23.4	22.8	34.0	29.3	37.8	27.0	30.5	28.6	31.7
Argentina	12.6	...	77.1	70.7	59.8	...	3.1	13.8	14.9	25.3	14.0	16.2	22.0	5.1	10.4	10.9	21.7	6.5	4.6	11.5	18.4
Turkmenistan		...	49.3	36.5	7.0	...	23.0	14.2	9.3	...	40.1	34.7	51.9	...	38.7	95.5	76.3	...	26.8	80.9	44.5
EEs Non-extractives		63.3	59.2	57.7	46.3	11.4	13.9	15.2	14.6	26.7	26.4	26.6	37.4	14.4	17.4	24.4	28.8	15.8	16.8	24.0	27.0

Note: *EE* emerging economy, *GDP* gross domestic product, *LDC* least developed country, *LMIC* lower- or middle-income country

Notes

1. Granger tests establish causality by using past independent variables to predict latter dependent variables.

References

Agrawal, Pradeep. 2001. The Relation Between Savings and Growth: Cointegration and Causality Evidence from Asia. *Applied Economics* 33 (4): 499–513.
Anoruo, Emmanuel, and Yusuf Ahmad. 2001. Causal Relationship Between Domestic Savings and Economic Growth: Evidence from Seven African Countries. *African Development Review* 13 (2): 238–249.
Arrow, Kenneth J. 1962. The Economic Implications of Learning by Doing. *Review of Economic Studies* 29 (3): 155–173.
Auerbach, Alan J., Kevin A. Hassett, and Stephen D. Oliner. 1993. Reassessing the Social Returns to Equipment Investment. Working Paper 4405, National Bureau of Economic Research, Cambridge, MA.
Becker, Gary S. 1962. Investment in Human Capital: A Theoretical Analysis. *Journal of Political Economy* 70 (5): 9–49.
Bernard, Andrew B., Stephen Redding, Peter K. Schott, and Helen Simpson. 2002. Factor Price Equalization in the UK? Working Paper 9052, National Bureau of Economic Research, Cambridge, MA.
Blomstrom, Magnus, Robert E. Lipsey, and Mario Zejan. 1993. Is Fixed Investment the Key to Economic Growth? Working Paper 4436, National Bureau of Economic Research, Cambridge, MA.
———. 1996. Is Fixed Investment the Key to Economic Growth? *Quarterly Journal of Economics* 111 (1): 269–276.
Carroll, Christopher D., and David N. Weil. 1994. Saving and Growth: A Reinterpretation. *Carnegie-Rochester Conference Series on Public Policy* 40: 133–192.
Cavalcanti, Tiago V. de V., Kamiar Mohaddes, and Mehdi Raissi. 2011. Growth, Development and Natural Resources: New Evidence Using a Heterogeneous Panel Analysis. *Quarterly Review of Economics and Finance* 51 (4): 305–318.
Chenery, Hollis B., and Michael Bruno. 1962. Development Alternatives in an Open Economy: The Case of Israel. *Economic Journal* 72 (285): 79–103.

Corden, W. Max, and J. Peter Neary. 1982. Booming Sector and De-Industrialisation in a Small Open Economy. *Economic Journal* 92 (368): 825–848.

Corrado, Carol, Charles Hulten, and Daniel Sichel. 2009. Intangible Capital and US Economic Growth. *Review of Income and Wealth* 55 (3): 661–685.

De Long, J. Bradford, and Lawrence H. Summers. 1991. Equipment Investment and Economic Growth. *Quarterly Journal of Economics* 106 (2): 445–502.

———. 1993. How Strongly Do Developing Economies Benefit from Equipment Investment? *Journal of Monetary Economics* 32 (3): 395–415.

Dutz, Mark A., Sérgio Kannebley Jr., Maira Scarpelli, and Siddharth Sharma. 2012. Measuring Intangible Assets in an Emerging Market Economy: An Application to Brazil. Policy Research Working Paper 6142, World Bank, Washington, DC.

Easterly, William, and Sergio Rebelo. 1993. Fiscal Policy and Economic Growth: An Empirical Investigation. *Journal of Monetary Economics* 32 (3): 417–458.

Fennel, S. 2014. The Role of Human Capital in Development. Unpublished manuscript, Economic and Labour Market Analysis Department, International Labour Organization, Geneva.

Frankel, Marvin. 1962. The Production Function in Allocation and Growth: A Synthesis. *American Economic Review* 52 (5): 996–1022.

Friedman, Milton. 1957. *A Theory of the Consumption Function*. Princeton: Princeton University Press.

Grossman, Gene M., and Elhanan Helpman. 1991. *Innovation and Growth in the Global Economy*. Cambridge, MA: MIT Press.

Harrod, Roy. 1948. *Towards a Dynamic Economics: Some Recent Developments of Economic Theory and Their Application to Policy*. London: Macmillan.

Hausmann, Ricardo, Jason Hwang, and Dani Rodrik. 2007. What You Export Matters. *Journal of Economic Growth* 12 (1): 1–25.

Heckscher, E. 1991. The Effect of Foreign Trade on the Distribution of Income. In *Heckscher–Ohlin Trade Theory*, edited and translated by Henry Flam and M. June Flanders, 43–69. Cambridge, MA: MIT Press.

Hirschman, Albert O. 1958. *The Strategy of Economic Development*. New Haven: Yale University Press.

Hulten, Charles R., and Janet X. Hao. 2012. The Role of Intangible Capital in the Transformation and Growth of the Chinese Economy. Working Paper 18405, National Bureau of Economic Research, Cambridge, MA.

Inklaar, Robert, and Marcel P. Timmer. 2013. Capital, Labour and TFP in PWT8.0. Unpublished manuscript, Groningen Growth and Development Centre, University of Groningen.

Ismail, Kareem. 2010. The Structural Manifestation of the "Dutch Disease": The Case of Oil Exporting Countries. Working Paper 10/103, International Monetary Fund, Washington, DC.

Kaldor, Nicholas. 1957. A Model of Economic Growth. *Economic Journal* 67 (268): 591–624.

———. 1966. *Causes of the Slow Rate of Economic Growth of the United Kingdom: An Inaugural Lecture*. Cambridge: Cambridge University Press.

———. 1967. *Strategic Factors in Economic Development*. Ithaca: Cornell University Press.

———. 1975. What is Wrong with Economic Theory. *Quarterly Journal of Economics* 89 (3): 347–357.

Kindleberger, Charles P. 1960. International Trade and United States Experience: 1870–1955. In *Postwar Economic Trends in the United States*, ed. Ralph E. Freeman, 337–373. New York: Harper & Brothers.

Kuznets, Simon. 1973. Modern Economic Growth: Findings and Reflections. *American Economic Review* 63 (3): 247–258.

Lewis, W. Arthur. 1954. Economic Development with Unlimited Supplies of Labour. *The Manchester School* 22 (2): 139–191.

Lin, Justin Yifu. 2011. New Structural Economics: A Framework for Rethinking Development. *World Bank Research Observer* 26 (2): 193–221.

Lin, Justin, and Ha-Joon Chang. 2009. Should Industrial Policy in Developing Countries Conform to Comparative Advantage or Defy it? A Debate Between Justin Lin and Ha-Joon Chang. *Development Policy Review* 27 (5): 483–502.

Linnemann, Hans, Pitou van Dijck, and Harmen Verbruggen. 1987. *Export-Oriented Industrialization in Developing Countries*. Singapore: Singapore University Press.

Mahmood, Moazam. 2007. Macro Drivers of Growth in Asia. Unpublished manuscript, Asian Employment Forum, International Labour Organization, Geneva.

Mahmood, Moazam, and Matthieu Charpe. 2013. Can Wage Cuts Raise Growth? Unpublished manuscript, Economic and Labour Market Analysis Department, International Labour Organization, Geneva.

Mankiw, N. Gregory, David Romer, and David N. Weil. 1992. A Contribution to the Empirics of Economic Growth. *Quarterly Journal of Economics* 107 (2): 407–437.

Marshall, Alfred. 1920. *Principles of Economics*. 8th ed. London: Macmillan.

McMillan, Margaret S., and Dani Rodrik. 2011. Globalization, Structural Change and Productivity Growth. Working Paper 17143, National Bureau of Economic Research, Cambridge, MA.

Mill, John Stuart. 1844. *Essays on Some Unsettled Questions of Political Economy*. London: John W. Parker.

———. 1848. *Principles of Political Economy, With Some of Their Applications to Social Philosophy*. Vol. 2 vols. London: John W. Parker.

Myrdal, Gunnar. 1957. *Economic Theory and Underdeveloped Regions*. London: Methuen.

Ohlin, Bertil G. 1935. *Interregional and International Trade*. Cambridge, MA: Harvard University Press.

Palley, Thomas I. 2011. The Rise and Fall of Export-Led Growth. Working Paper 675, Levy Economics Institute, Annandale-on-Hudson, NY.

Prebisch, Raúl. 1962. The Economic Development of Latin America and its Principal Problems. *Economic Bulletin for Latin America* 7 (1): 1–22. Originally published as *The Economic Development of Latin America and its Principal Problems* (New York: United Nations, Department of Economic Affairs, 1950).

Ricardo, David. 1821. *On the Principles of Political Economy and Taxation*. 3rd ed. London: John Murray.

Robinson, Joan. 1953. The Production Function and the Theory of Capital. *Review of Economic Studies* 21 (2): 81–106.

———. 1962. *Essays in the Theory of Economic Growth*. London: Palgrave Macmillan.

———. 1967. Growth and the Theory of Distribution. *Annals of Public and Cooperative Economics* 38 (1): 3–7.

Romer, Paul M. 1986. Increasing Returns and Long-Run Growth. *Journal of Political Economy* 94 (5): 1002–1037.

Rosenstein-Rodan, P.N. 1943. Problems of Industrialisation of Eastern and South-Eastern Europe. *Economic Journal* 53 (210/11): 202–211.

Sachs, Jeffrey D., and Andrew M. Warner. 1995. Natural Resource Abundance and Economic Growth. Working Paper 5398, National Bureau of Economic Research, Cambridge, MA.

———. 1999. The Big Rush, Natural Resource Booms and Growth. *Journal of Development Economics* 59 (1): 43–76.

Say, Jean-Baptiste. 1821. *A Treatise on Political Economy; Or, The Production, Distribution, and Consumption of Wealth*. Translated from the fourth edition of the French, by C. R. Prinsep. London: Longman, Hurst, Rees, Orme and Brown.

Schultz, Theodore W. 1963. *The Economic Value of Education*. New York: Columbia University Press.

Singer, Hans W. 1950. The Distribution of Gains between Investing and Borrowing Countries. *American Economic Review* 40 (2): 473–485.
Singer, Hans W., and Patricia Gray. 1988. Trade Policy and Growth of Developing Countries: Some New Data. *World Development* 16 (3): 395–403.
Solow, Robert M. 1956. A Contribution to the Theory of Economic Growth. *Quarterly Journal of Economics* 70 (1): 65–94.
———. 1994. Perspectives on Growth Theory. *Journal of Economic Perspectives* 8 (1): 45–54.
Stiglitz, Joseph E. 2011. Rethinking Macroeconomics: What Failed, and How to Repair it. *Journal of the European Economic Association* 9 (4): 591–645.
Tang, Chor Foon, and Kean Siang Ch'ng. 2012. A Multivariate Analysis of the Nexus Between Savings and Economic Growth in the ASEAN-5 Economies. *Margin: The Journal of Applied Economic Research* 6 (3): 385–406.
Tovias, Alfred. 1982. Testing Factor Price Equalization in the EEC. *Journal of Common Market Studies* 20 (4): 375–388.
UNCTAD (United Nations Conference on Trade and Development). 2013. *Trade and Development Report, 2013*. New York: United Nations.
Young, Alwyn. 1994. Lessons from the East Asian NICS: A Contrarian View. *European Economic Review* 38 (3–4): 964–973.

Part II

Three Policy Drivers of Development

The book has set out to explain the difference in per capita incomes amongst developing countries (DCs)—that is, what differentiates least developed countries (LDCs) from lower- and middle-income countries (LMICs) from emerging economies (EEs), and all of them from advanced economies (AEs).

The first empirical part of the book has identified three main empirical regularities that explain per capita incomes among DCs and set them apart from AEs. These empirical regularities have prevailed consistently for the same set of countries, observed over the past third of a century. Chapters 2, 3, and 4 have attempted to show both causality and robustness for these empirical regularities. If these three empirical regularities do indeed determine per capita incomes in large part, then each can be used to derive policy to leverage per capita incomes further, and more radically.

In moving from recognising these empirical regularities to deriving policy, the objective of the book is widened. It is not enough to explain the determination of just per capita incomes and their growth over time. A first-order normative imperative is to explain not just the average of per capita incomes, but also their distribution across different income groups within each country, and especially the distribution of income between the poor—those unable to meet even a required dietary allowance of at least 2250 calories per day needed to live—and the non-poor. So, the objective of the book widens from explaining the determinants of growth of per capita income to explaining the determinants of more inclusive growth.

Working towards that wider objective, recall from the first part of the book.

Growth

The first empirical regularity explains differences in per capita incomes in DCs, through their growth. The evidence suggests that it is not so much the quantum of gross domestic product (GDP) growth that sets DCs apart from each other in terms of their per capita incomes. It is the composition of their GDP growth, of the degree of productive transformation of their economy. Long-run GDP growth rates do climb up the income ladder, but the past decade and a half shows a significant convergence across the income ladder. The more abiding divergence between LDCs, LMICs, and EEs is seen in the composition of long-run GDP, in the development of one key sector, manufacturing, which climbs up the income ladder. Hence what explains catch-up in per capita incomes—or lack of it—is not so much the quantum of GDP growth, as the composition of this growth.

Employment

The second empirical regularity explains the differences in per capita incomes between DCs, through jobs and the labour market. Employment growth, an important explanatory variable for AEs, does not set DCs apart in terms of their per capita incomes. What sets different income categories of DCs apart from each other, LDCs, LMICs, and EEs, is job quality. Two key indicators of job quality—reductions in vulnerability and improvements in productivity—move up the income ladder. There is also evidence of a two-way relationship, with not just higher incomes allowing reductions in vulnerable jobs, but also transitioning from more vulnerable to waged jobs simultaneously, enabling higher productivity and therefore higher per capita incomes.

Further, these qualitative changes seem to move together, with job quality being better in manufacturing. This, despite the lower share of employment in manufacturing, a larger employment outflow from agriculture to services, and apparent limits to the employment absorption capacity of manufacturing. So again, what explains countries moving up the per capita income ladder, or their inability to do so, is not so much the quantum of employment growth, as it is job quality.

Macro Drivers

A third empirical regularity seeks to explain differences in per capita incomes between DCs through the classical macro drivers of growth and jobs—accumulation and exports. Accumulation of physical capital and savings was observed to explain differences in income across DCs. However, investment in human capital explains these income differences even more, setting apart clearly DCs from AEs. Further, this investment in human capital is seen to operate at both ends of skill scale, with a significant impact on per capita incomes explained by schooling. And at the upper end of the skill scale, per capita incomes also show a significant impact from more intangible knowledge-based capital.

In this second policy part of the book, each of these empirical regularities allows a major policy implication to be derived and illustrated with some country granularity.

Deriving Policy for More Inclusive Growth and Productive Transformation of the Economy

The empirical regularity between per capita incomes and the composition of growth highlights the need to put more caveats on growth, which allow countries better catch-up. A major caveat to growth must be its inclusion, so that there is growth for all income groups, especially for the poor. So, growth must be poverty-reducing. A second major caveat is that this growth must be based on productive transformation, as observed in Chap. 2. So, this policy chapter examines the policy needs for growth to be both poverty-reducing and structurally transformational.

Deriving Policy for Better Jobs

The empirical regularity between per capita incomes and job quality highlights the policy need to find a strategic intervention to leverage job quality. The demonstration of weaker job quality in informality gives a broad policy handle with which to improve jobs. Policy on informality is hence derived through an instrument to register not just enterprises, but also workers. Registration of workers is seen as a policy instrument enabling them to potentially access social protection, minimum wages, and national legislation on a raft of improved conditions and rights.

Deriving Policy for Leveraging the Macro Variables Driving Structural Transformation

The empirical regularity between per capita incomes and accumulation of both physical capital and human capital infers the policy need to examine country strategies to leverage investment in both physical and human capital. Country policy on investment in physical and human capital is examined not through de jure proclamations, but de facto policy as revealed by national income accounts, budgets, and effective resource allocation towards these expenditure heads. Domestic resource mobilisation is seen to be more important for such investment than inflows. A key strategic policy variable emerges as the interest rate structure and macro prudential policies that enable the lowering of this cost of borrowing.

5

Putting Caveats on Growth: Policy for Inclusion and Productive Transformation

Moazam Mahmood and Florence Bonnet

This first policy chapter on growth harks back to the first empirical chapter's finding on growth—that the quantum of growth does not explain developing countries (DCs) moving up the per capita *income ladder quite as well as the composition of this growth (Chap. 2). So, growth, to explain catch-up in country incomes, needs a caveat, which is that the composition of this growth must exhibit structural change. But arguably, and with a large literature to support it, the first-order normative condition on growth should be that growth in the first instance be poverty-reducing. If we are to prioritise the needs of the population, then the first priority should be meeting the caloric needs of the population falling below the required dietary allowance (RDA) needed to live.*

M. Mahmood (✉)
Lahore School of Economics, Lahore, Punjab, Pakistan

Capital University of Economics and Business, Beijing, China

F. Bonnet
International Labour Organization, Geneva, Switzerland

This puts two policy caveats on growth. That it should be poverty-reducing. And that it should be based on productive transformation of the structure of the economy. This chapter examines the policy conditions required to meet these two caveats on growth.

The objective of this volume has been to explain DC incomes and catch-up to higher incomes. Chapter 2 focused logically—and spurred by a large growth and development literature—on the growth of country incomes. However, just the quantum of growth in these incomes has not proved sufficient to explain why least developed countries (LDCs) have remained stuck below US$1000 per capita for the past third of a century, why lower- and middle-income countries (LMICs) have remained bracketed between US$1000 and US$4000, and why emerging economies (EEs) have remained bracketed between US$4,000 and US$12,000. The reason is that the growth rates of per capita incomes have begun to converge over time across LDCs, LMICs ,and EEs, so failing to explain why they have remained stuck in their income categories and not done better in catching up to higher incomes.

What the chapter found instead was that the composition of income growth explained country incomes and catch-up very well—specifically, the development of manufacturing. So, while income growth on its own does not explain country incomes and catch-up well, putting a caveat on growth—of the composition of this growth—explains these incomes well. So, one caveat, on growth explaining country incomes, emerges as productive transformation. Given this strong and long-holding empirical regularity, policy for catch-up in country incomes should be based on the policy drivers of productive transformation.

However, explaining aggregate country income and catch-up in it, while serving as a first useful abstraction, does not explain the distribution of this income across groups of the population, nor possible different rates of catch-up in the incomes of these different groups. The problem can be posited in terms of examining the evolution of the whole distribution of income within the country, that is, of all the different income groups. However, a prior, on basic humanitarian grounds, must be to examine the incomes of the poor—those unable to meet even the RDA of caloric intake per day. Poverty and hunger must be the first goal of development, as captured powerfully by becoming the first of the sustainable development goals (SDGs)—to end poverty by 2030.

Putting Caveats on Growth: Policy for Inclusion and Productive... 149

Therefore, while Chap. 2 has explained aggregate country income through not just the growth in it, but the composition of that growth, that is, through productive transformation, as a prior, what has to be explained is the income of the poor and what prevents its catch-up to the higher incomes of the non-poor.

Accordingly, this chapter will begin by examining the income of the poor, and what constrains it from rising to the income of the non-poor. It will then posit policy drivers for growth of the income of the poor. Then, the chapter will return to the policy drivers of aggregate incomes, which is productive transformation.

So, there are now two caveats on the composition of growth. First, that it needs to be inclusive, to establish its determinants, and what policy drivers can leverage them. And second, that growth needs to be based on productive transformation, and to establish what policy drivers can leverage that.

To that end, this policy chapter on inclusive growth is structured into four sections. Section 5.1 looks at some key determinants of poverty based on an empirical analysis of some 75 DCs. Section 5.2 looks at the policy needs to fill the income gap of the poor, through transfers and enhanced labour incomes. Section 5.3 looks at the non-income needs of the poor, and the role of public goods in meeting those needs. Strategic policy to fill the income and non-income gaps is discussed. Section 5.4 then looks at the policy needs for productive transformation.

In Sect. 5.1, the empirical analysis of poverty in DCs is based on identifying who the poor are. It shows the largest quantitative determinants to be a demographic drag, comprising the children and the elderly, and vulnerable workers. Both pull these populations below the poverty line.

In Sect. 5.2, identification of the poor then allows an estimation of the income gap, and what kinds of income would be needed to fill this gap. The young and the elderly, not being of working age, require more transfer incomes to fill their gaps, although they will of course also benefit from enhanced labour incomes of their employed family members. Vulnerable workers require enhanced labour incomes, through higher productivity, wages, and employment levels. Policy on transfers and enhancing labour incomes is examined in the light of the literature and country experiences.

In Sect. 5.3, non-income gaps to reduce poverty are identified in three key areas: health, education, and subsidies on consumption. The role of public goods in these areas is seen as being indispensable in filling the gaps for the poor in health, education, and nutrition.

Turning to the second caveat on growth, in Sect. 5.4, policy on productive transformation is examined. A strategic area focused on is country experiences in industrial catch-up, with educational attainments and capabilities playing key roles.

5.1 Some Key Determinants of Poverty

The Millennium Development Goals (MDGs) set out to halve poverty between 2000 and 2015. Table 5.1 estimates extreme poverty—defined according to the World Bank as US$1.90 needed to provide just the RDA of 2250 calories per day for an adult equivalent—for the same 110 DCs for the period 1990–2012. The table shows that in 1999, 33.8 percent of the population of these 110 DCs was in extreme poverty. By 2012, this population of the extremely poor had halved to 14.9 percent, meeting the MDG globally. And indeed, compared to 1990, this population of the extremely poor had gone down by more than two-thirds, from 46.9 to 14.9 percent. However, the global goal was met in all regions, except Africa, where extreme poverty dropped from 55.2 percent in 1999 to only 40.7 percent by 2012. Albeit, Africa made great strides over this MDG period, in halting and reversing the increase in poverty seen over the 1990s of 3 percent.

The SDG for eliminating extreme poverty between 2015 and 2030 poses the largest challenge for Africa with 41 percent of the global poor, followed by Asia with 12 percent, Latin America and the Caribbean with 6 percent, and Europe and Central Asia with 4 percent.

To meet this goal, the logical enquiry is to ask what jobs, earnings, and incomes have the poor come to rely on, and how they differ from the jobs, earnings, and incomes of the non-poor. If there is a significant difference between them, then these jobs, earnings, and incomes are indeed the determinants of poverty reduction.

To determine what jobs, earnings, and incomes the poor have come to rely on, and whether this differentiates them from those of the non-poor, what is needed is a decomposition of both in their relation to the labour market. Table 5.2 presents the results for 66 DCs.

Table 5.1 Poverty rates (percent)

	1990	1993	1996	1999	2002	2005	2008	2010	2011	2012
Poverty rate at US$1.90										
Developing countries (110)	46.89	43.13	34.59	33.81	29.47	25.23	19.09	16.68	14.93	14.93
Africa (44)	52.44	56.22	55.52	55.19	54.48	48.33	45.54	43.97	42.31	40.7
Asia and the Pacific (25)	58.71	49.24	38.15	36.88	30.03	25.43	16.46	12.8	10.28	12.23
Europe and Central Asia (19)	2.54	8.06	10.88	12.92	11.44	9.09	5.77	5.04	4.37	3.86
Latin America and Caribbean (20)	21.2	17	15.58	15.28	13.44	10.19	7.63	6.89	6.32	5.94
Arab states (2)	Survey data coverage is too low									
Poverty rate at US$3.10										
Developing countries (110)	67.17	67.68	58.77	57.41	52.26	50.4	38.78	34.97	32.52	36.23
Africa (44)	71.75	74.35	74.33	74.99	75.04	70.95	67.8	66.79	65.49	64.22
Asia and the Pacific (25)	82	77.18	66.81	64.52	56.6	54.32	38.71	32.82	29.06	36.25
Europe and Central Asia (19)	7.7	20.07	24.39	29.8	24.37	18.21	13.36	12.53	11.87	11.19
Latin America and Caribbean (20)	35.78	31.55	29.73	28.55	26.55	21.44	16.76	14.99	13.99	13
Arab states (2)	Survey data coverage is too low									
Poverty rate at US$5.00										
Developing countries (110)	80.24	82.97	77.3	76.31	71.91	71.05	59.36	55.3	52.78	57.76
Africa (44)	85.24	86.8	86.62	87.36	87.74	85.88	83.21	82.56	81.8	81.14
Asia and the Pacific (25)	92.33	91.02	85.35	83.31	77.17	76.21	61.72	55.47	51.67	60
Europe and Central Asia (19)	22.67	41.37	46.59	54.05	45.34	33.09	24.63	23.98	22.7	22.01
Latin America and Caribbean (20)	53.88	50.81	48.13	47.06	44.7	38.36	32.13	29.88	28.45	26.78
Arab states (2)	Survey data coverage is too low									

Source: Authors' estimations at the ILO, based on data from the World Bank, PovcalNet, April 2016 (available at http://iresearch.worldbank.org/PovcalNet/)

Table 5.2 Population in DCs, by poverty and employment status, 2012

	Non-poor			Poor			Total		
	Female (%)	Male (%)	Total (%)	Female (%)	Male (%)	Total (%)	Female (%)	Male (%)	Grand total (%)
Developing countries, US$1.90									
Dependant	72.12	51.77	61.80	77.11	62.11	69.60	72.96	53.47	63.10
Inactive, 15–64	41.28	19.40	30.19	34.67	17.07	25.86	40.17	19.02	29.47
Under 15 and over 65	29.04	30.55	29.80	41.69	44.06	42.87	31.17	32.77	31.98
Unemployed	1.80	1.82	1.81	0.76	0.97	0.87	1.63	1.68	1.65
Self-employed	12.43	22.08	17.33	18.08	28.31	23.19	13.38	23.11	18.30
Employers	0.75	2.57	1.67	0.31	1.17	0.74	0.68	2.34	1.52
Own-account workers	7.65	16.22	11.99	11.13	22.03	16.58	8.23	17.17	12.76
Unpaid contributing family workers	4.03	3.30	3.66	6.64	5.11	5.87	4.47	3.60	4.03
Wage and salaried workers	15.33	26.08	20.78	4.65	9.45	7.05	13.53	23.34	18.49
Other employed	0.12	0.07	0.10	0.17	0.14	0.15	0.13	0.08	0.10
Grand total	100.00	100.00	100.00	100.00	100.00	100.00	100.00	100.00	100.00
Developing countries, US$3.10									
Dependant	69.79	50.13	59.82	77.46	58.28	67.79	72.87	53.38	63.01
Inactive, 15–64	41.02	20.13	30.43	38.77	17.25	27.92	40.12	18.98	29.43
Under 15 and over 65	26.53	27.90	27.23	37.91	39.94	38.93	31.10	32.71	31.91
Unemployed	2.23	2.10	2.16	0.79	1.09	0.94	1.65	1.69	1.67
Self-employed	10.88	18.41	14.70	16.89	29.70	23.35	13.29	22.91	18.16
Employers	0.88	2.87	1.89	0.40	1.60	1.01	0.68	2.36	1.53
Own-account workers	6.81	13.10	10.00	10.22	22.88	16.60	8.18	17.00	12.64
Unpaid contributing family workers	3.20	2.44	2.81	6.27	5.22	5.74	4.43	3.55	3.99

(continued)

Table 5.2 (continued)

	Non-poor			Poor			Total		
	Female (%)	Male (%)	Total (%)	Female (%)	Male (%)	Total (%)	Female (%)	Male (%)	Grand total (%)
Wage and salaried workers	19.20	31.38	25.38	5.53	11.93	8.76	13.71	23.62	18.72
Other employed	0.13	0.08	0.11	0.12	0.09	0.10	0.13	0.08	0.10
Grand total	100.00	100.00	100.00	100.00	100.00	100.00	100.00	100.00	100.00
Developing countries, US$5.00									
Dependant	65.67	47.86	56.67	77.00	56.65	66.71	72.79	53.39	62.98
Inactive, 15–64	38.03	19.58	28.70	40.91	18.35	29.50	39.84	18.81	29.20
Under 15 and over 65	24.81	25.80	25.31	35.13	37.06	36.10	31.29	32.88	32.09
Unemployed	2.84	2.48	2.66	0.97	1.24	1.10	1.66	1.70	1.68
Self-employed	9.23	14.68	11.98	15.75	27.78	21.83	13.32	22.91	18.17
Employers	1.07	3.18	2.14	0.46	1.89	1.18	0.69	2.37	1.54
Own-account workers	5.92	9.97	7.96	9.56	21.15	15.42	8.20	17.00	12.65
Unpaid contributing family workers	2.24	1.53	1.88	5.72	4.74	5.23	4.43	3.55	3.98
Wage and salaried workers	24.95	37.37	31.23	7.13	15.49	11.36	13.76	23.62	18.74
Other employed	0.14	0.09	0.12	0.12	0.08	0.10	0.13	0.08	0.10
Grand total	100.00	100.00	100.00	100.00	100.00	100.00	100.00	100.00	100.00

Source: Authors' estimations at the ILO, based on data from the World Bank, PovcalNet, April 2016 (available at http://iresearch.worldbank.org/PovcalNet/)

Three main determinants of poverty stand out: (a) demographic drag, (b) vulnerable jobs, and (c) lack of productive transformation.

One, poverty has a strong demographic drag. Of the total population of the extremely poor, 70 percent were dependants. This was significantly higher than for the non-poor of whom 62 percent were dependants. So, while the total population of the poor and non-poor had a significant demographic drag of 63 percent, the poor were far more burdened by dependants. The dependants comprise the young, under 15 years of age, and the old, above 65 years of age. They also comprise the inactive, of working age, and the unemployed. Again, the demographic drag stood out for the poor. Almost two-thirds of the poor dependants were the young and the old, in contrast to the non-poor dependants at just under one half.

Economic dependency is in fact lower for the poor. The poor could less afford inactivity in working ages, or unemployment. The share of poor dependants who were inactive was a quarter, compared to the non-poor's share of 30 percent. Similarly, the share of poor dependants who were unemployed was only 1 percent, compared to the non-poor's share of 2 percent.

Two, the poor relied more on vulnerable forms of work. The agreed definition of vulnerability[1] is self-employment, which comprises own-account workers plus unpaid contributing family workers. The table shows that the poor relied the most on self-employment, whose share was 23 percent of their population. In contrast, the non-poor relied less on self-employment, whose share was 17 percent of their population.

Self-employment comprises own-account workers, unpaid contributing family workers, and employers. There was a contrast between the poor and the non-poor largely for unpaid contributing family workers. They had a 6 percent share of the poor self-employed, compared to a 4 percent share of the non-poor self-employed. Unpaid contributing family work was also supplied more by poor women, whose share was 7 percent, compared to poor men at 5 percent.

The reciprocal of vulnerable work is waged work. The poor had a very low share of waged workers, at just 7 percent of their total population. In contrast, the non-poor share of waged work was twice greater at 21 percent of their total population.

The poverty rates for these two determinants of poverty are equally telling. In terms of the demographic drag, one-quarter of all children under 14 years of age were poor, while 13 percent of the elderly above

64 years of age were poor. In terms of vulnerable jobs, over 21 percent of the self-employed were poor, compared to only 7 percent of those waged or salaried. Contributing family workers had the highest poverty rate, near a quarter being poor.

This contrast between the poor and the non-poor largely held for all regions. The only significant break from the pattern was for unemployment in Europe and Central Asia, with the share of the poor being higher than for the non-poor.

This contrast between the poor and the non-poor for extreme poverty at US$1.90, also held for moderate poverty at US$3.10 and near poverty at US$5.00. Again, the only significant break in the pattern was for unemployment in Europe and Central Asia, with the share of the poor being higher than for the non-poor.

Therefore, what appears to drive poverty strongly is a significantly higher demographic drag for the poor compared to the non-poor. And the poor rely much more on vulnerable forms of employment, like self-employment and unpaid family labour rather than waged employment.

This begs the question then, what sectoral development throws up this disparity between the jobs that the poor do compared to the non-poor.

Lack of structural transformation throws up poverty.

A good segue into sectoral development is to locate poverty spatially. Table 5.3 confirms the archetypical literature that poverty in DCs is a strongly rural phenomenon, but not exclusively (see, for instance, Lipton and Ravallion 1993; Odhiambo and Manda 2003). The total population

Table 5.3 Percentage of the poor/non-poor living in rural/urban areas

	Rural (%)	Urban (%)		Rural (%)	Urban (%)
DCs, US$1.90 PPP			DCs, US$3.10 PPP		
Non-poor	59.08	40.92	Non-poor	41.25	58.75
Poor	87.78	12.22	Poor	83.31	16.69
Grand total	63.86	36.14	Grand total	55.14	44.86
DCs, US$5 PPP			AEs, 60% of median income		
Non-poor	30.91	69.09	Non-poor	18.01	81.99
Poor	78.39	21.61	Poor	21.09	78.91
Grand total	56.10	43.90	Grand total	18.69	81.31

Note: *AE* advanced economy, *DC* developed country, *PPP* purchasing power parity
Source: Authors' estimations at the ILO, based on data from the World Bank, PovcalNet, April 2016 (available at http://iresearch.worldbank.org/PovcalNet/)

of the extremely poor in DCs was 88 percent rural and 12 percent urban. This preponderance of rural poverty gets weaker going up the income ladder, falling for moderate poverty to 83 percent and near poverty to 78 percent. For relative poverty in the advanced economies (AEs), it is reversed, with urban poverty predominating with a 79 percent share in their total poverty.

The explanation for both the preponderance of rural poverty in DCs and the disparity in jobs between the poor and the non-poor does appear to lie in sectoral development. Table 5.4 decomposes the poor and non-poor in 42 DCs by their broad sector of employment.[2] It is striking that of the total extremely poor, two-thirds were employed in agriculture, while only about one-third of the non-poor were employed there. In comparison, industry had a higher share of the non-poor at 21 percent, compared to the poor at 15 percent. As did services, with 42 percent of the non-poor, compared to 18 percent of the poor.

This preponderant proportion of the extremely poor trapped in agriculture applies to all regions, with Africa and Latin America and the Caribbean both at 68 percent of the poor, Asia at 63 percent, and Europe and Central Asia at 48 percent.

This is a finding based on the proportion of the total poor employed in agriculture. It can be cross-referenced by looking at the proportion of the total employment in agriculture, who were poor. A quarter of those employed in agriculture were poor, compared to just 12 percent of those employed in industry, and only 7 percent of those employed in services.

Then a Lewisian and post-Lewisian framework of productive transformation explains poverty quite well. As workers move out of a traditional low-productivity sector like agriculture, and move into higher-productivity sectors like industry and services, poverty goes down. The transformation takes place not just in terms of productivity, but more likely than not, also in the nature of the job, from vulnerable self-employment to more decent waged employment. The share of waged in total employment was near double in urban areas compared to rural areas, for DCs, especially in Africa and Asia and the Pacific.[3] Transformation of jobs becomes a key driver for poverty reduction, along with addressing the demographic burden of the poor.

Specifically, lack of trade and manufacturing generates more poverty.

Table 5.4 Decomposition of the poor and non-poor in DCs, by broad employment sector, 2012

Sector	Non-poor			Poor			Total		Grand total (%)
	Female (%)	Male (%)	Total (%)	Female (%)	Male (%)	Total (%)	Female (%)	Male (%)	
Agriculture	37.70	34.34	35.46	67.94	63.42	65.05	42.58	38.61	39.96
Industry	15.75	24.27	21.42	12.63	17.88	15.99	15.25	23.34	20.59
Services	46.26	41.19	42.89	19.25	18.48	18.76	41.90	37.86	39.23
Other	0.29	0.20	0.23	0.18	0.22	0.21	0.27	0.20	0.22
Grand total	100.00	100.00	100.00	100.00	100.00	100.00	100.00	100.00	100.00

Note: *DC* developing country, *PPP* purchasing power parity. All figures are based on US$1.90 PPP
Source: Authors' estimations at the ILO, based on data from the World Bank, PovcalNet, April 2016 (available at http://iresearch.worldbank.org/PovcalNet/)

The broad sectors of agriculture, industry, and manufacturing can be decomposed further into 14 specific sectors. Table 5.5 decomposes the poor and the non-poor by their specific sector of employment for 37 DCs.[4]

Again, near two-thirds of the total extremely poor were employed in agriculture, compared to just over a third of the total non-poor. The next two major specific sectors that the non-poor relied on were trade and manufacturing. Fifteen percent of the total non-poor were employed in trade, compared with 9 percent of the total poor. And 12 percent of the total non-poor were employed in manufacturing, compared to 7 percent of the total poor. A fourth possible specific sector employing any significant share of the total non-poor was general services, at 6 percent, compared to 3 percent of the total share of the poor.

The more effective productive transformation strategy indicated to reduce poverty would then be to focus on the development of these two sectors—trade and manufacturing.

Policy directions for the three determinants of poverty reduction include transfers, better jobs, and more productive transformation.

Given the weaknesses in jobs, earnings, and incomes that the poor have come to rely on, the question is: can gross domestic product (GDP) growth not simply reduce poverty over time?

Figure 5.1 plots country change in GDP over time against its change in poverty over time. There should be a negative relationship, with more countries in the positive-growth, negative-change (or drop)-in-poverty quadrant (top left of each panel) or in the negative-growth, positive-change (or increase)-in-poverty quadrant (bottom right of each panel). But the relationship fitted is positive, with almost as many countries in the negative-growth, negative-change (or drop)-in-poverty quadrant (bottom left of each panel), or in the positive-growth, positive-change (or increase)-in-poverty quadrant (top right of each panel).

Therefore, growth in itself has not been consistently poverty-reducing over the last 25 years. But there is evidence of policy working to ameliorate the three determinants of poverty over time.

The demographic drag of a higher share of dependants, children below working age, and the elderly above 64 years can benefit from increased labour income for the household, but will also require significant transfer income from the non-poor. Figure 5.2 shows that of the macro drivers of

Table 5.5 Decomposition of the poor and non-poor in DCs, by specific employment sector, 2012

Sector	Non-poor Female (%)	Non-poor Male (%)	Non-poor Total (%)	Poor Female (%)	Poor Male (%)	Poor Total (%)	Total Non-poor (%)	Total Poor (%)	Grand total (%)
Agriculture	38.93	34.68	36.10	67.21	62.67	64.29	36.10	64.29	40.35
Wholesale and retail trade	15.66	14.86	15.13	11.34	7.71	9.01	15.13	9.01	14.20
Construction	3.08	10.10	7.75	2.39	10.69	7.72	7.75	7.72	7.75
Manufacturing	11.71	12.38	12.16	8.84	6.93	7.61	12.16	7.61	11.47
Other services	9.28	5.07	6.48	3.85	3.47	3.61	6.48	3.61	6.04
Transport, storage, and communications	0.77	6.61	4.65	0.19	3.91	2.58	4.65	2.58	4.34
Hotels and restaurants	3.78	2.03	2.62	2.60	0.68	1.37	2.62	1.37	2.43
Public administration	4.12	5.09	4.76	0.99	1.31	1.19	4.76	1.19	4.23
Education	5.78	2.61	3.67	0.93	0.80	0.85	3.67	0.85	3.24
Mining and quarrying	1.16	1.28	1.24	0.55	0.85	0.74	1.24	0.74	1.17
Not classifiable	0.29	0.19	0.22	0.61	0.30	0.41	0.22	0.41	0.25
Health and social work	3.44	1.09	1.88	0.37	0.19	0.25	1.88	0.25	1.63
Financial intermediation	1.82	3.01	2.61	0.11	0.27	0.21	2.61	0.21	2.25
Electricity, gas, and water	0.18	1.01	0.73	0.04	0.23	0.16	0.73	0.16	0.65
Grand total	100.00	100.00	100.00	100.00	100.00	100.00	100.00	100.00	100.00

Note: *DC* developing country, *PPP* purchasing power parity. All figures are based on US$1.90 PPP
Source: Authors' estimations at the ILO, based on data from the World Bank, PovcalNet, April 2016 (available at http://iresearch.worldbank.org/PovcalNet/)

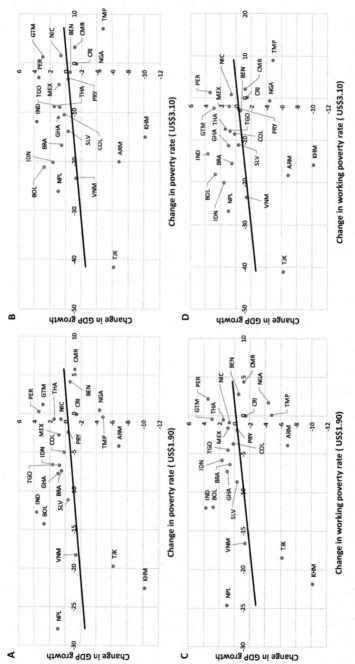

Fig. 5.1 Relationship between GDP growth and poverty rate. (Note: *GDP* gross domestic product. Source: Authors' estimations at the ILO, based on data from the World Bank, PovcalNet, April 2016 (available at http://iresearch.worldbank.org/PovcalNet/))

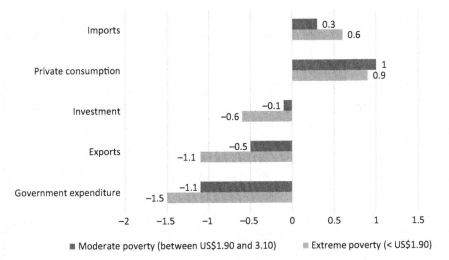

Fig. 5.2 Effect on poverty rate of 1 percentage point increase in share of GDP components, by poverty measure, 1991–2014 (percentage). (Note: *GDP* gross domestic product. Source: Authors' estimations at the ILO, based on data from the World Bank's World Development Indicators)

growth, government expenditure is the most poverty-reducing. Section 5.2 examines the role of transfers in poverty reduction, and formulates policy for it. Section 5.3 examines the non-income determinants of poverty, and looks at the role of provisioning of public goods, in the key areas of consumption, health, and education.

5.2 Closing the Income Gap for the Poor

This section examines the income gap, an estimate of how much additional income from labour and how much additional spending on social protection would be needed to eliminate poverty. The section examines how the income gap varies depending on the demographic and labour market position of the poor. This analysis is essential for understanding the relative importance of policy tools, primary being social protection and employment policies.

Eliminating poverty, however, calls for a broad range of policies such as governance arrangements, access to basic services, and well-designed rural development strategies, which cannot be directly captured through an analysis of the income gap. With these limitations in mind, Sect. 5.2 (a) provides estimates of the income gap for DCs at different levels of economic development. The main determinants of income gaps are then described in Sect. 5.2 (b). In particular, the extent to which poor households are primarily affected by high demographic and economic dependency ratios or by decent work deficits is assessed; such an analysis should be helpful in the process of formulating the most appropriate combination of policy responses. Based on the assessment of individuals' and households' demographic and economic characteristics, the concluding section, Sect. 5.2 (c), discusses different cases where, as part of combined policies, social protection or improved labour incomes might play a major role in filling the income gap.

(a) Estimating the Income Needed to Eliminate Poverty

The income needed to eliminate extreme poverty in DCs represents less than 1 percent of global income.

Estimates made here show that, in 2012, US$72 billion would have been needed to eliminate extreme poverty in DCs (Box 5.1).[5] The income gap for eliminating extreme poverty represents 0.16 percent of global income and 0.31 percent of DCs' income (Table 5.6). It represents 3.9 percent of LDCs' GDP when considering this group of countries alone. Although the income gap seems small when viewed from a global standpoint, it still represents a relatively high proportion of government expenditure and social protection budgets in most developing and in particular in LDCs and LMICs.[6]

To eliminate both extreme poverty and moderate poverty, nearly US$360 billion would be needed (econometric specifications available with the authors). This represents 1.7 percent of GDP in DCs, 0.4 percent in EEs, 3.1 percent in LMICs, and as much as 14.3 percent of GDP in LDCs (Table 5.6).

This picture for DCs masks significant differences both between and within countries.[7] Figure 5.3 shows that LDCs account for less than 4

Table 5.6 Global income gap, by region and poverty line, 2012

	Distribution of the income gap (%)		Income gap (% of GDP)		Income gap (% government expenditure)	
	US$1.90 PPP	US$3.10 PPP	US$1.90 PPP	US$3.10 PPP	US$1.90 PPP	US$3.10 PPP
DCs	100.0	100.0	0.31	1.65	1.46	7.27
LDCs	42.9		3.86	14.31	17.61	68.59
LMICs	38.6		0.53	3.11	2.67	14.14
EEs	18.5		0.07	0.40	0.24	1.39

Note: *DC* developing country, *EE* emerging economy, *GDP* gross domestic product, *LDC* least developed country, *LMIC* lower- or middle-income country, *PPP* purchasing power parity. Global and regional estimates based on 65 DCs (20 LDCs, 23 LMICs, and 24 EEs). See Table 5.12 in the Appendix for detailed data sources. Extreme poverty and extreme associated income gap are defined as the share of those with per capita income or consumption below US$1.90 PPP per day. Extreme and moderate poverty and extreme and moderate associated income gap are defined as the share of those with per capita income or consumption below US$3.10 PPP per day

Source: Authors' estimations at the ILO, based on national household survey data

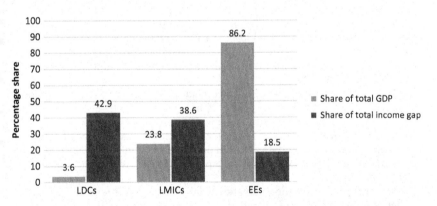

Fig. 5.3 Distribution of total GDP and extreme income gap in DC categories. (Note: *DC* developing country, *EE* emerging economy, *GDP* gross domestic product, *LDC* least developed country, *LMIC* lower- or middle-income country, *PPP* purchasing power parity. Global and regional estimates based on 65 DCs (20 LDCs, 23 LMICs, and 24 EEs). See Table 5.12 in the Appendix for detailed data sources. Extreme poverty and extreme associated income gap are defined as the share of those with per capita income or consumption below US$1.90 PPP per day. Source: Authors' estimations at the ILO, based on national household survey data)

percent of GDP in DCs but for 42.9 percent of total income gap in DCs. By contrast, EEs account for 86.2 percent of GDP in DCs but for 18.5 percent of the total income gap.

> **Box 5.1: Estimates of the Global Income Gap**
>
> The global income gap or global aggregate poverty gap is the minimum amount of income needed to bring all poor people out of poverty. It is estimated as the sum of the differences for all poor people between their current per capita expenditure on consumption or income (depending on the country) and the respective poverty lines. The global income gap therefore provides a minimum estimate of the amount by which labour incomes and social protection transfers should increase to end poverty, based on a static perspective. The term 'minimum' means that, as far as social protection transfers are concerned, the interpretation of this gap is only reasonable if the transfers could be made perfectly efficiently, which is highly implausible (Haughton and Khandker 2009). The analysis of the income gap takes on board the depth of poverty (or distance to the poverty line) not assessed when considering poverty rates for different groups. The estimate of the income gap for different population groups (such as in Fig. 5.3) considers the distance to the poverty line for each individual below the poverty line according to her or his demographic and labour market position.
>
> The analysis of the gap in DCs—total and for population groups—is based on national household surveys from 65 DCs representing more than 85 percent of the population from the different regions, including 20 LDCs, 23 LMICs, and 24 EEs. Data for the majority of countries (more than 80 percent) refer to the period 2010–13.
>
> The resulting distribution of the income gap for the different population groups (children less than 15 years old, employed aged 15–64 by employment status, unemployed, inactive able and unable to work, and persons aged 65 and over) calculated for each country for the latest year available was applied to the 2012 data adjusted on the World Bank's interactive computational tool, PovcalNet, and extrapolated to the world and regional populations.
>
> The comparison of the estimated total income gap presented in this chapter—based on extrapolated results from 65 DCs—with derived estimates from the broader set of countries available in the World Bank PovcalNet database, highlights a difference of less than 0.02 percent of GDP for the global income gap to end extreme poverty, the World Bank estimate being higher.
>
> Note: PovcalNet is available from the World Bank, at http://iresearch.worldbank.org/PovcalNet/povOnDemand.aspx.

The income gap represents over half of social protection budgets in many DCs.

Eliminating poverty through social transfers alone cannot be considered as a sustainable solution in the long run (ILO 2001, 2003) and would be a major budgetary challenge for most DCs. Indeed, the total cost of eliminating extreme poverty runs as high as the total current expenditure on public social protection—illustrated by the lower line in Fig. 5.4, panel A—in 14 out of 20 LDCs, for whom there was data. On average, the income gap for eliminating extreme poverty represents nearly 90 percent of total spending on social protection in LDCs. This figure comes to 26 percent in LMICs and represents less than 1 percent of current social protection spending in EEs. When considering the income gap for eliminating both extreme poverty and moderate poverty, it represents on average nearly 70 percent of total spending on social protection in all DCs but considering LDCs alone, their income gap represents more than 3 times the amount of money currently spent on social security benefits in LDCs.

High demographic and economic dependency ratios are important determinants of poverty.

The analysis of the composition of the income gap by age group and economic status confirms the importance of the demographic drag as an important determinant of poverty (Fig. 5.5). Children under 15, and the elderly people aged 65 and over, accounted for near half of the extreme income gap. Another 20 percent of the income gap was accounted for by inactive people of working age (15–64 years).

Child poverty accounted for 43 percent of the income gap in DCs, but for more than 50 percent of the income gap in LDCs. The working poor represented another 28 percent of the total income gap in DCs, but for 37 percent in LDCs. Amongst the working poor, the self-employed accounted for most of the income gap, rather than the waged, more than 90 percent in LDCs and LMICs.

Filling in the income gaps to end poverty for these major constituent groups logically requires a combination of increased labour incomes and social transfers. The extent of the need for income from social protection in these groups depends on the economic dependency ratio in the household and on current working conditions of the labour income earners. It

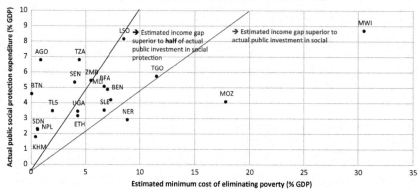

A. Extreme poverty in LDCs (< US$1.90 PPP per capita per day)

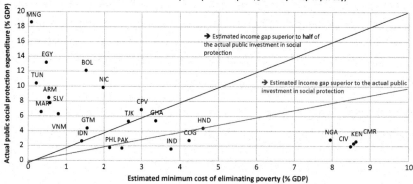

B. Extreme and moderate poverty in LMICs (< US$3.10 PPP per capita per day)

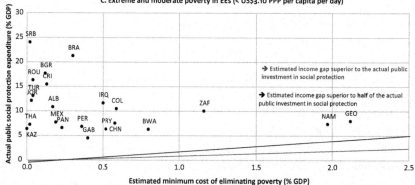

C. Extreme and moderate poverty in EEs (< US$3.10 PPP per capita per day)

(continued)

also depends on employment opportunities for people in the household able and willing to work. All these factors determine the potential for an improvement in labour incomes and their effective impact on poverty reduction for all household members.

The more unambiguous case for social protection and transfers is for the elderly and the disabled. People aged 65 and over represented 4 percent of the extreme income gap to in DCs (3 percent in LDCs and over 6 percent in EEs). People with disabilities unable to work represented another 0.4 percent of the extreme income gap in DCs. Altogether, the minimum financial implications of measures to eliminate extreme poverty for these two groups, which should be able to count on social protection, represented just 0.02 percent of GDP in DCs.

Children in poverty need to benefit from both an improvement in their parents' labour incomes and some level of transfers. The working poor may benefit from decent working conditions and still be below the poverty line, not because they earn less than the poverty line but because they share this labour income with many dependants. In such situations, social protection might be the sole or best answer at least in the short run. Section 5.2 (b) analyses seven socio-demographic and economic features of individuals and households for the poor, which are important elements

Fig. 5.4 Total income gap and expenditure on public social protection as a percentage of GDP, 2012. (Note: *EE* emerging economy, *GDP* gross domestic product, *LDC* least developed country, *LMIC* lower- or middle-income country, *PPP* purchasing power parity. In panel A, in countries on the right side of the red line, the estimated income gap to eliminate extreme poverty in LDCs is superior to the actual total public investment in social protection. In countries on the right side of the blue line, the estimated income gap accounts for more than half of actual public social protection expenditure, which is still above the proportion of social protection that reaches the poor in many countries (see Sect. 5.2). Country names associated with ISO3 codes and detailed data sources are presented in Table 5.12 in the Appendix. Source: Authors' estimations at the ILO, based on national household survey data for the income gap; and on data from ILO, Social Security Inquiry, April 2016 (available at http://www.ilo.org/dyn/ilossi/ssimain.home); OECD, Social Expenditure Database, April 2016 (available at http://www.oecd.org/social/expenditure.htm); ADB, Social Protection Index, April 2016 (available at http://spi.adb.org/spidmz/index.jsp); and European System of Integrated Social Protection Statistics, February 2016 (available at http://ec.europa.eu/eurostat/web/social-protection/overview) for social protection expenditure data)

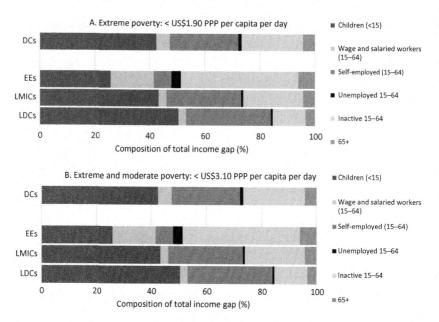

Fig. 5.5 Composition of the total income gap, 2012. (Note: *EE* emerging economy, *LDC* least developed country, *LMIC* lower- or middle-income country, *PPP* purchasing power parity. Global estimates based on 103 countries representing close to 85 percent of the world population. Source: Authors' estimations at the ILO, based on national household survey data)

for an appropriate mix of social protection policies and policies that boost labour incomes, discussed in Sect. 5.2 (c).

(b) Demographic and Economic Dependency Ratios and Decent Work Deficits

Poor people live in larger households with fewer members with labour incomes.

Poverty is strongly affected by household size and composition (OECD 2009a, b). Compared to the non-poor, the poor tend to live in relatively large households often without access to paid employment and in particular to wage and salaried employment, placing a heavy burden on labour income earners.[8] On average, people in extreme or moderate poverty in DCs live in households that have 7.8 persons, compared to 5.7 persons for the non-poor (Table 5.7).

Table 5.7 Size of household and percentage of household members in paid employment, latest year available

	Average household size		% of household members in paid employment		% of household members in wage and salaried employment		% of household members, own-account workers, or employers	
	Poor	Non-poor	Poor	Non-poor	Poor	Non-poor	Poor	Non-poor
Extreme poverty								
DCs	7.8	5.7	21.4	32.5	7.3	17.9	14.5	15.1
LDCs	8.2	6.6	24.0	30.6	5.0	10.8	20.0	21.0
LMICs	8.0	5.9	22.2	31.5	8.7	16.9	13.5	14.6
EEs	7.1	4.8	17.9	35.7	7.8	26.1	10.2	9.7
Extreme and moderate poverty								
DCs	7.3	5.4	23.0	34.2	8.5	20.0	14.9	14.7
LDCs	7.9	6.1	25.3	32.5	5.7	13.8	20.7	20.1
LMICs	7.3	5.6	23.8	33.2	9.8	18.7	14.0	14.5
EEs	6.7	4.6	19.9	37.2	9.9	27.6	10.1	9.6

Note: *DC* developing country, *EE* emerging economy, *LDC* least developed country, *LMIC* lower- or middle-income country, *PPP* purchasing power parity. Extreme poverty: <$1.90 PPP per capita per day. Extreme and moderate poverty: <$3.10 PPP per capita per day. Global estimates based on 103 countries representing close to 85 percent of the world population. Weighted by total population. Paid employment includes wage and salaried employment, own-account workers and employers. See Table 5.12 in the Appendix for detailed data sources

Source: Authors' estimations at the ILO, based on national household survey data

The deficit of labour income earners of working age in poor households is common to all regions, levels of development, and poverty lines. The extremely poor in DCs live in households with an average 21 percent of their working-age members in paid employment (Box 5.2) compared to 33 percent for the non-poor. Further, as noted earlier, poverty is associated with a deficit of wage and salaried employment. The incidence of wage and salaried employment is 2.5 times higher among the non-poor compared to the poor in DCs.

Box 5.2: Definition of Terms

Demographic dependency ratio. Demographic dependants include those under the age of 15 (child dependency) and over the age of 64 (old-age dependency). The productive part is made up of the population considered to be of working age, between 15 and 64 years. The ratio is expressed as a percentage. Total demographic dependency ratio = (number of people aged 0–14 and those aged 65 and over)/number of people aged 15–64 × 100. A high demographic dependency ratio may be an increased burden on the income earners within households and in a country.

Economic dependency ratio. This is based on the actual activity status of the household members rather than on their ages. A first version is calculated as the ratio of the household members outside the labour force (children, inactive aged 15–64, and people aged 65 and over) to those actually working or unemployed aged 15–64. A second and third version consider the ratios between those outside employment or outside paid employment and those in employment or in paid employment aged 15–64. Hence the economic dependency ratio measures the number of inactive household members for each active member or, alternatively, in its second and third versions, the number of non-working household members or non-labour income earners to household members in employment or in paid employment (15–64 years old).

Persons in employment are defined as all those of working age who, during a short reference period, were engaged in any activity to produce goods or provide services for pay or profit (see below). Persons in employment are wage and salaried workers and the self-employed. Self-employed persons include employers, own-account workers, and contributing family workers. Paid employment in this chapter includes all persons in employment except contributing family workers.

For pay or profit refers to work done as part of a transaction in exchange for remuneration payable in the form of wages or salaries for time worked or work done, or in the form of profits derived from the goods and services produced through market transactions, specified in the most recent international statistical standards concerning employment-related income (ILO 2013b). Contributing family workers are included as part of the employed, as persons who work for pay or profit payable to the household or family in market units operated by a family member living in the same or in another household.

Permanent contracts are defined as open-ended contracts, or as contracts of unlimited duration (ILO 2015a). They are considered as more secure as they allow visibility regarding the future evolution of work and income. Such arrangements still cover more than 50 percent of all wage and salaried workers but just above one out of four workers (including both wage and salaried workers and those in self-employment) (ILO 2015b).

The poor face significant working-time deficits—underemployment.

The proportion of workers working short hours, for pay or profit (less than 35 hours), or very short hours (less than 20 hours per week),[9] is systematically higher among the poor at 35 percent compared to the non-poor at 27 percent. This is true for both waged workers and for the self-employed, in LDCs, LMICs, and EEs (Fig. 5.6). Although the poor in self-employment are particularly badly hit by short working hours, more than half work less than 35 hours per week, compared to 19 percent of poor waged workers.[10]

In LDCs, LMICs, and EEs alike, it is women in particular who work short or very short hours for pay or profit, often for low pay. In DCs, almost 40 percent of all working women work less than 35 hours a week for pay or profit and those affected the most are self-employed women.[11] Women in LDCs and LMICs are the most affected by very short working hours, at least as far as employment (paid employment) is concerned.

Paradoxically, at the same time women in DCs may face longer working days, when both paid and unpaid work are considered. Women are more time-poor than men (Chant 2010). Indeed, gender gaps in the distribution of unpaid household and care work also imply that women are more likely to work shorter hours for pay or profit (ILO 2016).

In Asia, the poor are also subject to excessive working hours.

Working hours also tend to be more polarised for the poor than for the non-poor, whose working hours tend to cluster around standard working hours, in line with national regulations. While the practice of working excessive hours can improve earning potential and career prospects, it can also expose workers to safety and health risks (ILO 2011a, b; Lee et al. 2007). In addition to being more likely to be in underemployment, the poor in DCs are also more likely than the non-poor to face the risks associated with excessive hours without having the opportunity to gain from those extra hours (see Fig. 5.7).

In DCs in Asia and the Pacific, almost 60 percent of the extremely and moderately poor in wage and salaried employment worked more than 48 hours per week and more than 22 percent work more than 60 hours per week. In other regions, the proportion of the working poor who work excessive hours is typically lower than in Asia.

The jobs of the poor are less protected than those of the non-poor.

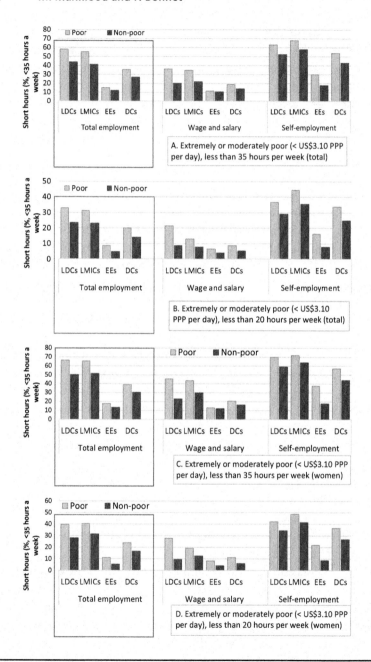

(continued)

Employees without a permanent employment contract tend to have less job stability and lower pay than those in regular full-time employment.[12] In addition, they have frequent periods of unemployment, which leads to sharp income fluctuations. Workers in unregulated, insecure employment arrangements, who are more likely to work without a contract and even more likely to work without a permanent contract, are also those most likely to be among the working poor. This is because such employment arrangements offer less pay (ILO 2015a). Without a formal employment contract, workers are more vulnerable to the non-application of employment laws and regulations and are also more likely to face difficult working conditions.

In 34 DCs for which data was available, poor wage and salaried workers were three times less likely to have a permanent contract than their non-poor counterparts. Less than 8 percent of the extremely poor had a permanent contract compared to more than 30 percent of the non-poor. For extreme and moderate poverty, only 10 percent of the poor in wage and salaried employment had a permanent contract compared to 33 percent of the non-poor (see also Fig. 5.8).

Poor people are less covered by employment-related social protection.

Affiliation to social protection through employment often depends on an explicit contract in formal enterprises or on a formally defined employment relationship between a dependent worker and an employer (ILO 2013a). As noted, in DCs only a minority of workers, especially among the poor, are covered by formal employment contracts that would entitle them to social protection (Fig. 5.9, panel A).[13] The high incidence of non-standard forms of employment among the poor is a major factor behind the lack of social protection coverage (ILO 2015b).[14]

Fig. 5.6 Short working hours and poverty in DCs (hours per week), latest year available. (Note: *DC* developing country, *EE* emerging economy, *LDC* least developed country, *LMIC* lower- or middle-income country, *PPP* purchasing power parity. Global weighted estimates based on 65 DCs, representing 74 percent of total employment. Hours of work refer to usual hours of work from all jobs when available, otherwise from main and second jobs. Panels A and B: common poverty line of US$3.10 PPP per day and per capita. The population of reference covers people in employment aged 15–64. Data is for the latest year available, which ranges between 2005 and 2013. One-fourth of the country data refers to 2005–09 and nearly 60 percent is for 2012 or 2013. Source: Authors' estimations at the ILO, based on national household survey data)

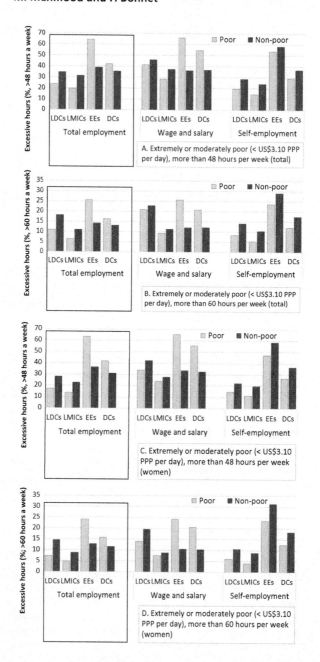

Less than 8 percent of the extreme or moderate working poor contribute to a pension scheme in DCs, compared to 37.2 percent of the non-poor (Fig. 5.9, panel B).[15] Affiliation rates are significantly higher in EEs compared to the LDCs and LMICs but remain low among the poor. Less than 2 percent of the poor are affiliated in LDCs, 3.2 percent in LMICs, and 11.2 in EEs.

With the exception of a few countries (particularly in Latin America), most self-employed workers do not contribute to a pension scheme. In DCs, on average 16 percent of the extremely and moderately poor in wage and salaried employment contribute to a pension scheme, compared to less than 3 percent of the self-employed.[16] The corresponding proportions are under 1 percent in both LDCs and LMICs.

There is a resultant significant deficit in social protection for the poor.

Considering all types of social protection benefits, either in cash or in kind, contributory and non-contributory, the proportion of the poor relying on social protection benefits[17] is on average lower than that of the non-poor. Based on a set of 30 DCs (representing nearly 70 percent of the population of DCs), the aggregate result shows that 47 percent of the moderate and extremely poor received some social protection benefits, compared to 57 percent of the non-poor.

The country results are more mixed. For moderate and extreme poverty, in 21 out of 30 DCs the proportion of the poor receiving benefits is higher than for the non-poor. While for the extremely poor, in 14 out of 30 countries the proportion of the poor receiving benefits exceed the non-poor.

However, the poor received a smaller share of the spending on social protection, significantly lower than their representation in the population.[18] On average the extremely and moderately poor, who constitute

Fig. 5.7 Excessive hours of work and poverty in DCs (hours per week), latest year available. (Note: *DC* developing country, *EE* emerging economy, *LDC* least developed country, *LMIC* lower- or middle-income country, *PPP* purchasing power parity. Global weighted estimates based on 47 DCs representing more than 74 percent of total employment. The population of reference covers people in employment aged 15–64. Data is for the latest year available, which ranges between 2005 and 2013. One-fourth of the country data refers to 2005–09 and nearly 60 percent is for 2012 or 2013. Source: Authors' estimations at the ILO, based on national household survey data)

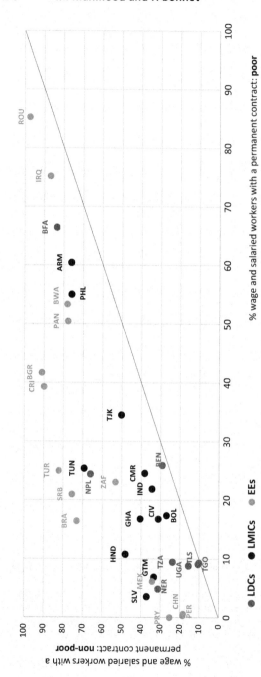

Fig. 5.8 Permanent contracts among wage and salaried workers: comparison between poor and non-poor (percentage), latest year available. (Note: *EE* emerging economy, *LDC* least developed country, *LMIC* lower- or middle-income country, *PPP* purchasing power parity. This figure covers wage and salaried workers aged 15–64. The dark grey dots are for LDCs, the black dots for LMICs, and the light grey dots for EEs. All of them refer to the extreme and moderate poverty line of US$3.10 PPP per capita per day. Any dot above the diagonal means that the proportion of the non-poor in wage and salaried employment with a permanent contract is higher than the corresponding proportion among the poor. Country names associated with ISO3 codes and detailed data sources are presented in Table 5.12 in the Appendix. Data is for the latest year available, which ranges between 2005 and 2013. One-fourth of the country data refers to 2005–09 and nearly 60 percent is for 2012 or 2013. Source: Authors' estimations at the ILO, based on national household survey data)

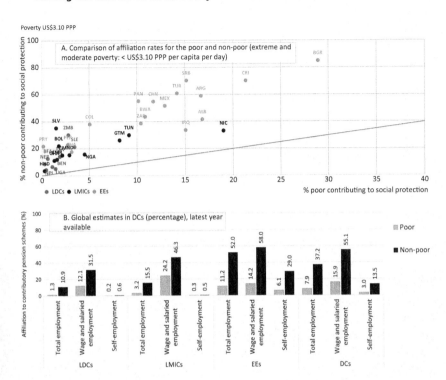

Fig. 5.9 Affiliation to contributory social protection (pension mainly), poor and non-poor workers (percentage of total employment), latest year available. (Note: *DC* developing country, *EE* emerging economy, *LDC* least developed country, *LMIC* lower- or middle-income country, *PPP* purchasing power parity. Contribution to social protection (at least for pensions). All dots refer to the extreme and moderate poverty line of US$3.10 PPP per capita per day. Any dot above the diagonal means that the proportion of the non-poor contributing to social protection (at least for pensions) is higher than the proportion among the poor. Country names associated with ISO3 codes and detailed data sources are presented in Table 5.12 in the Appendix. Panel B: Global estimates based on 34 DCs representing 75 percent of total employment. The population of reference covers people in employment aged 15–64. Data are for the latest year available, which ranges from 2007 to 2013. Source: Authors' estimations at the ILO, based on national household survey data)

42.0 percent of the total population, receive 21.1 percent of the total social protection benefits expenditure. The amount of social protection benefits received by the poor is on average seven times lower than the amount per beneficiary for the non-poor.

Some countries have very limited social protection provisions and associated resources for the poor in particular but also for the non-poor. This characterises most African countries with available data. For instance, coverage of the poor is less than 10 percent in Cameroon, Ethiopia, Ghana, Malawi, Nigeria, Sudan, Uganda, and Zambia; coverage of the non-poor is barely any higher. Those countries combine the highest poverty incidence (more than 60 percent),[19] limited investment in social protection (usually less than or around 5 percent of GDP) and among the lowest proportion of social protection resources going to the poor, compared to their representation in the population. In Ethiopia, Malawi, Uganda, the United Republic of Tanzania, and Zambia, extreme and moderate poverty rates are greater than 70 percent but the benefits received by the poor represent in some cases less than 25 percent of the total amount of social protection benefits.

South Africa stands apart as one of the few exceptions. Where, nearly 90 percent of the moderate and extremely poor receive social protection benefits compared to 50–60 percent of the non-poor. As in other LMICs and EEs from Latin America or Eastern Europe and Central Asia, in South Africa the incidence of poverty is lower than in low-income countries. More importantly, the proportion of those living below the poverty line and receiving social protection benefits is greater than 60 percent and higher than the proportion of beneficiaries among the non-poor. What characterises these countries is the broader scope of their national social protection systems, the significant amount of resources invested in social protection, and, over recent decades, the extension of social protection through mechanisms coping with high informality or low activity rates (ILO 2015b).[20]

Then the significantly higher coverage in countries such as the Russian Federation, Turkey, Colombia, Mexico, or Argentina demonstrates deliberate strategies adopted by governments to extend coverage to the poor and to redesign social protection systems to concentrate resources on targeted benefits (Fig. 5.10).

But the impact of existing levels of social protection on poverty prevention and reduction can be huge.

Social protection benefits play an important role in preventing and reducing poverty. In Figs. 5.11 and 5.12, the correlation between higher spending on social protection and lower poverty rates is positive. There are, however, important differences in the impact of social protection on poverty, observed across countries with similar levels of spending on

Putting Caveats on Growth: Policy for Inclusion and Productive... 179

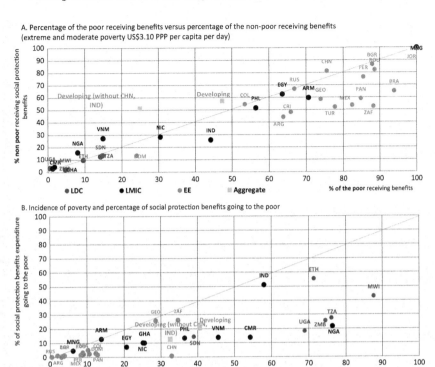

Fig. 5.10 Percentage of the poor and non-poor receiving benefits and proportion of social protection benefits expenditure going to the poor, latest year available. (Note: *EE* emerging economy, *LDC* least developed country, *LMIC* lower- or middle-income country, *PPP* purchasing power parity. The analysis of the shares of public expenditure on social protection benefits going to the poor versus the non-poor should take into consideration that many people are above the poverty threshold because they receive social protection benefits. Panel A compares the proportions of the poor (horizontal axis) and non-poor (vertical axis) receiving social protection benefits (any type). Any dots below the diagonal highlight a situation where the percentage of the poor receiving benefits (independently of the level of benefit received) exceeds the proportion of the non-poor. Panel B considers the incidence of poverty (or the proportion of the poor in total population, horizontal axis) compared to the share of the total value of social protection benefits going to the poor (vertical axis). Any dot below the diagonal means that the cumulative value of benefits from social protection received by the poor is lower than their representation in the total population and that the level of benefit per beneficiary is lower for the poor than for the non-poor. Country names associated with ISO3 codes and detailed data sources are presented in Table 5.12 in the Appendix. Source: Authors' estimations at the ILO, based on national household survey data)

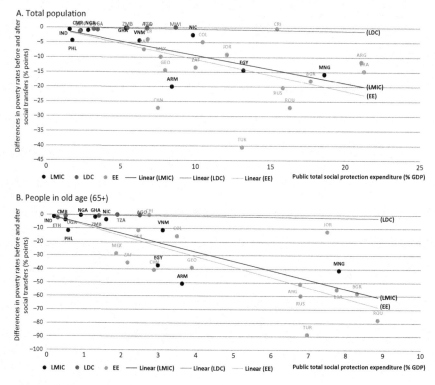

Fig. 5.11 Public social protection expenditure (percentage of GDP) and impact of social transfers (percentage points), latest year available. (Note: *DC* developing country, *EE* emerging economy, *GDP* gross domestic product, *LDC* least developed country, *LMIC* lower- or middle-income country, *PPP* purchasing power parity. The impact of social protection transfers is measured as the difference between poverty rates before and after social protection transfers. Only the direct reduction of income poverty through the transfer of purchasing power to the beneficiaries is considered here. Calculations based on a common poverty line of US$3.10 PPP per capita per day. In panel A, the figures relate total public social protection expenditure as a percentage of GDP to the impact for individuals of social protection transfers on poverty reduction (differences in poverty rates before and after social transfers in percentage points). In panel B, the horizontal axis presents public social protection benefits for older persons (either in cash or in kind) as a percentage of GDP and the vertical axis the differences (in percentage points) in poverty rates resulting from the income received from social protection (all types of benefits) for people aged 65 and over. In the latter case, all social protection transfers are taken into account and not only old-age or survivors' pensions or benefits in kind directed specifically to the elderly. Country names associated with ISO3 codes and detailed data sources are presented in Table 5.12 in the Appendix. DCs include 32 countries. Source: Authors' estimations at the ILO, based on national household survey data)

Putting Caveats on Growth: Policy for Inclusion and Productive... 181

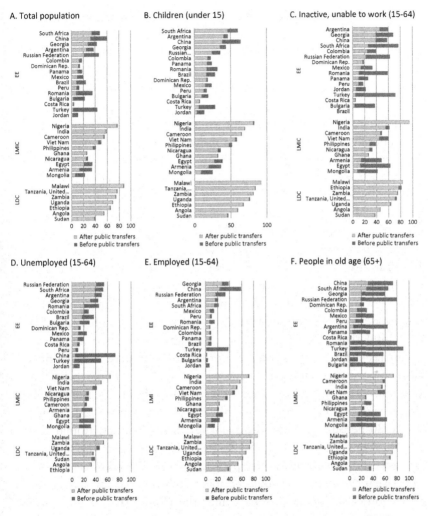

Fig. 5.12 Impact of social protection on poverty reduction and prevention by age group and economic status, country data (latest year available). (Note: *DC* developing country, *EE* emerging economy, *LDC* least developed country, *LMIC* lower- or middle-income country, *PPP* purchasing power parity. Common poverty line of US$3.10 PPP per capita per day all DCs. Impact on poverty reduction and prevention calculated on a per capita basis, to be consistent with other results presented in this report. This methodological choice explains some of the differences between these and other results published in Eurostat or OECD using the same original data. 'Inactive unable to work' are people with disability not in the labour force and not looking for work, being unable to work because of their disability (identified in household surveys). Source: Authors' estimations at the ILO, based on national household survey data)

social protection. The main factors for the varying impacts include societies' objectives of social protection[21] such as income maintenance versus poverty reduction; the difference in coverage and levels of benefits received by the poor and the non-poor; and the trade-off between the proportion of people covered and the level of benefit received, especially when resources are limited.

In DCs, the last decade has shown an encouraging expansion in the number of countries that have established cash transfer programs focusing on low-income and excluded groups (Hanlon et al. 2010; ILO 2014b; Fiszbein et al. 2013). Spending on social protection is, however, usually lower than in developed countries. Moreover, in many countries, social protection reaches a small proportion of the population, sometimes not primarily the poor. Even though social protection plays a role in reducing the income gap (reducing the distance to the poverty line) for direct beneficiaries, it does not necessarily significantly reduce the incidence of poverty. In the absence of social protection, extreme poverty would be, on average, 15 percentage points higher and extreme and moderate poverty would be 13 percentage points higher (Fig. 5.13).

Behind these aggregated numbers lie important disparities between countries and between population groups. The impact of social protection on poverty is significant in most EEs (Fig. 5.11). Differences in poverty rates before and after social protection transfers range from 10 to 14 percentage points in Argentina, Brazil, Mexico, and South Africa to above 20 percentage points in countries such as Turkey, Romania, and the Russian Federation (Fig. 5.12). In EEs in particular, the role played by social protection in poverty prevention and reduction is crucial and effective for people who should be able to rely on social protection as the main source of income, in particular the elderly (Fig. 5.11, panel B; Fig. 5.12, panel F) and people unable to work either permanently or temporarily (Fig. 5.12, panel C). People aged 65 and over are among those benefiting the most from social security transfers. For the 32 countries for which the information is available, extreme poverty rates among those aged 65 and over are 30 percentage points lower after social protection transfers and 23 percentage points lower when considering both extreme and moderate poverty. A number of countries have extended or reformed social protection programs as part of their overall development strategy. In Brazil, Mongolia, South Africa, and Turkey, and more

Putting Caveats on Growth: Policy for Inclusion and Productive... 183

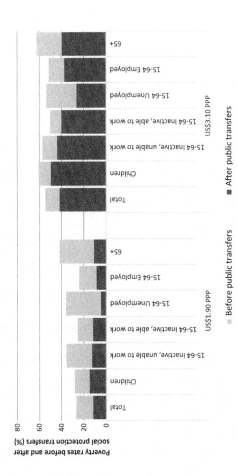

Fig. 5.13 Impact of social protection investment on poverty reduction and prevention (percentage), latest year available. (Note: *DC* developing country. The impact of social protection benefits on poverty reduction and prevention in the various subgroups of the population results not only from specific benefits targeting those groups but from all social protection benefits received by household members and equally shared between them. Public social protection expenditure covers all measures that provide benefits, whether in cash or in kind, to secure protection from a lack of work-related income (or insufficient income) caused by sickness, disability, maternity, employment injury, unemployment, old age, or death of a family member; lack of (affordable) access to healthcare; insufficient family support, in particular for children and adult dependants; general poverty; and social exclusion (ILO 2014b). Data is for the latest year available, which ranges from 2007 to 2013. Nearly 70 percent of the country data is for 2012 or 2013. The 32 DCs represent 72 percent of the total population of DCs. Source: Authors' estimations at the ILO, based on national household survey data)

recently in China, the impact on poverty reduction has been relatively high compared to that in other countries with similar proportions of GDP invested in social protection.

(c) The Mix of Policy Responses Needed to Close the Income Gap

Given the observed demographic and economic characteristics of poor households, policy to reduce and end poverty will have to be a logical mix of enhanced social transfers and labour income. The mix will depend on the characteristics of the household. Accordingly, in this section two sets of households are defined, and an appropriate policy mix of transfers and labour incomes is aimed at them.

In the first set of cases, high demographic and economic dependency ratios are the main determinants of poverty (cases 1–3 in Box 5.3). In the second set, decent work deficits for those in employment and unemployed are the main poverty determinants (cases 4 and 5 in Box 5.3). Each case calls for combined policies that include the extension of social protection and measures to improve labour incomes. In the first set of cases, social protection might play the major role, while employment policies should ideally be emphasised in the second set of cases. Finally, the role of social protection and labour incomes in addressing the income gap is quantified.

High demographic and economic dependency ratios as the main determinants of poverty imply social protection as the main policy response (cases 1–3).

The first set of cases is characterised by the poor whose reliance on incomes from labour is either non-existent (case 1) or limited (cases 2 and 3). The criterion used is a cut-off of less than a quarter of the household members of working age in paid employment. These cases represent the majority of the extremely and moderately poor and most of the income gap.

These three cases cover the poor who are the most exposed to high income gaps. In these cases, poverty arises mainly as a result of a high incidence in households of children and people of working age who are inactive (able or unable to work), unemployed, and elderly. The high incidence of demographic dependency, and in the short run, economic dependency, implies that social protection is probably the most immediate appropriate policy response. For those that face poor working conditions (cases 2 and 3) and for those unemployed or inactive but able and willing to work, decent work deficits have to be addressed, but, given the limited number of people of working age in the household, any employment-related policy should be combined with social protection transfers to ensure a sufficient impact on poverty reduction for the workers, the unemployed, and their families.[22]

> **Box 5.3: Simplified Cases and Most Appropriate Mix of Policy Responses**
>
> The five cases presented below are defined according to two dimensions: the proportion of household members aged 15–64 in paid employment (see definition in Box 5.2) and by employment status, with a distinction between people living in households relying solely on wage and salaried employment and those living in households relying exclusively on profit as employers or own-account workers.* Figure 5.14 presents for the different cases, the proportions of people concerned, their relative exposure to the higher income gap**, and the policy response that could play a major role as part of the mix of policy answers (lighter-shaded for social protection and darker-shaded for increase in labour incomes).

		(a) Proportion of household members aged 15–64 in paid employment				
		None	Less than 25 percent		More than 25 percent	
(b) Relative exposure to high income gap**	High	**Case 1** 17.4 percent of the extremely and moderately poor in DCs	Waged and salaried	**Case 2** 13.8 percent of the extremely and moderately poor in DCs	Waged and salaried	
			Self-employed	**Case 3** 21.0 percent of the extremely and moderately poor in DCs	Self-employed	
	Moderate	Main component of the mix of policy responses: ☐ High demographic and economic dependency ratios as the main determinants of poverty, and social protection as the main policy response (at least in the short run), combined with measures to address decent work deficits in cases 2 and 3. ■ Deficits in labour incomes as the main determinant of poverty, calling for policies enhancing full and productive employment and decent work.			Waged and salaried	**Case 4** 13.9 percent of the extremely and moderately poor in DCs
		* An additional 12.8 percent of the poor in DCs live in households with labour incomes from both self-employment as well as wage and salaried employment. These are included in the above cases. ** Relative exposure to the high income gap is considered high when the share of their income gap in the total income gap is greater than the proportion of the group in the poor population; and considered moderate otherwise.			Self-employed	**Case 5** 21.0 percent of the extremely and moderately poor in DCs

Fig. 5.14 Simplified cases and most appropriate policy responses. (Source: Authors' illustration)

Households in which less than 25 percent of the working-age members are in paid employment (cases 2 and 3) have a combination of high child demographic and economic dependency ratios and, obviously, significant decent work deficits for their unemployed members or those who are in employment. Measures to enhance labour incomes are clearly required, but the number of people concerned within the household is insufficient to provide income security for workers, the unemployed, and their dependants. For a significant impact on poverty reduction, social protection transfers are necessary—at least in the short run—to affect the income gap directly and to enhance individuals' skills and capabilities and, it is hoped, to improve school attendance for the numerous children (Aizer et al. 2016; Alderman and Yemtsov 2012). Complementary measures should ideally tackle the situation of the unemployed and of those who are inactive but able and willing to work to enhance their access to employment through active labour market policies, training and skills development, or asset accumulation (see McCord 2012; ILO 2014b; Bonnet et al. 2012; ILO and OECD 2013; Alderman and Yemtsov 2012).

Insufficient labour income as the main determinant of poverty implies enhancing the quantum and quality of employment as the main policy response, supported by social protection measures (cases 4 and 5).

The second set of cases is characterised by the poor whose reliance on labour income is high, cases 4 and 5, but have jobs that are predominantly informal and with individual income from labour that is insufficient to take care of more than two or three dependants. The criteria used is a cut-off of more than a quarter of household members of working age in paid employment.

In comparison to the first set of cases, the higher proportion of people in paid employment within households translates into lower levels of exposure to high income gaps, but the quality of employment becomes an essential factor.[23] Case 4 is where the working poor are largely self-employed, while case 5 is where the working poor are largely in waged employment. These two cases represent a minority of the poor in DCs. But recall that self-employment is predominant among the working poor, while waged employment is much higher for the non-poor.

Deficits in labour incomes among the working poor result from widespread underemployment in particular among the self-employed in DCs. In the case of wage and salaried workers, minimum wage policies are necessary. However, there is also a need here for policies which address the absence of a formally defined employment relationship through a contract and the high incidence of weak employment relationships with derogations on protection and entitlements (ILO 2015b).

For all the working poor, either in waged employment or self-employment, the deficits in labour incomes are associated with the high proportion of working poor in informal employment and the need for combined measures to enhance formalisation and to reduce decent work deficits in the informal economy (ILO 2014a). Informal employment also means an absence of employment-related social protection, with catastrophic financial consequences for workers and their families. The effective implementation of national social protection floors to reduce deficits in the informal economy and support the transition to better jobs and the gradual extension of coverage by contributory schemes should form part of targeted responses to this problem. Additionally, policies are needed to raise productivity for the self-employed. Chapter 7 on policies for jobs addresses these concerns further.

An estimated 64–72 percent of the income gap to be filled by social protection...

Based on this analysis, social protection becomes a key tool for reducing poverty. The proportion of the total income gap to be filled by social protection is determined based on:

- The economic dependency ratio within each household and the distance to the poverty line or poverty depth (methodology and assumptions available with the authors).
- Social protection is considered the sole option for people aged 15–64 with disabilities and unable to work and for people aged 65 and over.
- The amount of money necessary to raise all other population groups to the poverty line might then be found through a combination of social protection transfers and improvement in labour income either directly or indirectly (as, for instance, for children).

This gives an estimate of 68 percent of the moderate and extreme poverty gap that would have to be filled by social protection, with variations depending on population groups and country groups. The contribution of social protection ranges from 51 percent for wage and salaried workers, to 71 percent for children and to 100 percent (by definition) for the elderly and people with disabilities who are unable to work (Fig. 5.15). Which leaves a third of working poverty to be eliminated through an increase in labour. This includes increase in labour incomes, more hours of work for those underemployed and willing to work more, an increase in wages and profits along with measures in favour of a gradual formalisation of informal employment, and active labour market policies, notably training and retraining.

… which gives an estimated cost of social protection of 1.1 percent of GDP to eliminate both extreme and moderate poverty in DCs.

This gives an estimate of US$72 billion to end extreme poverty, and nearly US$360 billion to end extreme and moderate poverty, which would have been needed by DCs in 2012. While part of this total income gap has to be met by improving labour incomes, it is estimated that the minimum cost for social protection, assuming an unrealistic perfect targeting and delivery, would amount to just above US$50 billion to eliminate extreme poverty and to US$245 billion to eliminate both extreme and moderate poverty (econometric specifications available from the authors). This rep-

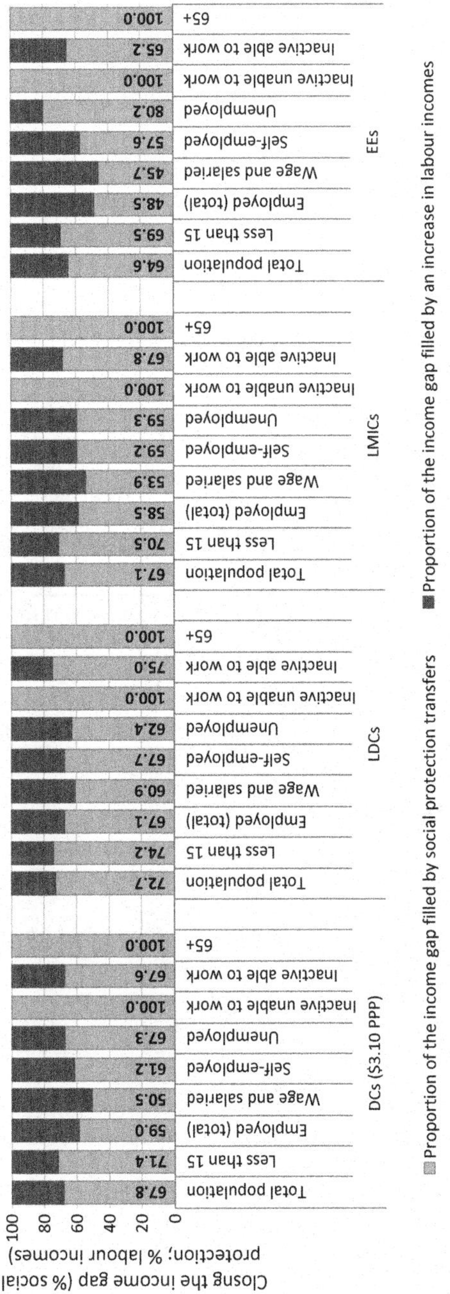

Putting Caveats on Growth: Policy for Inclusion and Productive... 189

Fig. 5.15 Proportions of the gap, respectively, filled by social protection transfers and increases in labour earnings, 2012. (Note: *DC* developing country, *EE* emerging economy, *LDC* least developed country, *LMIC* lower- or middle-income country, *PPP* purchasing power parity. Calculation for US$3.10 PPP. 103 countries covered, representing 85 percent of the global population. The proportion of the income gap calling for social protection transfers is determined for each household and applied to its household members. The share to be covered by an increase in labour income is the complement to 100 percent. Econometric specifications available from the authors. Source: Authors' estimations at the ILO, based on national household survey data)

resents 0.2 percent of GDP in DCs, 2.7 percent of GDP in LDCs, 0.4 percent of GDP in LMICs, and 0.05 percent of GDP in EEs to end extreme poverty. To end both moderate and extreme poverty, this comes to 1.1 percent of GDP in DCs.

In LDCs, where extreme poverty predominantly occurs, the additional estimated cost for social protection to end extreme poverty comes to 2.7 percent of GDP and over 9 percent of government expenditure (econometric specifications available from the authors). To end extreme and moderate poverty comes to more than 50 percent of current government expenditure in LDCs compared to 9.5 percent in LMICs and less than 1 percent in EEs (Table 5.8).

Whatever their level of income, countries have some discretion over the size of government expenditure (Fig. 5.16) (see ILO 2010a, b), which

Table 5.8 Additional investment in social protection to close the income gap, 2012

Income group	Income gap and minimum additional cost for social protection	Extreme poverty (<$1.90 PPP)		Extreme and moderate poverty (<$3.10 PPP)	
		% GDP	% government expenditure	% GDP	% government expenditure
DCs	Total income gap	0.31	1.46	1.65	7.27
	… additional cost of social protection	0.22	1.02	1.12	4.93
LDCs	Total income gap	3.86	17.61	14.31	68.59
	… additional cost of social protection	2.68	12.21	10.40	49.84
LMICs	Total income gap	0.53	2.67	3.11	14.14
	… additional cost of social protection	0.37	1.87	2.09	9.50
EEs	Total income gap	0.07	0.24	0.40	1.39
	… additional cost of social protection	0.05	0.16	0.26	0.90

Note: *DC* developing country, *EE* emerging economy, *GDP* gross domestic product, *LDC* least developed country, *LMIC* lower- or middle-income country, *PPP* purchasing power parity. 65 DCs covered, representing 85 percent of the global population. The 'additional cost of social protection' corresponds to a minimum, assuming unrealistic perfect targeting and delivery

Source: Authors' estimations at the ILO, based on national household survey data

Putting Caveats on Growth: Policy for Inclusion and Productive... 191

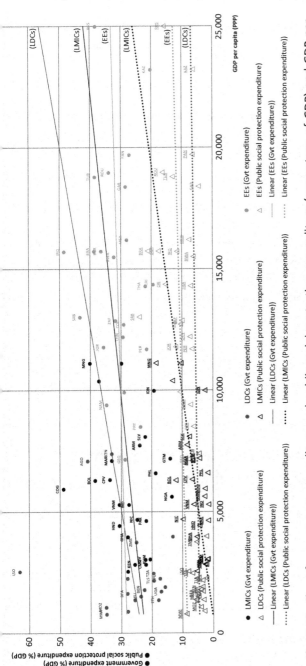

Fig. 5.16 Size of government expenditure and public social protection expenditure (percentage of GDP) and GDP per capita, latest available year. (Note: *EE* emerging economy, *GDP* gross domestic product, *LDC* least developed country, *LMIC* lower- or middle-income country, *PPP* purchasing power parity. For a given level of GDP per capita, the figure displays both the size of government expenditure (circles) and, as part of it, public social protection expenditure (triangles), the two indicators expressed as a percentage of GDP. Taking the examples of Brazil and Mexico, their GDP per capita are comparable (around US$16,000 PPP per capita per year) but both total government expenditure and public social protection spending are significantly lower in Mexico than in Brazil. The total size of government expenditure as a percentage of GDP amounts to 39 percent in Brazil compared to 28 percent in Mexico. While public social protection expenditure in Brazil constitutes more than half of the amount of government expenditure (55 percent), in Mexico, this ratio is lower by half (28 percent). Country names associated with ISO3 codes are presented in Table 5.12 in the Appendix. Source: Authors' estimations at the ILO, based on data from the IMF's World Economic Outlook Database, January 2016)

translates into a weak correlation between levels of GDP and the size of government. A very small government may mean a low capacity on the part of the authorities to raise and collect taxes and other revenue, usually concomitant with a high share of informal employment. It can, however, also be seen as offering room for improvement in government revenue and expenditure (relative to other countries of a similar level of development but higher levels of government expenditure). Comparing Mongolia to India, for instance, for the same level of GDP per capita, the proportion of GDP going to government expenditure, and specifically to social protection expenditure is significantly higher in Mongolia.

The introduction and enforcement of tax reforms to increase fiscal resources, including, in particular, enhancing the effectiveness and efficiency of tax collection, are part of the challenge. This may also call for revised spending programs, making them more adequate to societal preferences to increase the willingness of the taxpayer to pay taxes (ILO 2010a, b). Then, countries with a similar size of government resources may take very different decisions as to the share of these resources allocated to social protection (the triangles in Fig. 5.16). Figure 5.16 shows that some countries with relatively small governments, like 20 percent of GDP or less, decided to devote a significant share of these resources to financing social security programs, in some cases through innovative approaches (ILO 2014b; HelpAge International 2011; Ortiz et al. 2015).[24]

5.3 Non-income Dimensions of Poverty and the Role of Public Goods

While the income dimensions of poverty seem paramount, especially given the large budgets seen above needed to eliminate it, the non-income dimensions also emerge as fundamental. These are referred to in the literature, as non-income, in the sense that they do not enter private budgets, and are conventionally labelled public goods—even if not necessarily always publicly provided. This section prioritises education, health, and subsidies on key wage goods.

Jobs and earnings work primarily through income to trap people in poverty, both workers and their dependants. Hence vulnerability in work and the demographic drag are seen to be two main determinants of poverty. And vulnerability in work is seen to be correlated to lack of productive transformation, lower skill levels, and lower access to non-routine occupations.

These drivers of poverty work through two channels: constraints to the individual's productivity and constraints to the household's budget. Through one channel they constrain earning potential—constraining the productivity of the poor compared to the non-poor. Hence vulnerability in work, lack of development of higher-productivity sectors like industry and services, lack of education and training, and resultant lack of access to non-routine occupations all restrict the productivity of the poor compared to the non-poor. Then this earnings and productivity channel can be constrained not only by the income of the poor, which allows them access to education, health, and nutrition, but also by non-income access to education, health, and nutrition, through public provisioning of these goods.

The second channel through which these drivers of poverty work is through household budgets. Payment for education, and health, can substitute in the household budget for reduced caloric intake, driving up the incidence of poverty. Hence forced investment and savings to enhance future productivity and earning potential can drive households into immediate poverty. And of course, a higher price for wage goods like cereals reduces the purchasing power of the household and can drive it into poverty. Conversely, better provision of public goods like education, health, and subsidies on key wage goods like cereals can reduce the incidence of poverty.

The literature has long recognised these non-income dimensions of poverty, especially in the areas of education, health, and subsidies on wage goods. On the productivity side, education has long been linked to the ability of higher-skilled workers to convert other forms of capital like land and machinery into productive output (Lauder et al. 2006; Baldacci et al. 2008). More skilled workers are, by definition, better able to generate more output per unit of labour than other workers. This increase in productivity not only leads to higher economic growth (Romer 1990), but pro-poor growth. Investment in public education is considered a pathway to converting economic growth into more inclusive growth, that benefits the poor as much, or more than the wealthy (Bigsten et al. 2003). Increasing education and skill levels gives people access to higher productivity and higher paid employment. The ability to read and write is associated with higher waged employment, because of such job requirements (Mincer 1995) and lower poverty. Conversely, for workers with little or no education, jobs tend to be restricted to low wage sectors such as agriculture, and low regulation of working conditions, lowering both (Albin 1970). There are also intergenerational effects from education, helping break the chain of poverty being passed on across generations.

The link between health and poverty is also well established in the literature. People who are unwell, or poorly nourished, or have an injury, are far more likely than able-bodied people to be living in poverty. Weak access to public health systems can make bad health or an injury more burdensome for the poor (Wagstaff 2002). And then those who are in bad health or injured will not be able to work as productively, and so escape poverty, especially given lack of social protection coverage for such contingencies in much of the developing world. Giving rise to a health poverty trap, making it difficult for a person in bad health to escape poverty and access healthcare (McIntyre et al. 2006).

While there is a significant literature on the impact of weak access to public goods working through the productivity channel, there is less on the household budget channel lowering purchasing power. And much of it is more controversial.

Barham et al. (1995) acknowledge that weak access to public education can lead to private expenditures, with low-income households having to reduce other household expenditures. Similarly, out-of-pocket health expenditures for the poor reduce the purchasing power of the household budget and can reduce nutrition. Long-term illnesses can pile on debt for the poor.

But what can increase the purchasing power of the poor are subsidies on key wage goods, like cereals. And these are a standard tool for poverty reduction, albeit with problems of their own. An IMF (2008) study counted 28 countries with food subsidies in 2008, particularly prevalent in the Middle East and North Africa (Sdralevich et al. 2014).

The argument for universally available food subsidies, like *baladi* bread in Egypt, is that the poor spend the largest share of their budget on food.

Therefore, a subsidy on food would affect the poor more than the non-poor. However, the non-poor may well spend more on food in absolute terms, which gives rise to the criticism that the non-poor may benefit more from the food subsidy rather than the poor—calling for more targeted programs rather than universal subsidies. However, targeted programs are in turn costlier to implement. And the extent to which increased benefits accrue to the poor can be extremely variable across programs. Therefore, both universal wage-good subsidies and targeted programs can carry large government budgets. Nine of the 28 countries examined by the IMF (2008) had food and fuel subsidies of more than 3 percent of their GDP.

Access of the Poor to Public Education

So, weak access to public education can constrain the productivity of the poor and reduce the purchasing power of their household budgets. Conversely, pro-poor growth requires that the poor have better access to public education to overcome their lower level of education compared to the non-poor. The results found here unfortunately confirm much weaker access for the poor to public education.

There is only one cross-country dataset that disaggregates educational outcomes by income or wealth, a UNICEF series for out-of-school children by wealth quintiles by country. Figure 5.17 compares the percentage of children of school-going age that were out of school for the bottom quintile, relative to the other four quintiles. Figure 5.18 shows that the bottom quintile consistently had a higher share of children out of school across all country groups (lower income, lower middle, and upper middle income). There were only three exceptions out of 73 countries reported on—Kyrgyzstan, Ukraine, and Kazakhstan. All three exceptions fall in the Europe and Central Asian region. There was no data available for higher-income countries.

The out-of-school gaps were clearly much less for the upper middle-income countries (Fig. 5.17). Amongst the lower-middle countries, Nigeria had the largest gap, with over 70 percent of children in the lowest quintile out of school, compared to 20 percent for the rest of the population.

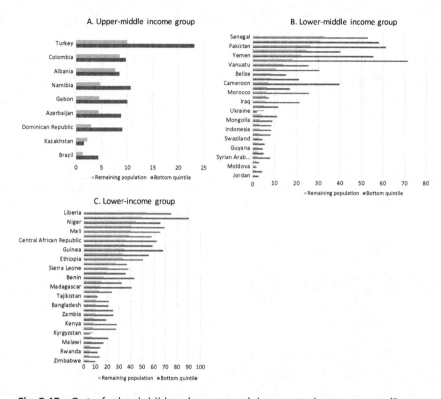

Fig. 5.17 Out-of-school children (percentage), by country income group. (Source: Authors' estimations at the ILO, based on data from UNICEF (available at https://data.unicef.org/))

Pakistan had the next highest gap of 60 percent of children in the lowest quintile out of school compared to 28 percent for the rest of the population. Cameroon and Yemen also stand out with large gaps. Amongst the lower-income group, Liberia, Chad, Burkina Faso, Niger, Guinea, the Central African Republic, and Mali had over 60 percent of children in the bottom quintile out of school. And in all cases, the gap for out-of-school children was significantly high.

This out-of-school gap, between the bottom quintile and the top four quintiles, is seen to be correlated to the provisioning of public education. Figure 5.19 shows the negative correlation of out-of-primary-school children from the bottom quintile to government expenditure on education

Putting Caveats on Growth: Policy for Inclusion and Productive...

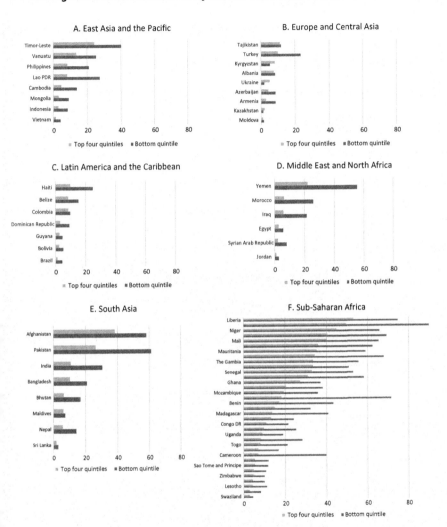

Fig. 5.18 Out-of-school children (percentage), by regional group. (Source: Authors' estimations at the ILO, based on data from UNICEF (available at https://data.unicef.org/))

as a share of GDP. As government expenditure goes down, out-of-school children go up, albeit there is a wide variation at the lower end of the share of children out of school, with some governments managing it with very low expenditures, like Zambia.

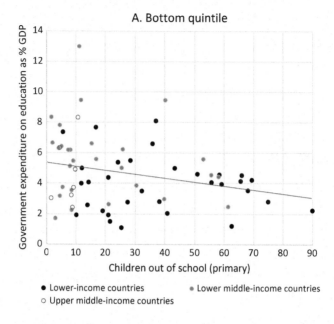

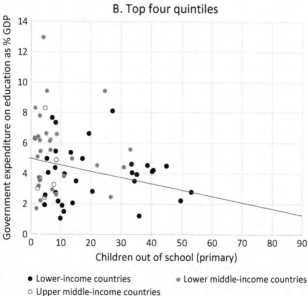

Fig. 5.19 Correlation between government expenditure on education and school attendance. (Note: *GDP* gross domestic product. Source: Authors' estimations at the ILO, based on data from UNICEF (available at https://data.unicef.org/))

Low government expenditures lead in turn to high pupil-teacher ratios, which have a positive correlation to children out of school at the primary level, as seen in Fig. 5.20. As the pupil-teacher ratio goes up, so do the children out of school. But again, there is a wide spread at the lower end of share of children out of school, with countries like Malawi and Rwanda achieving it despite high pupil-teacher ratios.

Access of the Poor to Public Health Provisions

Weak access to public health provisions can constrain the productivity of the poor and reduce the purchasing power of their household budgets. Leading to a health poverty trap, with illness taxing the household's budget on expenditure for private healthcare, in turn pressuring the budget for nutrition. The results found here reconfirm severe constraints in the access of the poor to public health provisions.

A World Bank survey of health indicators permits disaggregation by quintile.[25] It addresses financial constraints for women in accessing healthcare facilities, for the bottom quintile compared to the top four quintiles. Of the 54 countries examined, all had a significantly higher proportion of the bottom quintile facing more financial constraints compared to the top four quintiles. The sole exception was São Tomé and Príncipe where both were about equal.

A more specific health gap for the poor was in percentage of births with skilled assisted delivery. Figure 5.21 shows significantly lower assisted births for the bottom quintile compared to the rest of the population, in all regions, except Europe and Central Asia. There were also a few country exceptions in Asia and the Pacific for Thailand and Mongolia, and in Latin America and the Caribbean for Barbados and Argentina.

A key outcome indicator for health is children-under-five mortality rates per 1000 live births, seen in Fig. 5.22. For the bottom quintile, child mortality was significantly higher compared to the rest of the population, for all countries reported, except Syria and the Maldives. Both the highest mortality rates and the largest gaps were found in sub-Saharan Africa, notably in Cameroon and Guinea. But large gaps were also found in Asia, in India and Pakistan.

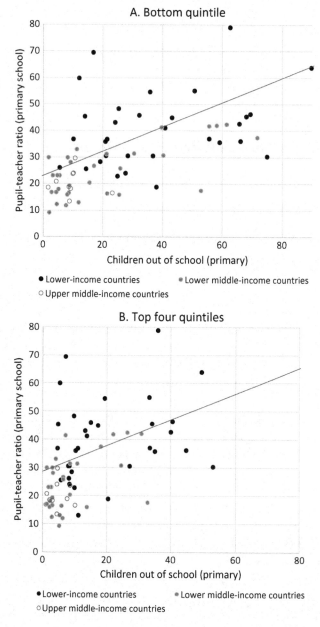

Fig. 5.20 Correlation between pupil-teacher ratio in primary school and school attendance. (Source: Authors' estimations at the ILO, based on data from UNICEF (available at https://data.unicef.org/))

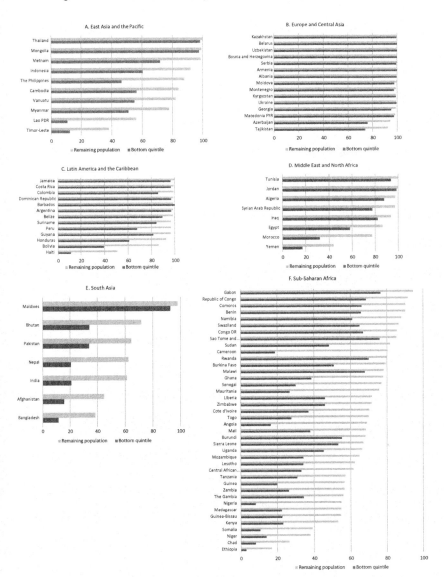

Fig. 5.21 Assistance during delivery (any skilled personnel) (percentage of births). (Source: Authors' estimations at the ILO, based on data from the World Bank, ASPIRE: The Atlas of Social Protection Indicators of Resilience and Equity, April 2016 (available at http://datatopics.worldbank.org/aspire/))

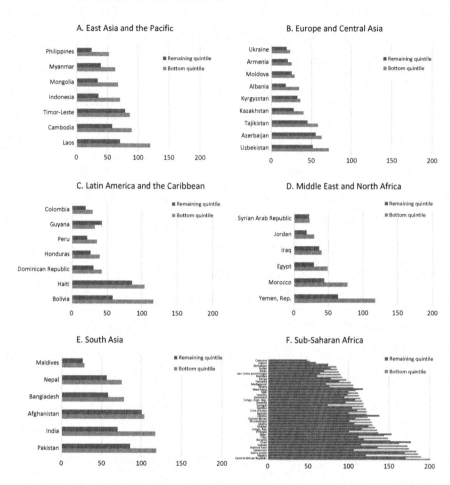

Fig. 5.22 Under-five mortality rate (per 1000 live births). (Source: Authors' estimations at the ILO, based on data from the World Bank, ASPIRE: The Atlas of Social Protection Indicators of Resilience and Equity, April 2016 (available at http://datatopics.worldbank.org/aspire/))

This grievous gap between the poor and non-poor in child mortality has less of a link to the government budget on health, given institutional weaknesses, and more of a link to actual public provision of health staff. So, Fig. 5.23 shows that child mortality for the bottom quintile has no correlation with government expenditure on health. There is, for instance, a huge spread at 100 deaths per 1000 live births between, say, Senegal

Putting Caveats on Growth: Policy for Inclusion and Productive... 203

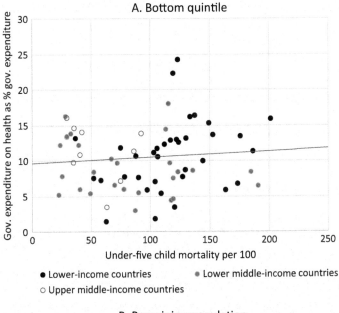

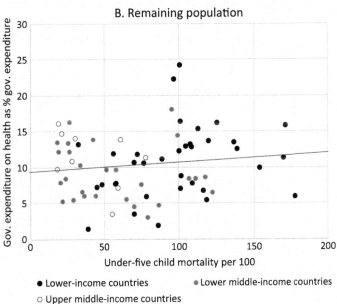

Fig. 5.23 Correlation between government expenditure on health (percentage) and under-five child mortality. (Source: Authors' estimations at the ILO, based on data from the World Bank, ASPIRE: The Atlas of Social Protection Indicators of Resilience and Equity, April 2016 (available at http://datatopics.worldbank.org/aspire/))

and Mozambique spending about 8 percent of their GDP on public health and Rwanda and Uganda spending over 20 percent, with the same outcome.

If government expenditure on health does not explain child mortality outcomes, private expenditure could. But Fig. 5.24 shows that out-of-pocket expenditure is also not very well correlated to child mortality for the bottom quintile.

What does explain child mortality well for the bottom quintile is the density of medical staff per 1000 of the population. Figure 5.25 shows a good negative correlation. As staff density increases, child mortality for the bottom quintile drops.

The Impact of Subsidies on Wage Goods on Poverty

Despite the expense of universal subsidies on wage goods, and their leakages, there is evidence of their impact on the poor. The evidence is of improved nutrition, through the public distribution system in India (Kaul 2014), and the Egyptian food subsidy program (McDermott 1992). This chapter attempts to evaluate the impact of food subsidies on the incidence of poverty.

Table 5.9 gives the size of the budgets for food subsidy programs in 25 countries. These range for most countries at under 1 percent of GDP, but with seven outliers at between 2 and 3 percent mostly in the Middle East and North Africa.

Three of these countries afforded data which allowed an assessment of the impact of their food subsidy program on poverty, shown in Table 5.10.

Indonesia's Raskin program allowed eligible households to buy a maximum of 15 kg rice per month at 75–80 percent below the market price. Indonesia's poverty rate for 2010 was calculated at 15.9 percent of the population. This poverty rate was based on the subsidised price of rice for the poor. The table shows that removal of the subsidy, and loss of purchasing power would raise the poverty rate to 17.14 percent of the population. Hence the subsidy on rice lowers the poverty rate by 1.24 percent of the population of the country. And about 80 percent of the poor do

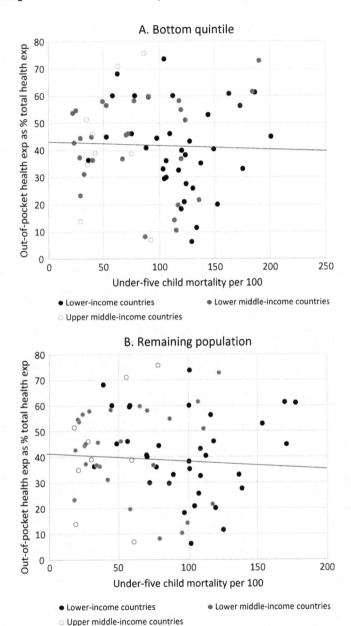

Fig. 5.24 Correlation between out-of-pocket health expenditure (percentage of total health expenditure) and under-five child mortality. (Source: Authors' estimations at the ILO, based on data from the World Bank, ASPIRE: The Atlas of Social Protection Indicators of Resilience and Equity, April 2016 (available at http://datatopics.worldbank.org/aspire/))

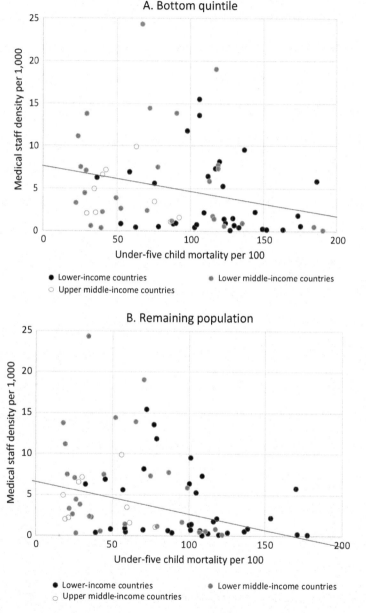

Fig. 5.25 Correlation between medical staff density and under-five child mortality. (Source: Authors' estimations at the ILO, based on data from the World Bank, ASPIRE: The Atlas of Social Protection Indicators of Resilience and Equity, April 2016 (available at http://datatopics.worldbank.org/aspire/))

Table 5.9 Government expenditure on food subsidies as a percentage of GDP

Country	Year	Expenditure (% of GDP)	Region
Djibouti	2011	<0.1	Africa
Senegal	2013	0.1	Africa
Mauritius	2012	0.3	Africa
Morocco	2013	0.7	Africa
Ethiopia	2007	0.1	Africa
Mauritania	2011	0.8	Africa
Algeria	2011	1.9	Africa
Tunisia	2013	1.9	Africa
Sudan	2011	0.22	Africa
Egypt	2011	2.4	Africa
Saudi Arabia	2011	0.13	Arab states
Syria	2011	2.75	Arab states
Jordan	2012	1	Arab states
Kuwait	2011	0.75	Arab states
Bahrain	2011	0.7	Arab states
Lebanon	2011	<0.1	Arab states
Qatar	2011	<0.1	Arab states
United Arab Emirates	2011	<0.1	Arab states
Iraq	2011	3.3	Arab states
India	2012	0.8	Asia and the Pacific
The Maldives	2010	1.8	Asia and the Pacific
Timor-Leste	2008	5.8[a]	Asia and the Pacific
Bangladesh	2011	0.75	Asia and the Pacific
Indonesia	2010	0.25	Asia and the Pacific
The Philippines	2009	<0.1	Asia and the Pacific

Note: *GDP* gross domestic product
[a] Percentage of non-oil GDP
Source: Authors' estimations at the ILO, based on data from the IMF's World Economic Outlook Database, 2016

get the subsidy. However, leakages are still high, and only 20 percent of the subsidy goes to the poor, while 80 percent goes to the non-poor.

The Philippines' National Food Authority has a universal subsidy which lowers the market price of rice by 20 percent, with no rationing of quantity. Table 5.10 shows that the poverty rate in the Philippines, based on the subsidised price of rice was near 12 percent of the population. Removal of this subsidy is estimated to increase the poverty rate to near 12.5 percent of the population. This half percent lower poverty rate is enabled by 54 percent of the poor getting the subsidy. However, again as

Table 5.10 Impact of food subsidies on poverty

Country	Year	Subsidy program	Subsidised products	A: Poverty rate with food subsidies (%)	B: Poverty rate without food subsidies (%)	Impact of food subsidies on poverty reduction (B−A) (%)	% of subsidies received by the poor	% of the poor who received any subsidies	Expenditure (% of GDP)
Indonesia[a]	2010	Raskin	Rice	15.90	17.14	1.24	20.88	79.86	0.25 (2010)
The Philippines[a]	2009	NFA	Rice	11.98	12.46	0.48	20.78	54.27	0.05 (2009)
Iraq[b]	2007	Public distribution system	Basket of goods[c]	3.37	7.43	4.06	3.23	99.71	3.3 (2011)
Egypt[d]	2005	Ration cards Baladi bread	Sugar, oil, rice and tea Baladi bread	25.2	34	8.8	Not available	Not available	2.4 (2011)

Eligible households can purchase up to 15 kg per month at 75–80% lower than the market price.
NFA sells rice about a fifth cheaper than non-NFA ordinary rice. NFA rice subsidies are universal, with unlimited purchase.
In-kind ration card system through which the government provides subsidised commodities to almost a fifth of the population.
Ration cards allow 80% of Egyptian households to buy set quotas of specific commodities at subsidised prices from specific outlets.
Baladi bread is sold at 5 piasters (about US$0.01) per loaf, with no entitlement restrictions and distribution on a first-come-first-served basis.

(continued)

Table 5.10 (continued)

Country	Subsidy program	Year	Subsidised products	A: Poverty rate with food subsidies (%)	B: Poverty rate without food subsidies (%)	Impact of food subsidies on poverty reduction (B−A) (%)	% of subsidies received by the poor	% of the poor who received any subsidies	Expenditure (% of GDP)
Egypt[d]	Ration cards *Baladi* bread	2005	Sugar, oil, rice, and tea *Baladi* bread	19.6	26.6	7	18	Subsidised flour = 40% *Baladi* bread = 70%	1.7 (2005)

Ration cards allowed about 60% of Egyptian households to buy set quotas of specific commodities at subsidised prices from specific outlets.

Baladi bread is sold at 5 piasters (about US$0.01) per loaf, with no entitlement restrictions and distribution on a first-come-first-served basis.

Note: *GDP* gross domestic product, *NFA* National Food Authority, *PPP* purchasing power parity

[a] Poverty rate at US$1.90 2011 PPP
[b] Poverty rate at US$1.25 2005 PPP
[c] Includes wheat flour, rice, sugar, vegetable oil, chick peas, white beans, lentil, tea, milk (powered), salt, soap, detergent, infant formula (powered), weaning cereal, tomato paste, and white flour, 16 items in total
[d] Poverty rate at moderate poverty line (as defined by the World Bank)

Source: Authors' estimations at the ILO, based on data from the World Bank's World Development Indicators, PovcalNet (available at http://iresearch.worldbank.org/PovcalNet/), and 'Egypt's Food Subsidies: Benefit Incidence and Leakages' (unpublished manuscript, World Bank, Washington, DC, 2010); and IMF, World Economic Outlook Database

in Indonesia, only 20 percent of the subsidy goes to the poor, with the other 80 percent going to the non-poor.

The Iraqi public distribution system provides a basket of subsidised food commodities in kind to near one-fifth of the population. Table 5.10 shows that the poverty rate based on this subsidy was 3.4 percent in 2007. Removing the subsidy is estimated to more than double the poverty rate to 7.4 percent of the population. Virtually all the poor get the subsidy, but 97 percent of the subsidy goes to the non-poor. While the case of Iraq as a conflict state may be special, the impact of the subsidy remains significant.

Finally, the World Bank (2010) estimates that Egypt's ration card system which, allowed 60 percent of Egyptian households to buy a basket of commodities at subsidised prices in 2005, combined with universal *baladi* bread subsidies, has reduced poverty by almost 9 percent of the population in 2005.

5.4 Policy on Productive Transformation

Chapter 2 argued that increase in aggregate incomes, and catch-up in them, between LDCs, LMICs, EEs, and AEs, required not just growth of GDP, but growth with a caveat—that is, growth with productive transformation. This chapter has argued on top of that, that a humanitarian prior to catch-up in aggregate country incomes must be a catch-up in the incomes of the poor with the non-poor. This puts a caveat on GDP growth of being more inclusive and poverty-reducing. Policy has been derived to cut this income gap of the poor, based on transfers and increases in the labour incomes of the poor. Policy has also been derived to cut the non-income gaps of the poor, through provisioning of public goods in three key areas, education, health, and consumption subsidies on wage goods.

So, a substantive part of policy for poverty reduction has to be based on transfers from the non-poor to the poor. However, an equally substantive part of policy for poverty reduction has to be based on increasing the labour incomes of the non-poor, through increases in productivity, wages, and less vulnerable forms of employment. Chapter 3 showed that these improvements in labour market outcomes are also enabled by productive transformation, as workers move from less productive to more productive sectors. They were also simultaneously seen to reduce their vulnerability, in large part, moving from contributing family work, and self-employment to waged employment.

Figure 5.26 confirms the enhanced labour incomes part of the poverty reduction strategy by showing that productive transformation is indeed poverty-reducing. It shows that reduction in country poverty is for the most part correlated to a drop in the share of agriculture in GDP, and an increase in the shares of industry and services. So, productive transformation allows catch-up not only in aggregate country incomes, but also catch-up in incomes between the poor and the non-poor. Productive transformation is poverty-reducing.

So, policy now needs to be derived for productive transformation.

The policy debate on productive transformation is vast in its literature and surprisingly short on fundamental disagreements. Three notions add critical value for policy.

One, the departure from comparative advantage creates more room for the state to intervene with industrial policy.

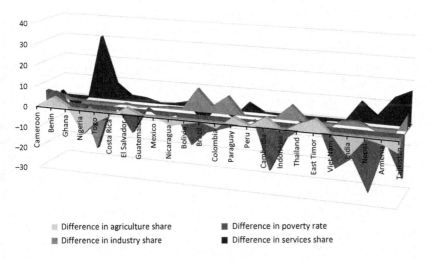

Fig. 5.26 Change in GDP sector share. (Note: *GDP* gross domestic product. Source: Authors' estimations at the ILO, based on data from the World Bank's World Development Indicators and PovcalNet (available at http://iresearch.worldbank.org/PovcalNet/))

Two, education and skills constrain the development of manufacturing.

Three, the notion of institutions as an enabler of productive transformation has evolved from the classic study of Japan's MITI to a set of enabling intangibles called social capabilities. Both skills and social capabilities may well explain the extent of departure from comparative advantage, and the degree and success of country strategy to leapfrog.

Departing from Comparative Advantage

Schumpeter (1934) was the early non-interventionist in markets and the economy. Economics was a natural self-regulating mechanism when undisturbed by social and other meddlers. He saw a cycle of innovation with new businesses replacing old ones in creative destruction. This gave booms and recessions, which were inevitable, and could not be corrected without disturbing the creation of new wealth.

Young (1928) was the early challenger to this classical view of exogenous improvements. Improvements occur in Young's representative firm, through growth of roundabout methods of production, which are channelled through prices to the market.

Rosenstein-Rodan, Hirschman, and Kaldor follow with more explicit grounds for intervention. Rosenstein-Rodan (1943) envisaged a 'big push' in investment for economic development. Hirschman (1981) favoured market disequilibria to stimulate growth. Kaldor's first law argues that a higher manufacturing growth rate gives a higher GDP growth rate (see Kaldor 1966, 1967, 1975; Thirlwall 1983).

Lin's (2012) schematic into three waves of development theory and his debate with Chang (see Lin and Chang 2009), frame the notion of departure from comparative advantage very neatly. Lin's first wave of structuralist economics that emerged from the Latin American experience of the 1940s represents the first concerted departure from the theory of comparative advantage. An income gap between countries was explained by structural difference between them due to market failures. These market imperfections, and the need to reduce the gap between industrialised and DCs, urged Keynesian government intervention, and structural reforms.

The explicit argument against country production being determined by its comparative advantage was captured by Singer (1950) and Prebisch

(1962). They found that countries focusing on primary products, given their comparative advantage in them, faced declining terms of trade in the long run. This became the argument for import-substituting industrialisation.

A theoretical argument was added by Scitovsky (1954) that industrial policy was needed for underinvestment in some sectors.

The clinching argument for industrial policy came from Chang (1993) and Stiglitz (1996), based on the country experiences of initially Japan and Korea, and then eight economies called the 'East Asian miracle'.[26] They draw on the economic and political conditions in these countries that make for successful industrial policy.

Park and Chan (1989) emphasised interlinkages between industry and services, especially for employment generation, while Kuznets (1968) noted for 14 AEs and EEs that their production structures had undergone a profound transformation over 60 years of their history. Hence the grounds for industrial policy for a productive transformation of the economy, which is not given by comparative advantage.

The weaknesses in import-substituting industrialisation, particularly in Latin America, prompted what Lin (2012) calls a 'second wave' of policy reaction, with renewed emphasis on the essential function of markets in allocating resources and providing incentives for development. This approach ignored structural differences between countries, and expected structural change to happen spontaneously in the development process. Advocated by international financial institutions in the 1990s, the Washington Consensus advocated development policy based on liberalisation, privatisation, and price flexibility, and downplayed the role of the government in steering economic growth and technological change (Cimoli et al. 2009).

However, this second wave of development theory ignored that industrial policy had been successfully employed in the past in the countries that were now developed industry leaders, including the US, Germany, and Japan, and more recently the newly industrialising economies of East Asia, and the more vibrant EEs like China and Brazil (Cimoli et al. 2009). These countries had nurtured technology-intensive industries to jump-start their production, diffuse the benefits of technological learning across the rest of the economy, and boost growth. So, the remarkable achievements in growth in the twentieth century ignored the basic tenets of the Washington Consensus, which paid insufficient attention to the heterogeneity and specific characteristics among individual countries. As a result, a third wave of development theory emerged, which Lin (2012) characterises as the 'new structuralist economics.'

The essence of the new structuralist economics is that (a) factor endowments determine a country's comparative advantage and (b) the production structure of the country should be based on factor endowments and so, on comparative advantage. But (c) these factor endowments change over time, with the level of development, moving continuously from low income to high income. And (d) the government plays an active role in changing these factor endowments.

The debate between Lin and Chang brings out a key policy variable, in the degree of departure that is possible from comparative advantage (see Lin and Chang 2009; Lin 2011). Both recognise that climbing up the ladder is a hard slog that involves more than getting the prices right. It requires intelligent industrial policy, organisation building, and accumulation of technological capabilities through research and development, training, and production experience. They agree that in climbing up the ladder, a country can skip some rungs with the help of industrial policy, but that it can slip and fall if it tries to skip too many rungs. Comparative advantage does determine a country's climbing ability, and to skip rungs. The disagreement between them lies in the number of rungs that can be skipped, being small for Lin, to be comparative advantage-conforming, and larger for Chang, being comparative advantage-defying.

The strategic policy question then must be, what determines the number of rungs that can be skipped, which is the degree of departure from comparative advantage.

Education and Skills as a Major Determinant of the Degree of Departure from Comparative Advantage

According to the Lin–Chang framework, factor endowments give comparative advantage, and these factor endowments can change with policy intervention. The question then is, what factor endowments constrain productive transformation, and are also amenable to policy intervention?

Recalling from Chap. 2, the lowest rung on the productive transformation ladder was the collective inability for LDCs to raise their shares in manufacturing above 10 percent of GDP over the past third of a century. This can be taken as a test of a discrete jump up from the lowest rung of the productive transformation ladder. From amongst this group of LDCs with an average manufacturing share of under 10 percent of GDP, what factor endowments would allow them to raise this share discretely?

Nübler (2011) shows a determining variable to be education levels. In Table 5.11, LDCs with average years of schooling below 4.5 years had manufacturing shares below 8 percent of GDP. Only LDCs with average years of schooling above 4.5 broke out of that barrier and raised their shares in manufacturing above 9 percent of GDP and indeed up to 12 percent of GDP.

The role of skills, and education levels, and the constraints they place on adoption of new technology has been recognised by Lall (2001), and in the context of Africa by the ADEA (2013) Triennale report. The report emphasises three sub-themes: common core skills for all, mass development of technical and vocational skills, and building knowledge and innovation-based economies and societies.

Table 5.11 Characteristics of different country groups

				Group characteristics			
	AYS	Average MVA	AYS	Non-schooled	Primary	Secondary	Polarised 'missing middle'
Group 1	2.8	7.8	<4.5	High	Low	Low <20%	No
Group 2	3.8	7.6	<4.5	High	Very	High	Yes
Group 3	5.7	12	>4.5	Low	High	Varies	No
Group 4	5.2	9.2	>4.5	Low	High	Varies	Yes

Note: *AYS* average years of schooling, *MVA* manufacturing value-added
Source: Irmgard Nübler, 'Promoting Catching-Up Growth and Productive Transformation in LDCs: A New Approach', in 'Growth, Employment and Decent Work in the Least Developed Countries: Report of the ILO for the Fourth UN Conference on the Least Developed Countries' (International Labour Office, Geneva, 2011)

But Ansu and Tan (2011) point out a vicious cycle which constrains education and skill levels especially in the case of the low-income economies of sub-Saharan Africa. Investing in education and skills is costly and exceeds the capacity of government to finance for the levels required—which in turn impedes economic growth, further limiting the resources available for skills and training. Their proposed strategy is to initially meet specific sectoral demands for skills, only following with universal improvements in skills, and orienting the educational system towards science and technology, especially in tertiary education.

Social Capabilities as Intangibles Par Excellence, as a Major Determinant of Departure from Comparative Advantage

While average years of schooling provides a hard parameter that constrains policy departure from comparative advantage, a more intangible but broader parameter emerges in the notion of social capabilities. Abramovitz (1986) introduces the notion by examining catch-up phases in today's developed countries, noting that rapid change was not always in the more technologically advanced countries, but in those with more advanced social capabilities. He further noted that these social capabilities to absorb more advanced technologies were not given, but acquired and embodied in societies.

Nübler (in ILO 2014c) puts the country's educational attainment structure at the base of the social capabilities pyramid. Lall and Chang give social capabilities a more complex structure. Lall (1992) puts technological capabilities at the national level, and innovatively at the firm level. Chang et al. (2014) recognise the tradition of economic historians who have regarded the manufacturing sector, especially the capital goods sector, as the learning centre of capitalism in technological terms (see also Rosenberg 1963, 1982; Kaldor 1967; Cohen and Zysman 1988; Rowthorn and Wells 1987; Park and Chan 1989). Hence industrial policies that promote the manufacturing sector become important elements of a national learning strategy. Promoting activities in advanced knowledge communities, creates opportunities for workers to acquire new sets of technological and business knowledge. This in turn expands options for firms to diversify into new products.

Hidalgo and Hausmann (2009) liken a capability to a building block or Lego piece, a product is a Lego model, and a country is equivalent to a bucket of Lego. Countries can then make products for which they have all the necessary capabilities. Chang (2011) emphasises that these productive capabilities have a collective nature, resulting from the interdependence between learning and production, with a variety of actors. The result is an *industrial commons*, with interdependence between a set of industries which contribute advanced materials, components, subsystems, and manufacturing systems (Tassey 2010).

Of course, the social capability and industrial commons approach changes the nature of traditional industrial policy in many ways. For a start, the interdependence implies that industrial policy is no longer focused on just manufacturing and services but also on productive transformation of agriculture. The capital goods produced in manufacturing feed and enable technical change in agriculture. Second, the old-style industrial policy, where the government was often the producer itself, is not so relevant, as its effective policies (Bianchi and Labory 2006). Amsden and Singh (1994) note the plurality of policies, where the state promoted intense competition among firms in Korea, but MITI created cartels in Japan. Both policies were tailor-made to achieve the same objective of long-term productivity growth. Third, Stiglitz (2003) points out that rents can be made into productive capital goods by investing them in production and infrastructure.

But industrial policy still essentially remains based on the recognition that shifting production from certain goods to others that contribute more towards improvements in productivity, income, and wages, in particular tradeables and industrial products (Hausmann et al. 2007; Rodrik 2010). Switching to activities, products, and technologies with steeper learning curves becomes important.

And some of the traditional instruments of industrial policy abide. Nunn and Trefler (2010) note that tariff structures that protect education-intensive activities, with a skill bias are observed to be positively correlated to long-run per capita GDP growth. And Astorga et al. (2014) note that empirical evidence from Latin America shows that depreciation of real exchange rates, unless accompanied by industrial and technology policies to accelerate learning, could not close the technology gap.

Appendix

Table 5.12 List of household surveys consulted

Country (ISO3 code)	Name of survey	Year
Albania (ALB)	Living standards measurement survey	2012
Angola (AGO)	Inquérito integrado sobre o bem estar da população, 2008/09	2009
Argentina (ARG)	Encuesta Permanente de Hogares	2012
Armenia (ARM)	Household integrated living conditions survey	2012
Benin (BEN)	Enquête modulaire intégrée sur les conditions de vie des ménages au Bénin	2011
Botswana (BWA)	Botswana core welfare indicators survey, 2009/10	2009
Bhutan (BTN)	Bhutan living standards survey, 2003	2003
Bolivia, Plurinational State of (BOL)	Encuesta de hogares	2012
Brazil (BRA)	Pesquisa Nacional Por Amostra de Domicilios	2012
Bulgaria (BGR)	European Union statistics on income and living conditions	2012
Burkina Faso (BFA)	Questionnaire unifié des indicateurs de base du bien-être	2003
Cabo Verde (CPV)	Inquérito às despesas e receitas familiares	2001
Cambodia (KHM)	Socioeconomic survey	2009
Cameroon (CMR)	Troisième enquête camerounaise auprès des ménages	2007
China (CHN)	Chinese household income project	2008
Colombia (COL)	Encuesta nacional de calidad de vida	2012
Congo (COG)	Questionnaire des indicateurs de base du bien-être	2005
Costa Rica (CRI)	Encuesta Nacional de Hogares	2012
Côte d'Ivoire (CIV)	Enquête Niveau de Vie des ménages	2002
Dominican Republic (DOM)	Encuesta Nacional de Ingresos y Gastos de los Hogares	2007
Egypt (EGY)	Household Income, Expenditure and Consumption Survey	2008
El Salvador (SLV)	Encuesta de Hogares de Propositos Multiples	2012
Ethiopia (ETH)	Ethiopia rural socioeconomic survey	2010
Gabon (GAB)	Direction Générale de la Statistique et des Etudes Economiques, Questionnaire des indicateurs de base du bien-être	2005

(continued)

Table 5.12 (continued)

Country (ISO3 code)	Name of survey	Year
Georgia (GEO)	Integrated household survey	2013
Ghana (GHA)	Ghana Living Standards Survey	2013
Guatemala (GTM)	National survey of living conditions	2011
Honduras (HND)	Encuesta hogares	2011
India (IND)	National sample survey (66th round, 2009/10)	2010
Indonesia (IDN)	National social and economic household survey (SUSENAS)	2010
Iraq (IRQ)	Household social and economic survey	2007
Jordan (JOR)	Household income, expenditure and consumption survey	2010
Kazakhstan (KAZ)	Sampling household survey, 2003	2003
Kenya (KEN)	Kenya integrated household budget survey	2005
Lesotho (LSO)	Lesotho household budget survey	2002
Malawi (MWI)	Integrated household survey	2010
Mali (MLI)	Enquête légère intégrée auprès des ménages	2006
Mexico (MEX)	Encuesta nacional de ingresos y gastos de los hogares	2012
Mongolia (MNG)	Household social and economic survey	2011
Morocco (MAR)	Enquête nationale sur le niveau de vie des ménages	2007
Mozambique (MOZ)	Inquérito aos agregados familares sobre orçamento familiar	2002
Namibia (NAM)	National household income and expenditure survey	2009
Nepal (NPL)	Nepal living standards survey	2010
Nicaragua (NIC)	Encuesta nacional de hogares sobre medición de nivel de vida	2009
Niger (NER)	National survey on household living conditions and agriculture	2011
Nigeria (NGA)	General household survey (panel)	2012
Pakistan (PAK)	Core welfare indicators questionnaire	2005
Palestine (PSE)	Expenditure and consumption survey	2011
Panama (PAN)	Encuesta de niveles de vida	2008
Paraguay (PRY)	Encuesta permanente de hogares	2012
Peru (PER)	Encuesta nacional de hogares	2013
Philippines (PHL)	Labour force survey/Family income and expenditure survey	2009
Romania (ROU)	European Union statistics on income and living conditions	2012
Russian Federation (RUS)	Russian Federation longitudinal monitoring survey, Higher School of Economics	2013
Senegal (SEN)	Enquête de suivi de la pauvreté au Sénégal	2001
Serbia (SRB)	Living standards measurement survey	2007
Sierra Leone (SLE)	Integrated household survey	2003

(continued)

Table 5.12 (continued)

Country (ISO3 code)	Name of survey	Year
South Africa (ZAF)	National income dynamics study	2012
Sudan (SDN)	Household income, expenditure and consumption survey	2009
Tajikistan (TJK)	Tajikistan living standards measurement survey	2009
Thailand (THA)	Household socioeconomic survey	2010
Timor-Leste (TLS)	Standards of living survey	2007
Togo (TGO)	Questionnaire des indicateurs de base du bien-être	2011
Tunisia (TUN)	Enquête nationale sur le budget, la consommation et le niveau de vie des ménages	2010
Turkey (TUR)	European Union statistics on income and living conditions	2012
Uganda (UGA)	Uganda national household survey	2009
United Republic of Tanzania (TZA)	Tanzania National Panel Survey, 2012/13	2013
Vietnam (VNM)	Viet Nam household living standard survey	2008
Zambia (ZMB)	Living conditions monitoring survey report	2010

Notes

1. According to the ILO and the International Conference of Labour Statisticians.
2. This data for decomposition of the poor by sector of employment was not available for AEs.
3. Authors' estimations at the ILO, based on data from the World Bank, PovcalNet, April 2016 (available at http://iresearch.worldbank.org/PovcalNet/).
4. Again, data for the decomposition of the poor by their specific sector of employment was not available for AEs.
5. Extreme poverty is defined as incomes or expenditure on consumption below US$1.90 per day, in PPP terms.
6. Less than 2 percent of government expenditure is needed to eliminate extreme poverty in DCs, but more than 9 percent in the case of Africa and over 25 percent in low-income countries. These proportions translate to 7.3 percent of total government expenditure required to eliminate extreme and moderate poverty in DCs, 31.3 percent in Africa, and over 100 percent in low-income countries alone. In view of current govern-

ment expenditure and public expenditure on social protection—6.2 percent of GDP in DCs (ILO 2014c), 8.6 percent worldwide (ILO 2014b)—this gap in income relative to global and regional GDP might be seen as reasonable, leading one to question why the gap still exists at all. This notwithstanding, huge disparities remain between regions and countries in terms of gaps and ability to cover the associated costs; the limited share of those social protection benefits reaching the poor (ADB 2016); the sustainability of an approach based only on social protection; and workers' legitimate expectations for decent working conditions, including decent levels of labour income. For data on countries' ability to cover these costs, see the World Bank's ASPIRE dataset, available at http://datatopics.worldbank.org/aspire/

7. The minimum cost of eliminating extreme poverty exceeds 5 percent of GDP in Malawi (16.0 percent), Mozambique (9.1 percent), Niger (5.3 percent), and Togo (5.0 percent). In these four countries, this minimum cost ranges from 32.5 to 77.6 percent to eliminate both extreme and moderate poverty. In other regions, the minimum cost of eliminating extreme and moderate poverty exceeds 3 percent of GDP in Timor-Leste (12.4 percent), Nepal (5.6 percent), Cambodia (4.6 percent), India (3.8 percent), and Honduras (4.6 percent) and represents more than the total public investment in social protection.

8. The relationship between family size and poverty, however, is quite complex. As children grow up and become economically active, they make valuable contributions to households. There are also good reasons for having large families as part of a livelihood strategy whereby children are expected to take care of parents in their old age, especially in the absence of any form of pension provision.

9. It should be noted that, while there is no official definition, ILO (2015b) and Messenger and Wallot (2015) define 'very short hours' as those below 15 hours per week.

10. For the non-poor, short working hours (less than 35 hours per week) adversely affect 43 percent of those self-employed and 14 percent of wage and salaried workers.

11. In DCs, more than 36 percent of women below the poverty threshold in self-employment (including contributing family workers) work less than 20 hours per week, and the majority (nearly 60 percent) work less than 35 hours per week.

12. Taking the case of developed countries, comparative European research shows a significant association between poverty rates and contractual

work status. Logistic regression shows that this disparity is largely explained by the difference in wages between temporary and permanent workers, rather than by the individual and household characteristics of those in temporary work (Ray et al. 2014). Evidence from DCs also associates the absence of permanent contracts with higher risks of poverty, including higher risks of chronic poverty (Chronic Poverty Advisory Network 2013).

13. Many of the self-employed are not covered by social protection laws and regulations for contributory social security and when they are, this is too often through weak mechanisms such as voluntary coverage. This rarely converts into effective coverage (ILO 2015b). Dependent workers in non-standard forms of employment are often excluded from coverage either by law or in practice. Reasons for their exclusion may derive directly from the terms of the contract or indirectly because of its duration below a minimum defined threshold, an insufficient number of hours worked and other reasons that include the type of employer (households in the case for domestic workers) and the size of enterprises. All these factors tend to affect the poor more than the non-poor (ibid.). For those covered under the law, the limited ability to contribute, the irregularity and unpredictability of income (factors not compatible with usual affiliation modalities and the long period of contribution required), and the critical priority of basic daily needs are major reasons for de facto exclusion from social insurance coverage. Other reasons range from the lack of awareness of entitlements to the inappropriateness of the benefits and of ways to contribute, the lack of confidence in institutions, and the level of effectiveness and efficiency of national institutions to deliver benefits and services (Schmitt and De 2013; ILO 2015b).

14. Independent of poverty status, an earlier ILO (2015b) report showed significantly lower affiliation rates among the self-employed compared to wage and salaried workers (at the global level, 52 percent of wage and salaried workers are affiliated to a pension scheme compared to 16 percent of the self-employed), but also the significant negative impact of being in non-standard forms of employment on current social protection coverage by contributory schemes. There is indeed a very high correlation between the fact of having a formalised permanent contract and the affiliation to social protection among wage and salaried workers. Affiliation rates appear to be significantly lower among workers in part-time employment compared to those in full-time employment (whether in dependent or independent employment).

15. Where extreme poverty is concerned, 6.5 percent of the extremely poor in DCs are currently affiliated to a pension scheme compared to 31.4 percent of the non-poor.
16. Corresponding affiliation rates among the non-poor are respectively 55.1 percent for wage and salaried workers and 13.5 percent for the self-employed earning a living above the poverty threshold.
17. Social protection benefits include both individual benefits—unemployment (including severance pay), old-age benefits and retirement grants, survivor benefits (including death grants), sickness benefits, disability benefits, education-related allowances, where applicable—and household benefits (family- and child-related allowances in cash and value of child-related allowances in kind, housing allowances and other social allowances in cash or value of other social allowances in kind not elsewhere classified).
18. To be considered with caution, as many people are above the poverty threshold because they receive social protection benefits.
19. Considering both the extremely and moderately poor (<$3.10 PPP per capita and per day).
20. The South African Child Support Grant, although means-tested, covers more than half of all children under the age of 18 (10.8 million children in 2012). The expenditure on child benefits (1.2 percent of GDP) is above the world average (0.4 percent of GDP) and not far from the average in developed countries and European countries (1.4 percent). South Africa reaches nearly universal coverage of people in old age (90 percent of this extension resulting from the gradual extension of the non-contributory old-age grant). The Bolsa Família program in Brazil is the largest program providing child benefits in absolute terms. It reaches around 14 million families and covers about a quarter of Brazil's population—at an annual cost of less than 0.5 percent of GDP (ILO 2014b). It is estimated that 10 percent of the change in inequality compared to the 1990s is due to the Bolsa Família (Barros et al. 2010).
21. These range from social policy along the lines designed by Otto von Bismarck and the primary objective of income maintenance based on social insurance, with eligibility for earnings-related benefits depending on the contribution record, to that of William Beveridge with flat-rate benefits provided universally, financed by taxation and a declared objective of prevention of poverty (Morel and Palme 2012).
22. Unfortunately, this rationale does not fit current trends in social assistance, and certainly not in Africa where the focus tends to be on the

elderly or households without any working-age adults. In most programs, if there is one working-age adult—regardless of the number of dependants—households tend to be excluded from these schemes.
23. Employment quality is imperfectly assessed through the different statuses in employment. This must be considered in the light of the analysis of decent work deficits presented in Sect. 5.2. Results show that the self-employed tend to be affected by decent work deficits even more than wage and salaried workers (limited access to social protection, higher exposure to short hours, but also extensive hours of work—particularly in DCs). Section 5.2 also shows, however, that wage and salaried employment is not protected from facing decent work deficits.
24. Data available from ILO Social Security Inquiry, http://www.ilo.org/dyn/ilossi/ssimain.home, accessed on 30 April 2016.
25. See the World Bank's ASPIRE dataset, available at http://datatopics.worldbank.org/aspire/
26. While there is a prolific literature on the 'East Asian miracle', Chang (1993) and Stiglitz (1996) have been seminal. For Japan, see, for example, Dore (1973); for Korea, see Wade (2003).

References

Abramovitz, Moses. 1986. Catching Up, Forging Ahead, and Falling Behind. *Journal of Economic History* 46 (2): 385–406.
ADB (Asian Development Bank). 2016. *The Social Protection Indicator: Assessing Results for Asia*. Manila: ADB.
ADEA (Association for Development of Education in Africa). 2013. Promoting Critical Knowledge, Skills and Qualifications for Sustainable Development in Africa: How to Design and Implement an Effective Response by Education and Training Systems. Proceedings of the 2012 ADEA Triennale on Education and Training in Africa, Tunis, African Development Bank.
Aizer, Anna, Shari Eli, Joseph Ferrie, and Adriana Lleras-Muney. 2016. The Long-Run Impact of Cash Transfers to Poor Families. *American Economic Review* 106 (4): 935–971.
Albin, Peter S. 1970. Poverty, Education, and Unbalanced Economic Growth. *Quarterly Journal of Economics* 84 (1): 70–84.
Alderman, Harold, and Ruslan Yemtsov. 2012. Productive Role of Safety Nets. Social Protection and Labour Discussion Paper 1203, World Bank, Washington, DC.

Amsden, Alice H., and Ajit Singh. 1994. The Optimal Degree of Competition and Dynamic Efficiency in Japan and Korea. *European Economic Review* 38 (3–4): 941–951.

Ansu, Yaw, and Jee-Peng Tan. 2011. Skills Development for Economic Growth in Sub-Saharan Africa: A Pragmatic Perspective. In *Good Growth and Governance in Africa: Rethinking Development Strategies*, ed. Akbar Noman, Kwesi Botchwey, Howard Stein, and Joseph E. Stiglitz, 462–498. Oxford: Oxford University Press.

Astorga, Rodrigo, Mario Cimoli, and Gabriel Porcile. 2014. The Role of Industrial and Exchange Rate Policies in Promoting Structural Change, Productivity and Employment. In *Transforming Economies: Making Industrial Policy Work for Growth, Jobs and Development*, ed. José M. Salazar-Xirinachs, Irmgard Nübler, and Richard Kozul-Wright, 79–111. Geneva: International Labour Office.

Baldacci, Emanuele, Benedict Clements, Sanjeev Gupta, and Qiang Cui. 2008. Social Spending, Human Capital, and Growth in Developing Countries. *World Development* 36 (8): 1317–1341.

Barham, Vicky, Robin Boadway, Maurice Marchand, and Pierre Pestieau. 1995. Education and the Poverty Trap. *European Economic Review* 39 (7): 1257–1275.

Barros, Ricardo, Mirela de Carvalho, Samuel Franco, and Rosane Mendonça. 2010. Markets, the State, and the Dynamics of Inequality in Brazil. In *Declining Inequality in Latin America: A Decade of Progress?* ed. Luis Felipe López-Calva and Nora Lustig, 134–174. Washington, DC: Brookings Institution Press.

Bianchi, Patrizio, and Sandrine Labory, eds. 2006. *International Handbook on Industrial Policy*. Cheltenham: Edward Elgar.

Bigsten, Arne, Bereket Kebede, Abebe Shimeles, and Mekonnen Taddesse. 2003. Growth and Poverty Reduction in Ethiopia: Evidence from Household Panel Surveys. *World Development* 31 (1): 87–106.

Bonnet, Florence, Catherine Saget, and Axel Weber. 2012. Social Protection and Minimum Wages Responses to the 2008 Financial and Economic Crisis: Findings from the ILO/World Bank Inventory. Employment Working Paper 113, ILO, Geneva.

Chang, Ha-Joon. 1993. The Political Economy of Industrial Policy in Korea. *Cambridge Journal of Economics* 17 (2): 131–157.

———. 2011. Institutions and Economic Development: Theory, Policy and History. *Journal of Institutional Economics* 7 (4): 473–498.

Chang, Ha-Joon, Antonio Andreoni, and Ming Leon Kuan. 2014. Productive Capabilities Transformation: Institutions, Linkages and Policies for Manufacturing Growth and Employment. Background Paper, International Labour Organization, Geneva.

Chant, Sylvia, ed. 2010. *The International Handbook of Gender and Poverty: Concepts, Research, Policy*. Cheltenham: Edward Elgar.

Chronic Poverty Advisory Network. 2013. Working Out of Chronic Poverty: A Policy Guide. http://www.odi.org/sites/odi.org.uk/files/odi-assets/publications-opinion-files/8515.pdf. Accessed 30 Mar 2016.

Cimoli, Mario, Giovanni Dosi, Richard Nelson, and Joseph E. Stiglitz. 2009. Institutions and Policies Shaping Industrial Development: An Introductory Note. In *Industrial Policy and Development: The Political Economy of Capabilities Accumulation*, ed. Mario Cimoli, Giovanni Dosi, and Joseph E. Stiglitz, 19–38. Oxford: Oxford University Press.

Cohen, Stephan S., and John Zysman. 1988. *Manufacturing Matters: The Myth of the Post-Industrial Economy*. New York: Basic Books.

Dore, Ronald. 1973. *British Factory–Japanese Factory*. London: Allen & Unwin.

Fiszbein, Ariel, Ravi Kanbur, and Ruslam Yemtsov. 2013. Social Protection, Poverty and the Post-2015 Agenda. Policy Research Working Paper 6469, World Bank, Washington, DC.

Hanlon, Joseph, Armando Barrientos, and David Hulme. 2010. *Just Give Money to the Poor: The Development Revolution from the Global South*. Sterling VA: Kumarian Press.

Haughton, Jonathan, and Shahidur R. Khandker. 2009. Measures of Poverty. In *Handbook on Poverty and Inequality*, ed. Jonathan Haughton and Shahidur R. Khandker, 67–82. Washington, DC: World Bank.

Hausmann, Ricardo, Jason Hwang, and Dani Rodrik. 2007. What You Export Matters. *Journal of Economic Growth* 12 (1): 1–25.

HelpAge International. 2011. Financing Social Pensions in Low- and Middle-Income Countries. Pension Watch: Briefings on Social Protection in Older Age, Briefing No. 4, HelpAge International, London.

Hidalgo, César A., and Ricardo Hausmann. 2009. The Building Blocks of Economic Complexity. *PNAS* 106 (26): 10570–10575.

Hirschman, Albert O. 1981. *Essays in Trespassing: Economics to Politics and Beyond*. New York: Cambridge University Press.

ILO (International Labour Organization). 2001. Reducing the Decent Work Deficit: A Global Challenge; International Labour Conference, 89th Session 2001. Report of the Director-General, International Labour Office, Geneva.

———. 2003. *Working Out of Poverty; International Labour Conference, 91st Session 2003. Report of the Director-General, International Labour Office, Geneva.*

———. 2010a. *Extending Social Security for All: A Guide Through Challenges and Options.* Geneva: International Labour Office.

———. 2010b. *World Social Security Report 2010/11: Providing Coverage in Times of Crisis and Beyond.* Geneva: International Labour Office.

———. 2011a. *Final Report: Tripartite Meeting of Experts on Working-Time Arrangements (Geneva, 17–21 October 2011).* Geneva: International Labour Office.

———. 2011b. *Working Time in the Twenty-First Century: Report for Discussion at the Tripartite Meeting of Experts on Working-Time Arrangements (17–21 October 2011).* Geneva: International Labour Office.

———. 2013a. *The Informal Economy and Decent Work: A Policy Resource Guide Supporting Transitions to Formality.* Geneva: International Labour Office.

———. 2013b. Resolution I: Resolution Concerning Statistics of Work, Employment and Labour Underutilization. Resolution adopted by the 19th International Conference of Labour Statisticians, Geneva, 11 October.

———. 2014a. *Report V(1): The Transition from the Informal to the Formal Economy; International Labour Conference, 104th Session, 2015.* Geneva: International Labour Office.

———. 2014b. *World Social Protection Report 2014/15: Building Economic Recovery, Inclusive Development and Social Justice.* Geneva: International Labour Office.

———. 2014c. *World of Work Report 2014: Developing with Jobs.* Geneva: International Labour Office.

———. 2015a. *Non-Standard Forms of Employment: Report for Discussion at the Meeting of Experts on Non-Standard Forms of Employment (Geneva, 16–19 February 2015).* Geneva: International Labour Office.

———. 2015b. *World Employment and Social Outlook 2015: The Changing Nature of Jobs.* Geneva: International Labour Office.

———. 2016. *Women at Work: Trends 2016.* Geneva: International Labour Office.

ILO (International Labour Organization) and OECD (Organisation for Economic Co-operation and Development). 2013. Addressing Employment, Labour Market and Social Protection Challenges in G20 Countries: Key Measures Since 2010. Background Paper Prepared for the G20 Task Force on Employment, ILO and OECD, Geneva and Paris.

IMF (International Monetary Fund). 2008. *Fuel and Food Price Subsidies: Issues and Reform Options*. Washington, DC: IMF, Fiscal Affairs Department.

Kaldor, Nicholas. 1966. *Causes of the Slow Rate of Economic Growth of the United Kingdom: An Inaugural Lecture*. Cambridge: Cambridge University Press.

———. 1967. *Strategic Factors in Economic Development*. Ithaca: Cornell University Press.

———. 1975. What is Wrong with Economic Theory. *Quarterly Journal of Economics* 89 (3): 347–357.

Kaul, Tara. 2014. Household Responses to Food Subsidies: Evidence from India. Unpublished manuscript, University of Maryland, College Park.

Kuznets, Simon. 1968. *Toward a Theory of Economic Growth*. New York: Norton.

Lall, Sanjaya. 1992. Technological Capabilities and Industrialisation. *World Development* 20 (2): 165–186.

———. 2001. *Competitiveness, Technology and Skills*. Cheltenham: Edward Elgar.

Lauder, Hugh, Phillip Brown, Jo-Anne Dillabough, and A.H. Halsey, eds. 2006. *Education, Globalization, and Social Change*. Oxford: Oxford University Press.

Lee, Sangheon, Deirdre McCann, and Jon C. Messenger. 2007. *Working Time Around the World: Trends in Working Hours, Laws and Policies in a Global Comparative Perspective*. Abingdon: Routledge.

Lin, Justin Yifu. 2011. New Structural Economics: A Framework for Rethinking Development. *World Bank Research Observer* 26 (2): 193–221.

———. 2012. *New Structural Economics: A Framework for Rethinking Development and Policy*. Washington, DC: World Bank.

Lin, Justin, and Ha-Joon Chang. 2009. Should Industrial Policy in Developing Countries Conform to Comparative Advantage or Defy it? A Debate Between Justin Lin and Ha-Joon Chang. *Development Policy Review* 27 (5): 483–502.

Lipton, Michael, and Martin Ravallion. 1993. Poverty and Policy. Policy Research Working Paper 1130, World Bank, Washington, DC.

McCord, Anna. 2012. Skills Development as Part of Social Protection Programmes. Background Paper Prepared for the *Education for All Global Monitoring Report 2012: Youth and Skills; Putting Education to Work*, UNESCO, Paris.

McDermott, Ann K. 1992. Targeting Cereals Subsidies: Case Studies of Morocco, Algeria, Egypt, and Tunisia. CMR Working Paper 7, USAID, Washington, DC.

McIntyre, Diane, Michael Thiede, Göran Dahlgren, and Margaret Whitehead. 2006. What Are the Economic Consequences for Households of Illness and of Paying for Healthcare in Low- and Middle-Income Country Contexts? *Social Science and Medicine* 62 (4): 858–865.

Messenger, Jon C., and Paul Wallot. 2015. The Diversity of "Marginal" Part-Time Employment. INWORK Policy Brief 7, International Labour Office, Geneva.

Mincer, Jacob. 1995. Economic Development, Growth of Human Capital, and the Dynamics of the Wage Structure. Department of Economics Discussion Paper 744, Columbia University, New York.

Morel, Nathalie, and Joakim Palme. 2012. Financing the Welfare State and the Politics of Taxation. In *The Routledge Handbook of the Welfare State*, ed. Bent Greve, 401–409. Abingdon: Routledge.

Nübler, Irmgard. 2011. Promoting Catching-Up Growth and Productive Transformation in LDCs: A New Approach. In *Growth, Employment and Decent Work in the Least Developed Countries: Report of the ILO for the Fourth UN Conference on the Least Developed Countries*, 61–74. Geneva: International Labour Office.

Nunn, Nathan, and Daniel Trefler. 2010. The Structure of Tariffs and Long-Term Growth. *American Economic Journal: Macroeconomics* 2 (4): 158–194.

Odhiambo, Walter, and Damiano Kulundu Manda. 2003. Urban Poverty and Labour Force Participation in Kenya. Paper presented at the World Bank Urban Research Symposium, Washington, DC, December 15–17.

OECD (Organisation for Economic Co-operation and Development). 2009a. In-Work Poverty: What Can Governments Do? Policy Brief, September, OECD, Paris.

———. 2009b. Is Work the Best Antidote to Poverty? In *Employment Outlook 2009: Tackling the Jobs Crisis*, 165–210. Paris: OECD.

Ortiz, Isabel, Matthew Cummins, and Kalaivani Karunanethy. 2015. Fiscal Space for Social Protection: Options to Expand Social Investments in 187 Countries. Extension of Social Security Working Paper 48, International Labour Office, Geneva.

Park, Se-Hark, and Kenneth S. Chan. 1989. A Cross-Country Input-Output Analysis of Intersectoral Relationships Between Manufacturing and Services and Their Employment Implications. *World Development* 17 (2): 199–212.

Prebisch, Raúl. 1962. The Economic Development of Latin America and its Principal Problems. *Economic Bulletin for Latin America* 7 (1): 1–22. Originally published as *The Economic Development of Latin America and its Principal Problems*. New York: United Nations, Department of Economic Affairs, 1950.

Ray, Kathryn, Paul Sissons, Katy Jones, and Sandra Vegeris. 2014. Employment, Pay and Poverty: Evidence and Policy Review. Joseph Rowntree Foundation, York.

Rodrik, Dani. 2010. Diagnostics Before Prescription. *Journal of Economic Perspectives* 24 (3): 33–44.

Romer, Paul. 1990. Human Capital and Growth: Theory and Evidence. *Carnegie-Rochester Conference Series on Public Policy* 32 (1): 251–286.

Rosenberg, Nathan. 1963. Technological Change in the Machine Tool Industry, 1840–1910. *Journal of Economic History* 23 (4): 414–443.

———. 1982. *Inside the Black Box: Technology and Economics*. Cambridge: Cambridge University Press.

Rosenstein-Rodan, P.N. 1943. Problems of Industrialisation of Eastern and South-Eastern Europe. *Economic Journal* 53 (210/11): 202–211.

Rowthorn, Robert E., and J.R. Wells. 1987. *De-Industrialization and Foreign Trade*. Cambridge: Cambridge University Press.

Schmitt, Valerie, and Loveleen De. 2013. *Social Protection Assessment Based National Dialogue: A Good Practices Guide; Approaches and Tools Developed in East and South-East Asia from 2011 to 2013*. Bangkok: International Labour Office, Regional Office.

Schumpeter, Joseph A. 1934. *The Theory of Economic Development: An Inquiry into Profits, Capital, Credit, Interest, and the Business Cycle*. Cambridge, MA: Harvard University Press.

Scitovsky, Tibor. 1954. Two Concepts of External Economies. *Journal of Political Economy* 62 (2): 143–151.

Sdralevich, Carlo, Randa Sab, Younes Zouhar, and Giorgia Albertin. 2014. Subsidy Reform in the Middle East and North Africa: Recent Progress and Challenges Ahead. Middle East and Central Asia Departmental Paper 14/3, International Monetary Fund, Washington, DC.

Singer, Hans W. 1950. The Distribution of Gains Between Investing and Borrowing Countries. *American Economic Review* 40 (2): 473–485.

Stiglitz, Joseph E. 1996. Some Lessons from the East Asian Miracle. *World Bank Research Observer* 11 (2): 151–177.

———. 2003. *Globalisation and Its Discontents*. New York: Norton.

Tassey, Gregory. 2010. Rationales and Mechanisms for Revitalizing US Manufacturing R&D Strategies. *Journal of Technology Transfer* 35 (3): 283–333.

Thirlwall, A.P. 1983. A Plain Man's Guide to Kaldor's Growth Laws. *Journal of Post Keynesian Economics* 5 (3): 345–358.

Wade, Robert. 2003. *Governing the Market: Economic Theory and the Role of Government in East Asian Industrialization*. Princeton: Princeton University Press.

Wagstaff, Adam. 2002. Poverty and Health Sector Inequalities. *Bulletin of the World Health Organisation* 80 (2): 97–105.

World Bank. 2010. Egypt's Food Subsidies: Benefit Incidence and Leakages. Unpublished Manuscript, World Bank, Washington, DC.

Young, Allyn A. 1928. Increasing Returns and Economic Progress. *Economic Journal* 38 (152): 527–542.

6

Policy for Jobs: Reducing Informality

6.1 Introduction

The first empirical part of this book observes that to explain differences in per capita incomes between developing countries (DCs)—between least developed countries (LDCs), lower- and middle-income countries (LMICs), and emerging economies (EEs)—and their catch-up to advanced economies (AEs), what matters is not just the quantum of change, but the quality and composition of the change. This generalisation is based on three empirical regularities, on growth, jobs, and the macro drivers of growth and jobs. Each empirical regularity from the first part of the book is used in symmetry to infer policy in the second part of the book.

The first empirical regularity on growth observes that catch-up in per capita incomes for DCs is determined less by the rate of gross domestic product (GDP) growth and more by the composition of that growth. The development of manufacturing explains long-run movement up the per capita income ladder, with LDCs stuck for the past third of a century with single-digit manufacturing shares in GDP, LMICs in the mid-twenties, and EEs in the mid-thirties.

This gives one caveat on growth to derive policy in Chap. 5, that it should be based on productive transformation. However, the chapter noted that this explains growth of average per capita incomes in a country. Important as that is, it does not explain growth of the distribution of incomes, how different income groups have fared in the country over time. And the first-order normative imperative was argued to be an explanation for the differences in growth of incomes between the poor and the non-poor. Which put a second caveat on growth policy—that it be poverty-reducing and hence more inclusive.

This allowed the first policy chapter, on growth (Chap. 4), to infer policy on inclusion and productive transformation. Poverty was seen to be determined very strongly by a demographic drag, vulnerability in jobs, and productive transformation. The demographic drag inferred a strong role for transfer incomes, from the non-poor to the poor. The vulnerability in jobs inferred the need for enhancing labour incomes, through an increase in employment and job quality. Job quality was tagged to be closely linked to informality, which this chapter on jobs now picks up on empirically. Productive transformation was also seen to be poverty-reducing, leading back to policy needs for this.

The second empirical regularity on jobs observes that catch-up in per capita incomes for DCs is determined less by the quantum of employment growth because of the phenomena of the working poor. The poor, comprising large parts of the labour force, are virtually uncovered by any significant social protection. Hence, they cannot afford not to work. So those that cannot find formal, or decent jobs, are forced to accept work in less formal, less decent jobs, which can be onerous and arduous in terms of working conditions, less productive, less remunerative, and certainly less covered and monitored by rights. Then, catch-up in terms of the metrics of per capita incomes and employment is determined less by employment growth and more by job quality. Success and distress in the labour market is indicated less by job growth and more by job quality. Indeed, the finding is that key metrics of job quality, such as vulnerability, and the working poor climb up the per capita income ladder, their shares in employment improving from LDCs, further for LMICs, and farthest for EEs.

It was also observed that there was evidence of a two-way relationship between job quality and per capita incomes. Job quality was not just a derivative of moving up the income ladder for DCs, as a sort of trickle-down function of higher-income DCs being able to afford better jobs. Indeed, the improvement of job quality through reduction in vulnerability, with more waged employment, was seen to be strongly associated with increases in productivity and per capita incomes. Hence structural change results in the simultaneous movement of workers from lower- to higher-productivity sectors, and from more vulnerable self-employment to less vulnerable waged employment.

These empirical findings allow this policy chapter on jobs to focus on this one strategic variable of improving job quality. That is, the compulsion of the poor, unable to find formal regulated employment, to accept informal, less or unregulated jobs, arduous and less productive jobs with lower remuneration. Job quality and productivity weakens with lack of regulation, in going from formality to informality. Formalisation then becomes a necessary condition for improving job quality and productivity.

This chapter argues that formalisation policy should be based on registration of workers, as well as registration of enterprises. Registration of workers allows entitlements to rights that govern working conditions and remuneration through minimum wages. A more open question is how entitlement to rights increases productivity. The observation from the empirical chapter on jobs (Chap. 3) is that less vulnerable, waged jobs have higher productivity. This policy chapter on jobs finds evidence for the broader generalisation that formality through registration and entitlement to rights raises productivity. The data is weak, but the best available so far. The rationale for this increase in productivity based on enhanced entitlements comes from two strands of literature, higher nutrition affording higher effort and productivity, and higher incentives to retain a higher part of the product pushing up effort and productivity again.

Finally, the third empirical regularity observed in the macro drivers of growth and employment in Chap. 4 was that catch-up in per capita incomes is determined not just by the quantum of investment but also by the composition of this investment. So, investment in physical capital is as important as investment in human capital. This implies macro policy on both forms of investment as seen ahead in Chap. 7. It also comes full circle, linking the policy need for investment in human capital and knowledge-based capital imperative for poverty reduction and productive transformation inferred in Chap. 5, with the requirements to raise productivity argued in the present chapter and with evidence of the impact of such investment on technical change and catch-up seen in Chap. 7.

6.2 The Emerging Complexity and Significance of Informality in DCs

The initial view of informality, shaped by the International Labour Organization's (ILO) report on Kenya, was of a simple dualism in the labour market (ILO 1972). Weak GDP growth led to weak growth in formal sector employment that was insufficient to absorb the faster rate of population growth, giving rise to employment in a residual informal sector. The informal sector was considered a subsistence sector, unrelated to the formal sector. Informal employment acted as the lowest safety net, and was seen as a temporary phase with higher GDP growth in the long run providing sufficient formal employment to match demographic growth.

This initial concept of informality viewed it as a homogenous sector comprising refuge labour seeking informal employment as a last resort. This conceptual homogeneity of the informal sector was broken up by De Soto (1989) and the Legalist school in the 1980s and 1990s, arguing that it comprised not just refuge labour, but what we can term here, 'refuge capital'. Microenterprises chose to be informal to avoid the transaction costs of registration and formalising.

The strict dualist segregation of the formal sector having no links with the informal sector was also broken up by the Voluntarist school of Maloney (2004) and the Structuralist school of Portes et al. (1989). They argued that since microenterprises could reduce their costs of production by avoiding registration and taxation, larger capitalist firms in the formal sector sought to reduce their own production costs by subcontracting to these informal microenterprises, connecting the formal and informal sectors through supply chains.

This differentiation of informality justifies our characterising it here as part refuge labour, and part refuge capital. Indeed, the definition of informality adopted by the 17th International Conference of Labour Statisticians in 2003 (see ILO 2004) is in keeping with this notion when it uses three operational criteria:

- Informal employment without legal protection
- Informal employment without social protection
- Informal employment both inside the informal sector and outside it as well

So, informality is defined as all employment relationships that are not subject to national labour legislation, income taxation, social protection, or entitlement to certain benefits like sick leave, maternity leave, severance pay, and dismissal without notice.

Table 6.1 illustrates the complexity of the components of informality as set out by the first ILO (2011, 2013) estimation exercise. The usual decomposition of employment status is into own-account workers, employers, contributing family workers, waged employees, and members of production cooperatives (often left out because of its low numbers). Each of these forms of employment can be formal and informal, except contributing family workers who are, by definition, informal. But further, these forms of employment can now be envisaged to be in three kinds of production units, which are formal enterprises, informal enterprises and households. This gives a three-by-nine matrix. Informal employment then comes to comprise:

- Informal contributing family workers in both formal and informal enterprises, by definition
- Informal own-account workers, reckoned to be in informal enterprises and household production units
- Informal waged employees in formal and informal enterprises and household production units
- Informal members of production cooperatives

Based on this careful ILO methodology, stipulated as yet for only non-agricultural employment, Table 6.1 estimates informality for LDCs,

Table 6.1 Average share of informal employment in total non-agricultural employment

Production units	Own-account workers Informal	Own-account workers Formal	Employers Informal	Employers Formal	Contributing family workers Informal	Employees Informal	Employees Formal	Members of production cooperatives Informal	Members of production cooperatives Formal
LDCs, jobs by status in employment (% in non-agricultural employment)									
Formal sector enterprises					1.68	10.75			
Informal sector enterprises	36.18		0.44		7.70	11.08	3.92	4.55	
Households	0.00					2.17			
LMICs, jobs by status in employment (% in non-agricultural employment)									
Formal sector enterprises					0.25	12.79			
Informal sector enterprises	29.45		1.08		7.04	25.78	2.26	0.00	
Households	0.59					2.00			
EEs, jobs by status in employment (% in non-agricultural employment)									
Formal sector enterprises					0.50	13.71			
Informal sector enterprises	17.60		1.57		1.74	5.69	1.72	0.00	
Households	0.02					2.03			
Overall average, jobs by status in employment (% in non-agricultural employment)									
Formal sector enterprises					0.41	13.33			
Informal sector enterprises	22.36		1.37		3.84	13.50	1.95	0.04	
Households	0.24					2.02			

Note: *EE* emerging economy, *LDC* least developed country, *LMIC* lower- or middle-income country
Source: Author's estimations at the ILO, based on data from ILO, *Statistical Update on Employment in the Informal Economy* (Geneva: International Labour Office, 2011); and ILO, *Measuring Informality: A Statistical Manual on the Informal Sector and Informal Employment* (Geneva: International Labour Office, 2013)

Table 6.2 Informal employment as a percentage share of total non-agricultural employment, by country (ILO estimates)

Country	Informal employment	Formal employment
LDCs		
Lesotho	34.9	65.1
Liberia	60.0	40.0
Madagascar	73.6	26.4
Mali	81.8	18.2
Tanzania	76.2	23.8
Uganda	69.4	30.6
Zambia	69.5	30.5
Average	74.5	25.5
LMICs		
Armenia	19.8	80.2
Bolivia	75.1	24.9
El Salvador	66.4	33.6
Honduras	73.9	26.1
India	83.6	16.4
Indonesia	72.5	27.5
Moldova	15.9	84.1
Nicaragua	65.7	34.3
Pakistan	78.4	21.6
Paraguay	70.7	29.3
Philippines	70.0	30.0
Sri Lanka	62.1	37.9
Vietnam	68.2	31.8
West Bank and Gaza	57.1	42.9
Average	79.0	21.0
EEs		
Argentina	49.7	50.3
Brazil	42.2	57.8
China	32.6	67.4
Colombia	59.6	40.4
Costa Rica	43.8	56.2
Dominican Republic	48.5	51.5
Ecuador	60.9	39.1
Macedonia FYR	12.6	87.4
Mexico	53.7	46.3
Panama	43.8	56.2
Peru	69.9	30.1
Serbia	6.1	93.9
South Africa	32.7	67.3

(continued)

Table 6.2 (continued)

Country	Informal employment	Formal employment
Uruguay	39.8	60.2
Venezuela	47.8	52.2
Average	42.9	57.1
DCs, overall average	57.1	42.9

Note: *DC* developing country, *EE* emerging economy, *LDC* least developed country, *LMIC* lower- or middle-income country

Source: Author's estimations at the ILO, based on data from ILO, *Statistical Update on Employment in the Informal Economy* (Geneva: International Labour Office, 2011); and ILO, *Measuring Informality: A Statistical Manual on the Informal Sector and Informal Employment* (Geneva: International Labour Office, 2013)

LMICs, EEs, and an overall average for DCs. Table 6.2 also gives the country estimates for informality among LDCs, LMICs, and EEs, and estimates for informal employment into a surprisingly significant average share of non-agricultural employment. For the sample of 36 countries for which this estimation could be made, the average of the informal employment share for DCs comes out as 57 percent. The share of informal employment is very high for LDCs at 75 percent and LMICs at 79 percent, and much lower for EEs at 43 percent.

Table 6.3 gives a parallel estimate of informal employment as share of non-agricultural employment, made by Jütting and de Laiglesia (2009). This estimate is for a slightly earlier period, prior to 2000, whereas the ILO dataset is for the period 2004–10. Assuming some comparability between the two, given slow change in informality over time, both estimates give the same average share of informal employment of between 54 and 55 percent. The ILO estimate is significantly higher for eight countries out of the common sample of 23, and significantly lower for five countries. Given these two independent estimates of informal employment, both show that informality is significant, only falling below 20 percent of non-agricultural employment for just Russia, Serbia, Armenia, Macedonia, and Moldova, in the sample. Otherwise it ranges between one-third for China and 95 percent for Chad in the sample.

Therefore, of major concern is the abiding significance of informal employment as a share of non-agricultural employment across DCs. If there is a single strategic policy priority, it should be to improve the job quality of this majority of workers, whose working conditions can be considered a priori, *definitionally, to be much weaker than for formal workers.*

Table 6.3 Informal employment as a percentage share of total non-agricultural employment, by country (ILO and OECD estimates)

Country	OECD estimates	ILO estimates (2004–10)	Difference in estimates
Algeria		41.3	
Argentina	53.3	49.7	3.6
Armenia		19.8	
Bolivia[a]	63.5	75.1	−11.6
Brazil	51.1	42.2	8.9
Chad	95.2		
China		32.6	
Colombia[a]	38.4	59.6	−21.2
Costa Rica[a]	44.3	43.8	0.5
Dominican Republic[a]	47.6	48.5	−0.9
Ecuador	74.9	60.9	14
Egypt	45.9		
El Salvador[a]	56.6	66.4	−9.8
Guinea	86.7		
Haiti	92.6		
Honduras[a]	58.2	73.9	−15.7
India[a]	83.4	83.6	−0.2
Indonesia[a]	77.9	72.5	5.4
Iran	48.8		
Kenya	71.6		
Kyrgyzstan	44.4		
Lebanon	51.8		
Macedonia FYR		12.6	
Mali	81.8	81.8	0
Mexico	50.1	53.7	−3.6
Moldova	21.5	15.9	5.6
Morocco	67.1		
Nicaragua		65.7	
Pakistan[a]	64.6	78.4	−13.8
Panama	49.4	43.8	5.6
Paraguay[a]	65.5	70.7	−5.2
Peru	67.9	69.9	−2
The Philippines[a]	72	70	2
Romania	22		
Russia	8.6		
Serbia		6.1	
South Africa	50.6	32.7	17.9
Sri Lanka		62.1	
Syria	30.7		

(continued)

Table 6.3 (continued)

Country	OECD estimates	ILO estimates (2004–10)	Difference in estimates
Thailand	51.5		
Tunisia	35		
Turkey	33.2		
Uruguay		39.8	
Venezuela	49.4	47.8	1.6
Vietnam		68.2	
West Bank and Gaza	43.4	57.1	−13.7
Yemen	51.1		
Zambia[a]	58.3	69.5	−11.2
Average	55.4	53.6	1.8

Note: [a]OECD estimates for these countries were taken before 2000, whereas the ILO estimates were taken in 2004–10, depending on the year for which the data was available

Source: Author's estimations, based on data from Johannes P. Jütting and Juan R. de Laiglesia, eds. *Is Informal Normal? Towards More and Better Jobs in Developing Countries* (Paris: OECD Development Centre, 2009)

6.3 Registration of Informal Workers as Well as Informal Enterprises as a Strategic Policy Benefitting the Bulk of Informal Workers

Then given the observed significance of informal employment, and its definitionally associated lack of rights, conditions of work, and social protection, registration of informal employment becomes a key strategic policy for catch-up in the labour market. And given the low levels of productivity associated with vulnerable forms of employment that inhabit informality, registration should also lead to catch-up in productivity and per capita incomes, as seen ahead. However, the first question that arises is how to register informal employment. This can be done through two channels, registering enterprises and registering workers themselves. There are arguments for doing both.

There is an argument for registering enterprises.

The argument for registering enterprises is twofold. Formalisation would bring enterprises into the tax net and raise public revenues. And formalisation of enterprises would also formalise the workers employed. The first argument certainly holds, but the second need not be a sufficient condition to formalise all the workers employed by formalised enterprises.

The first argument can be seen from the share of firms formally registered when they began operations in the country—estimates based on the World Bank's Enterprise Survey for 2009 of more than 130,000 firms in 130 countries.[1] Of currently registered firms, 88 percent on average were already registered when they began operations. The lowest percentage was just over half for Malaysia, while a number of countries had near full registration.

What these estimates miss out is calculating the number and share of unregistered firms as comparators. But they do show the importance of registration—that a significant proportion of unregistered firms can be observed to have registered over time. On average, 20 percent of currently registered firms began operations without registration, but have since felt the need to register. So, policy can be observed to have worked, to have brought a fifth of firms into the tax net and raised some revenues.

But there is also evidence that registering firms need not be a sufficient condition to register their workers. Hence policy should have a dual focus on also registering informal workers themselves.

The formal registration of enterprises, however, need not imply a compulsion to formally register all their workers. Because the decomposition of estimates made for informal employment in non-agriculture shows a significant share of informal employment in formal enterprises.

Table 6.1 shows that the bulk of informal workers are waged employees. For DCs, the average informal employment share is 57 percent, comprised largely of employees with 31 percentage points, followed by own-account workers with 23 percentage points, and contributing family labour with 4 percentage points. So, the registration of unregistered waged employees would stand to benefit more than half the informal employment in non-agriculture.

It would also be imperative to register informal waged workers themselves rather than just registering their enterprises. Table 6.1 shows that, for DCs, the share of informal waged workers in informal enterprises at

13 percent of non-agricultural employment was as high as the share of informal waged workers in formal enterprises also at 13 percent. So clearly while registration of informal enterprises is important and necessary, it is not a sufficient policy to cover all informal workers. Half of all waged employees in informality in the formal enterprises would be left uncovered unless the workers themselves were registered. Formalising informal enterprises can clearly resist formalising all their workers as the evidence shows.

6.4 Assessing the Impact of Registering Informal Workers

There is evidence that registration of workers has the potential to significantly improve (a) rights, (b) social protection, (c) productivity and remuneration, and (d) poverty. There is also evidence that these four dimensions of job quality move together. The direction of causality seems to favour the argument that improvement of rights and social protection, through registration of workers, has great potential to also leverage gains in productivity, remuneration, and hence also poverty. There are three strands of literature and observations that support this direction of causality. First, registration of waged workers brings them into the purview of national legislation on rights, wages, and social floors. And this is by no means a definitional argument. Second, that registration of self-employed workers strengthens their access to rights and enhances their entitlement to assets and output, which increases the incentive to raise inputs and outputs—raising productivity and remuneration. Third, enhanced incomes and nutrition further increase productivity and incomes in a virtuous, but not unending, spiral.

Registration of informal waged workers brings them into the purview of national legislation on rights, wages, and social floors.

Informal waged workers by definition have weaker recourse to rights and social floors, since they are not registered by the enterprise they work for, nor are they registered with a social protection program, which is often the same thing as being registered with the enterprise. Registration of waged workers brings them into the purview of national legislation on rights, wages, and social floors. However, the act of registration should not be seen as a definitional enhancement of their recourse to labour legislation and social floors. There must be evidence that the formalisation of informal waged workers is observed to enhance their rights, remuneration, and welfare.

The rights gap in the informal economy is especially serious with respect to freedom of association, the right to organise, and to bargain collectively (Trebilcock 2005; ILO 2002). There is a systematic denial of the right to organise to certain groups of workers even by countries that have ratified conventions that give these rights (ILO Convention Numbers 87 and 98). This lack of representation and voice features strongly for workers in the informal economy, and is the most broadly manifest in lower wages compared to formal employment. It is also manifest in a more extreme form in onerous working conditions and straight exploitation, through forced labour, including debt bondage and trafficking, child labour including hidden and more hazardous forms of it, and discrimination, especially against women, workers with disabilities, and migrants.

There is well-researched, if scattered, micro-level country evidence of improvement in the broader manifestation of the rights gap, through improvement of wages by formalisation of employment, particularly for Latin America where there has been a concerted drive towards formalisation of employment in the last decade or so. Argentina's increase in wage inequality over the 1990s has been reversed in the 2000s, in part ascribed to a process of labour formalisation. An Oaxaca-Blinder decomposition of income allows Beccaria et al. (2014) to distinguish between a returns effect and a redistributive effect, both showing significance. Maurizio (2015) extends the study to Brazil, finding that in parallel to Argentina's reversal of wage inequality in the 2000s, Brazil's formalisation of labour has reached all categories of workers, been accompanied by real minimum wage increases, and so had an equalising effect. A collaborative study by ECLAC and ILO (2014) extends these results to nine countries in the region. Between 2009 and 2013, the share of formal employment increased in these countries, accompanied by a large reduction in earnings inequality. Increased formality resulting from the creation of new jobs and the formalisation of informal jobs has particularly benefitted wage earners, workers with intermediate levels of education, and women.

There is also evidence from a World Institute for Development Economics Research micro study for Vietnam over 2005–13, which shows increased real wages, and an increased share of wages in value added, for firms that shift out of the informal economy (see Boly 2015).

Equally meticulous micro-level evidence comes showing improvement in contractual conditions for formalised workers, from Vietnam and Brazil. In Vietnam, a comparison between formal and informal firms shows that registration of firms is seen to lead to a decrease in the use of casual labour (Rand and Torm 2012). In Brazil, Fajnzylber et al. (2011) show that the act of becoming fully registered leads to firms using more contract-based labour with formal guarantees, rather than more casual employment relationships based on personal and social relations.

A more general improvement in working conditions was also observed in formalising small and medium manufacturing enterprises in Vietnam, spurred by their increased visibility (Rand and Torm 2012).

Registration of self-employed workers strengthens their access to rights, enhances entitlements to assets and output, which increases their incentives to raise inputs and outputs—raising productivity and remuneration.

Estimates of productivity in the informal economy reckon it to be much lower than productivity in the formal economy. Table 6.4 gives the instances of four economies for which this comparison could be made. Informal economy productivity ranged from just 27 percent of formal economy productivity in Kyrgyzstan to 83 percent in Peru.

Table 6.4 Productivity ratios

Country	Share of informal sector employment	Share of informal sector GDP	Year 1	Year 2	Productivity ratio (%)
Kyrgyzstan	70.4	38.8	2011	2007	27
Colombia	60.8	33.5	2011	2007	32
Turkey	41.5	29.1	2011	2007	58
Peru	58.3	53.7	2011	2007	83

Note: *GDP* gross domestic product
Source: Author's estimations at the ILO, based on data from ILOSTAT

La Porta and Shleifer (2008) using a log scale index on the World Bank Enterprise Survey found that informal enterprises have a productivity of 7.6, some 83 percent, compared to small formal enterprises with 9.1, medium formal enterprises with 9.4, and big formal enterprises with 9.7.

A major intended impact of formalisation is to raise productivity and incomes for the individual and the economy. While formalising waged employment will raise the productivity of those informal waged workers, who comprise 31 percentage points of total informal employment of 57 percent of non-farm employment in DCs (Table 6.1). That still leaves the informal self-employed comprising another 23 percentage points of the total non-farm informal employment, whose productivity needs to be raised.

The literature is quite clear that formal firms have higher productivity, compared to informal firms, largely based on their access to physical capital, or formal sector credit (see La Porta and Shleifer 2008). In fact, employees across formal and informal sector firms are considered broadly homogenous in terms of human capital. So, it is the physical capital of the owners and managers that distinguishes between formal and informal firms, driving the quality of their inputs and access to finance. Hence typically a Mexican study shows that one Peso invested in an informal firm earns a half of what it would in a formal firm (Busso et al. 2012).

The question then is that since the productivity of formal firms is empirically observed to be significantly higher than for informal firms, the productivity of both waged workers comprising 56 percent of informal employment and self-employed workers comprising the other 44 percent of informal employment should increase with their formalisation. The near equal shares of both waged and self-employed workers would imply that the average productivity is based evenly on both. The mechanism for the increase in productivity needs to be elaborated, more so for the self-employed.

The productivity of waged workers would rise with their registration and that of their firms. The access of the registered firm to more human and physical capital would raise the capital-labour ratio, inputs and outputs, to increase the productivity of the newly registered firm and its workers.

The question then is, what factors would raise the productivity of a newly registered self-employed worker?

Registration of the own-account workers (the self-employed) and contributing family workers (the unpaid) can yield great benefits for them in the medium to longer term. Registration of self-account workers and contributing family workers will, first, establish them as legal entities with entitlements. These entitlements can have a large range, from defining clearer ownership of working capital and non-land assets (as opposed to entitlements to owned property and land which presumably exists), entitlements to product and income produced, entitlements to participate in public and private programs for social protection, both contributory and non-contributory, entitlements to participate in other public welfare programs, and entitlements to workers' rights extended to self-employment,

This impact of property rights and entitlements echoes De Soto's (2000) seminal claim that strong and clear property rights, formalised rather than informal, are necessary for economic efficiency and for more inclusive growth with the poor. Unreported, unrecorded economic activity in the informal sector creates a titling void, depriving it of access to a formal system that gives legal ownership to property. The lack of legal ownership restricts access to formal credit markets. It also restricts access to legal recourse in the case of disputes, not just on property, but on the goods and services produced.

Hence registration of the self-employed, comprising own-account workers and contributing family workers, can be viewed as the thin edge of the wedge, to leverage their entitlements to property and to the income produced, to participate in public programs, and to have access to public goods and services. This argument is amply demonstrated in agriculture, where clear entitlements to land and tenancy rights, and its products, creates the incentive to increase investment and output, raising productivity (Lawry et al. 2014). The case of China being the classic example, where post-1978, Deng Xiao Ping reforms gave communal peasants the right to the product of their plots under the Household Responsibility system, increasing their inputs and productivity. That is the single most important factor credited with the massive reduction in poverty in China (Mahmood et al. 2012).

Applied to the non-farm informal economy, the argument for entitlement through property rights has its critics, who basically aver that the institutions of informality provide a solidarity and support network (Cao 2012). This loss of support through formalisation may not be compensated by the gains from formalised property rights (van Elk et al. 2014). This criticism is partly misplaced, in that registration, entitlement, and property rights should not be denied to the informal economy, in principle, when the formal economy gains manifestly by them. The point however is taken that the policy for formalisation should ensure that the potential gains accrue, which is a question for the following section of this chapter, on what policies have been observed to work better, or worse.

Enhanced incomes and nutrition further increase productivity and incomes in a virtuous but not unending spiral.

Registration and formalisation of waged workers and enterprises is observed to enhance wages, and conditions of work like security of contracts and labour force participation that secure and increase income. Registration and formalisation of workers enhance productivity and incomes for both waged and self-employed workers. This has the potential to set off an upwards spiral of increased nutrition and reduced poverty, leading in turn to increased productivity and incomes.

Evidence of increased nutrition is provided by the reduction in the poverty rate because that is measured as the population's consumption of a required dietary allowance of 2250 calories per adult equivalent per day. The poverty line of US$1.90–2.00 prices the cost of buying this basket of goods in each country's local prices, made internationally comparable through a purchasing power parity index.

Table 6.5 shows that 50 percent of the variation in poverty across countries is explained by the variation in their shares of informal employment in total employment. The higher the share of informal employment, the higher the population falling under the poverty line. This result is pretty robust, since it weakens considerably if any part of formal employment, even in the informal sector, is considered, with the correlation dropping to a quarter or below.

Figure 6.1 estimates poverty rates in formal employment compared to informal employment and again finds that formality lowers poverty,

Table 6.5 Correlations with informality

Type of employment	Correlation between informal employment and...	
People in informal employment	Poverty US$1.90–2.00	0.49
	Poverty total < US$2.00	0.51
	Poverty total < US$4.00	0.51
	Productivity	−0.49
People in formal employment in informal sector	Poverty US$1.90–2.00	0.26
	Poverty total < US$2.00	0.17
	Poverty total < US$4.00	0.22
	Productivity	−0.22
People employed in the informal sector	Poverty US$1.90–2.00	0.62
	Poverty total < US$2.00	0.63
	Poverty total < US$4.00	0.65
	Productivity	−0.55
People in informal employment outside informal sector	Poverty US$1.90–2.00	−0.06
	Poverty total < US$2.00	−0.09
	Poverty total < US$4.00	−0.09
	Productivity	−0.12

Source: Author's estimations at the ILO, based on data from the ILO's Global Employment Trends and informality estimates for the years for which data is available

across LDCs, LMICs, and EEs. This also applies to total employment through a rare estimate made here, as well as the usual non-agricultural employment. Hence nutrition improves and poverty falls, with an increase in formal employment.

Further, this is not a one-off effect. There has long been both theory and evidence that improved nutrition raises labour input, and therefore productivity (see Leibenstein 1957; Myrdal 1968; Bliss and Stern 1978). While low nutrition reduces productivity. Indeed, Leibenstein even set a consumption floor on the wage, below which the wage could not fall, because of the level of nutrition that the wage could afford, would not permit any significant labour input. Therefore Mirrlees (1975) and Stiglitz (1976) both show that an increase in the wage/remuneration at low levels of nutrition and consumption will initially

Policy for Jobs: Reducing Informality   251

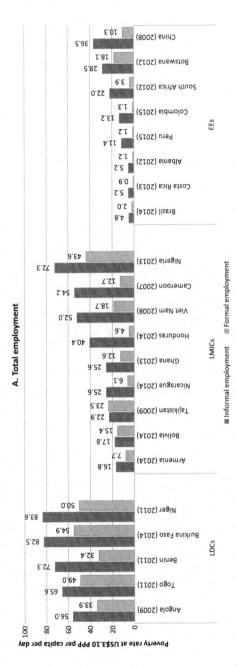

Fig. 6.1 Poverty rates among workers in informal and formal employment. (Note: *PPP* purchasing power parity. Extreme and moderate poverty = <$3.10 PPP per capita per day. Source: Calculations by Florence Bonnet at the ILO, based on national household survey data)

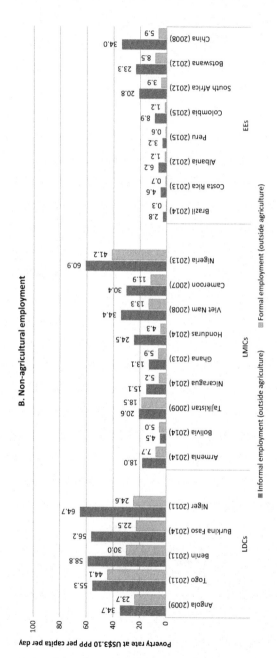

Fig. 6.1 (continued)

give a wage-productivity ratio increasing at an increasing rate. However, with higher levels of nutrition and consumption, this wage-productivity ratio will only increase at a declining rate.

So, registration and formalisation of employment can unleash a further dynamic, enhance productivity and incomes, raising consumption and nutrition, which enable further increases in productivity and therefore incomes. This upward spiral of productivity, consumption, and productivity again does end at higher levels of consumption.

The jump up in productivity, going from informality to formality, working through the three channels, of rights, entitlements, and nutrition, can be seen in Table 6.5. Productivity is inversely correlated to the share of informal employment in total employment. A half of the variation in productivity between countries is explained by the variation in their share of informal employment.

6.5 Policy to Register Informal Workers and Enterprises

So, registration of workers and enterprises emerges as a strategic policy to leverage better labour market outcomes, and catch-up in per capita incomes through higher productivity. Workers come under the purview of rights and social protection legislation and programs, both waged and potentially the self-employed. Waged workers benefit from gaining the key strengths of representation and collective bargaining, enabling their wages to rise. Labour force participation goes up, increasing employment incomes. Contractual conditions also improve, and with them, security of incomes.

Self-employed workers improve their productivity and incomes. This results from the registration and improvement in entitlements to property and outputs, which in turn raises the incentives to increase inputs, outputs, and productivity.

An additional channel that raises productivity and incomes is improved nutrition. The increased productivity and incomes through the formalisation effect afford higher consumption and nutrition, driving down poverty. The higher nutrition enables for a time higher labour inputs, outputs, and productivity.

Given these improved outcomes in labour markets and catch-up in per capita incomes, policy to register workers and enterprises becomes key.

Much of the policy experience that countries have has been for registering enterprises. Experience in registering workers has been limited to extension of health and other forms of social protection. However, there are some very recent innovative programs that bring uncovered workers into the purview of national legislation such as India's National Rural Employment Guarantee Act 2005 in the case of propping up the rural minimum wage. Along with Brazil's Bolsa Família and Mexico's Oportunidades, these are largely categorised as non-contributory social protection programs. While not strictly formalisation programs, they act to bring some of the benefits of formalisation to informal workers and their households. Their efficacy is examined in the next section.

The Efficacy of Policies to Register Enterprises

Policy to register enterprises can be put into two categories: price mechanisms and non-price logistical mechanisms.

Price Mechanisms

To recall the model of informality dubbed here as refuge capital, firms can seek to evade the perceived high transaction costs of formalisation, in terms of taxes due to the state, and compliance with national legislation on key workers' rights, including representation and collective bargaining, wages and dismissals, key working conditions like occupational safety and health and contributions to workers' social benefits. Call them (C).

The major benefits to firms from formalisation would be access to the formal credit market, largely taken to be cheaper than the informal credit market. Formalisation would also increase access to public goods and services. Call them (B).

In addition to these explicit benefits of formalisation, firms can also gain potential benefits, from improved entitlements to property and their product, which creates incentives for upscaling inputs, outputs, productivity, and incomes. Also lump them with (B).

But the important point to note is that while the costs of formalisation (C) are certain, the benefits (B) are not and have to be realised.

(i) The sine qua non mechanism of registering enterprises is through lowering the cost of registration, by a rate (ΔR). If firms use a strict cost-benefit analysis, then they will register to formalise only if this reduction in the nominal cost of registration, $\Delta R(R)$, is greater than the transaction costs, that is

$$\Delta R(R) \geq C$$

On the face of it, this is unlikely to be the case, leading only to a trickle from informality to formality (see, for instance, La Porta and Shleifer 2014). However, the global evidence presented above showed that some 20 percent of currently registered firms transited from informality to formality. Hence firms must be weighing the reduction in costs of registration plus the possibility of increased benefits against the transaction costs, that is

$$\Delta R(R) + B \geq C$$

Illustrative rules of the thumb are that the reduction in the cost of registration (ΔR) has to be at least 50 percent (see van Elk et al. 2014).

(ii) A more innovative mechanism, since the reduction in the registration fee $\Delta R(R)$ cannot be very large, because the registration fee R itself cannot be very large in comparison to the transaction costs (C), is to reduce these transaction costs, by a rate (ΔC). So, firms will now weigh the reduction in registration costs and increased benefits against reduced transaction costs, that is

$$\Delta R(R) + B \geq C - \Delta C(C), \text{ or}$$
$$\Delta R(R) + B \geq 1 - \Delta(C)$$

The reduction in transaction costs (ΔC) comes largely from reduction in state taxes, and reduction in employer contributions to social security.

The most prominent case study for this reduction in transaction costs is the case of the monotax called *Monotributo*, in Argentina. In 1998, the government introduced a simplified scheme for small taxpayers, comprising a single monthly tax, replacing income tax and value tax, and including social security and social work contributions (van Elk et al. 2014). Since its creation, the volume of registered taxpayers has increased continuously, going up from just over a half million to 2 million over this period. This has not only increased the formalisation of firms, but also increased the number of workers with health benefits and pension protection.

Brazil's SIMPLES program also relies on reduction of transaction costs to induce formalisation of enterprises (Fajnzylber et al. 2011). The program targets firms employing under five workers, and again simplifies and replaces a set of government taxes and social security contributions, with single monthly payment. It also reduced the amount to be paid, to 3–5 percent of gross revenues for microenterprises, and 5–7 percent for small firms. The reduction in the tax burden is estimated to be about 8 percent. An important feature is that this program has made the social security contribution independent of the amount of wage bill. Instead it is determined as a fixed percentage of total revenues, creating an incentive to increase employment, and to register and formalise existing unregistered workers.

SIMPLES is estimated to have a good impact on informality, with up to a 12 percent increase in licenses to operate, and a 7 percent increase in registration with the tax authorities.

A similar window to reduce transaction costs to induce formalisation of enterprises in Brazil, aims at allowing the self-employed to formalise. This Individual Microentrepreneur (MEI) program targets firms with one employee or less, and annual revenues of under US$36,000.[2] The program again has one fixed amount to be paid every month. But this is adjusted according to the minimum wage, and includes taxes and social security contributions. The MEI addresses 10 million informal entrepreneurs in Brazil, and over a three-year period from its inception in 2008 had managed to register 1.4 million workers.

A Colombian variant of this program to reduce transaction costs to induce formalisation gives a sunset clause after which the reduction gradually disappears at the end of six years.[3] Law 1429 also envisages periodic amnesties for companies that failed annual renewals in the past. This Law 1429 can be credited with a 10 percent increase in registration in the year after its inception in 2011. Cumulatively, some 232,000 small companies are estimated to have benefitted from the discounts to the trade register under this law. However, the sunset clause in the law has also been criticised for having only a temporary effect, rather than a long-run one.

If the Latin American experience has been a positive one in pointing to the efficacy of reducing transaction costs in inducing formalisation, the experience from Asia reinforces the same policy message, but with a negative argument. The Asian experiences of Vietnam, Sri Lanka, and Bangladesh have been not to rely on reducing transaction costs, with little resultant impact on informality and formalisation.

Panel data evidence from Vietnamese small and medium enterprises in manufacturing, shows the reluctance of many firms to formalise, because they perceive high recurrent costs associated with it (Rand and Torm 2012). The perception of the survey comparing formal and informal firms was that, informal firms did not just see formalisation as entailing the cost of registration (R), but also other costs of entitlement including occupational safety and health. So, there does not seem to have been any concerted policy to reduce the transaction costs of formalisation (C), with weak results in formalisation. Firms could perceive the benefits of formalisation (B), but the transaction costs (C) remained prohibitive.

Bangladesh attempted, similarly, a registration drive for businesses in information and communication technology, but based merely on enhancing the efficiency of the registration system (see Di Giorgio and Rahman 2013). So the drive probably reduced some costs of registration (ΔR), but did not reduce any transaction costs entailed by formalisation (C).

A randomised controlled trial showed the result of the drive to be essentially zero.

A similar experiment in Sri Lanka, which offered only information about the registration process, and cost reimbursement, some (ΔR), had no effect on the formalisation rate (see Bruhn and McKenzie 2013a). In fact, the study itself points to the need to provide further incentive payments, to spur formalisation, that is, (ΔC). It even estimated that a payment of approximately two months' profit would be sufficient to induce the firm to register.

Non-price Mechanisms

Given that price mechanisms have to reduce transaction costs substantively to induce incentives for both firms and the self-employed to register, the argument for non-price mechanisms weakens. But it has its adherents.

Bolivian data shows that formalisation of firms is affected by distance to the tax office (McKenzie and Sakho 2010). A Brazilian case study shows that formalisation is less successful in remote and less populous areas (see Bruhn and McKenzie 2013b). The MEI program in Brazil tries to overcome this by registration through a web portal, but other logistical requirements remain, like banking, loans transactions, and administrative invoices (Santiago 2011).

However, a specific outreach program to remote municipalities in Brazil's Minas Gerais state shows the ineffectiveness of such purely logistical programs, unaccompanied by significant cost reduction incentives (Bruhn and McKenzie 2013b). This program extended a one-stop shop, the Minas Facil Expresso office, with a reduction in registration fee (ΔR) to start-ups and expanding businesses in 822 remote municipalities in the state. A study found a statistically significant negative effect, with a decrease in registration and no significant changes in tax revenues. So, neither the logistical facilitation nor the reduction in registration fee were sufficient inducements for firms to formalise.

So if the reduction in logistical costs is (ΔL), then neither this plus the reduction in registration fee (ΔR) was sufficient to induce formalisation, without the reduction in transaction costs (ΔC) like tax liabilities. Then the criteria for formalisation of firms become:

$$(\Delta L) + (\Delta R) + B \geq C - \Delta C(C)$$

And reduction in transaction costs (ΔC) emerges as the key variable to induce formalisation of firms.

6.6 Policy to Register Informal Workers

Policy to register informal firms should in theory result in registration of all the workers employed by the firm. However, the estimates made in Table 6.1 showed as many informally employed workers in formal firms as in informal firms, with 13 percentage points each, out of total non-agricultural informal employment of 57 percent. Further, the self-employed comprised another 23 percentage points out of this informal employment of 57 percent.

So, a majority of the workers in informal employment, 13 percent plus 23 percent, making 36 percentage points out of total non-agricultural informal employment of 57 percent, have to be targeted individually. Policy has to focus not just on registering enterprises, but also the workers themselves.

Any significant policy to register workers directly has been to extend some form of social protection to them. Indeed, that metric of social protection coverage is the often used proxy for estimating informal employment in many countries.

Non-contributory social protection programs are on the rise, more so than contributory programs in DCs.

Contributory social protection and comprehensive coverage for health, pensions, and unemployment benefits, as in much of the AEs, can be the goal for DCs. But progress on it has been piecemeal on both counts: the contributory mechanism and the comprehensiveness of the programs.

The mechanism for financing social protection programs in the standard model upheld is contributory, with the employer, the worker, and the state each contributing. This standard model of contributory social protection is alive and well in the AEs as Fig. 6.2 shows. Coverage in these AEs has gone up from under 80 percent in 1990 to near universal by 2013. Contributory social protection has inched up too, from about 62 percent to 65 percent over this period. However, the larger increase in

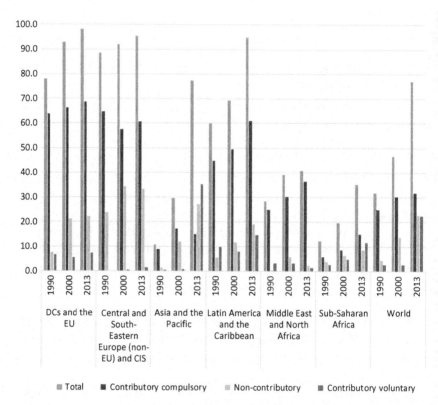

Fig. 6.2 Old-age pension and survivors' legal coverage, 1990–2013. (Note: Global estimates based on 178 countries in 2013, 173 countries in 1990 and 2000, weighted by the working-age population. Source: Calculations by Florence Bonnet at the ILO, based on data from ILO, *World Employment and Social Outlook 2015: The Changing Nature of Jobs* (Geneva: International Labour Office, 2015); data on legal and social protection coverage from the ILO Research Department, International Social Security Association, European Commission, United Nations, ILO Trends Unit (Trends Econometric Models), and national legislation and statistical offices)

coverage has come from non-contributory programs, which have shot up from under 5 percent in 1990 to over 20 percent by 2013.

This has also been the pattern, but much more pronounced in other regions, with contributory programs pushing up overall coverage, but non-contributory programs pushing up overall coverage much more. Indeed, in Asia and the Pacific, and in sub-Saharan Africa, non-contributory coverage has come to near equal and in Asia exceed contributory coverage. As a result, global coverage by 2013, of just under 80 percent, comprised contributory coverage of about 30 percent, non-contributory coverage of about 22 percent, and voluntary contributory coverage of another 22 percent.

Many of these non-contributory transfer (NCT) programs provide some of the key benefits and impact of formalisation.

The nature of the NCT programs is also notable. Comprehensive social protection programs cover key areas like health, pensions, and unemployment benefits. Coverage in these key areas requires not just the funding, but an institutional structure to reach the workers. In the formal economy, the institutional structure operates through the enterprise. In the informal economy, the enterprise being unregistered, the institutional structure cannot operate through it. It is confronted with unregistered and therefore unknown workers and households. NCT programs therefore must be more strategic in:

- Choosing their key areas, largely health and pensions, rather than unemployment benefits, when there may be no employment relationship for the self-employed, and no registration of contract for the informally employed.
- Choosing for outreach, either (i) self-selection or (ii) registration of the worker or the household
- Making a transfer to the worker or the household
- Bringing the worker or the household under the purview of specifically relevant pieces of national legislation on rights, welfare, and public programs.

As a result, these NCT programs have the effect of providing some of the benefits of formalisation as discussed in the first part of this chapter. They are not strict formalisation, but akin to it, in providing some of the key impact, and in challenging terrain very difficult to outreach with the standard model of formalisation and social protection.

There are a variety of such successful NCT programs, operating in DCs. Four have been chosen to illustrate briefly their strategic aim, impact, and social diversity in providing some of the benefits of formalisation in areas (a) to (d).

Supporting the Rural Minimum Wage in India: The Mahatma Gandhi National Rural Employment Guarantee Act

Workfare programs have a long history, and debate on whether provision of basic income should be a right, or earned through work. The Mahatma Gandhi National Rural Employment Guarantee Act (MNREGA) is the current and most unusual of the NCTs operating.[4] The program provided 100 days of work at the minimum wage to one adult member of a rural household applying for it. The program uses the labour provided for rural public infrastructure.

The program has a recurrent annual budget of about 0.5 percent of GDP. It was generating approximately 2.3 million days of employment in 2012/13. It was affecting close to 50 million households through these jobs.

The most important impact of the program is that, it is estimated to have increased the real wage income of the rural poor by about 20 percent in 2009/10 (Ghose 2012). As a result, the program has played a major role in propping up the rural wage floor, and reducing gender wage gaps (Borah and Bordoloi 2014). And rural poverty is estimated to have been reduced by 12–16 percentage points in that year.

The ingenuity of the program lies in its tackling the huge informal rural labour market in India. A standard formalisation program would have been daunted by the multiple challenge of outreach, of incentives to register workers and households, of monitoring their rural wages, and of mechanisms for enforcement and compliance.

MNREGA tackled these challenges adroitly. Incentives to register are tackled through self-selection. As are controlling program leakages, with only the poor accepting to work at the minimum wage, which deters leakages to richer workers and households. Bringing millions of rural workers and households into the purview of national legislation on the minimum wage, and when monitoring and enforcement would be near impossible with the standard model of formalisation. By large-scale hiring at the minimum wage, MNREGA sets a demonstration effect which has effectively propped up the rural minimum wage, bringing all rural workers into the purview of national legislation on it. The bargaining power of rural workers has been enhanced, a key feature of formalisation. Indeed, propping up the rural minimum is reckoned to have affected the urban age as well.

The program in effect formalises 50 million households a year.

Large-Scale Social Transfers to the Poor, Reversing Rising Income Inequality: Bolsa Família in Brazil

Two large DCs stood out as having the highest income inequality in the world, with Gini coefficients of over 0.6. These were Brazil and South Africa. Brazil reversed its high Gini at the turn of the decade 2010. This change in the secondary distribution of income has been strongly contributed to by its large-scale income transfer program, Bolsa Família. South Africa's Gini has continued to rise in the absence of any such effective and large-scale transfer programs.

Bolsa Família is a traditional conditional cash transfer (CCT) program. It provides households with per capita incomes below R$137 with a transfer varying between one-sixth and over 100 percent of this domestic poverty line (Wetzel 2013; Berg 2009). The condition is that the household's children attend school and health clinics. The program is reckoned to have reached 14 million households, and a population of 50 million, which is a quarter of the total population. The annual budget of the program comes to about 0.5 percent of GDP.

Ten years after the program's operation, extreme poverty is estimated to have been halved, from 9.7 percent of the population to 4.3 percent. The Gini coefficient is estimated to have dropped from 0.6 to 0.527. While Brazil is a big spender on social sectors, with 22 percent of GDP spent on education, health, social protection, and social security, this 0.5-percent-of-GDP Bolsa Família program is largely credited with having a greater impact on its reduction in poverty and inequality.

The ingenuity of Bolsa Família lies in its tackling the low incomes of a large informal, self-employed and employed population. Registration of this population would be daunting, especially with no incentives. Bringing the population into the purview of national legislation on education and health would again be difficult for lack of incentives. The program effects all three objectives of formalisation, raising incomes, registering households, and bringing them under the purview of national legislation on education and health.

The lack of an effective workfare program like MNREGA, or a transfer program like Bolsa Família, has meant that South Africa's Gini coefficient, already above 0.6, has continued to rise. The country's largest labour market intervention, the Expanded Public Works Program, its second five-year phase, has not met its objective of halving unemployment by 2014 (Meth 2011).

Raising Enrolment and Human Capital Among the Poor: Progresa/Oportunidades in Mexico

The CCT program, Progresa, earlier called Oportunidades, again transfers income to poor households, in return for their children attending school, health, and nutrition clinics (World Bank 2014; Behrman and Parker 2011). The program provides between half and three quarters of the minimum wage to households, predominantly women, and two-thirds rural. It reached close to 6 million households—a quarter of the country's population.

Progresa is credited with a third of the decrease in rural poverty, and much of the increase in enrolment.

A critical factor responsible for the success of the CCTs in Brazil and Mexico is that not only was the demand generated for more enrolment and health clinic attendance but also the supply of facilities and services matched. The CCT in Bolivia, with similar aims as Bolsa Família and Progresa, seems to have foundered in public provisioning of education and healthcare (McGuire 2013).

Conversely, South Africa's child support grant similarly aimed as Bolivia's CCT, at reducing the impact of poverty on school enrolment, appears to be doing well (Case et al. 2005). Longitudinal data shows take up by a third of all eligible-age children. The grant appears to be reaching the poorer households of the surveyed area. Children receiving the grant were significantly more likely to attend school than the equally poor control group. So, the grant appeared to be helping overcome the impact of poverty on enrolment.

Universalising Healthcare with NCTs: Thailand

This Universal Coverage Scheme (UCS) targeted the 30 percent of the uninsured population left uncovered by two earlier schemes (Yiengprugsawan et al. 2010). Initially the scheme had two types of payment, fee exemption and THB30 (about US$0.75) co-payment. Subsequently even the co-payment was abolished. The UCS registers members at a primary healthcare facility, for first access, except in emergencies, and acts as a gatekeeper for higher-level hospitals.

Empirical studies of illness expenditure show that the UCS substantially reduces the financial burden of healthcare among the poor, especially catastrophic medical payments that lead to impoverishment. The UCS has so boosted the use of primary healthcare facilities. As such, the scheme is seen to have reduced inequity in healthcare.

This NCT program targets the large poorer population unable to get standard health insurance. As such, it registers this population, giving them access to public health facilities. This provides a significant benefit for this informal population, effectively formalising them in healthcare.

6.7 Is This Dual Strategy for Formalisation the Way Forward for Improving Jobs, Incomes, and Catch-Up in DCs?

Job quality emerges as the primary metric for judging labour market outcomes. It is indicative of individual welfare, and is a driver of productivity and incomes at the micro level. At the macro level, better job quality, productivity, and incomes drive up consumption and aggregate domestic demand—which provides a useful balance with exogenous demand in driving growth.

With so much of development strategy riding on job quality, the boundary of informality in the labour market becomes critical, because it distinctly weakens job quality. And early estimates of informal employment, by the ILO and by this chapter, made for the non-agricultural sectors, show it to be vast, dominating the labour market. These estimates also show informal employment to be complex, occurring not just in unregistered informal enterprises, but equally in formal enterprises. And the largest share of informal employment is observed to be self-employment.

This empirical analysis has two important implications for jobs policy. One, that registration of workers and enterprises can provide strategic leverage in reducing informality. This brings enterprises and workers under the purview of national legislation, raising revenues, bargaining power, entitlements, wages, productivity, and access to public goods. Two, registration has to be of both workers and enterprises.

Policy experience shows that registration of enterprises is seen to hinge strongly on reducing transaction costs substantively, rather than just reducing registration fees and logistical costs of registration.

Policy experience of registering workers through a standard model of formalisation is extremely limited, given the challenges of outreach, especially to the self-employed. Here, however, NCT programs are seen to be quite effective. In registering workers, raising wages, bringing informal workers into the purview of national legislation, effecting transfers, scaling up the programs, and affecting significant portions of the target population. Indeed, these NCTs can be observed to have had an impact on macro outcomes like poverty and inequality. So, while these NCTs are not the standard forms of formalisation, they effectively have that impact.

Notes

1. Data available at http://www.enterprisesurveys.org
2. For more detail, see Santiago (2011); Neri and Fontes (2010); Brazil, Ministry of Social Welfare (2011); and van Elk et al. (2013).

3. For more detail, see Colombia, Confecámaras (2011) and Universidad Externado de Colombia (2011).
4. See www.mnrega.nic.in for more detail.

References

Beccaria, Luis, Roxana Maurizio, and Gustavo Vazquez. 2014. Recent Changes in Wage Inequality in Argentina: The Role of Labour Formalization and Other Factors. Unpublished manuscript, Universidad Nacional de General Sarmiento, Buenos Aires.

Behrman, Jere R., and Susan W. Parker. 2011. The Impact of the PROGRESA/Oportunidades Conditional Cash Transfer Program on Health and Related Outcomes for the Aging in Mexico. Working Paper 34, University of Pennsylvania, Population Aging Research Center, Philadelphia, PA.

Berg, Janine. 2009. Brazil Conditional Transfers as Response to the Crisis: The Bolsa Família Programme. *ILO Notes on the Crisis*, International Labour Office, Geneva.

Bliss, Christopher, and Nicholas Stern. 1978. Productivity, Wages and Nutrition. *Journal of Development Economics* 5: 331–362.

Boly, Amadou. 2015. On the Effects of Formalization on Taxes and Wages: Panel Evidence from Vietnam. Working Paper 42, United Nations University World Institute for Development Economics Research, Helsinki.

Borah, Kabita, and Rimjhim Bordoloi. 2014. MGNREGA and Its Impact on Daily Waged Women Workers: A Case Study of Sonitpur District of Assam. *IOSR Journal of Economics and Finance* 4 (4): 40–44.

Brazil. Ministry of Social Welfare. 2011. *Los desafíos de la seguridad social en Brasil en el contexto actual*. Brasília: Secretary of Social Welfare Policies.

Bruhn, Miriam, and David McKenzie. 2013a. Entry Regulation and Formalization of Microenterprises in Developing Countries. Policy Research Working Paper 6507, World Bank, Washington, DC.

———. 2013b. Using Administrative Data to Evaluate Municipal Reforms: An Evaluation of the Impact of Minas Fácil Expresso. Policy Research Working Paper 6368, World Bank, Washington, DC.

Busso, Matías, Maria Victoria Fazio, and Santiago Levy Algazi. 2012. (In)Formal and (Un)Productive: The Productivity Costs of Excessive Informality in Mexico. Working Paper 341, Inter-American Development Bank, Washington, DC.

Cao, Lan. 2012. Informal Institutions and Property Rights. *Brigham-Kanner Property Rights Conference Journal* 1: 263–279.
Case, Anne, Victoria Hosegood, and Frances Lund. 2005. The Reach and Impact of Child Support Grants: Evidence from KwaZulu-Natal. *Development Southern Africa* 22 (4): 467–482.
Colombia. Confecámaras. 2011. Impacto de la formalización empresarial en Colombia. Colección Cuadernos de Análisis Económico no. 1, Confecámaras, Bogota.
De Soto, Hernando. 1989. *The Other Path: The Invisible Revolution in the Third World*. New York: Basic Books.
———. 2000. *The Mystery of Capital: Why Capitalism Triumphs in the West and Fails Everywhere Else*. New York: Basic Books.
Di Giorgio, Giacomo, and Aminur Rahman. 2013. SME Registration Evidence from a Randomised Control Trial in Bangladesh. Policy Research Working Paper 6382, World Bank, Washington, DC.
ECLAC (Economic Commission for Latin America and the Caribbean) and ILO (International Labour Organization). 2014. *The Employment Situation in Latin America and the Caribbean: Employment Formalization and Labour Income Distribution*. New York: United Nations.
Fajnzylber, Pablo, William F. Maloney, and Gabriel V. Montes-Rojas. 2011. Does Formality Improve Micro-Firm Performance? Evidence from the Brazilian SIMPLES Program. *Journal of Development Economics* 94 (2): 262–276.
Ghose, Ajit K. 2012. Addressing the Employment Challenge: India's MGNREGA. Employment Working Paper 105, International Labour Organization, Geneva.
ILO (International Labour Organization). 1972. *Employment, Incomes and Equality: A Strategy of Increasing Productive Employment in Kenya*. Geneva: International Labour Office.
———. 2002. Decent Work and the Informal Economy. Report VI submitted to the 90th Session of the International Labour Conference, Geneva, June.
———. 2004. *Final Report of the 17th International Conference of Labour Statisticians*. Geneva: International Labour Office.
———. 2011. *Statistical Update on Employment in the Informal Economy*. Geneva: International Labour Office, Department of Statistics.
———. 2013. *Measuring Informality: A Statistical Manual on the Informal Sector and Informal Employment*. Geneva: International Labour Office.
Jütting, Johannes P., and Juan R. de Laiglesia, eds. 2009. *Is Informal Normal? Towards More and Better Jobs in Developing Countries*. Paris: OECD Development Centre.

La Porta, Rafael, and Andrei Shleifer. 2008. The Unofficial Economy and Economic Development. *Brookings Papers on Economic Activity* 39 (2): 275–352.

La Porta, Rafael, and Andrei Shleifer. 2014. Informality and Development. *Journal of Economic Perspectives* 28 (3): 109–126.

Lawry, Steven, Cyrus Samii, Ruth Hall, Aaron Leopold, Donna Hornby, and Farai Mtero. 2014. The Impact of Land Property Rights Interventions on Investment and Agricultural Productivity in Developing Countries: A Systematic Review. Campbell Systematic Review 1 Campbell Collaboration, Oslo.

Leibenstein, Harvey. 1957. *Economic Backwardness and Economic Growth*. New York: Wiley.

Mahmood, Moazam, Dic Lo, and Yu Yongding. 2012. The Macro Drivers of Growth in China. Unpublished manuscript, International Labour Organization, Geneva.

Maloney, William F. 2004. Informality Revisited. *World Development* 32 (7): 1159–1178.

Maurizio, Roxana. 2015. Transitions to Formality and Declining Inequality: Argentina and Brazil in the 2000s. *Development and Change* 46 (5): 1047–1079.

McGuire, James W. 2013. Conditional Cash Transfers in Bolivia: Origins, Impact, and Universality. Paper presented at the Annual Meeting of the International Studies Association, San Francisco, April 3–6.

McKenzie, David, and Yaye Seynabou Sakho. 2010. Does It Pay Firms to Register for Taxes? The Impact of Formality on Firm Profitability. *Journal of Development Economics* 91 (1): 15–24.

Meth, Charles. 2011. Employer of Last Resort? South Africa's Expanded Public Works Programme (EPWP). Working Paper 58, Southern Africa Labour and Development Research Unit, University of Cape Town.

Mirrlees, James A. 1975. A Pure Theory of Underdeveloped Economies. In *Agriculture in Development Theory*, ed. Lloyd G. Reynolds, 84–106. New Haven: Yale University Press.

Myrdal, Gunnar. 1968. *Asian Drama: An Inquiry into the Poverty of Nations*. New York: Pantheon.

Neri, Marcelo, and Adriana Fontes. 2010. Informalidad y trabajo en Brasil: Causas, consecuencias y políticas públicas. *Cadernos Adenauer* 11 (2): 16–23.

Portes, Alejandro, Manuel Castells, and Lauren A. Benton. 1989. *The Informal Economy: Studies in Advanced and Less Developed Countries*. Baltimore: Johns Hopkins University Press.

Rand, John, and Nina Torm. 2012. The Benefits of Formalization: Evidence from Vietnamese Manufacturing SMEs. *World Development* 40 (5): 983–998.

Santiago, Silas. 2011. Microempresas e empresas de pequeno porte: Brasil: A experiência do Simples Nacional e do Microempreendedor Individual. Unpublished manuscript, Comitê Gestor do Simples Nacional, Brasília.

Stiglitz, Joseph E. 1976. The Efficiency Wage Hypothesis, Surplus Labour, and the Distribution of Income in LDCs. *Oxford Economic Papers* 28 (2): 185–207.

Trebilcock, Anne. 2005. Decent Work and the Informal Economy. Discussion Paper 4, United Nations University World Institute for Development Economics Research, Helsinki.

Universidad Externado de Colombia. 2011. ¿La ley 1429 de 2010 ha formalizado el empleo en Colombia? Boletín del observatorio del mercado de trabajo y la seguridad no. 13, Universidad Externado de Colombia, Bogota.

van Elk, Koos, Jan de Kok, Jessica Duran, and Gert-Jan Lindeboom. 2013. Improving the Formalisation of Informal Enterprises: A Search for Case Studies. Unpublished manuscript, Panteia, Zoetermeer.

———. 2014. Enterprise Formalization: Fact or Fiction? A Quest for Case Studies. Research paper, International Labour Organization (ILO) and Gesellschaft für Internationale Zusammenarbeit (GIZ) GmbH, Geneva and Eschborn.

Wetzel, Deborah. 2013. Bolsa Família: Brazil's Quiet Revolution. World Bank. http://www.worldbank.org/en/news/opinion/2013/11/04/bolsa-familia-Brazil-quiet-revolution. Accessed on 5 December 2017.

World Bank. 2014. A Model from Mexico for the World. World Bank. http://www.worldbank.org/en/news/feature/2014/11/19/un-modelo-de-mexico-para-el-mundo. Accessed on 5 December 2017.

Yiengprugsawan, Vasoontara, Mathew Kelly, Sam-ang Seubsman, and Adrien C. Sleigh. 2010. The First 10 Years of the Universal Coverage Scheme in Thailand: Review of its Impact on Health Inequalities and Lessons Learnt for Middle-Income Countries. *Australasian Epidemiologist* 17 (3): 24–26.

7

Macro Policy for Drivers of Growth and Jobs

7.1 Introduction

This third policy chapter on macro drivers, in symmetry with the policy chapters on growth and jobs (Chaps. 4 and 5), is also based on the findings of the empirical chapter on macro drivers (Chap. 6)—that accumulation of physical capital explains per capita *incomes in developing countries (DCs) and their catch-up to advanced economies (AEs) as much as human capital.*

This policy chapter then examines macro policy which enables increases in both types of investment—in gross fixed capital formation and in human capital through education and investment in knowledge-based intangible capital.

The third empirical regularity, that the quantum of accumulation is as important as the composition of accumulation—that is investment in both physical and human capital explains per capita incomes—leads to a broad policy implication for both physical capital and human capital.

Country policy on investment in physical and human capital is examined not through de jure proclamations, but de facto policy as revealed by national income accounts, budgets, and effective resource allocation towards these expenditure heads. Domestic resource mobilisation is seen to be more important for such investment, rather than inflows.

On investment in physical capital, the chapter finds that looser monetary policy and interest rate structures climb the per capita income ladder. Hence the lower cost of borrowing is seen to enable higher levels of investment. However, this lower cost of borrowing is seen to be enabled in turn by more stringent macroprudential regimes, tightening fiscal policy, and controlling inflation, which subsequently allow lower interest rate structures. Therefore, good governance of macro fundamentals, through both fiscal and monetary policy, is seen to enable higher levels of investment. Further, sequencing is seen to be at the heart of this policy, in that reversing the sequence to loosen monetary policy prior to lowering inflation would simply raise the nominal interest rates and therefore not be sustainable.

On investment in human capital, the key enabling policy variable is seen to be government expenditure on both basic and tertiary education.

But the chapter ends on a note of caution. While stressing that investment in both physical and human capital has been observed to work, to explain higher per capita incomes, there is a broader policy argument to be made for more balanced growth. Balance in the reliance between the drivers of investment, exports, and consumption leads to a better balance between incentives to raise productivity and incomes and incentives to raise domestic aggregate demand.

7.2 Accumulation of Physical Capital

In Chap. 4 it was found that investment and savings shares explained per capita incomes consistently and well in moving up the per capita income ladder, virtually in lockstep from least developed countries (LDCs) to lower- and middle-income countries (LMICs) to emerging economies (EEs). Investment and savings were not only well correlated to gross domestic product (GDP) per capita and growth in GDP per capita, but they also Granger-caused it in the largest number of countries.

Table 7.1 Total investment as a percentage of GDP

Group	1990	Observ.	2000	Observ.	2007	Observ.	2012	Observ.
LDCs	15.69	35	15.79	35	18.42	35	17.81	35
LMIs	27.69	27	25.99	27	25.44	27	22.85	27
EEs	24.82	38	25.76	38	28.75	38	28.17	38
AEs	24.36	43	23.35	43	23.22	43	20.42	43
DCs	25.28	113	23.85	113	30.33	113	32.65	113

Note: *AE* advanced economy, *DC* developing country, *EE* emerging economy, *GDP* gross domestic product, *LDC* least developed country, *LMIC* lower- or middle-income country. GDP figures are country averages weighted by the PPP share of that income group's GDP, as provided by the IMF
Source: Author's estimations at the ILO, based on data from the IMF's World Economic Outlook Database

Table 7.1 summarises the more complex results from Chap. 4. For LDCs, investment as a share of GDP has been the lowest between 1990 and 2012, ranging between 16 and 18 percent. For LMICs it has been higher, ranging between 23 and 28 percent of GDP. While for EEs, investment as a share of GDP has been the highest, and consistently increasing, from 25 to 28 percent.

The major market incentive explaining investment climbing up the per capita *income ladder has been the cost of borrowing.*

A number of factors can be called upon to explain why investment as a share of GDP climbs up the per capita income ladder so consistently, going up from LDCs to LMICs to EEs. Since this is private investment, the major market incentive determining this should be the cost of borrowing to invest, which is the opportunity cost of capital. Tables 7.2 and 7.3 do indeed show this to be the case. Table 7.2 gives the average real interest rate structure for LDCs, LMICs, and EEs for the period 2000 to 2012. It shows that LDCs have had the highest real interest rate over this period, ranging between 11 and 12 percent. LMICs have had somewhat lower real interest rates over this period, ranging between 6 and 8 percent, while EEs have had the lowest real interest rates over this period, ranging between 5 and 6 percent.

However, while real interest rates are given by the central banks, influenced by global market assessments of country risk, and country inflation rates combining to give the real interest rates, the cost of lending actually faced by investors can deviate from this. Table 7.3 however

Table 7.2 Real interest rates

Group	1990	Observ.	2000	Observ.	2007	Observ.	2012	Observ.
LDCs	4.28	16	10.80	16	11.87	16	10.56	16
LMIs	−6.82	18	8.41	18	5.98	18	6.79	18
EEs	4.26	26	5.58	26	4.97	26	6.17	26
AEs	3.34	21	2.98	21	3.36	21	3.58	21
DCs	0.94	60	7.82	60	7.11	60	7.53	60

Note: *AE* advanced economy, *DC* developing country, *EE* emerging economy, *LDC* least developed country, *LMIC* lower- or middle-income country. Figures are unweighted averages
Source: Author's estimations at the ILO, based on data from the World Bank's World Development Indicators

Table 7.3 Lending interest rates

Group	1990	Observ.	2000	Observ.	2007	Observ.	2012	Observ.
LDCs	21.09	19	22.67	19	20.19	19	19.09	19
LMIs	20.66	19	18.38	19	13.90	19	12.57	19
EEs	21.37	27	16.88	27	11.88	27	10.60	27
AEs	...	...	9.05	25	7.55	25	5.43	25
DCs	21.07	65	19.01	65	14.90	65	13.65	65

Note: *AE* advanced economy, *DC* developing country, *EE* emerging economy, *LDC* least developed country, *LMIC* lower- or middle-income country. Figures are unweighted averages
Source: Author's estimations at the ILO, based on data from the World Bank's World Development Indicators

shows that the lending interest rate structure, faced by investors, also explains investment climbing up the income ladder well. The table shows that between 1990 and 2012, LDCs faced lending interest rates ranging between 19 and 23 percent. LMICs faced lower lending interest rates over this period, ranging between 13 and 21 percent, while EEs faced the lowest lending interest rates over this period, ranging between 21 and 11 percent.

So, as the band range of lending interest rates falls going up the per capita income ladder, it has enabled higher private investment levels. The policy question then is: what factors have enabled EEs and LMICs to lower their real and lending interest rates below those of LDCs, so lowering their borrowing costs?

Factors That Have Lowered the Borrowing Costs for Countries with Higher Per Capita Incomes

(a) Higher savings enable lower costs of capital.

A higher supply of domestic savings should, ceteris paribus, lower the cost of capital. A number of country studies and cross-country comparisons support this argument. Bean et al. (2015) note that the fall in both short-term and long-term interest rates in the AEs, but especially long-term rates since the 1990s, are not due to the current crisis, but an increasing propensity to save. The integration of China, with its high marginal propensity to save, into global financial markets is reckoned to have put additional downward pressure on real interest rates. Schmidt-Hebbel et al. (1994) in a survey of DCs, note the importance of savings to finance capital accumulation. Country studies as for Lesotho show clearly evidence of Granger causality from savings to investment and growth (see Sekantsi and Kalebe 2015).

Conversely, if lower interest rates are not supported by higher savings, the International Monetary Fund (IMF) (1983) argues that interest rate repression may lead to capital outflows and foreign exchange shortages, both lowering investment, rather than enhancing it.

Table 7.4 then summarily recalls the evidence from Chap. 4, that indeed savings do climb up the per capita income ladder in DCs. So

Table 7.4 Gross domestic savings as a percentage of GDP

Group	1990	Observ.	2000	Observ.	2007	Observ.	2012	Observ.
LDCs	9.65	31	16.13	31	19.73	31	17.15	31
LMIs	22.41	33	23.00	33	25.68	33	24.48	33
EEs	26.40	42	28.66	42	36.11	42	37.14	42
AEs	23.75	43	23.01	43	23.08	43	21.05	43
DCs	24.50	106	26.61	106	32.57	106	32.82	106

Note: *AE* advanced economy, *DC* developing country, *EE* emerging economy, *GDP* gross domestic product, *LDC* least developed country, *LMIC* lower- or middle-income country. GDP figures are country averages weighted by the PPP share of that income group's GDP, as provided by the IMF
Source: Author's estimations at the ILO, based on data from the World Bank's World Development Indicators

LDCs had the lowest range of savings as a share of GDP, between 1990 and 2012, ranging from 10 to 20 percent. LMICs had a higher range of savings over this period, between 22 and 26 percent of GDP, while EEs had the highest range of savings over this period, between 26 and 37 percent of GDP.

So, for DCs, the supply of savings climbing up the per capita income ladder have supported the lowering of real lending interest rates, which have enabled investment rates to also climb up the per capita income ladder.

(b) Lower interest rates also have to be enabled by lower inflation.

The macro objective spelled out in the first policy chapter (Chap. 5) was growth of GDP, with two caveats on it—inclusive growth for poverty reduction and growth that results in productive transformation. Therefore, increased investment in physical capital is needed to raise growth of aggregate incomes and especially for the poor to reduce their poverty.

Increased private investment is seen to be facilitated considerably by the market incentive of lower costs of capital, through lower interest rates. DCs with higher per capita incomes, EEs and LMICs, compared to LDCs, have managed to lower their real and lending interest rates through a supply-side factor of higher savings. A second pre-eminent factor enabling lower interest rates has to be demand-side macro policy, largely observed to be preoccupied with controlling inflation. And a major instrument to control inflation in DCs is conventional monetary policy through higher interest rates. Hence lower interest rates have to be enabled through lower inflation.

This is an argument based on policy sequencing. First, note that lower interest rates enable higher investment and higher growth. But second, if there is excess demand in the economy, or supply-side bottlenecks, lower interest rates will fuel inflation rather than increases in output. So, inflation will not allow an increase in output, and therefore spur growth, but will hurt growth instead. And inflation will erode incomes, logically eroding lower incomes critically dropping them below the poverty line. So, inflation hurts not just growth, but inclusive growth and poverty reduction.

So, the argument for policy sequencing is that, there has to be an acknowledgement that inflation hurts growth of incomes, especially the incomes of the poor. Hence inflation has to be controlled through higher interest rates as needed. With control of inflation, lower interest rates can be afforded, which can be used to raise investment and growth.

Inflation targeting through interest rates has come to be largely accepted.

The neoclassical position on demand management—of managing inflation—is well summed up by Bean et al. (2015). The four major central banks of the AEs—the US Federal Reserve, the Bank of England, the European Central Bank, and the Bank of Japan—have sought to keep inflation in their economies low and stable, using as their main instrument the official policy interest rate, as Fig. 7.1 shows. The argument is that if inflation and inflationary expectations are already at their desired rate, then keeping to this inflation target requires the central bank to set its policy rate so that aggregate demand is equal to the 'natural' or potential level of output. This is the Wicksellian natural rate of interest, and comprises the natural real rate of interest and the inflation target.

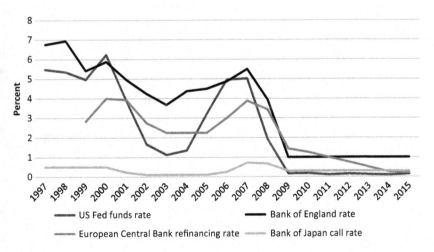

Fig. 7.1 Official policy rates. (Source: Author's calculations at the ILO, based on data from the central banks' websites; and Charles Bean, Christian Broda, Takatoshi Ito, and Randall Kroszner, 'Low for Long? Causes and Consequences of Persistently Low Interest Rates', Geneva Reports on the World Economy 17 (ICMB, Geneva; CEPR, London, 2015))

If inflation is above the target, then the central bank will need to choose a policy rate above the natural rate, to bring inflation down to the target. Conversely, if inflation is below the target, the central bank will need to lower the policy rate, to bring inflation up to the target.

Figure 7.1 shows that the policy interest rates for these four AEs have been falling since the 1990s, and after the onset of the financial crisis in 2009, have been close to the lower zero bound, to raise aggregate demand to its potential level of output.

Many DCs have been struck by macroeconomic crises in the past three decades. In the 1980s, oil price rises, large-scale international borrowing, and subsequent debt crises plunged many DCs into macro crises. Then in the late 1990s, there was a new spate of crises from Mexico in 1995, the Asian crisis in 1997/98, Russia in 1998, and a return to Latin America in Brazil in 1999. Ferreira et al. (1999) note the commonality between these crises in DCs. They were preceded by large increases in current account deficits, often increasing fiscal deficits, with a fear of default or devaluation leading to reversal of capital inflows. These necessitated a reduction in expenditures, through contractionary fiscal and monetary policy, leading to recession.

Macro policy to manage aggregate demand in these crisis-hit countries came to be called stabilisation policy (Crockett 1981), with four explicit instruments. These were (a) exchange rate pegging, (b) monetary targeting, (c) inflation targeting, and (d) inflation reduction without an explicit nominal anchor (Mishkin 1998). Macro experience has favoured the last two instruments, both using interest rate policy.

A country can peg the value of its exchange rate to that of a large low inflation country, which effectively controls its fiscal and monetary policy. The peg constrains domestic economic policy, like monetary expansion to that of the country pegged to. So, Argentina cured its bouts of hyperinflation above 1000 percent, by pegging to the US dollar in 1990, bringing the inflation rate down to 5 percent by 1994 and growth rates of near 8 percent. However, the strength of the peg is also its weakness in not allowing any independent domestic policy to respond to domestic concerns (Mishkin 1998).

Monetary targeting is based on Milton Friedman's money growth rate rule, of a chosen monetary aggregate like M2 targeted to grow at a constant rate (Mishkin 1998). In practise, no central bank sticks to a rule, and in fact adjusts monetary targeting to domestic needs like output growth and exchange rate considerations—a prime example of monetary targeting being Germany, which has used this instrument for more than two decades with very low rates of inflation.

Inflation targeting has become the monetary policy instrument of choice, especially of late, while pre-emptive monetary policy without a nominal anchor argues for preventing inflation even before it can occur. This 'just-do-it' policy has been successfully used in the US, with the Federal Reserve able to bring down inflation from double digits in 1980, to around 3 percent by 1991 (Mishkin 1998).

The impact of inflation targeting, on inflation itself, is generally reckoned to be effective. Average inflation in both EEs and AEs is considered substantially lower after the adoption of the inflation-targeting regime (Fraga et al. 2004). A survey of 36 DCs shows that, compared to non-targeting countries, the DCs that adopted inflation targeting experienced greater drops in inflation and in growth volatility (Gonçalves and Salles 2008). Another sample survey of 50 EEs and DCs found that inflation-targeting countries saw less inflation. Tightened monetary policy was seen to constrain aggregate demand, helped by exchange rate policy, but not so much fiscal policy (Habermeier et al. 2009).

So, there is less dispute about the empirical evidence of the efficacy of inflation targeting, although there are some dissidents (see, for instance, Ball and Sheridan 2005). There is more of a debate at setting too low an inflation target and thereby hurting growth too early in the inflation game as argued by Anwar et al. (2013). Easterly and Bruno (1998) give a very high inflation rate of 40 percent, where it becomes inimical to growth. The IMF gives lower threshold levels of 1–3 percent for AEs and 7–11 percent for DCs (Khan and Senhadji 2000).

And the poor do need to be protected from macroeconomic shocks.

Ferreira et al. (1999) consider the impact of macroeconomic shocks on the poor to be considerable. A macroeconomic crisis is characterised by (a) a decline in the gross national product over a 12-month period, (b) a doubling of the country rate of inflation to over 40 percent over a 12-month period, or (c) both. The shock can affect the living standards and welfare of poor households and communities through changes in relative prices, changes in aggregate demand lowering employment and wage rates, and changes in the rates of return on assets through the inflation tax.

While inflation erodes the incomes of the poor self-employed and the waged, it is wage incomes that do not adjust so easily to inflation, as empirical evidence from Latin America shows (see Cardoso 1992).

But it is important to separate out the need for lower inflation from the stabilisation programs carried out by DCs on advice from the IMF during the 1980s and 1990s.

The policy discussion in this book strictly separates the need for lower inflation—seen to be well targeted through conventional monetary policy on interest rates—from broader stabilisation programs based on cuts in public expenditure and especially social expenditures. Typical responses to crises are policies for restoration of internal and external balances, largely through fiscal consolidation. There are a number of surveys of the impact of such IMF and World Bank-advocated programs on growth distribution and poverty in the DCs. Most show a negative impact in the short run.

For instance, Garuda (2000) measures the effects of 58 IMF programs during 1975–91 on the Gini coefficients and income of the poorest quintiles, over two to five years following the program's initiation. The study finds evidence of significant deterioration in income distribution and the incomes of the poor in IMF program countries relative to their non-program counterparts where external imbalances were severe.

Przeworski and Vreeland (2000) find a negative impact of IMF programs on economic growth, for as long as the countries remain in the program.

Easterly (2000) finds that structural adjustment, as measured by the number of adjustment loans from the IMF and the World Bank, reduces the growth elasticity of poverty reduction. The poor benefit less from output expansion in countries with many adjustment loans, than in countries with few adjustment loans. There does not seem to be an equivalent impact on negative growth however. So, the poor suffer less from an output contraction in countries with many adjustment loans, than in countries with few adjustment loans.

Protection of the poor and the vulnerable, especially in times of crisis and macro shocks, and adjustment policy, then has to focus on the social floor, much as advocated in this book in Chap. 5, on filling the poverty gap. Ferreira et al. (1999) propose a two-part agenda to minimise negative effects on the poor. The first part is to have an effective public safety net before the crisis. The second part comprises policy that returns to counter-cyclicality as soon as internal and external macroeconomic balances are restored, managing fiscal reductions to protect items of importance for the poor, reinforcing safety nets to cope with the additional demand for support, and rebuilding social capital in poor communities.

In *Poor Economics*, Banerjee and Duflo (2011) have a very comprehensive checklist for policy intervention for evidence-based poverty reduction in eight areas: hunger, health, education, population, risk, borrowing, entrepreneurship, and savings.

Lustig (1999) is concerned with the impact of economic crises on not just poverty rates in Latin America, but also long-run and irreversible damage to the human capital of the poor. She advocates socially responsible macroeconomic policy with fiscal adjustment to protect the income of the poor during times of crises, and to simultaneously contribute to lower chronic poverty.

(c) And indeed, inflation has been brought down in DCs, more so going up the income ladder

Given the imperative of staving off higher inflation, for both growth of income and poverty reduction, this has been achieved better by higher-income DCs, so allowing them to keep their interest rates lower than low-income DCs.

Table 7.5 shows that all DCs had annual inflation rates of 20 percent and above in 1990. EEs and LMICs have had the sharpest drop in inflation down to 10 percent or below by 2000, and finally to near 6 percent by 2012. In LDCs, inflation raged upwards to 28 percent by 2000, finally coming down to 8 percent by 2012.

It does appear that DCs in general, but higher-income DCs more so, have attempted to reign in their internal and external balances.

Table 7.5 Percentage change in inflation, average consumer prices

Group	1990	Observ.	2000	Observ.	2007	Observ.	2012	Observ.
LDCs	19.99	41	27.61	41	7.10	41	7.79	41
LMIs	19.74	30	5.21	30	6.22	30	5.50	30
EEs	24.06	38	10.57	38	5.49	38	6.09	38
AEs	20.03	43	2.38	43	3.16	43	2.56	43
DCs	21.28	109	15.50	109	6.30	109	6.57	109

Note: *AE* advanced economy, *DC* developing country, *EE* emerging economy, *LDC* least developed country, *LMIC* lower- or middle-income country. Figures are unweighted averages
Source: Author's estimations at the ILO, based on data from the IMF's World Economic Outlook Database

Table 7.6 Government budget balance as a percentage of GDP

Group	1990	Observ.	2000	Observ.	2007	Observ.	2012	Observ.
LDCs	...	...	...	...	−4.09	16	−3.66	16
LMIs	...	...	...	...	−4.21	25	−5.75	25
EEs	...	...	...	...	0.83	32	−1.38	32
AEs	...	...	...	...	−0.68	47	−5.10	47
DCs	...	...	...	...	−0.45	83	−2.70	83

Note: *AE* advanced economy, *DC* developing country, *EE* emerging economy, *GDP* gross domestic product, *LDC* least developed country, *LMIC* lower- or middle-income country. GDP figures are country averages weighted by the PPP share of that income group's GDP, as provided by the IMF
Source: Author's estimations at the ILO, based on data from the World Bank's World Development Indicators

Table 7.6 shows government budget balances for 2007 and 2012. EEs have kept their budget balance in a range between 1 and −1 percent. LMICs have kept their budget balance between −4 and −6 percent, while LDCs have kept their budget balance at about −4 percent.

Table 7.7 shows the current account balance for a longer period, from 1990 to 2012. EEs have kept their current account balance between −1 percent and positive, with distinct improvement over time. LMICs have kept their current account balance between 1 percent and negative, with a worsening over time, while LDCs have kept their current account balance between −1 and −6 percent, with a worsening over time.

Table 7.8 gives government debt from 2000 to 2012. EEs have reduced their debt from 47 to 37 percent. LMICs have reduced their debt from

Table 7.7 Current account balance as a percentage of GDP

Group	1990	Observ.	2000	Observ.	2007	Observ.	2012	Observ.
LDCs	−6.80	42	−1.35	42	−1.61	42	−4.39	42
LMIs	−2.04	36	0.75	36	−0.21	36	−3.23	36
EEs	−0.95	44	3.93	44	2.56	44	0.14	44
AEs	−0.22	43	−0.60	43	0.08	43	1.40	43
DCs	−1.62	122	2.57	122	1.32	122	−1.46	122

Note: *AE* advanced economy, *DC* developing country, *EE* emerging economy, *GDP* gross domestic product, *LDC* least developed country, *LMIC* lower- or middle-income country. GDP figures are country averages weighted by the PPP share of that income group's GDP, as provided by the IMF
Source: Author's estimations at the ILO, based on data from the IMF's World Economic Outlook Database

Table 7.8 General government gross debt as a percentage of GDP

Group	1990	Observ.	2000	Observ.	2007	Observ.	2012	Observ.
LDCs	...	...	101.13	40	45.30	40	42.12	40
LMIs	...	...	76.15	36	54.97	36	52.01	36
EEs	...	...	47.10	48	33.00	48	36.53	48
AEs	...	...	65.23	48	68.92	48	96.62	48
DCs	...	...	56.98	124	39.60	124	41.12	124

Note: *AE* advanced economy, *DC* developing country, *EE* emerging economy, *GDP* gross domestic product, *LDC* least developed country, *LMIC* lower- or middle-income country. GDP figures are country averages weighted by the PPP share of that income group's GDP, as provided by the IMF
Source: Author's estimations at the ILO, based on data from the IMF's World Economic Outlook Database

76 to 52 percent, while LDCs have reduced their debt from 100 to 42 percent.

Of course, reining in these internal and external balances will have come at a price, hurting the poor more, as feared above. However, a new breed of macroprudential policy has also emerged, which may not dampen growth so much through interest rate hikes.

Macroprudential policies may limit the reliance on raising interest rates and so constrain growth less.

Macroprudential policies have emerged in the wake of the financial crisis. Their objective remains to be the counteracting of financial imbalances. The role of setting interest rates is to stabilise the components of aggregate demand, such as consumption and investment. Macroprudential policies aim to lean against excessive asset growth during booms, and to smooth out long-term loan growth (Shin 2013). They tackle financial imbalances by preventing credit and debt from mounting too rapidly. They work on the supply and demand for credit. On the supply side, macroprudential tools bolster banks' resilience against credit losses. On the demand side, they bolster the resilience of households by reducing credit growth (Guibourg et al. 2015).

These tools mitigate the risk of excessive credit growth, risk of excessive leveraging, liquidity risk, and critically, the risk of large and volatile capital flows (Lim et al. 2011). EEs have particularly come to be wary of capital inflows shocking the often small size of their domestic economies and their degree of openness. The problem emerged with the Asian crisis, where large-scale capital inflows and loans denominated in foreign currencies reversed and had to be paid for with depreciating exchange rates, leading to huge deleveraging of domestic assets, and bankruptcies for firms and banks (Mahmood and Aryah 2001). Now some Eastern European and Latin American countries have used caps on foreign currency lending and other liquidity-related measures to address excessive credit from capital inflows (Lim et al. 2011).

Evidence on the impact of macroprudential policies is still preliminary, but apparent advantages show them to be less blunt than monetary tools and more flexible than fiscal tools. If the financial imbalances are specific to a particular sector, then a mortgage cap can be more efficient than monetary policy. Introducing such a simple macroprudential rule that links reserve requirements to credit growth, dampens the need for optimal monetary policy to raise interest rates in the face of expansionary shocks (Alpanda et al. 2014; Leduc and Natal 2015). They are reckoned to reduce the accelerator effect and so lend a hand to monetary policy which requires a smaller response through change in the nominal interest rate (Quint and Rabanal 2013).

EEs have used these macroprudential instruments more than AEs, and indeed, their reliance on foreign direct investment (FDI) is seen to be waning. Table 7.9 shows that FDI flows rose in EEs to peak at 4 percent of GDP by the time of the crisis, before tapering off to 3 percent by 2012.

Table 7.9 FDI net inflows as a percentage of GDP

Group	1990	Observ.	2000	Observ.	2007	Observ.	2012	Observ.
LDCs	0.10	39	2.16	39	2.91	39	3.16	39
LMIs	0.71	35	0.63	35	3.25	35	1.86	35
EEs	0.81	42	2.73	42	4.24	42	3.09	42
AEs	1.02	41	4.51	41	4.12	41	1.66	41
DCs	0.75	116	2.11	116	3.92	116	2.74	116

Note: *AE* advanced economy, *DC* developing country, *EE* emerging economy, *GDP* gross domestic product, *LDC* least developed country, *LMIC* lower- or middle-income country. GDP figures are country averages weighted by the PPP share of that income group's GDP, as provided by the IMF
Source: Author's estimations at the ILO, based on data from the World Bank's World Development Indicators

Nor is this an effect of the financial crisis, because FDI in LDCs has continued to rise over the crisis period.

(d) Reducing the interest rate spread in DCs

The cost of borrowing can also be brought down by reducing the spread in the interest rate structure. The spread is the difference between the interest rate at which banks themselves borrow money, and the interest rate at which they lend to their borrowers. The spread raises the cost of borrowing. Some evidence shows the spreads to be systemically higher in DCs. If so, that would reduce investment, and bringing the spread down would spur it.

Further, a higher spread also works as a disincentive for savings, because it lowers the deposit rate, which it pays on savings kept with the bank.

The spread between the interest rates paid by banks for borrowing money and the interest rates that they in turn charge to lend it out should be indicative of the risk of default (Nkusu 2003). While the spread can vary between banks within an economy, it is more useful to consider variation in spreads between economies,[1] and why some economies manage to achieve lower spreads on average, compared to others.

A better macroeconomic environment reduces spreads.

Inflation clearly leads to higher spreads. With inflation and monetary depreciation, borrowers can reimburse banks less than the amount of the loan, in real terms. Banks can then be expected to cover this loss in profits by increasing their lending rate and widening their interest margin.

Demirgüç-Kunt et al. (2003) find, in a survey of 1400 banks across 72 countries, that inflation has a robust positive impact on bank margins. Inflation was also found to be positively correlated to banking spreads in a number of country studies like Malawi (see Chirwa and Mlachila 2004), Indonesia (see Raharjo et al. 2014), and a panel of 18 countries in Africa (see Crowley 2007).

A stable macroeconomic environment, with low inflation, low interest rates, low volatility of interest rates, exchange rates, trade or budget deficits, and overall uncertainty surrounding macroeconomic performance, all affect the spread of interest rates. Macroeconomic instability is positively associated with interest margins, because it increases the risk premiums faced by banks.

Afanasieff et al. (2002) find for Brazil, using both cross-sectional and panel data, that these macro variables explain interest rate spreads far more than microeconomic variables.

Ultimately it becomes a vicious circle, because economic growth lowers banking spreads, which induce higher investment and economic growth in turn. So Demirgüç-Kunt et al. (2003) and Afanasieff et al. (2002) both find a negative correlation between the banking spread and economic growth.

But an improvement in the macroeconomic environment is observed to help reduce not just the real interest rate, but also the banking spread, raising the incentive for higher investment and growth.

Market power too can raise the banking spread.

In a free market economy, the interest rate spread should be negatively correlated to factors affecting the level of competition. Less competition gives banks more market power and can lead to wider spreads and so higher profit margins.

Demirgüç-Kunt and Huizinga (1998) find from a survey of bank-level data for 80 countries that the market concentration ratio is correlated with bank margins and profits. Demirgüç-Kunt et al. (2003), for a survey of 1400 banks across 72 countries, find that tighter regulation on bank entry and bank activities boosts the cost of financial intermediation.

This could imply that opening up the banking sector to foreign banks—which are well capitalised, come with advanced technology, and better management—could improve competition, and reduce spreads.

But, Demirgüç-Kunt and Huizinga (1998) also find that this competitive effect does not improve with the entry of foreign banks in DCs. Foreign banks have had higher interest margins and profits compared to domestic banks, while the opposite held in AEs.

Detragiache et al. (2008) go further and argue that in poor countries, domestic banks are better than foreign banks at monitoring soft-information customers, so foreign bank entry may hurt these customers and worsen welfare. They find that in such poor countries, higher foreign bank penetration lowers private sector credit.

But regulatory frameworks reflecting the state of domestic governance appear to be the pre-eminent policy variable for lowering the cost of credit and enhancing volume.

Demirgüç-Kunt et al. (2003) find that institutional indicators of economic freedom and protection of property rights explain cross bank net interest margins the most robustly.

The argument is one of information asymmetry resulting in moral hazard and adverse selection as set out by Stiglitz and Weiss (1981). Banks do not usually have as much information about their clients' transactions as the clients themselves. Therefore, banks require collateral to overcome the risks of making the wrong choice of client and a bad outcome. So, in the case of loan default, the legal risk surrounding collateral repossession shapes financial contracts affecting banking spread (Galindo 2001).

Djankov et al. (2006) find strongly in support of this argument from a sample of 129 countries. In economies where the legal framework and judicial institutions in charge of contract enforcement and creditor rights protection worked efficiently, banks reduced their lending rates and narrowed their margins due to less legal risk.

La Porta et al. (2008) trace weakness in institutions of governance to the origins of the country's legal framework. They find the two most distinct philosophies of law and regulation to be civil law of French legal origin and common law of English legal origin. Of the two, they find civil law to afford relatively less investor protection, more state involvement in economic activities, more regulation, and less independent judicial systems. This leads to relatively weaker enforcement of contracts, and property rights. Beck et al. (2004), testing for a sample of 4000 firms from 38 countries, find a good correlation between such legal tradition and firms' access to external finance.

7.3 Investment in Human Capital

Chapter 4 found that human capital and knowledge-based capital explain per capita incomes and their growth in complement with physical capital very well. AEs particularly stood out in that their GDP growth comprised a near quarter of total factor productivity (TFP), taken as a proxy for technical change, after allowing for increases in physical capital, labour, and human capital. In comparison, DCs had a smaller TFP of about 17 percent. And what accounted for the higher TFP in AEs was not higher shares in physical capital, which were lower in fact, but human capital, which was much higher at 11 percent of GDP, compared to DCs with less than half that at 4 percent of GDP.

Human capital itself was further differentiated between lower-level skills associated with basic education, labelled as human capital, and higher cognitive skills and services labelled as intangibles or knowledge-based capital. Human capital was seen to have stronger Granger causality on GDP in LDCs, while knowledge-based capital had stronger Granger causality on GDP in EEs.

(a) Accumulation of human capital through basic education is critical, but badly managed in LDCs.

   Policy should focus on outcome variables.
   Barro's (2001) classic finding on the growth effects of education were based on a panel of 100 countries observed from 1965 to 1995. Growth is positively related to the starting level of average years of school attainment, more for adult males.[2] But growth is insignificantly related to male schooling at the primary level. Indeed, Barro (1991), Barro and Lee (1993, 1996, 2013), and Barro and Sala-i-Martin (2004) have

consistently used years of schooling as their main explanatory variable, in preference to school enrolment as used by Mankiw et al. (1992) or Caselli et al. (1996).[3]

So, what matters for growth is the outcome variable, of educational attainment, rather than input variables like enrolment.

Table 7.10 corroborates this through the gross enrolment ratios for primary, secondary, and tertiary education, for LDCs, LMICs, and EEs. The table shows that while LDCs and LMICs have improved their enrolment ratios at the primary level between 1990 and 2012, there was not much to distinguish between LDCs, LMICs, and EEs by 2012. All of them have had enrolment ratios above 100 percent since 2007, with above-age students inflating the primary enrolment ratios.

While public expenditures do not justify the outcome variables in education, especially in LDCs.

Table 7.10 Gross enrolment ratios

	1990	Observ.	2000	Observ.	2007	Observ.	2012	Observ.
Primary								
LDCs	69.30	35	83.14	35	101.77	35	109.51	35
LMIs	95.94	32	99.01	32	102.86	32	105.62	32
EEs	107.04	38	107.67	38	105.65	38	104.70	38
AEs	100.69	41	102.20	41	101.94	41	101.69	41
DCs	91.08	105	96.85	105	103.51	105	106.58	105
Secondary								
LDCs	14.27	22	20.47	22	29.24	22	38.89	22
LMIs	62.74	22	63.59	22	73.15	22	79.08	22
EEs	70.21	36	80.17	36	88.76	36	92.41	36
AEs	87.95	39	101.54	39	101.84	39	103.92	39
DCs	52.77	80	59.19	80	68.10	80	74.02	80
Tertiary								
LDCs	1.85	26	2.73	26	5.14	26	8.49	26
LMIs	15.61	22	19.21	22	25.71	22	29.49	22
EEs	21.67	26	31.56	26	47.73	26	52.12	26
AEs	26.21	37	46.26	37	58.15	37	65.36	37
DCs	12.90	74	17.76	74	26.22	74	30.06	74

Note: *AE* advanced economy, *DC* developing country, *EE* emerging economy, *LDC* least developed country, *LMIC* lower- or middle-income country. Figures are unweighted averages

Source: Author's estimations at the ILO, based on data from the World Bank, EdStats

Table 7.11 Public expenditure on education as a percentage of GDP

Group	1990	Observ.	2000	Observ.	2007	Observ.	2012	Observ.
LDCs	...	...	2.87	24	3.70	24	4.12	24
LMIs	...	...	3.58	22	3.30	22	3.51	22
EEs	...	...	4.33	29	4.65	29	5.28	29
AEs	...	...	4.97	35	4.86	35	5.11	35
DCs	...	...	4.00	75	4.05	75	4.44	75

Note: *AE* advanced economy, *DC* developing country, *EE* emerging economy, *GDP* gross domestic product, *LDC* least developed country, *LMIC* lower- or middle-income country. GDP figures are country averages weighted by the PPP share of that income group's GDP, as provided by the IMF
Source: Author's estimations at the ILO, based on data from the World Bank, EdStats

Public expenditures should be a major indicator of both input and outcome variables in education. Much of the social policy debate revolves around expenditures. However, Table 7.11 shows that in 2012, LDCs had increased their share of GDP going to education above 4 percent, above LMICs at 3.5 percent, albeit below EEs at 5.3 percent.

But the outcome variables do not reflect the same ordering as the expenditure variables. Table 7.12 shows the survival rate to the last grade of primary education. Indeed, LDCs reduced their survival rate marginally between 2000 and 2012, to just below 58 percent. LMICs increased their survival rate significantly over this period to 90 percent, and EEs to 93 percent.

Similarly, Table 7.13 shows that the out-of-school rate for children at the secondary level was near halved between 2000 and 2012, by LMICs to 10 percent, and for EEs to 6 percent. However, LDCs were only able to bring down their out-of-secondary-school rate by a quarter over this period, to 39 percent.

As a result, the outcome variable of average years of total schooling at the age of 15 years or plus does not also reflect the ordering of the shares of expenditures on education across LDCs, LMICs, and EEs. Table 7.14 shows that LDCs increased their years of total schooling by the lowest number of years, 1.6, between 1990 and 2010, to reach 4.3 years. LMICs increased their years of total schooling by 1.8 years, to reach 7.8, over this period, while EEs increased their years of total schooling by 2.3 years over this period.

Table 7.12 Survival rate to the last grade of primary school

Group	1990	Observ.	2000	Observ.	2007	Observ.	2012	Observ.
LDCs	...	...	58.24	21	59.35	21	57.60	21
LMIs	...	...	83.60	25	86.29	25	90.18	25
EEs	...	...	90.22	27	91.33	27	92.70	27
AEs	...	...	96.54	24	96.31	24	97.32	24
DCs	...	...	78.75	73	80.40	73	81.74	73

Note: *AE* advanced economy, *DC* developing country, *EE* emerging economy, *LDC* least developed country, *LMIC* lower- or middle-income country. Figures are unweighted averages
Source: Author's estimations at the ILO, based on data from the World Bank, EdStats

Table 7.13 Out-of-school rate (percent) for children of lower secondary school age

Group	1990	Observ.	2000	Observ.	2007	Observ.	2012	Observ.
LDCs	...	...	50.81	9	42.30	9	38.84	9
LMIs	...	...	19.46	15	11.52	15	9.82	15
EEs	...	...	10.57	21	6.24	21	5.71	21
AEs	...	...	3.59	33	2.41	33	3.19	33
DCs	...	...	21.58	45	15.21	45	13.70	45

Note: *AE* advanced economy, *DC* developing country, *EE* emerging economy, *LDC* least developed country, *LMIC* lower- or middle-income country. Figures are unweighted averages
Source: Author's estimations at the ILO, based on data from the World Bank, EdStats

Keeping LDCs still trapped below threshold education levels needed for productive transformation.

The policy chapter on growth, Chap. 4, observed that one of the determinants of productive transformation, of increasing the share of manufacturing above 10 percent, was an increase in average years of schooling above 4.5. Sheridan (2014) too notes that countries need to achieve a minimal level of human capital before transitioning from a reliance on primary exports to manufacturing-based ones. Table 7.14 shows LDCs to still be trapped below 4.5 years of schooling by 2010, while LMICs had been well above this threshold before 1990.

The expenditures on education must switch from the objective of enrolment to attainment—which brings in the quality of schooling.

Table 7.14 Average years of total schooling, children aged 15 or above

Group	1990	Observ.	1995	Observ.	2000	Observ.	2005	Observ.	2010	Observ.
LDCs	2.68	28	3.03	28	3.38	28	3.82	28	4.30	28
LMIs	6.03	35	6.49	35	6.90	35	7.31	35	7.76	35
EEs	6.71	36	7.35	36	7.82	36	8.44	36	8.96	36
AEs	8.94	36	9.40	36	9.91	36	10.25	36	10.55	36
DCs	5.33	99	5.82	99	6.24	99	6.73	99	7.22	99

Note: *AE* advanced economy, *DC* developing country, *EE* emerging economy, *LDC* least developed country, *LMIC* lower- or middle-income country. Figures are unweighted averages
Source: Author's estimations at the ILO, based on data from the World Bank, EdStats, Barro–Lee Dataset

Clearly, educational expenditures, especially in LDCs, are targeting enrolment, rather than attainment, whereas attainment matters more in moving countries up the value-added and income ladder. So, educational expenditures must aim not just at getting children into school, but also in keeping them there. Keeping children in school for longer, given the pull of child labour at low levels of household income, implies schools with proximity, basic amenities, teachers, and teaching.

The policy debate now turns on the differences in cognitive skills, which are the knowledge capital of countries, in explaining growth (Hanushek 2016). Both cognitive and non-cognitive skills are considered to be formed early in the lifecycle, accounted for by racial, ethnic, and family background-led gaps in schooling (Carneiro and Heckman 2003). The evidence points to early skills and ability which beget future skills and ability. The development of these early cognitive and non-cognitive skills depends crucially on school quality, where DCs still have a huge gap with AEs (Hanushek 2013).

In fact, direct measures of labour force quality from international mathematics and science test scores provide the best correlates to growth (Hanushek and Kimko 2000). These are a direct function of school quality.

While there should not be a policy trade-off between school coverage and school quality, there may well be a debate on an initial trade-off between universalising coverage in basic education and moving to higher levels of education (see, e.g. Jiminez et al. 2012). However, the role of tertiary education in generating knowledge-based capital emerges as critical.

7.4 Accumulation of Knowledge-Based Capital as the Intangible That Explains Critical Differences in Growth

Education and training enhance skills, increase productivity, and account well for growth as observed in Chap. 4. But there has been a growing realisation that just adding more years of schooling, without increasing cognitive skills, shows little systematic influence on growth (Hanushek 2013, 2016). Cognitive skills are an enhancement of knowledge.

The World Bank has constructed a knowledge economy index (KEI) that benchmarks countries' performance on four aspects of the knowledge economy: favourability towards knowledge development, education, innovation, and information and communication technology (Pillay 2011). The KEI proves to be a good predictor of future economic growth. It focuses attention on tertiary education and research institutions in low-income countries, generating a pool of experts capable of adapting to—and in turn generating—science and technology.

In fact, while tertiary education has not been regarded in the literature and practice as being poverty alleviating, a simulation of sub-Saharan African countries shows that expansion of tertiary education leads to faster technological catch-up, GDP growth, and poverty reduction (Bloom et al. 2006).

The knowledge economy has been operationalised into the notion of intangible capital. Intangible capital does not have a physical or financial embodiment. It is simply intellectual or knowledge-based capital (OECD 2011).

Ferreira and Hamilton (2010) calculate intangible capital as the difference between total wealth and tangible capital both produced and natural. They show that this estimate of intangible capital explains output per worker better than human capital.

One classification of intangible capital groups it into three types, computerised information such as software and databases, innovative property like research and development (R&D) copyrights, and human economic competencies such as organisational know-how that increases enterprise efficiency. Such classifications of intangible capital show that it explains about a quarter of labour productivity growth in the US and the larger countries of the EU (van Ark et al. 2009).

Using one element of such intangible capital, patent applications, shows it to explain per capita incomes across DCs well. Table 7.15 shows patent applications between 1990 and 2012 for LDCs, LMICs, and EEs. The table shows LDCs stuck in a very low band range for non-resident applications barely climbing to a maximum of 218 by 2012, while LMICs more than quadrupled their applications to near 21,000, over this period, and EEs more than doubled their applications to near 91,000. Resident applications show a similar trend differentiating between LDCs, LMICs, and EEs.

A direct contributor to such intangible capital is R&D expenditure. Griffith et al. (2004) stress that R&D expenditure has two roles. It stimulates innovation, and it enhances technology transfer through absorptive capacity.

Table 7.16 shows again a clear differentiation across LDCs, LMICs, and EEs. Between 2000 and 2012, R&D expenditure remains below 0.5 percent of GDP in LDCs. In LMICs, it also rises slowly to 0.7 percent of GDP over this period, while in EEs, R&D expenditure doubles to 1.4 percent of GDP.

Policy to Promote R&D and Human Capital-Based Growth

While expenditure on R&D is important, and clearly explains countries moving up the per capita income and value-added ladder, the policy question for DCs becomes one of directing it through either the public or the private channel. Rather than debating this theoretically on the pros and cons of public versus private expenditures, the experience of what works is handier.

Grossman (2007) examines the positive and normative implications of two alternative measures to promote R&D-based growth. One measure is to provide R&D subsidies to private firms. An alternative measure is publicly provided education targeted to the development of science and engineering skills. The finding is that R&D subsidies to firms may be detrimental to both productivity and earnings inequality. In contrast,

Table 7.15 Patent applications by non-residents and residents

	1996	Observ.	2000	Observ.	2007	Observ.	2012	Observ.
Non-residents								
LDCs	146	4	195	4	209	4	218	4
LMIs	4715	19	4474	19	17,757	19	20,907	19
EEs	8357	26	18,609	26	57,702	26	72,899	26
AEs	37,497	36	46,179	36	74,269	36	90,963	36
DCs	6440	49	11,618	49	37,117	49	45,711	49
Residents								
LDCs	24	6	49	6	23	6	49	6
LMIs	1117	18	1493	18	3821	18	5698	18
EEs	8523	25	16,998	25	92,351	25	315,056	25
AEs	81,894	36	105,064	36	121,702	36	124,428	36
DCs	4941	49	9422	49	48,039	49	157,749	49

Note: *AE* advanced economy, *DC* developing country, *EE* emerging economy, *LDC* least developed country, *LMIC* lower- or middle-income country. Figures are weighted by the relative population within that income group
Source: Author's estimations at the ILO, based on data from the World Bank's World Development Indicators

Table 7.16 R&D expenditure as a percentage of GDP

Group	1990	Observ.	2000	Observ.	2007	Observ.	2012	Observ.
LDCs	...	...	0.28	4	0.26	4	0.40	4
LMIs	...	...	0.59	12	0.69	12	0.70	12
EEs	...	...	0.76	22	1.06	22	1.43	22
AEs	...	...	2.24	37	2.34	37	2.51	37
DCs	...	...	0.72	38	0.97	38	1.25	38

Note: *AE* advanced economy, *DC* developing country, *EE* emerging economy, *GDP* gross domestic product, *LDC* least developed country, *LMIC* lower- or middle-income country. GDP figures are country averages weighted by the PPP share of that income group's GDP, as provided by the IMF
Source: Author's estimations at the ILO, based on data from the World Bank's World Development Indicators

publicly provided education targeted to R&D skills is found to be unambiguously growth promoting, and neutral with respect to the earning distribution.

Park (2006) makes the point that not only is the level of human capital important, but also its dispersion across the population distribution. Examining data for 95 AES and DCs, he finds that both the dispersion index and the index of human capital positively influence productivity growth. Given limited resources for investment in human capital, this finding implies that an education policy that created more dispersion in human capital will promote more growth. Again, publicly funded education will tend to create more dispersion of human capital than privately funded education.

Recalling the results from Table 7.10 on tertiary education. LDCs are seen to be particularly weak in expanding its coverage across the age group. LMICs and EEs have been much more successful in this expansion.

7.5 While Accumulation Is Important, Policy Balance Is Also Needed Between the Macro Drivers of Growth

Accumulation of physical and human capital explains DCs moving up the per capita income ladder and the rate of catch-up to the AEs. Observation of empirics in Chap. 4 and policy in this chapter have shown

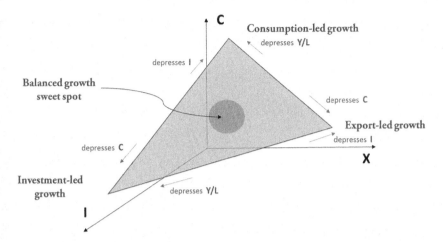

Fig. 7.2 Balance between the determinants of growth. (Source: Author's illustration)

this. But the all-too-reliant investment-led models of the early Soviet Union, and China till recently, are a reminder of the need for balance between the three major macro drivers of growth—investment, consumption, and exports.[4] The critical role of government expenditures has already been examined in Chap. 5.

The argument for balance between these three macro drivers of growth comes from examining the objectives of each of these three macro drivers, investment, consumption, and exports. Figure 7.2 illustrates the three macro drivers, their economic objectives, and the tensions and trade-offs between them.

The figure in three space plots a macro driver on each axis, exports on the x-axis, consumption on the y-axis, and investment on the z-axis. If country policy moves more towards export-led growth, the upside is that productivity will increase, to reduce unit labour costs and increase competitiveness. However, the trade-off is that this export-led growth will also depress domestic consumption. If, alternatively, country policy moves towards consumption-led growth, this will depress productivity. And the trade-off is that this consumption-led growth will depress domestic investment. The third alternative is investment-led growth, which will increase productivity up to a point after which diseconomies of scale step in, and productivity will be weaker compared to export-led growth. And the trade-off is that this investment-led growth will depress consumption.

Hence the need, in tennis parlance, for a policy 'sweet spot'.

Notes

1. Bank-specific factors include bank size, loan ratios, return on average assets, and operating costs. See, for example, Were and Wambua (2014).
2. Women's education not being well utilised, except through a well-observed drop in fertility rates.
3. See, for example, the survey article in Schütt (2003).
4. Well illustrated by the Feldman–Mahalanobis model for the former Soviet Union and the Raj–Sen and Bhaduri models for China.

References

Afanasieff, Tarsila Segalla, Priscilla Maria Villa Lhacer, and Márcio I. Nkane. 2002. The Determinants of Bank Interest Spread in Brazil. Working Paper 46, Banco Central do Brazil, Brasília.

Alpanda, Sami, Gino Cateau, and Césaire Meh. 2014. A Policy Model to Analyze Macroprudential Regulations and Monetary Policy. Working Paper 6, Bank of Canada, Ottawa.

Anwar, Sarah, Anis Chowdhry, and Iyanatul Islam. 2013. Inflation Targeting in Developing Countries Revisited. VOX, CEPR's Policy Portal. http://voxeu.org/debates/commentaries/inflation-targeting-developing-countries-revisited. Accessed 5 Dec 2017.

Ball, Laurence, and Niamh Sheridan. 2005. Does Inflation Targeting Matter? In *The Inflation-Targeting Debate*, ed. Ben S. Bernanke and Michael Woodford, 249–276. Chicago: University of Chicago Press.

Banerjee, Abhijit V., and Esther Duflo. 2011. *Poor Economics: A Radical Rethinking of the Way to Fight Global Poverty*. Philadelphia: Perseus Books.

Barro, Robert J. 1991. Economic Growth in a Cross Section of Countries. *Quarterly Journal of Economics* 106 (2): 407–443.

———. 2001. Human Capital and Growth. *American Economic Review* 91 (2): 12–17.

Barro, Robert J., and Jong-Wha Lee. 1993. International Comparisons of Educational Attainment. *Journal of Monetary Economics* 32 (3): 363–394.

———. 1996. International Measures of Schooling Years and Schooling Quality. *American Economic Review* 86 (2): 218–223.

———. 2013. A New Data Set of Educational Attainment in the World, 1950–2010. *Journal of Development Economics* 104: 184–198.

Barro, Robert J., and Xavier Sala-i-Martin. 2004. *Economic Growth*. 2nd ed. Cambridge, MA: MIT Press.

Bean, Charles, Christian Broda, Takatoshi Ito, and Randall Kroszner. 2015. Low for Long? Causes and Consequences of Persistently Low Interest Rates. Geneva Reports on the World Economy 17, International Center for Monetary and Banking Studies and Centre for Economic Policy Research, Geneva and London.

Beck, Thorsten, Aslı Demirgüç-Kunt, and Ross Levine. 2004. Law and Firms' Access to Finance. Working Paper 10687, National Bureau of Economic Research, Cambridge, MA.

Bloom, David, David Canning and Kevin Chan. 2006. Higher Education and Economic Development in Africa. Unpublished manuscript, World Bank, Human Development Sector, Africa Region, Washington, DC.

Cardoso, Eliana. 1992. Inflation and Poverty. Working Paper 4006, National Bureau of Economic Research, Cambridge, MA.

Carneiro, Pedro, and James Heckman. 2003. Human Capital Policy. Working Paper 9495, National Bureau of Economic Research, Cambridge, MA.

Caselli, Francesco, Gerardo Esquivel, and Fernando Lefort. 1996. Reopening the Convergence Debate: A New Look at Cross-Country Growth Empirics. *Journal of Economic Growth* 1 (3): 363–389.

Chirwa, Ephraim W., and Montfort Mlachila. 2004. Financial Reforms and Interest Rate Spreads in the Commercial Banking System in Malawi. *IMF Staff Papers* 51 (1): 96–122.

Crockett, Andrew D. 1981. Stabilization Policies in Developing Countries: Some Policy Considerations. *Staff Papers* 28 (1): 54–79.

Crowley, Joseph. 2007. Interest Spreads in English-Speaking African Countries. Working Paper 07/101, International Monetary Fund, Washington, DC.

Demirgüç-Kunt, Aslı, and Harry Huizinga. 1998. Determinants of Commercial Bank Interest Margins and Profitability: Some International Evidence. Policy Research Working Paper 1900, World Bank, Washington, DC.

Demirgüç-Kunt, Aslı, Luc Laeven, and Ross Levine. 2003. The Impact of Bank Regulations, Concentration, and Institutions on Bank Margins. Policy Research Working Paper 3030, World Bank, Washington, DC.

Detragiache, Enrica, Thierry Tressel, and Poonam Gupta. 2008. Foreign Banks in Poor Countries: Theory and Evidence. *Journal of Finance* 63 (5): 2123–2160.

Djankov, Simeon, Caralee McLeish, and Andrei Shleifer. 2006. Private Credit in 129 Countries. Report 40720, World Bank, Washington, DC.

Easterly, William. 2000. The Effect of IMF and World Bank Programs on Poverty. Unpublished manuscript, World Bank, Washington, DC.

Easterly, William, and Michael Bruno. 1998. Inflation Crises and Long-Run Growth. *Journal of Monetary Economics* 41 (1): 3–26.

Ferreira, Susana, and Kirk Hamilton. 2010. Comprehensive Wealth, Intangible Capital, and Development. Policy Research Working Paper 5452, World Bank, Washington, DC.

Ferreira, Francisco, Giovanna Prennushi, and Martin Ravallion. 1999. Protecting the Poor from Macroeconomic Shocks: An Agenda for Action in a Crisis and Beyond. Unpublished manuscript, World Bank, Washington, DC.

Fraga, Arminio, Ilan Goldfajn, and André Minella. 2004. Inflation Targeting in Emerging Market Economies. In *NBER Macroeconomics Annual 2003*, ed. Mark Gertler and Kenneth Rogoff, 365–400. Cambridge, MA: MIT Press.

Galindo, Arturo. 2001. Creditor Rights and the Credit Market: Where Do We Stand? Working Paper 448, Inter-American Development Bank, Research Department, Washington, DC.

Garuda, Gopal. 2000. The Distributional Effects of IMF Programs: A Cross-Country Analysis. *World Development* 28 (6): 1031–1051.

Gonçalves, Carlos Eduardo S., and João M. Salles. 2008. Inflation Targeting in Emerging Economies: What Do the Data Say? *Journal of Development Economics* 85 (1–2): 312–318.

Griffith, Rachel, Stephen Redding, and John Van Reenen. 2004. Mapping the Two Faces of R&D: Productivity Growth in a Panel of OECD Industries. *Review of Economics and Statistics* 86 (4): 883–895.

Grossman, Volker. 2007. How to Promote R&D-Based Growth? Public Education Expenditure on Scientists and Engineers versus R&D Subsidies. *Journal of Macroeconomics* 29 (4): 891–911.

Guibourg, Gabriela, Magnus Jonsson, Björn Lagerwall, and Christian Nilsson. 2015. Macroprudential Policy: Effects on the Economy and the Interaction with Monetary Policy. *Sveriges Riksbank Economic Review* 2: 29–46.

Habermeier, Karl, İnci Ötker-Robe, Luis Jacome, Alessandro Giustiniani, Kotaro Ishi, David Vávra, Turgut Kışınbay, and Francisco Vazquez. 2009. Inflation Pressures and Monetary Policy Options in Emerging and Developing Countries: A Cross Regional Perspective. Working Paper 09/01, International Monetary Fund, Washington, DC.

Hanushek, Eric A. 2013. Economic Growth in Developing Countries: The Role of Human Capital. *Economics of Education Review* 37: 204–212.

———. 2016. Will More Higher Education Improve Economic Growth? *Oxford Review of Economic Policy* 32 (4): 538–552.

Hanushek, Eric A., and Dennis D. Kimko. 2000. Schooling, Labour-Force Quality, and the Growth of Nations. *American Economic Review* 90 (5): 1184–1208.

IMF (International Monetary Fund). 1983. Interest Rate Policies in Developing Countries. Occasional Paper 22, IMF, Washington, DC.

Jiminez, Emmanuel, Vy Nguyen, and Harry Anthony Patrinos. 2012. Stuck in the Middle? Human Capital Development and Economic Growth in Malaysia and Thailand. Policy Research Working Paper 6283, World Bank, Washington, DC.

Khan, Mohsin S., and Abdelhak Senhadji. 2000. Threshold Effects in the Relationship Between Inflation and Growth. Working Paper 00/110, International Monetary Fund, Washington, DC.

Leduc, Sylvain and Jen-Marc Natal. 2015. Monetary and Macroprudential Policy in a Leveraged Economy. Working Paper 2011-15, Federal Reserve Bank of San Francisco, San Francisco, CA.

Lim, Cheng Hoon, Francesco Columba, Alejo Costa, P. Kongsamut, A. Otani, M. Saiyid, Torsten Wezel, and X. Wu. 2011. Macroprudential Policy: What Instruments and How to Use Them? Lessons from Country Experiences. Working Paper 11/238, International Monetary Fund, Washington, DC.

Lustig, Nora. 1999. Crises and the Poor: Socially Responsible Macroeconomics. Presidential address at the Fourth Annual Meeting of the Latin American and Caribbean Economic Association, Santiago, October 22.

Mahmood, Moazam, and Gosah Aryah. 2001. The Labour Market and Labour Policy in a Macroeconomic Context: Growth, Crisis, and Competitiveness in Thailand. In East Asian Labour Markets and the Economic Crisis: Impacts Responses and Lessons, Gordon Betcherman and Rizwanul Islam, 245–292. New York: World Bank and International Labour Organization.

Mankiw, N. Gregory, David Romer, and David N. Weil. 1992. A Contribution to the Empirics of Economic Growth. *Quarterly Journal of Economics* 107 (2): 407–437.

Mishkin, Frederic S. 1998. Strategies for Controlling Inflation. Working Paper 6122, National Bureau of Economic Research, Cambridge, MA.

Nkusu, Mwanza. 2003. Interest Rates, Credit Rationing, and Investment in Developing Countries. Working Paper 03/63, International Monetary Fund, Washington, DC.

OECD (Organisation for Economic Co-operation and Development). 2011. New Sources of Growth: Intangible Assets. Project Brief, OECD. https://www.oecd.org/sti/inno/46349020.pdf. Accessed 5 Dec 2017.

Park, Jungsoo. 2006. Dispersion of Human Capital and Economic Growth. *Journal of Macroeconomics* 28 (3): 520–539.

Pillay, Pundy. 2011. Higher Education and Economic Development: Literature Review. Centre for Higher Education Transformation, Wynberg.

Porta, La, Florencio Lopez-de-Silanes Rafael, and Andrei Shleifer. 2008. The Economic Consequences of Legal Origins. *Journal of Economic Literature* 46 (2): 285–332.

Przeworski, Adam, and James Raymond Vreeland. 2000. The Effect of IMF Programs on Economic Growth. *Journal of Development Economics* 62 (2): 385–421.

Quint, Dominic, and Pau Rabanal. 2013. Monetary and Macroprudential Policy in an Estimated DSGE Model of the Euro Area. Working Paper 13/209, International Monetary Fund, Washington, DC.

Raharjo, Pamuji Gesang, Dedi Budiman Hakim, Adler Hayman Manurung, and Tubagus N.A. Maulana. 2014. The Determinants of Commercial Banks' Interest Margin in Indonesia: An Analysis of Fixed Effect Panel Regression. *International Journal of Economics and Financial Issues* 4 (2): 295–308.

Schmidt-Hebbel, Klaus, Luis Serven, and Andres Solimano. 1994. Saving, Investment, and Growth in Developing Countries: An Overview. Policy Research Working Paper 1382, World Bank, Washington, DC.

Schütt, Florian. 2003. The Importance of Human Capital for Economic Growth. Unpublished Manuscript, Institute for World Economics and International Management, Bremen.

Sekantsi, Lira P., and Kalebe M. Kalebe. 2015. Savings, Investment and Economic Growth in Lesotho: An Empirical Analysis. *Journal of Economics and International Finance* 7 (10): 213–221.

Sheridan, Brandon J. 2014. Manufacturing Exports and Growth: When Is a Developing Country Ready to Transition from Primary Exports to Manufacturing Exports? *Journal of Macroeconomics* 42: 1–13.

Shin, Hyun Song. 2013. Adapting Macroprudential Approaches to Emerging and Developing Economies. In *Dealing with the Challenges of Macro Financial Linkages in Emerging Markets*, ed. Otaviano Canuto and Swati R. Ghosh, 17–55. Washington, DC: World Bank.

Stiglitz, Joseph E., and Andrew Weiss. 1981. Credit Rationing in Markets with Imperfect Information. *American Economic Review* 71 (3): 393–410.

van Ark, Bart, Janet X. Hao, Carol Corrado, and Charles Hulten. 2009. Measuring Intangible Capital and its Contribution to Economic Growth in Europe. Working Paper 3, European Investment Bank, Luxembourg.

Were, Maureen, and Joseph Wambua. 2014. What Factors Drive Interest Rate Spread of Commercial Banks? Empirical Evidence from Kenya. *Review of Development Finance* 4 (2): 73–82.

8

Regularities Redux: Success Stories and Traps—What Has Worked for Developing Countries?

8.1 The Findings Explaining Differences in Per Capita Incomes Across DCs and Growth in These Per Capita Incomes

This book has focused not on the diversity of the 145 developing countries (DCs) examined, but on their commonalities. Their diversity is acknowledged, in different paths to moving up the per capita income ladder. However, economic and social analysis and implied policy must out of necessity seek generics—some commonalities between similar countries on what factors impel their movement up the income ladder.

The volume has used a yardstick for development based on returns to the individual's work. The returns attempt to capture a host of development variables critical to catch-up. The returns have to be sustainable in the long run and therefore supported by productivity, human capital, and capability. The returns must permit the household to escape absolute and relative poverty. The returns must inevitably comprise a social floor both in work and out of work, to complement weak returns from the market. The returns will reflect bargaining power in the determination of primary returns to the individual through the market, and secondary returns through transfers.

The use of this metier has allowed us to group these 145 DCs by per capita income, into least developed countries (LDCs) below US$1000, lower- and middle-income countries (LMICs) between US$1000 and US$4000, and emerging economies (EEs) between US$4000 and US$12,000. The book has then sought to explain the differences between these income groups, observed consistently for the same set of countries over the past third of a century, in terms of differences in key variables in their growth, jobs, and macro policy paths.

The book finds that three empirical regularities—in growth, jobs, and macro drivers—explain significant differences in per capita incomes between DCs and growth in these incomes over time. All three regularities infer the generalisation that what explains development is not so much the quantum of change, but the composition of change.

(a) In growth, there is a long-run difference in gross domestic product (GDP) growth per capita, which increases going up the income ladder. However, in the last decade or so, GDP per capita growth rates have converged across income groups. The more abiding difference over the last third of a century between these income groups has been in the composition of their growth, with the share of manufacturing in GDP consistently moving in lockstep up the income ladder. That said, competition in manufacturing has been brutal over this period, with gainers and losers in each income group. Moreover, factor endowments have also given different growth paths, not always favouring manufacturing. Despite this, productive transformation, moving from low-productivity sectors like agriculture, to higher-productivity sectors like industry—especially manufacturing and services—explains differences between income groups.

(b) In the labour market, again, employment growth does not explain long-run differences between income groups. Employment growth is seen to be more demographically given in DCs with low social protection compelling much of the poorer working-age population to work in any kind of job, good or bad. What explains the differences between income groups consistently is job quality. The three major indicators of job quality used internationally to benchmark both the

Millennium Development Goals and the Sustainable Development Goals—vulnerability, the working poor, and labour productivity—all improve consistently, moving up the income ladder. There is also evidence of this being not just a one-way relationship, with higher-income DCs affording better job quality. Transition from vulnerability to waged employment is seen to lead to higher labour productivity, and incomes, especially via productive transformation.

(c) In the macro drivers of growth and jobs, again, the quantum of change explains differences between income groups, but the composition of change explains it further. Accumulation in terms of investment and savings do explain differences between income groups. Savings are especially seen to constrain LDCs' incomes. But the composition of accumulation, through human capital and knowledge-based capital explain differences between income groups better. Exports do not consistently explain differences between income groups, but are observed to help some countries more than others. Again, the composition of exports matters more.

The three regularities have been used to infer policy for DCs to catch up, moving up the income ladder, towards advanced economies (AEs)—but with caveats.

(d) Growth, in per capita incomes for catch-up, has one caveat—of productive transformation, the necessity of moving from lower-productivity sectors to higher-productivity sectors. But this explains growth in average per capita income, and not growth in the distribution of these incomes across different groups, especially between the poor and the non-poor. So, what is needed is an explanation of the determinants of relative growth of incomes between the poor and the non-poor, which puts a fundamental prior caveat on explaining growth and inferring policy—that it be inclusive and poverty-reducing.

Global poverty is observed to have three main determinants: a demographic drag, vulnerability in jobs, and lack of productive transformation. Policy for more inclusive growth then becomes a complex combination of more transfer incomes for households with a relatively greater demographic drag, and more labour incomes for households with relatively greater vulnerability in employment. And the need to enhance labour incomes circles back to the need to enhance productivity through productive transformation, but also through within-sector technical change, especially for the vast majority of the working poor self-employed in agriculture.

Policy for productive transformation is seen to stem on the number of rungs that can be skipped going up the value-added ladder. This represents a departure from production and trade based on factor endowments given by neoclassical theory. And the number of rungs skipped has to be based on a prior educational attainment. Countries below a threshold of 4.5 years of schooling are seen to be trapped in the lowest manufacturing shares of GDP, in single digits in the long run. So, while there can be a growing laundry list of enabling policies culled from successive waves of industrialisation up to the present, it will founder unless the years of schooling is upped significantly.

(e) Policy for jobs is inferred from the empirical regularity observed in the importance of job quality rather than quantity. What drives this empirical regularity is the lack of social protection in DCs, impelling the poor—the vast majority of whom do not have formal jobs, as noted in the policy chapter on inclusive growth (Chap. 4)—to accept any jobs in the informal economy, with much weaker working conditions. Job quality then is strongly determined by the extent of informality in the labour market, which makes it imperative to estimate the extent and complexity of informal employment and levy policy to effectively reduce it.

This jobs policy chapter accordingly estimates and maps informal employment across the income groups of LDCs, LMICs, and EEs, based on a first methodology and estimation by the ILO. The existence of as much informal employment in the formal sector's registered enterprises, as in the informal sector's unregistered enterprises, implies the need to register not just enterprises but also workers themselves. And the effectiveness of policies mooted for registering both workers and enterprises is examined. Registration works arguably not only by bringing waged workers into the purview of national legislation, enhancing those working conditions, but also raises the productivity of the self-employed through increased incentives for higher inputs and outputs, by formalising claims in these markets.

(f) Policy for the macro drivers of growth and jobs is inferred from the empirical regularity observed on both the quantum and composition of accumulation, through investment in both physical and human capital. The quantum of private accumulation, in savings and investment, is seen to be leveraged by one major policy variable, the cost of borrowing, which falls going up the income ladder from LDCs to LMICs to EEs. The lower cost of borrowing is seen to be aided in turn by two determinants, a higher supply of savings and an improved set of macro fundamentals indicated by lower inflation rates. Higher inflation is arguably inimical not only to inclusive growth, hurting the incomes of the poor, but also to private accumulation, by causing banks to raise the nominal interest rate and their spread. Hence the policy recommendation here is heterodox, favouring neoclassical theory and the Washington consensus in the need for better-sequenced macro policy to lower inflation through management of fundamentals, before lowering interest rates. Only so can there be sustainable lowering of the long-run cost of borrowing, to aid accumulation.

Investment in human capital is seen to be impelled at two levels. Investment is needed in primary and secondary education, raising human capital. And investment is needed in tertiary education and in research and development, raising knowledge-based capital, usually dubbed 'intangibles'. Investment in secondary education particularly sets apart LDCs, from LMICs, from EEs, harking back to the need seen earlier for raising productivity and incomes through productive transformation, and the fundamental constraint placed on this by school attainment. Investment in knowledge-based capital is seen to clearly set AEs apart from the DCs, with double the share of expenditure on research and development.

8.2 Explaining Country Success or Traps Over Time

These empirical regularities explain differences in per capita incomes across DCs, and growth in these per capita incomes, over the past third of a century. Hence, productive transformation, job quality, the composition of accumulation, transfers, and government expenditures consistently explain country differences in per capita incomes. They become policy variables to raise per capita incomes across DCs, hastening income convergence between them, and with AEs, which are still farther away.

A more stringent test of these findings would be to observe which countries have been more successful over the past third of a century, and which ones more trapped in their trajectories over this period. This allows correlating the policy variables to success or traps, to see which variables give more consistent explanations of success and traps over the past third of a century.

The measure of success or traps could be the political one of graduation from each country's income group. This is the political measure used by the UN system to examine, for example, the graduation of LDCs into LMICs and EEs. Similarly, graduation could be examined from each income group.

Graduation may be a good political measure of success or a trap, but it is not a good economic measure. The reason is that some countries could be bunched on the income boundaries, and therefore find it easier to graduate compared to those deeper inside the boundaries. A fairer measure of success or traps is to see which countries have managed to double their per capita incomes between 1980 and now. Rather than let the fallout from the 2008 crisis affect the examination of long-run trends in the policy variables, the end year used is 2007. Then success and traps are measured through four categories of countries. The most successful countries are considered those that have at least doubled their per capita incomes between 1980 and 2007. The next category of success is countries that have increased their per capita incomes by between 50 and 100 percent over this period. The next category of success or trap is countries that have increased their per capita incomes by between 0 and 50 percent over this period. And the fourth category is countries that have lowered their per capita incomes over this period.

This more stringent test was permitted by data for almost all these policy variables to be tested. And the results show that virtually all the policy variables tested gave good, consistent explanations of the trajectory of successful and trapped countries over the past 25 years. These then are the policy variables that have indeed been observed to work—to propel development or trap it.

Productive Transformation

Table 8.1 tests for productive transformation in terms of sectoral change. It finds that sectoral change in agriculture, industry, and manufacturing consistently explains the degrees of success and entrapment. Going down the ladder from success to entrapment between 1980 and 2007, for the group of countries that doubled their per capita incomes, the drop in the share of agriculture in GDP was the largest at 15 percentage points. For the countries that increased their per capita incomes between 50 and 100 percent over this period, the drop in the share of agriculture was lower at 13 percentage points. For the countries that increased their per capita incomes between 0 and 50 percent over this period, the drop in the share of agriculture was lower still at 7 percentage points. And for the countries that lowered their per capita incomes over this period, the drop in the share of agriculture was the lowest at 1 percentage point. So, the drop in agricultural share of GDP is correlated to success.

Table 8.1 Average change in value-added share as a percentage of GDP

	Δ Agriculture	Δ Industry	Δ Manufacturing	Δ Services
GDP per capita growth	2007–1980	2007–1980	2007–1980	2007–1980
>1	−15.37	6.55	1.19	8.82
Between 0.5 and 1	−12.84	3.81	−1.32	9.01
Between 0 and 0.5	−6.96	0.77	−2.8	6.33
≤0	−0.89	−4.74	−3.07	5.7

Note: *GDP* gross domestic product
Source: Author's estimations at the ILO, based on data from the World Bank's World Development Indicators

Equally consistently, the increase in industrial shares and manufacturing shares in GDP are correlated to success. The increase in the services shares is a little less consistently correlated to success. This increase in the service shares was high for the two most successful groups of countries, and lower for the two least successful or entrapped groups.

Therefore, the productive transformation of the economy from agriculture to industry and manufacturing, consistently explains success and entrapment between 1980 and 2007.

However, Table 8.2 is a reminder of the need for productive transformation to also comprise technical change in each sector. The table shows the sectoral change in employment shares. The drop in agricultural employment share is correlated to success consistently. The increase in the share of industrial employment in total employment is also large at 2 percentage points for the most successful countries that doubled their per capita incomes. It then drops to a negative range of about 1 percentage point reduction for the other less successful and entrapped categories. The increase in the share of employment in services is pretty consistently correlated to success. Hence the constraints on employment absorption in industry are seen quite clearly, despite its more consistent role in leading in GDP growth. This is a good reminder of the need for productive transformation to comprise increasing productivity and productive employment in each sector.

Table 8.2 Average change in employment shares

	Δ Share of employment in agriculture	Δ Share of employment in industry	Δ Share of employment in services
GDP per capita growth	2007–1991	2007–1991	2007–1991
>1	−10.92	2.47	8.44
Between 0.5 and 1	−5.78	−0.45	6.23
Between 0 and 0.5	−5.95	−0.17	6.13
≤0	−3.06	−0.71	3.77

Note: *GDP* gross domestic product
Source: Author's estimations at the ILO, based on data from the World Bank's World Development Indicators

Job Quality

Table 8.3 tests for job quality. It finds that job quality very consistently explains success and entrapment. The drop in the share of vulnerable employment between 1980 and 2007 goes consistently down the success ladder, from 10 percentage points reduction for the most successful countries that doubled their per capita incomes, to 2 percentage points increase for the least successful or entrapped countries that lowered their per capita incomes.

The drop in the share of the US$1.25 working poor in total employment also consistently goes down the success ladder, from a 25 percentage point drop for the most successful countries that doubled their per capita incomes, to a 3 percentage point drop for the least successful or entrapped countries that lowered their per capita incomes. Similarly, the drop in the US$2 working poor also goes down consistently from success to entrapment.

The growth rate of labour productivity also goes down consistently from success to entrapment. This is definitional because that is the criteria used to measure success—the growth rate of GDP per capita.

Accumulation of Physical and Human Capital

Tables 8.4 and 8.5 look at physical investment and human capital. Table 8.4 finds that the increase in the share of investment in GDP has been the largest at 8 percentage points for the most successful countries

Table 8.3 Average change in selected labour market variables

Δ Share of vulnerable employment	Δ Share of working poor (<$1.25)	Δ Share of working poor (<$2)	Δ Aggregate labour productivity	Productivity growth rate (%)
2007–1991	2007–1991	2007–1991	2007–1991	2007–1980
−9.67	−24.81	−27.06	11,682.7	99.45
−4.43	−14.69	−15.82	5037.75	41.12
−3.99	−8.32	−8.79	1864.24	16.42
2.75	−2.63	−0.67	−860.51	−13.19

Source: Author's estimations at the ILO, based on data from the World Bank's World Development Indicators

Table 8.4 Average change in aggregate demand components as a percentage of GDP

	Δ Savings	Δ Gross fixed capital formation	Δ Exports	Δ Imports
GDP per capita growth	2007–1980	2007–1980	2007–1980	2007–1980
>1	23.33	8.08	24.07	7.12
Between 0.5 and 1	6.32	−0.31	11.24	4.39
Between 0 and 0.5	2.76	0.24	7.76	3.84
≤0	−7.49	1.92	1.81	10.5

Note: *GDP* gross domestic product
Source: Author's estimations at the ILO, based on data from the World Bank's World Development Indicators

Table 8.5 Average change in selected human capital variables

	Δ Average years of schooling	Δ Secondary gross enrolment	Δ Tertiary gross enrolment
GDP per capita growth	2007–1980	2007–1980	2007–1980
>1	2.39	41.53	16.19
Between 0.5 and 1	2.55	26.99	21.49
Between 0 and 0.5	2.27	18.27	15.91
≤0	2.16	4.64	5.96

Note: *GDP* gross domestic product
Source: Author's estimations at the ILO, based on data from the World Bank's World Development Indicators

that doubled their per capita incomes. Going down the success ladder to entrapment, the increase in investment drops discretely, albeit not so consistently to a band range between 0.3 percentage point drop and 2 percentage point increase.

The increase in the savings share of GDP is consistently correlated to success, going from a high of a 23 percentage point increase for the most successful countries that doubled their GDP per capita, consistently stepping down to a 7 percentage point drop for the least successful and entrapped countries.

Table 8.5 finds that the increase in average years of schooling creeps down slightly going down the success ladder, but not very consistently for the two most successful categories. The increase in average years of schooling goes from a range of 2.4 to 2.6 for the two most successful categories of countries that at least increased their incomes by 50 percent between 1980 and 2007, down to 2.3 for countries that increased their per capita incomes between 0 and 50 percent, further inching down to 2.2 for the least successful and entrapped countries that lowered their per capita incomes.

Table 8.5 also finds that the increase in the secondary enrolment ratio goes down very consistently, going down the success ladder. The increase in the enrolment ratio drops from a high of 42 percentage points for the most successful countries that doubled their per capita incomes, very consistently and significantly down to 4 percentage points for the least successful and entrapped countries that lowered their per capita incomes.

Table 8.5 finds that the increase in the tertiary enrolment ratio, as an indicator of knowledge-based capital, does not behave very consistently for the three more successful categories of countries. It varies in the band range of 16 to 22 percentage points for the countries that increased their per capita incomes. However, for the least successful and entrapped countries that lowered their per capita incomes, the increase in tertiary enrolment ratios drops down to 6 percentage points.

Exports

Table 8.4 also tests for exports. And it finds that the increase in export share in GDP does drop consistently, going down the success ladder to entrapment. The increase in the export share of GDP drops from 24 percentage points for the most successful countries that double their GDP per capita, down consistently to 2 percentage points for the least successful and entrapped countries that lowered their GDP per capita.

Social Protection

Table 8.6 tests for social protection expenditures. It finds that increases in public expenditure per capita for social protection have been consistently correlated to success. The growth rate of expenditures per capita is the highest at 272 percent for the most successful countries that doubled their per capita incomes. And this growth rate goes down consistently to 71 percent for the least successful and entrapped countries that lowered their per capita incomes.

Table 8.6 Average growth in public social protection expenditure per capita

	Public social protection expenditure per capita growth 2007–1990
GDP per capita growth	
>1	271.94
Between 0.5 and 1	204.1
Between 0 and 0.5	129.57
≤0	71.03

Note: *GDP* gross domestic product
Source: Estimations by Moazam Mahmood and Florence Bonnet at the ILO, based on national household survey data

In sum, what has worked for development for the past quarter of a century has been less the quantum of change and more the composition of this change. It has been the composition of growth in terms of productive transformation of the economy. It has been improvements in job quality. It has been investment in physical capital, but very importantly investment in human capital and knowledge-based capital. And it has been investment in social protection expenditures providing an economic and social floor for the individual and the economy.

CPSIA information can be obtained
at www.ICGtesting.com
Printed in the USA
LVOW13*1605100618
580224LV00012B/493/P